WILDFLOWERS OF CALIFORNIA

A MONTH-BY-MONTH GUIDE

The publisher gratefully acknowledges the generous support of the General Endowment Fund of the University of California Press Foundation.

WILDFLOWERS OF

CALIFORNIA

A Month-by-Month Guide

Laird R. Blackwell

UNIVERSITY OF CALIFORNIA PRESS

University of California Press, one of the most distinguished university presses in the United States, enriches lives around the world by advancing scholarship in the humanities, social sciences, and natural sciences. Its activities are supported by the UC Press Foundation and by philanthropic contributions from individuals and institutions. For more information, visit www.ucpress.edu.

University of California Press
Oakland, California

Library of Congress Cataloging-in-Publication Data

Blackwell, Laird R. (Laird Richard), 1945–
    Wildflowers of California : a month-by-month guide / Laird R. Blackwell.
        p.   cm.
    Includes bibliographical references and indexes.
    ISBN 978-0-520-27205-7 (cloth : alk. paper)—ISBN 978-0-520-27206-4 (cloth : alk. paper)
    1. Wild flower—California—Identification.   2. Wild flowers—California—Pictorial
works.   I. Title.
QK149.B586   2012
582.1309794—dc23
                                                                                            2011024363

26 25 24 23 22
10 9 8 7 6 5 4 3

The paper used in this publication meets the minimum requirements of ANSI/NISO Z39.48-
1992 (R 1997) (Permanence of Paper).∞

Cover photograph: Poppies and goldfields along Hite's Cove Trail on the south fork of the Merced River.
Note: All photographs were taken by the author.

For my beautiful, wise, loving wife, Melinda, and for our wonderful granddaughters Isla and Ava, who are being raised with laughter and adventure and nature's wonder.

CONTENTS

ACKNOWLEDGMENTS

I wish to thank all my students over the years who have kept me young and all the authors and colleagues who have kept me learning. Thanks to Melinda whose work with troubled kids and healing horses is as joyful and important as a meadow of flowers. And thanks to all the amazing and professional people at University of California Press who have been so graceful and able in this midwife process, with special thanks to Hannah Love and Francisco Reinking, and to Jean Blackburn at Bytheway Publishing Services. I am pleased and proud to have this book produced and published by such a fine press.

Face to face with the sunflower,
Cheek to cheek with the rose,
We follow a secret highway
Hardly a traveller knows,
The gold that lies in the folded bloom
Is all our wealth;
We eat of the heart of the forest
With innocent stealth.
We know the ancient roads
In the leaf of a nettle,
And bathe in the blue profound
Of a speedwell petal.

MARY WEBB, *POEMS AND THE SPRING OF JOY*, 1929

Let knowledge grow from more to more,
But more of reverence in us dwell;
That mind and soul, according well,
May make one music as before.

ALFRED, LORD TENNYSON, "IN MEMORIAM," 1849

THERE IS SOMETHING about wildflowers that touches us in a place too deep for words. A single flower, especially one at home in the wild, can take us back to seeing with the fresh eyes of a child; a whole landscape bursting with bloom can move us to laughter and tears of gratitude. It's almost impossible not to smile in the presence of a flower, not to feel more vital, more real. There is something about wildflowers that calls us to be more human, to live more honestly, to focus on what really matters, to laugh more, to care more.

Every state has its wildflower treasures. California is especially blessed—such diversity of habitats and such abundance of species and stunning floral displays. From seaside to desert, from Central Valley grasslands to snow-cloaked peaks, from rolling foothills to redwood forests, from granite Yosemite to volcanic Lassen and Shasta, from the "urban" Santa Monica Mountains to the wild and remote Klamath and Siskyou Mountains, from below sea level in Death Valley to the alpine summit of Mount Whitney—what a wonderland for us and for the flowers, each place a sacred heritage, a joy and a responsibility. As our population and land use grow, we run the risk of destroying the very treasures that keep us "grounded" and give us meaning beyond our own ideas and productions. Already so many wild places and wild gardens have been lost to all but memory. Inexorably we push, we spread, we build. It is all part of our struggle to be human, to find a place, to leave a mark; but we also know that what we are losing is a vital part of our journey, too: a part of our humanness, a part of our "place."

There are many people working each day to preserve our wild heritage and our future; it is soul work, a gift to all of us whether we recognize it yet or not. Thank goodness for those who dedicate their lives to such work—it is vital to our survival and our being. Perhaps if we all took the time to focus on what really matters in our lives, we would love more, we would sing more, and we would follow the call of the flowers more. This book is intended as an encouragement to follow that call and as a friend and guide along the way.

Wildflower Seasons in California

Let's imagine that it is now late January or part way into February in California. Depending on where you are in the state, there may have been a few scattered flowers in bloom over the winter (in some years, more than a few), but the fabulous, massive blooming that California is known for has been on hiatus for several months now. These last few weeks you have been hungering for the return of the flowers—for their vibrant colors and sweet aromas, and for the enthusiastic buzzing and whirring life that they bring in their wake. In our modern world of such rapid change and such uncertainty in so many aspects of our life, it is comforting to have some constancy, something solid that you can depend on and look forward to. Though the wildflowers certainly offer change and uncertainty (you never really know what kind of blooming year lies ahead or what wildflower surprises you will find just around the corner), they also bring predictability and reassurance. Every year—year after year—the flowers return to brighten and lighten our lives. And they return in particular places and particular times (with some variability, of course, depending on precipitation and temperature, among other factors).

There will be some sparse blooming years and some prolific ones; there will be golden years and purple ones; but how wonderful to know that every year, like clockwork, in late January or February a few "old faithfuls" will explode into bloom again in a few special, low-elevation places on the coast, in the coast ranges, in the Central Valley, and in the deserts to start the inexorable journey of the flowers across the months and across the state. From the first **footsteps of spring** along the coast in January or February to the last golden **rabbit brush** hoorah in the mountains in September or October, each month has its special flowers and its dazzling flower hot spots to feed your hunger and titillate your taste. Get out and enjoy it—it's a floral feast not to be missed!

Purpose and Organization of This Book

This book is intended to help you know when and where to see WOW—spectacular wildflower displays and gorgeous, fascinating flowers. For the purposes of this book, I have divided the state into 10 major geographical regions. There are many ways to do this, of course, but I have chosen a simple, widely used classification:

1. Northwest Mountains
2. Coast and Coast Ranges
3. Transverse Ranges—east of Los Angeles
4. Central Valley
5. Foothills of the Sierra
6. Cascades
7. High Sierra
8. Northeastern Corner
9. East of the Sierra
10. Southern Deserts

Places

In all, 67 flower hotspots (organized by these geographical regions) are described with directions to get there, the best blooming times, and lists of some of the wildflower treasures you can expect to find there—great displays and especially interesting, unique, beautiful, or frequent flowers. For each spot I have chosen a flower to feature—a flower that is common, occasional, or rare in this place that I especially like. This choice is entirely subjective. For more extensive lists of flowers for many of the places, check the bibliography, bookstores, the California Native Plant Society, or online. Of course, with so many incredible places for wildflowers in California, I could only select a few of my favorite spots to highlight. In the back of the book is a list and map of about 300 other good wildflower spots—places where some of the flowers in the book can also be found.

Months

Following the descriptions and map of the 67 hotspots, you will find descriptions of the months from late January–February through September. A few of the non-natives and escapees from cultivation and even a few natives bloom all winter, but for the most part, in most years, almost nothing begins blooming after September, and very little is in bloom in November and December. Note, however, that in some years, with enough rain and sun, the desert and sometimes the coast can be surprisingly flowery in November and December; for example, Anza-Borrego can be abloom with **windmills, brittlebush, chuparosa, desert trumpet**, and **creosote bush,** among others. But most years, the months of major blooming in California are January through September, so for each of these nine months there is a general description of flowering and flower places, then a list of special wildflower hot spots.

Flowers

With almost 6,000 species of wildflowers in California, this book can only feature a sampling. I have included over 600 of my favorites—flowers whose beauty or fascination would lead me to go out of my way to see them.

Following the introduction to each month come the descriptions and photos of the flowers that usually first bloom somewhere in California in this month. Of course, their first month of blooming will vary a bit from year to year, but most years you should be able to find significant blooming of these flowers beginning in this month in the place(s) indicated (and most likely in other places as well). In October, probably no new species will begin blooming, but there will be some beautiful flowers that began blooming a month or two earlier that are still hanging on as fall is in the air. Since most flowers bloom for at least several weeks, if you're looking for flowers to see in a particular month, be sure to check the earlier sections for MONTHS as well. The flowers included in each month are sequenced by color (blue, red, yellow, white, then green or brown), and then alphabetically by common name within each color. For each flower there is a photo taken in the field without artificial light or filters (except ultraviolet), then a brief description of the flower and plant; a note of particular interest; habitat; and examples of locations and blooming times. Locations in the central or southern parts of the state are in *italics*. It should be noted that the elevation ranges given are approximations, and that the locations given are not, in most cases, very specific, so you will probably have to do some searching—but that's half the fun! If you want more specific places to look for certain flowers, check the wonderful Calflora.org website, which has reports of specific flower sightings going back decades.

For several of the MONTHS, following the presentation of the wildflowers are photos and descriptions of a few non-native species of interest.

Indices

You should be able to find the names of all the flowers in this book, including scientific and common alternative names, in the Scientific Names index and the Common Names index.

When, Where, What, and Wow (How to Use This Book)

1. It is March, and you want to know where to go to see great wildflowers. Turn to March in the MONTHS section and check the places highlighted (organized by geographical area). Also be sure to look back at the late January–February section because flowers that start blooming then will probably still be blooming in March. You could also leaf through the PLACES section and find places where March is mentioned under the "Blooming" heading.

2. It is May, and you want to know what flowers you can find blooming this month. Turn to May in the MONTHS section and leaf through the flower descriptions and photos. For each flower there will be at least one place listed where it will be first blooming this month, as well as several other places it will start blooming in later months. You will also want to check April for flowers that began blooming then but are still blooming in May.

3. You want to know where and when to go to see great wildflowers in the Mojave Desert. Turn to the Mojave Desert part of the PLACES section and read the general description and the descriptions of the specific places in that geographical area (which will include the best blooming times).

4. You want to know where and when you can see one of your favorite flowers—**rock fringe**. Find "rock fringe" in the Index of Common

Names and turn to the indicated page where you will find a photo and description, including a list of several places you can find this flower, and for each place, the best time to find it in bloom.

5. You love wildflowers, but you're not sure which ones you want to go see. Leaf through the photos in the MONTHS section, choose some favorites, and read their descriptions to find out where and when to go to see them.

Using a Month-by-Month Guide—Benefits, Limitations, and Caveats

The two main purposes for a month-by-month wildflower guide are to help readers know where and when to go to find spectacular wildflower displays, and to help them know where and when to go to locate particular species in bloom. One of the great comforts and pleasures of "wildflowering" is the flowers' relative predictability—year after year, the same species bloom in the same places at about the same times, for some of the factors that most influence blooming times—soil type, latitude, and elevation—remain constant (at least in the human scale of time). How wonderful it is, for example, to know that every year in the Tahoe area in early May at Sagehen Meadows, you will find an incredible "lake" of acres and acres of deep-blue **camas lily** in peak bloom. This predictability is a delight to anticipate and a joy to experience, and this month-by-month guide will help you do both—if you turn to May in the MONTHS section, you will find the camas lily bloom in Sagehen Meadows as one of the highlighted flower displays of the month, and the description of the camas lily will list Sagehen Meadows as one of its prime locations, with May–June as the blooming period.

However, there can be some "disturbances" to this predictability, so there are some limitations to a wildflower guide with a month-by-month approach. Some of the other main factors affecting blooming time—temperature patterns, the amount and timing of precipitation, and snow distribution—are highly variable, both from year to year and from place to place, sometimes even from one site to a neighboring site.

I have already cautioned the reader that such variations can dramatically delay or accelerate blooming times, sometimes by as much as several weeks. This means that, depending on the year, the month indicated in this guide for the first blooming of a species might be off by at least a month in either direction (for example, the spectacular camas lily bloom in Sagehen Meadows referred to above didn't peak until mid-June in 2011, which was an extremely heavy snow year in the Sierra). But the guide can still be extremely useful: if you know that the season is delayed or accelerated, you can expand your search in the guide to a month later or a month earlier.

Place-to-place variability in climate conditions offers other challenges for using this guide. Larger-scale differences in environmental conditions between places (for example, elevation and latitude) will have considerable effects on blooming time—for the most part species at higher elevations or further north will bloom later—but these differences will be reflected in the lists of blooming places and times in the species descriptions. For example, you will find **baby blue eyes** under February because its first blooming in California will usually be in late February along the shore (for example, at Manchester Beach) and in the desert (for example, Anza-Borrego), but the description will also indicate that it can be found beginning to bloom in late March and early April along the Hite's Cove Trail in the foothills, and not until May in Six Rivers National Forest in the northwest mountains. If you are in one of the later-blooming areas, you will have to look through the earlier months to find the description and photo of the flower (of course, you could also look for "baby blue eyes" in the index).

More localized differences in environmental conditions (for instance, exposure: north-facing slopes being heavy with snow while nearby south-facing slopes are snow-free) can also alter blooming times considerably, sometimes by several weeks. Some species only grow on one exposure, but those that grow on more than one will start blooming at very different times at sites with different exposures within the same area. This guide does not reflect or account for this local variability, so it may lead you to expect to find a certain species in bloom in a certain month, but on this particular exposure you'll find the plants still in bud or already gone to seed.

So, the caveat to using this month-by-month guide to find flowers blooming in the field or to find descriptions of flowers you find blooming in the field is to be flexible—check several adjacent months in the guide, not just the current month. When the guide corresponds to your experience, celebrate the neat predictability. When you are surprised to find a species in bud or in fruit that the guide led you to expect would be in bloom, accept the guide as just a guide, appreciate nature's complexity, and enjoy the buds or fruits . . . and maybe try to find a different exposure!

As you become more aware of how to tell a "normal" blooming year from a delayed or accelerated one, and as you become more familiar with the local variations in environmental conditions, you will know better how to adapt your use of the guide so it will be of the greatest usefulness and enjoyment for you.

A Few Last Words

Please respect the flowers, the land, and other people who want to enjoy both—don't pick, trample, litter, or enter private property without permission. Also, respect yourself and your safety—watch out for poison oak, rattlesnakes, ticks, steep drop-offs, weather changes, and getting lost. You want your wildflowering experience to be When, Where, What, and WOW . . . not OW!

This book includes some of California's most spectacular wildflower places and many of its showiest and most intriguing flowers, but of course this is only a taste of the wildflower wonders this glorious state has to offer. I hope you will use this book as a guide and a starting place for a lifetime of wildflower exploration and adventure. For more information and ideas about places and flowers, check on-line "hot spot" sites (such as Carol Leigh's at calphoto.com—currently on hiatus—or the Theodore Payne Organization's at theodorepayne.org/hotline.html); check the wonderful websites at calflora.org or calphotos.berkeley.edu; contact CNPS and other organizations; talk to locals, or just wander. I would love it if you would let me know of any great discoveries you make (lblackwell@sierranevada. edu).

—Laird R. Blackwell

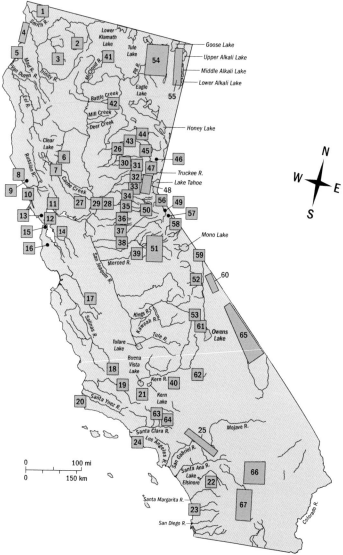

Map of 67 special wildflower places, or "hotspots," discussed in numerical order in this section.

SPECIAL WILDFLOWER PLACES

Once you have lived on the land, been a partner with its moods, secrets, and seasons, you cannot leave. The living land remembers, touching you in unguarded moments, saying, "I am here. You are part of me."

BEN LOGAN, *THE LAND REMEMBERS*, 1999

We shall not cease from exploration, and the end of all our exploring will be to arrive where we started and know the place for the first time.

T.S. ELIOT, "LITTLE GIDDING" FROM *FOUR QUARTETS*, 1943

FOR WILDFLOWER LOVERS who have been blessed with the opportunity and desire to explore the amazingly diverse state of California in search of wildflower treasures, we all have our own special California places and special flowers that we feel somehow are uniquely ours, that are forever linked to some memorable experience, some powerful emotion, some delicious surprise.

I can remember so vividly so many wildflower scenes: struggling for hours up 13,000-foot Mount Dana in Yosemite and finding at the very top an intensely blue **sky pilot**, a gorgeous floral piece of the deep blue sky; driving up a dirt road toward Wind Wolves Natural Preserve and being astonished at the dazzling field of **blue dicks, purple owl's-clover, sky lupine**, and **bird's-eye gilia** seemingly extending for miles all the way to the green, rolling hills behind, painted with patches of blazing yellow **hillside daisy**; breathlessly asking hikers returning from the shoulder of Ring Mountain if the rare **Tiburon mariposa lily** was in bloom yet and receiving an enthusiastic "yes" and then sprinting up the trail to find several in their full glory; hiking along the Winnemucca Lake trail at Carson Pass on a bright, warm, sunny summer day and reaching the famous seeps where shoulder-high jungles of **tiger lily, lupine, bluebells, monkey flower, paintbrush, corn lily, elephant's head**, and so many more took my breath and speech away; driving sadly up blackened Big Tajunga Canyon (victim of horrific fires the previous summer) in the San Gabriel Mountains to be amazed and exhilarated by a solid hillside of vibrant color—of **wishbone bush, wild canterbury bells, stinging lupine**, and **wide-throated monkeyflower**—bringing life to the charred ruins; looking out from 170th Street outside Lancaster near the California Poppy Reserve in mid-April to see an amazing ocean of acres and acres of satiny orange **California poppy** flowing and glowing for miles across the landscape in the afternoon sun; kneeling in the grassy fields at Salt Point State Park to see up close the intricate, miniature gardens of **blue-eyed grass, cream cups, rosy butter-and-eggs, tidy tips, sea thrift**, and **rosy onion**, all with a backdrop of the deep blue ocean and the startling yellow-flowered, succulent-leaved **coast dudleya** on the rocks by the water; walking up a sandy, barren wash in Anza-Borrego in early March to find a living canvas of **sand verbena, chuparosa, barrel cactus, phacelia**, and **Bigelow's monkeyflower**; in May being stunned by mile after mile of creamy **bush monkeyflower** along the walls of Feather River Canyon and by miles of several species of pink **clarkia** along the slopes of Kern River Canyon; standing alone at dusk on the edges of a bog in Butterfly Valley surrounded by hundreds of bizarre, insect-eating **pitcher plants** and being thankful I wasn't an insect, but not being entirely confident I wasn't next on the menu.

These experiences, these places, these flowers all go into making us who and what we are. I hope that this book will help you expand and deepen your experience of California's glorious flowers and magical flower places, and in the process, maybe even help you know yourself a little better.

NORTHWEST MOUNTAINS

Middle fork Smith River with fireweed

EAST OF THE COAST RANGES and west of the Cascade Mountains in northern California is an amazing and fascinating jumble of mountain ranges going in all directions, crisscrossing the northwest corner of the state. The Siskyou, the Klamath, the Trinity, the Scott, the Marble, the Salmon: mountain ranges everywhere, creating a vast, wild mountainous region. It is easy to understand how the last member of the Yahi—Ishi—and whole tribes could remain hidden for so long in this country.

Great rivers—the Smith, the Klamath, the Salmon, the Trinity—cut canyons through dense forests and bring sparkling life. This country boasts the most diverse conifer forests in the world and is home to a great diversity of wildflowers, including numerous endemics.

Although there are some highways through this area and a few easily accessible wildflower spots, reaching most of this terrain will require some driving on narrow roads (some paved) or some hiking to find the best spots and the most interesting flowers. I have featured three spots that are relatively easily accessible, though the Trinity Alps will probably require some hiking, and Kangaroo Lake and the Smith River will require some "back-country" driving and walking.

When

In the low-elevation forests along the rivers, the flowers will peak from May through June, while up in the higher mountains, peak blooming will be in July and August.

1) Smith River and Siskyou Mountains (to about 7,500 feet)

FEATURED FLOWER: **California harebell**. In July, these delightful, pale blue, airy flowers dangle and dance along forest trails.

DRIVING DIRECTIONS: U.S. Route 199 between Crescent City and the Oregon border follows the middle fork of the Smith River. A smaller road follows the even wilder south fork. There are numerous dirt roads going north and south into the Siskyou Mountains. Of special wildflower interest are the Little Jones Creek Road (10.5 miles east of Gasquet) climbing for about 10 miles to Bear Basin Butte Botanical Area, and the Middle Fork Gasquet Road going north from Gasquet for about a mile to the Stony Creek Trail.

WALKING DIRECTIONS: At the end of the Little Jones Creek Road, the gate may be locked, so you'll need to walk the last half mile to the lookout atop Bear Basin Butte. You may not want to walk in if there are people renting the cabin (indicated by a posted sign). Floristically interesting trails off U.S. 199 include the Stony Creek Trail, the Myrtle Creek Trail west of Gasquet, and the Darlingtonian Trail just west of Gasquet. All of these trails are passable by easy, level strolling.

DESCRIPTION: All three forks of the Smith River are glorious, sparkling, usually emerald pathways through this remote land. The trails mentioned above, and many others, take you to lush forest floor vegetation—ferns, mosses, and mostly large-leaved herbs such as **trillium, lily, rhododendron,** and **azalea.** The Darlingtonian Trail and the Myrtle Creek Trail take you to masses of **pitcher plant.** Bear Basin Butte is a treeless rock outcropping with a wide variety of flowers and expansive views.

BLOOMING: From June through August, with peak blooming from mid-June through July.

GLORIOUS GARDENS: **Thimbleberry, yerba santa, western trillium, tobacco brush, pitcher plant, Washington lily, hot-rock penstemon, fireweed, Labrador tea, leopard lily, western azalea, rhododendron, queen's cup, twinflower, California harebell, pussypaws, windflower, redwood kecki-ella, fuchsia.**

SPECIAL FLOWERS NOT IN PROFUSION: **One-sided wintergreen, Indian pink, alumroot, calypso orchid, Merten's coralroot, giant trillium, red ribbons, phantom orchid, bear grass.**

2) Kangaroo Lake Botanical Area (about 6,000 feet)

FEATURED FLOWER: **Scott Mountain phacelia.** In late June and July, clusters of this rare, ground-hugging, white **phacelia** with the jet black anthers are found occasionally along the Fen Trail.

DRIVING DIRECTIONS: From Interstate 5 (I-5) just south of Yreka, take California State Route 3 (SR-3) south to just beyond Callahan, then bear left on Gazelle Road for about eight miles, then turn right on Rail Creek Road to its end at Kangaroo Lake Campground.

WALKING DIRECTIONS: The Fen Trail starts off Rail Creek Road just before the "Campground" sign and climbs mildly for about a mile up to a junction with the Pacific Crest Trail.

DESCRIPTION: This lovely one-mile trail climbs gently up the serpentine outcrops (actually "ultramafic"—serpentine and peridotite), through co-nifer forest and across creeks and Darlingtonian fens.

BLOOMING: From June through August, with peak blooming in July.

GLORIOUS GARDENS: **Pitcher plant, marsh marigold, crimson columbine, Nuttall's larkspur, spreading phlox, Sierra sedum, dirty socks, Tolmie's pussy ears, blue flax.**

SPECIAL FLOWERS NOT IN PROFUSION: **Scott Mountain phacelia, beargrass, bush cinquefoil, Mount Eddy lupine, Lee's lewisia, red heather, fringed grass-of-Parnassus.**

3) Trinity Alps (about 2,400–9,000 feet)

FEATURED FLOWER: **Lewis monkeyflower.** In July and August, these large, pink-to-rose faces smile at you from along creeks and rivers throughout the Alps.

DRIVING DIRECTIONS: From Weaverville, SR-3 north and SR-299 west linking to SR-96 and Cecilville Road circle the Trinity Alps. Coffee Creek Road west of SR-3 takes you into the interior.

WALKING DIRECTIONS: Trails start from SR-299 west from Weaverville, from SR-3 north from Weaverville, from Coffee Creek Road, and from Cecilville Road west of Callahan. Some of the best trails for wildflowers are Union Creek, Long Canyon, Bear Basin, and Caribou Lakes.

DESCRIPTION: This is a rather isolated area with rugged peaks and canyons, lakes, two major rivers—the Trinity and the south fork of the Salmon—with many tributaries, extensive pine and fir forests, and a few permanent ice fields. With only one road entering, this is an area more for foot and horse travel than for driving. The predominantly Sierran flora only 60 miles from the Pacific Ocean is unique.

BLOOMING: From May to September, with peak blooming from mid-July to mid-August.

GLORIOUS GARDENS: **Leopard lily, crimson columbine, queen's cup, beargrass, Copeland's owl's-clover, pasqueflower, swamp laurel, red heather, Tolmie's saxifrage, creek dogwood, Indian warrior, alpine buttercup, Sierra primrose, heart-leaf arnica, Bigelow's sneezeweed, arrowleaf senecio, Tolmie's pussy ears, candy flower, white heather, Lewis monkeyflower, bleeding heart, explorer's gentian, common yellow monkeyflower, marsh mallow, rock fringe, scarlet gilia, monkshood, windflower, spiraea, coiled-beak lousewort, coltsfoot, cow parsnip, Kelley's tiger lily, Washington lily, western trillium.**

SPECIAL FLOWERS NOT IN PROFUSION: **Pitcher plant, Lee's lewisia, phantom orchid, pipevine, red-flowering currant, few-flowered bleeding heart, pink mountain heather, giant trillium, hairy honeysuckle, fire-cracker flower, scarlet fritillary, hiker's gentian, bush poppy, California Indian pink, showy polemonium, alpine buttercup, fringed grass-of-Parnassus, fringe cups, calypso orchid, Merten's coralroot, red larkspur, alpine gentian, broad-leaf twayblade, mock orange.**

COAST AND COAST RANGES

Sea thrift at Salt Point

WHENEVER YOU DRAW near the Pacific coast, it feels different, it smells different, it tastes different—even the air changes to a softer, more languid caress, spiced with the pungent odor of salt and the sea.

The flowers, too, are different on the coast—beach "strollers" staying clear of the incoming tides and flourishing in the sand and salt, tenacious hangers-on gripping shifting dunes with all their might, bluff dwellers with their "hair" streaming in the sea breezes. The narrow strip of beach and bluff boasts many fascinating species found in few other places. Perhaps it is the sea spray in the air or the blankets of dripping fog (especially in the northern part of the coast), but the flowers of the coast seem to have an intensity of color and a special vitality—it is a great place for saturated color and lingering fragrance and crispness of bloom. Whether you are enveloped in fog or standing clear on a bright, sunny day, the flowers are striking, intense, and luscious.

From Torrey Pines just north of San Diego all the way north to Eureka and the Dunes of Arcata, you will find beautiful, multihued gardens huddling in the sand and nestled on the grassy bluffs looking out over the sea. Mixed in will be occasional rocky cliffs with tenacious individual plants hanging on for dear life and patches of dense, dark woods (sometimes redwoods) reaching all the way to the beach, harboring strange and exotic deep-woods dwellers, some frantically seeking the smallest ray of sun, others calmly feeding on others for their nourishment.

As you move inland to the east, the hills are now brushy or forested, steep ranges where you will find some unique flowers and many old friends familiar from the Cascades and Sierra far to the east. This coastal strip of beach, bluff, and range is a fascinating place of intersections, of meeting places, of edges. For us—the visitors, the guests—the smell of the sea seems to blend with the smell of the flowers, the rolling of the water seems to merge with the windblown rippling of the blossoms, and something deep in us stirs in response.

Be sure to visit Bear Valley and Boggs Lake to see unusual flowers and spectacular displays, and stroll through the dense "jungles" of **azalea**, **rhododendron**, and **lily** in the coastal scrub of Kruse Rhododendron State Park. The redwood forests of Redwood National Park and in Muir Woods on Mount Tamalpais are heavy with misty mystery and timelessness and are rich with intriguing flowers. Don't miss the amazing gardens on San Bruno Mountain, which include several rare species, and be sure to see the rare and stunning **Tiburon mariposa lily** near the top of Ring Mountain and the several dune specialists, such as **crisp dune mint**, **magenta verbena**, and **dune wallflower**, at Nipoma-Guadalupe Dunes and the Dunes at Arcata. In the southern coast ranges, the Santa Rosa Plateau, the Carrizo Plain, along SR-58 (especially at Shell Creek), and Wind Wolves Natural Preserve boast spectacular spring wildflower displays.

When

As early as late January and February, you will probably find reliable harbingers of spring all along the coast. With the arrival of March, these early areas have even more blossoms, and now the blooming will begin to spread inland to the valleys in the coast ranges, including the stunning display of thousands of the rare **adobe lily** at Bear Valley and the carpets of **ground pink** and the stands of rich, dark **chocolate lily** on the Santa Rosa Plateau. In April and May, new species come to the coast, and the coast ranges explode into bloom, including the **azalea** and **rhododendron** jungles at Kruse Rhododendron State Park and the stunning **Tiburon mariposa lily** near the top of Ring Mountain. With June, July, and August, there is still some wonderful blooming along the coast and in the coast ranges (for example, the vernal pool plants at Boggs Lake), but the peak of blooming will have moved on into the higher mountains of the Cascades, the Sierra, and the Transverse and Peninsular ranges.

Northern

4) Redwood National and State Parks (to about 500 feet)

FEATURED FLOWER: **Windflower**. In April and May, these delicate flowers bring great patches of white to the dark undergrowth of the coastal redwoods.

DRIVING DIRECTIONS: Between Eureka and Crescent City, U.S. Route 101 and various spur roads penetrate the deep redwood forests—Jedediah Smith (along U.S. 199) and Del Norte and Prairie Creek along U.S. 101. Be sure to take the "scenic alternative," which includes the Avenue of the Giants.

WALKING DIRECTIONS: There are numerous walking and hiking trails off the main roads in all of these areas that will take you a short or long way into these magnificent forests.

DESCRIPTION: Even only a few yards off a main road on a trail into the redwoods, you will feel like you have entered a mysterious and ancient land. The forest is dense, the trees can tower over 300 feet above you, and the undergrowth is luxuriant with jungles of ferns and wonderful wildflowers that somehow manage to thrive in this land of little light.

BLOOMING: From February through August, with peak blooming of most species from March through May, but some (especially **leopard lily**) from June through August.

GLORIOUS GARDENS: **Leopard lily, western azalea, rhododendron, wind-**

flower, skunk cabbage, redwood sorrel, western dogwood, alumroot, starflower, western trillium, California harebell, false lily-of-the-valley.
SPECIAL FLOWERS NOT IN PROFUSION: **Red clintonia, bleeding heart, salmonberry, fringe cups, calypso orchid, giant trillium, firecracker flower, Indian pipe, Columbia lily.**

5) Dunes of Arcata (to about 50 feet)

FEATURED FLOWER: **Coast buckwheat**. From May well into the fall, the dunes a bit back from the shore are decorated with great gardens of these large white-to-rose, ball-shaped heads of crepe-papery flowers.
DRIVING DIRECTIONS: From U.S. 101 at Arcata, drive west on SR-255 toward Samoa. After a few miles, turn right to the Ma-Le'l Dunes parking area, and a little further south on SR-255, turn right on Stamps Lane and follow the "Friends of the Dunes" signs.
WALKING DIRECTIONS: Take the trails from the parking areas into the dunes and out to the beach.
DESCRIPTION: These two areas and the Lamphere-Christensen Dunes just north (a restored and protected area accessible only with permission from Friends of the Dunes) provide a glimpse of some of the interesting northern California dune plants.
BLOOMING: From May through August, with peak blooming from May into July.
GLORIOUS GARDENS: **Coast buckwheat, beach primrose, yellow sand verbena, sea rocket, sea thrift, Johnny-nip, seaside daisy.**
SPECIAL FLOWERS NOT IN PROFUSION: **White ladies tresses, beach silky pea, Douglas spiraea, beach silvertop, beach morning glory.**

6) Bear Valley (about 1,300–3,500 feet on Walker Ridge)

FEATURED FLOWER: **Adobe lily**. In March, masses of thousands and thousands of these rare and beautiful flowers create a pink haze from a distance and stunning displays of intense pink lilyness from up close.
DRIVING DIRECTIONS: From Williams, drive about 18 miles west on SR-20, then turn right (north) on Bear Valley Road. There may be some nice wildflower displays along the road through the rocky canyon, but the most spectacular displays will probably be in the fields to the west of the road after about seven to seven and a half miles from SR-20. To get to Walker Ridge, drive 6.2 miles west on SR-20 from the intersection with Bear Valley Road, then turn right on Walker Ridge Road.
WALKING DIRECTIONS: Most of the Bear Valley wildflower fields are behind fences. To get close to the showiest spring wildflower displays (including the famous **adobe lily**), you will need to go on a guided hike or to get per-

mission from the landowners, or stay in a small, signed area. You can wander freely along Walker Ridge Road (it is a popular place for hunting, however, so wear something colorful and be careful).

DESCRIPTION: With all the fences, this is not the best place to get up close and personal with the flowers, but in good years it does have wonderful carpets of spring wildflowers to see from a distance, highlighted by the amazing masses of the rare and extremely showy, pink **adobe lily** in mid-March.

BLOOMING: From late February through early June, with the peak blooming in mid-March through May.

GLORIOUS GARDENS: **Adobe lily, large blue-eyed Mary, buck brush, large-flowered star tulip, Indian warrior, bird's-eye gilia, red maid, redbud, blue dicks, cream cup, goldfields, Fremont's camas.**

SPECIAL FLOWERS NOT IN PROFUSION: **Douglas violet, western wallflower, volcanic onion, serrated onion, yellow fairy lantern, superb mariposa lily, bitterroot, Parish's purple nightshade, chaparral currant, royal larkspur.**

7) Boggs Lake (about 2,800 feet)

FEATURED FLOWER: **Two-horned downingia**. From late May into June, you will find thousands of these gorgeous, multicolored, vernal pool flowers in openings in the grass growing in the now mostly dried lake bottom.

DRIVING DIRECTIONS: From Lakeport along the western shore of Clear Lake, drive 7.7 miles south on SR-29, then turn left on Bottle Rock Road. After 4.4 miles, turn left on Harrington Flat Road, and after about one-half mile, park in the designated area on your left with the "Enter" sign.

WALKING DIRECTIONS: Start at the trailhead with the interpretive signs and follow the trails down to and around the lake. Watch out for rattlesnakes, poison oak, and ticks, and be especially careful of the **downingia** and other vernal pool plants as you walk carefully onto the dried lake bottom.

DESCRIPTION: This is probably the largest vernal pool in northern California, home to many fascinating, specially adapted plants as well as some wonderful birds. The liquid song of the red-winged blackbirds will accompany you on your circuit around the lake, and you are likely to see various ducks, geese, herons, and other enchanting waterfowl. You may also hear the ominous rattle of rattlesnakes.

BLOOMING: From March through July, with the peak blooming for most flowers, including several species of **downingia**, from late May into June.

GLORIOUS GARDENS: **Indian warrior, two-horned downingia, toothed downingia, needle navarretia, butter-and-eggs.**

SPECIAL FLOWERS NOT IN PROFUSION: **Winecup clarkia, golden fairy lantern, Indian pink, foothill penstemon, hyacinth brodiaea, false Solomon's seal.**

8) Kruse Rhododendron State Reserve (to about 100 feet)

FEATURED FLOWER: **Pacific rhododendron**. In May, these amazing, rosy pink flowers are dense on the tall shrubs bordering the trail: sometimes looking you right in the face, sometimes looking down at you from high above.

DRIVING DIRECTIONS: From Fort Ross, drive 9.3 miles north on SR-1, then turn right at the sign onto the dirt road. After about four-tenths of a mile, park in the area designated for the Phillips Gulch Trail.

WALKING DIRECTIONS: Head uphill on the trail above the parking area where you can meander along the very short Rhododendron Loop Trail.

DESCRIPTION: A delightful stroll through coastal scrub and **rhododendron** and **azalea** bushes.

BLOOMING: From May into June, with the **rhododendron** and **azalea** usually in peak bloom in mid-May.

GLORIOUS GARDENS: **Pacific rhododendron, western azalea, wood violet, Pacific starflower.**

SPECIAL FLOWERS NOT IN PROFUSION: **Columbia lily, red clintonia, Nootka rose, red-flowering currant, bi-colored lotus, California yellow-eyed grass, salal.**

9) Salt Point State Park (to about 500 feet)

FEATURED FLOWER: **Coast dudleya**. In late May and June, clinging to the rocks by the sea stunning rosettes of fleshy green and red leaves contrast with stalks of bright yellow flowers.

DRIVING DIRECTIONS: From Jenner, drive 20 miles north on SR-1 to the Salt Point State Park, which is on both sides of the highway. After a couple of miles, as you come out into a large clearing and get a view of the ocean, park on the east side of the road near the "Call Box" sign.

WALKING DIRECTIONS: Cross the highway and follow the use trails across the bluff and down to the beach. You can also head east from your car along the trail up into the hills.

DESCRIPTION: Whether it is a warm, clear, sunny spring day or (not unlikely) a not-so-warm, foggy one, this is a marvelous spot for salty air and sea breezes and luscious wildflower gardens. Take the time to explore this place carefully, sometimes on your hands and knees, and you will be rewarded with fascinating seaside plants and patches of intense color.

BLOOMING: Late February through June, with two peak bloomings, first in February and March, and then again in May and June.

GLORIOUS GARDENS: **Cream cups, sea fig, yellow bush lupine, rosy butter-and-eggs, tidy tips, seaside daisy, California poppy, goldfields, footsteps of spring, coast dudleya, Douglas iris, Fremont's camas, coast sun cup, seaside dandelion, coast cucumber, sea thrift, dwarf brodiaea, wild flax, rosy onion, California buttercup, milkmaids.**

SPECIAL FLOWERS NOT IN PROFUSION: **Checkerbloom, western blue-eyed grass, Tolmie's pussy ears, blue blossom, California phacelia, field chickweed, maple-leaf mallow, bi-colored lotus, celery-leaf lovage, Johnny-nip, self-heal.**

10) Bodega Head (to about 100 feet)

FEATURED FLOWER: **White baby blue eyes**. In February and March, numerous patches of this unusual white variety of the endearing early-spring bloomer decorate the grassy bluffs above the beach.

DRIVING DIRECTIONS: From SR-1 in Bodega Bay, turn west following the signs to Bodega Head. At the bottom of the hill (about three-tenths of a mile) turn right and continue another 3.5 miles to the parking area at the end of the road.

WALKING DIRECTIONS: Follow the trail north from the parking lot along the bluffs above the ocean. From time to time, you can take side trails down to the beach.

DESCRIPTION: This is the classic Pacific Ocean bluff hike, crossing wind-blown mats of bluff flowers with occasional descents to the rocky beaches. This is a great place to watch the surf and to find wonderful displays of early spring bloomers.

BLOOMING: February through April, with wonderful displays of some of northern California's earliest bloomers in February into March.

GLORIOUS GARDENS: **Coastal California buttercup, white baby blue eyes, seaside lupine, sea rocket, sea thrift, footsteps of spring, sea fig, wild cucumber, dune tansy.**

SPECIAL FLOWERS NOT IN PROFUSION: **Seaside daisy, coast barberry, California buttercup, purple morning glory, beach strawberry, silver dune lupine, dune knotweed, narrow-leaf gilia, Pacific silverweed.**

11) China Camp State Park (to about 50 feet)

FEATURED FLOWER: **Foothill shooting star**. In February and March, patches of these intense rose-colored, upside-down, inside-out, nodding flowers adorn the grassy banks.

DRIVING DIRECTIONS: From Novato just north of San Francisco, drive south on U.S. 101 several miles to Los Ranchitos, then turn left (east) on North San Pablo Road and follow the signs a few miles to China Camp. The road crosses open fields and runs along San Pablo Bay.

WALKING DIRECTIONS: There are several trails across open fields, along forest edges, and down to the bay. Probably the most interesting trails for wildflowers are the Shoreline Trail (about three miles round-trip) and the Turtle Back Nature Trail (about one and a half miles round-trip).

DESCRIPTION: Even on days when the fog lies heavy in San Francisco Bay, China Camp is often a sanctuary of sunshine. You can enjoy the warmth of grassy fields or the coolness of forest edges and the breeze coming off the water. Even in late February, the grassy fields will shine with sun (cup) and butter (cup), and your safety is guarded by warriors (Indian) in the woods.
BLOOMING: February through August, with some interesting early bloomers in February and March; the peak blooming is in April and May.
GLORIOUS GARDENS: **Indian warrior, milkmaids, foothill shooting star, coast suncup, California buttercup, blue dicks, blue-eyed grass.**
SPECIAL FLOWERS NOT IN PROFUSION: **Ground iris, bush monkeyflower, false lupine, checkerbloom.**

Central and Southern

12) Ring Mountain (603 feet)

FEATURED FLOWER: **Tiburon mariposa lily**. This endangered plant only occurs on Ring Mountain; its large, dazzling, yellow-green-purple-brown mottled flowers decorate the rocks in serpentine grasslands near the top from mid-May into June.
DRIVING DIRECTIONS: From SR-1 in Corte Madeira, head east on Paradise Drive. After about one and a half miles, park along the right side of the road near the gated dirt road with the information sign.
WALKING DIRECTIONS: Walk along the dirt road to the right to the "Information" sign, then head up the Loop Trail. There are several trails coming into and out of the Loop Trail—just keep working your way up toward the summit.
DESCRIPTION: The houses along this little open space remind you of the hard work and perseverance it took many people to keep a significant portion of this mountain undeveloped, and the rare, endangered **Tiburon mariposa lily** protected. You will walk through some forested areas, but most of the hike will be across open, serpentine grasslands.
BLOOMING: March through July, with most flowers in peak bloom in March and April.
GLORIOUS GARDENS: **Oakland star tulip, Tiburon mariposa lily, Douglas iris, checkermallow, California buttercup, elegant brodiaea, long-rayed hyacinth, soap plant, everlasting pea, ruby chalice clarkia, coyote mint, coast suncup.**
SPECIAL FLOWERS NOT IN PROFUSION: **Western blue-eyed grass, California Indian pink, tidy tips, globe gilia, large-flowered star-tulip, pitted onion, California false lupine.**

13) Mount Tamalpais and Muir Woods (to 2,571 feet)

FEATURED FLOWER: **Slink pod (fetid adder's tongue).** In February and March, you will find (if you look carefully) scattered patches of these odd, striped flowers on erect stems in the shade of the redwoods; when they go to fruit, you will see downright bizarre, limp and snaking, seedpod-bearing stems.

DRIVING DIRECTIONS: Just a few miles north of the Golden Gate Bridge across the Bay from San Francisco, head west on SR-1 where it separates from U.S. 101. Follow the signs to Mount Tamalpais and Muir Woods. There are several trailheads along the road on Mount Tamalpais; the signs for Muir Woods will take you down off the main Mount Tamalpais road into a hollow, low on the western side of the mountain.

WALKING DIRECTIONS: Wander to your heart's content on the extensive network of trails both in Muir Woods and on the slopes of Mount Tamalpais.

DESCRIPTION: With sufficient time and energy, you could do a loop beginning in the dark, mysterious redwoods of Muir Woods, and then ascend to the brushy slopes and sometimes open vistas of Mount Tamalpais, and return to the deep woods of Muir. For those hungry for spring, Muir Woods and the lower parts of Mount Tamalpais boast some wonderful wildflower displays as early as mid-to-late February.

BLOOMING: February through July, with some fascinating early bloomers in February and March, and the peak bloom for most species in March through May.

GLORIOUS GARDENS: **Fremont's camas, redwood sorrel, California blackberry, hoary manzanita, western trillium, coltsfoot, milkmaids, California poppy, wild cucumber.**

SPECIAL FLOWERS NOT IN PROFUSION: **Slink pod**, grand hound's tongue, **bush monkeyflower, checkerbloom, coast sun cup, foothill saxifrage, thimbleberry, bush poppy.**

14) Mount Diablo (to 3,849 feet)

FEATURED FLOWER: **Mount Diablo globe lily**. In May and June, the golden "light" from these exquisite yellow globes shines only on Mount Diablo and surrounding hills, and in a few places across the Carquinez Straits in Solano County.

DRIVING DIRECTIONS: In the East Bay across from San Francisco, Mount Diablo lies just southeast of Walnut Creek. There are several ways to access the summit, including Mount Diablo Road off I-680, and Walnut Avenue and then Oak Grove off Ygnacio Valley Road in Walnut Creek. To get to the Mitchell Canyon Trail, take Ygnacio Valley Road east, turn right on Clayton Road, then right on Mitchell Canyon Road. There is an entrance fee.

WALKING DIRECTIONS: There are several trails up the sides and around the summit. The Mitchell Canyon Trail is a wonderful "comprehensive" trail that can be a short, level, mile or two stroll (to see the endemic **Mount Diablo globe lily**) or a strenuous, all-day hike of over 15 miles.

DESCRIPTION: As an isolated peak in the central Coast Ranges rising almost 3,800 feet above the surrounding valleys, Mount Diablo is quite a conspicuous feature of the East Bay area, visible from many miles away in all directions. Practically any hike on the mountain will involve grasslands, chaparral, or oak woodlands, with a good chance of encountering one or more of the mountain's many springs. The Mitchell Canyon Trail takes you past all of these, and traverses woods and grassy hills for a good part of the way.

BLOOMING: February through June, with peak blooming from March into April.

GLORIOUS GARDENS: **Milkmaids, California buttercup, blue dicks, fiddleneck, miner's lettuce, foothill shooting star, wild cucumber, Indian warrior, baby blue eyes, Chinese houses, California blackberry, coyote mint, western wallflower.**

SPECIAL FLOWERS NOT IN PROFUSION: **Mount Diablo globe lily, red larkspur, giant trillium, aquatic buttercup, live forever, virgin's bower, royal larkspur, alumroot, wood strawberry, fan violet, red ribbons, lace parsnip, narrow-leaf milkweed, bird's-eye gilia, blue fiesta flower, fragrant fritillary, stream orchid, clustered broomrape, serrated onion, Oakland star tulip, glassy onion.**

15) San Bruno Mountains (to 1,314 feet)

FEATURED FLOWER: **Franciscan wallflower.** In March and April, you will find numerous stands of this creamy, four-petaled beauty, all the more alluring because of its rarity.

DRIVING DIRECTIONS: Heading north from San Jose toward San Francisco on U.S. 101, take the Bayshore Boulevard/Brisbane exit near South San Francisco. Turn west (left) on Guadalupe Canyon Parkway, and after 1.9 miles, turn right into the San Bruno Mountain Park entrance and follow the signs to trailhead parking.

WALKING DIRECTIONS: From the parking area, hike up the Summit Loop Trail. There are several trails branching off this trail that you could take to shorten or lengthen your hike. The entire 3.1 miles of the Summit Loop Trail is well worth the effort.

DESCRIPTION: Within a few minutes of entering the eucalyptus and fern coastal scrub "jungle," you will only faintly remember that you are near a major city. When you see the amazing displays of flowers, you will forget completely! From creek-fed hollows to open, grassy fields with expansive views of the city, this is a magical place. Especially in March and April, it is a glorious wildflower haven.

BLOOMING: From February through June, with a fabulous spring blooming in March and April.

GLORIOUS GARDENS: **Mission bells, rose rock cress, footsteps of spring, checkerbloom, lace parsnip, California blackberry, Franciscan wall-flower, coast sun cup.**

SPECIAL FLOWERS NOT IN PROFUSION: **Johnny jump-up, western dog violet, coast barberry, San Bruno manzanita, California phacelia, meadow chickweed, giant trillium, blue blossom, Watson's willowherb, California hedgenettle.**

16) Edgewood Preserve and Pulgas Ridge Open Area (about 225–820 feet)

FEATURED FLOWER: **Ruby chalice clarkia.** In May these delicate, red-spotted, pink blooms glow when backlit by a low, late-afternoon sun.

DRIVING DIRECTIONS: From the intersection of U.S. 101 and SR-92 in San Mateo, drive 4.3 miles west on SR-92, then turn left (south) on I-280. After 3.3 miles, take the Edgewood Road exit and drive east (left) on Edgewood Road for about one mile. For Pulgas Ridge, turn left onto Crestview Drive, then immediately left on Edmonds to the parking area, on the right. For Edgewood Park, turn right off Edgewood Road just beyond Crestview and into the parking lot for the park.

WALKING DIRECTIONS: For either area, wander at your leisure on the network of trails. In Edgewood Park, the Serpentine Trail is especially good for flowers.

DESCRIPTION: The trails in both areas go through oak woodlands and across open serpentine grasslands. The Serpentine Trail in Edgewood Park is especially interesting, alternating between quiet oak hollows and open ridge tops buffeted by freeway noise. The flowers seem all the more precious in such close proximity to the urban bustle.

BLOOMING: From February through June, with most flowers in peak bloom from mid-March through April.

GLORIOUS GARDENS: **Ruby chalice clarkia, California buttercup, blue dicks, foothill shooting star, yellow carpet, soap plant, common phacelia, tidy tips.**

SPECIAL FLOWERS NOT IN PROFUSION: **Coast sun cup, western blue-eyed grass, wild cucumber, Fremont's death camas, Ithuriel's spear, globe lily, golden mariposa lily, Indian warrior, red-flowering currant, purple morning glory, chia, fragrant fritillary, chick lupine, rosy onion, pitted onion.**

17) Pinnacles National Monument (about 825–3300 feet)

FEATURED FLOWER: **Woolly blue curls.** In May and June these "furry" shrubs with the spectacular, long-"antennaed" purple flowers on rosy spikes accompany you along many of the trails.

DRIVING DIRECTIONS: For the west entrance, drive about 11 miles east on SR-146 from Soledad on U.S. 101. For the east entrance (which is not connected to the west entrance), from King City on U.S. 101, take County Road G13 east, then SR-25 north to the Bear Gulch entrance spur road.

WALKING DIRECTIONS: There are several wonderful trails; of particular interest for wildflowers are the Juniper Canyon Trail, the Bear Gulch Trail, the High Peaks Trail, the Balcony Cliff Trail, the Chelone Peaks Trail, and the Rim Trail. Check with the Visitors' Center (on the east entrance road) for information.

DESCRIPTION: Competing with the beautiful wildflower displays are the dramatic rock formations, caves, waterfalls, and raptors!

BLOOMING: From late February into June, with most flowers in peak bloom from March through May.

GLORIOUS GARDENS: **Padres' shooting star, foothill shooting star, Johnny jump-up, western wallflower, wild cucumber, woolly Indian paintbrush, fiddleneck, milkmaids, common phacelia, blue dicks, Indian warrior, white fiesta flower, virgin's bower, black sage, California poppy, bush monkeyflower, Chinese houses, California buckeye, pitcher sage, woolly blue curls, elegant clarkia, butterfly mariposa lily, golden yarrow, crinkled onion, grand hound's tongue.**

SPECIAL FLOWERS NOT IN PROFUSION: **Pacific sedum, stinging lupine, whispering bells, blue fiesta flower, California hedgenettle, Booth's evening primrose, fuchsia, clustered broomrape, bush poppy, scarlet monkeyflower, volcanic onion, death camas, lanceleaf dudleya, Douglas spineflower, bitterroot, fairy fan, naked broomrape, Parry's larkspur, pipevine, wine-cup clarkia.**

18) SR-58 from Santa Margarita to McKittrick (to about 1,000 feet)

FEATURED FLOWER: **Lindley's blazing star**. In March and April, just west of McKittrick as the road begins to climb the Temblor Range, you will be dazzled by the burning orange patches of this stunning flower—a richer, more blazing orange than the fiddlenecks and perhaps even than the poppies also growing on the hills.

DRIVING DIRECTIONS: From Santa Margarita (just northeast of San Luis Obispo) on U.S. 101, drive east on SR-58 for about 75 miles to McKittrick. Be sure to turn north on Shell Creek Road toward the Santa Margarita end of the road.

WALKING DIRECTIONS: Most of this route is fenced, but there is plenty of delicious wildflowering to be done along the road edges.

DESCRIPTION: This is a spectacular drive in the spring when the grasslands, rolling hills, and oak woodlands of the Caliente Range and the Temblor Range are exploding with swaths, patches, and carpets of pink, purple, yellow, orange, white, and blue. In good years, the field at the intersection of SR-58 and Shell Creek Road can be an amazing floral tapestry.

BLOOMING: From late February through May, with most flowers in peak bloom in March and April.

GLORIOUS GARDENS: **Padre's shooting star, California poppy, goldfields, hillside daisy, fiddleneck, common phacelia, foothill popcorn flower, blue dicks, baby blue eyes, Lindley's blazing star, sky lupine, tidy tips, purple owl's-clover, prickly phlox, thistle sage, bush poppy, sticky monkeyflower, chia, bush lupine, tufted evening primrose, tansy-leaf phacelia, Bigelow's coreopsis, speckled clarkia.**

SPECIAL FLOWERS NOT IN PROFUSION: **Bladderpod bush, scarlet bugler, Booth's evening primrose, purple sand verbena, cream cups, golden layia.**

19) Carrizo Plain (about 500 feet)

FEATURED FLOWER: **Parry's larkspur.** In April and May in a good year, large stands of these lovely, pale blue delphiniums add their subtle color and interesting form to the grassland gardens.

DRIVING DIRECTIONS: Access is from the north (turn south from SR-58) or south (turn north from SR-166). Much of the Soda Lake Road, which travels the entire length of the plain, is paved, though several miles in the middle are not (and so should be avoided in wet weather). Branching off the main road are numerous dirt roads offering adventure and surprise!

WALKING DIRECTIONS: Wander to your heart's content across the unfenced grasslands and flowery meadows (being careful, of course, to value each individual even among a field of thousands).

DESCRIPTION: This is the largest remaining undeveloped piece of California grasslands. It nestles safely between two north-south–running mountain ranges. In good years, the spring wildflower displays are stunning, with carpets, tapestries, patches, masses, and "seas" of all sorts of spring bloomers—some are amazing uninterrupted displays of one species (for example, **hillside daisy, tidy tips, desert dandelion, common phacelia, purple owl's-clover, goldfields**) while others are multispecies paradises.

BLOOMING: From March through May, with the peak bloom in late March through April.

GLORIOUS GARDENS: **Hillside daisy, Bigelow's coreopsis, tidy tips, goldfields, desert dandelion, common phacelia, thistle sage, purple owl's-clover, fiddleneck, Parry's larkspur, red maids, western wallflower, yellow carpet, wild cucumber, bird-cage evening primrose.**

SPECIAL FLOWERS NOT IN PROFUSION: **Baby blue eyes, cream cups, California four o'clock, bladderpod bush, desert trumpet, yellow throats, white layia.**

20) Nipomo-Guadalupe Dunes (to about 50 feet)

FEATURED FLOWER: **Beach evening primrose**. For most of the spring and summer, these delightful, bright yellow, silver-dollar-size flowers brighten up the sand in areas just inland from the fore dunes, at least partly sheltered from the often-strong sea breezes.

DRIVING DIRECTIONS: From U.S. 101 at Pismo Beach, take the SR-1 exit and drive south. There are four access points to the dunes: at Grover Beach, Oceano, Oso Flaco Lake, and Guadalupe.

WALKING DIRECTIONS: Walk to your heart's content along the beach and in the dunes above the beach. The Oso Flaco Lake access is especially interesting—there is a causeway across the lake that turns into a trail through the dunes.

DESCRIPTION: This dune complex of the central coast has been called "the most unique and fragile ecosystem in California." It certainly is interesting—for the unusual and difficult environmental conditions and for the specialized plants that have adapted to them, including several uncommon varieties and subspecies.

BLOOMING: January through July, with most flowers in peak bloom from March through May.

GLORIOUS GARDENS: **Sea rocket, yellow sand verbena, beach evening primrose, milkmaids, dunes paintbrush, giant coreopsis, prickly phlox, silver dune lupine, common phacelia, butter-and-eggs, thin-leaved ice plant, nettle, purple sand verbena, blue dicks, coast paintbrush, California blackberry.**

SPECIAL FLOWERS NOT IN PROFUSION: **Dune wallflower, southern pink, clustered broomrape, magenta sand verbena, Hooker's evening primrose, crisp dune mint, beach morning glory, beach strawberry, seaside daisy, twinberry.**

21) Wind Wolves Natural Preserve (about 640–6,005 feet)

FEATURED FLOWER: **Hillside daisy**. In March and April, dense masses of these brilliant "sunflowers" splash fields, steep hillsides, and canyon walls with brilliant yellow "paint."

DRIVING DIRECTIONS: From Gorman, drive north on I-5 about 22 miles to the SR-166 exit, then drive west on SR-166 about 10 miles and turn left at the "Wind Wolves" sign. The entrance is about three miles up the road, and the trailheads are a bit further. The preserve is open to the public only on weekends.

WALKING DIRECTIONS: The Spring Wildflower Trail is an easy, level walk through amazingly dense fields of flowers in March and April; the San Emigdio Canyon Trail is a bit more of a hike but also has wonderful flowers.

DESCRIPTION: The preserve extends from the western edge of the San Joaquin Valley up into the eastern slopes of the Temblor Range. The **fiddleneck, blue dicks, lupine,** and **purple owl's-clover** are so thick in the low grasslands in spring that you can see great swathes of blue and purple and orange from miles away, but even this amazing display is matched in brilliance by the startling yellow "paint" of the **hillside daisy** on the canyon walls in the upper hills.

BLOOMING: Late February through May, with most flowers in peak bloom in March and April.

GLORIOUS GARDENS: **Hillside daisy, blue dicks, sky lupine, bird's-eye gilia, purple owl's-clover, stork's bill, white fiesta flower, common phacelia, arroyo lupine, fiddleneck, tansy-leaf phacelia.**

SPECIAL FLOWERS NOT IN PROFUSION: **Bladderpod bush, whispering bells, white keckiella, scarlet monkeyflower, our Lord's candle, coyote mint, Kennedy's mariposa lily, elegant clarkia, thistle sage, crinkled onion.**

22) Santa Rosa Plateau (about 1800 feet)

FEATURED FLOWER: **Chocolate lily.** From late February through March, clusters of these amazingly dark, rich, chocolaty flowers decorate the grassy fields, especially dramatic because not much else is yet in bloom.

DRIVING DIRECTIONS: From I-15 just south of Lake Elsinore, take the Clinton Keith Road exit and drive west about four miles to the Visitors' Center. There is a trailhead here and others within the next two or three miles along Clinton Keith Road.

WALKING DIRECTIONS: There are several trails of interest, but the Waterline Road Trail (for the **chocolate lily**) and the Vernal Pools Trail (for **spotted downingia, splendid mariposa lily,** and **ground pink**) are probably the most rewarding for spring flowers.

DESCRIPTION: Just a few miles west of the freeway and all the urban sprawl, this plateau stands out as an oasis of wildness with grasslands, oak woods, hills, creeks, and several remarkable vernal pools. The trails are mostly level strolls.

BLOOMING: From late February through June, with most flowers in peak bloom from March into May.

GLORIOUS GARDENS: **Chocolate lily, Padre's shooting star, ground pink, manroot, Johnny jump-up, goldfields, blue dicks, yellow carpet, red maids, tidy tips, rusty popcorn flower, chick lupine, black sage, bush monkeyflower, soap plant, splendid mariposa lily, spotted downingia, wine-cup clarkia, California poppy, golden yarrow, milkmaids.**

SPECIAL FLOWERS NOT IN PROFUSION: **Toothed downingia, narrow-leaf milkweed, cobweb thistle, elk thistle, powdery dudleya, California peony, southern pink, golden stars, western azalea, stinging lupine, widethroated monkeyflower, southern sun cup, canchalagua, needle navarretia, foothill saxifrage, fringed woodland star, Vasey's prickly pear,**

Parish's purple nightshade, checkerbloom, chaparral currant, brittle-bush, alkali heliotrope, climbing penstemon.

23) Torrey Pines State Park (to about 100 feet)

FEATURED FLOWER: **Sea dahlia.** In March through May, these rare (in California), cheery, yellow sunflowers dance in the sea breeze with the blue Pacific a lovely contrast in the background.

DRIVING DIRECTIONS: On U.S. 101, just a mile or so south of Del Mar (north of San Diego).

WALKING DIRECTIONS: There are several relatively short trails, all of which are wonderful, though the Guy Fleming Trail is particularly beautiful for flowers and ocean views.

DESCRIPTION: This is a densely vegetated bluff with coastal scrub and oak woods that rises above the ocean. Although the trails are, for the most part, gradual and easy, at times you might feel that you, as well as the flowers, are clinging to the cliffs and celebrating the magnificent view and ocean breezes. So close to the ocean moisture, it might be surprising to find several species of yuccas and cacti.

BLOOMING: From late February through May, with most flowers in peak bloom from March through April.

GLORIOUS GARDENS: **Sea dahlia, bladderpod bush, wild cucumber, black sage, ground pink, Parish's purple nightshade, common phacelia, purple sand verbena, milkmaids, southern sun cup, Padre's shooting star, coast paintbrush, Johnny jump-up.**

SPECIAL FLOWERS NOT IN PROFUSION: **Climbing milkweed, stinging lupine, California four-o'clock, virgin's bower, Mojave yucca, bush poppy, brittlebush, white fiesta flower, fringed woodland star, powdery dudleya, large-flowered phacelia.**

TRANSVERSE RANGES

Giant coreopsis in the Santa Monica Mountains

TO STAND ON A BEACH on the southern California coast anywhere from Santa Barbara south to San Diego is to experience the drama of worlds colliding, of barriers and edges. Looking west, you see the waters of the Pacific crashing on the beaches; looking east you see steeply rising mountains cutting the coast off from the inland desert. The Transverse Ranges— from the Santa Ynez Mountains just north of Santa Barbara, to the Santa Monica Range bisecting the greater Los Angeles area, to the San Gabriel Mountains, San Bernardino Mountains, and Little San Bernardino Mountains—and the Peninsular Ranges—from the San Jacinto Mountains west of Palm Springs to the Cuyamaca Mountains and Otay Mountains east of San Diego—create a considerable barrier between the world of beach and water and the world of hot desert sands.

The Transverse Ranges run more-or-less west to east (hence "transverse"), unlike the vast majority of California ranges that run north(west) to south(east). The Santa Ynez and Santa Monica mountains are low (though steep), but the San Gabriel and San Bernardino are "serious" mountains, peaking at over 10,000 feet, creating a bulky and majestic barrier. Much of the terrain, even in the lower elevations, is steep, covered with coastal scrub, chaparral, oak woodlands, and grasslands. Though the topography is a sharp edge, the plants suggest otherwise, for many plants that also occur on the coast (for example, **coastal paintbrush, bush poppy, stinging lupine, California sun cup**), and many that also occur in the desert (for example, **Parry's phacelia, wild canterbury bells, whispering bells, our Lord's candle**) can be seen quite a way up the mountains. And if you're familiar with the flowers of the northern California mountains, you might be surprised to find quite a few of those old friends (for example, **crimson columbine, great red paintbrush, snowplant, western wallflower, Richardson's geranium**) growing here too, especially at the higher elevations.

What a joy to find such a diversity of flowers and, on the western side, with the gorgeous blue Pacific as a backdrop! And what a godsend to the urban throngs below to have such a sanctuary in their backyard—wild places of peace, beauty, and quiet where the flowers (and animals) live on their own terms, unshaped, for the most part, by human values and constraints. Of course, it is the humans who have to stand up and insist that this continues in the face of ever-expanding human pressure and demands.

When

The lower elevations of the Santa Ynez and Santa Monica Mountains near the beach reach their peak bloom in March and April (though some plants can bloom all year)—the blazing yellow **giant coreopsis** are dazzling on the lower slopes of the Santa Monica Mountains in these spring months, while lower canyons like Solstice come alive with **hummingbird sage, bush sunflower, our Lord's candle, Parry's phacelia**, and **purple night-**

shade. Even the lower slopes of the San Gabriels and San Bernardinos, especially in burn areas, can be aglow in spring with **coastal wishbone bush, wild canterbury bells, Cucamonga manroot**, and **wide-throated monkeyflower.** In May into June, the lower and especially the middle elevations of many of these mountains are vibrant with such dazzlers as **large-flowered phacelia, our Lord's candle, climbing penstemon, speckled clarkia, golden yarrow, bush mallow**, and **tall purple sage.**

The best months for the higher elevations will, of course, be later, with displays peaking in July and August but continuing to some degree well into fall.

24) Santa Monica Mountains (to 3,111 feet)

FEATURED FLOWER: **Giant coreopsis.** From late February through May, the stretch of coast at the base of the western part of the Santa Monica Mountains is ablaze with extensive colonies of these large "sunflowers" on their "tree trunk" stems.

DRIVING DIRECTIONS: SR-1 west of Santa Monica runs along the base of the mountains; several narrow, winding roads climb steeply up into the mountains, notably those switchbacking up Topanga Canyon, Tuna Canyon, Malibu Canyon, and Coral Canyon.

WALKING DIRECTIONS: There are numerous trails throughout the area, many with spectacular views of the ocean. Among the best trails for wildflowers are Solstice Canyon, Mishe Mokwa, and Charmlee Wilderness Park.

DESCRIPTION: This is a sweet little mountain range (the highest peak is 3,111 feet), all the sweeter for its location—bisecting the greater Los Angeles area and rising directly up from the Pacific coastline. Much of the area is coastal scrub, chaparral, and oak woodland.

BLOOMING: Late February through July (a few plants are in bloom even later), with most flowers in peak bloom from March through May.

GLORIOUS GARDENS: **Giant coreopsis, prickly phlox, bush mallow, tall purple sage, bush monkeyflower, our Lord's candle, common phacelia, Indian warrior, coast paintbrush, ground pink, bladderpod bush, California buttercup, annual sunflower, black sage, Johnny jump-up, western wallflower, golden yarrow, California blackberry, manroot, virgin bower.**

SPECIAL FLOWERS NOT IN PROFUSION: **Parry's phacelia, hummingbird sage, southern pink, fuchsia-flowered gooseberry, stinging lupine, woolly blue curls, scarlet monkeyflower, large-flowered phacelia, chaparral currant, checkerbloom, California four o'clock, chocolate lily, California peony, thick-leaved yerba santa, California hedgenettle, Matilija poppy, butterfly mariposa lily.**

25) San Gabriel Mountains and San Bernardino Mountains (to 10,064 feet)

FEATURED FLOWER: **Wild canterbury bells**. In March through May in burn areas (all too frequent here), these tall plants with the large, stunningly blue-purple, vaselike flowers often join with other opportunists like **coastal wishbone bush** and **wide-throated monkeyflower** to bring life and hope back to charred slopes.

DRIVING DIRECTIONS: I-15 divides the San Gabriel Mountains and the San Bernardino Mountains. The main road traversing the San Gabriels is the Angeles Crest Highway (SR-2); while the Rim of the World Highway (SR-18) does the same in the San Bernardinos. There are many roads entering both ranges, including Mount Gleeson Road into Big Tujunga Canyon, Little Tujunga Road, San Gabriel Canyon Road (SR-39), Glendora Mountain Road, and Mount Baldy Road. All these roads are steep and winding.

WALKING DIRECTIONS: There are numerous trails through both these ranges. Some of the best for wildflowers are the Sierra Madre to Mount Wilson Trail, the Upper and Lower Winter Creek trails, and the Toll Road.

DESCRIPTION: The average elevation here is about 4,500 feet, but the highest points are over 10,000 feet. Though the higher slopes can be heavy with snow in the winter, they can be brutally hot in the summer. There are springs and streams and a few lakes, but much of this terrain is hot and dry scrub and chaparral, so be prepared and be cautious. Big Bear Lake and Lake Arrowhead are well known and well developed, which can be an annoyance but also can be a convenience and a delight.

BLOOMING: March through October, with peak blooming from April through July.

GLORIOUS GARDENS: **Crimson columbine, giant red paintbrush, California fuchsia, Parry's phacelia, wild canterbury bells, whispering bells, baby blue eyes, coastal wishbone bush, Wood's rose, prickly phlox, California buckwheat, our Lord's candle, elegant clarkia, bush monkeyflower, coastal paintbrush, western wallflower, bush poppy, blazing star, wide-throated monkeyflower, scarlet bugler, golden yarrow, large-flowered phacelia, climbing penstemon, speckled clarkia, lanceleaf dudleya, Indian warrior, red maids, foothill shooting star, cow parsnip, manroot, California four o'clock.**

SPECIAL FLOWERS NOT IN PROFUSION: **White-veined wintergreen, snowplant, stinging lupine, Matilija poppy, California sun cup, scarlet monkeyflower, southern pink, Rothrock's nama, blazing star, California peony, red larkspur, striped mariposa lily, eupatorium, Mojave prickly pear.**

CENTRAL VALLEY

Tidy tips, goldfields, and clover at Vina Preserve

THIS LONG, BROAD VALLEY, nestled between the foothills of the Sierra and southern Cascades to the east and the coastal ranges to the west and running much of the length of northern California (where it is called the Sacramento Valley) and central and a bit of southern California (where it is called the San Joaquin Valley), provides a huge, nearly flat palette for nature's floral artistry. The Central Valley also, however, has proved to be fertile ground for agriculture, business, and settlement, so what used to be an endless floral sea is now just a few scattered islands—preserves, sanctuaries, and a few small, "empty" fields.

As you stand in Jepson Prairie, Phoenix Park, or Vina Preserve (by arrangement) or another less-well-known one of these floral "islands" amid farming and development, imagine what this was like 100 years ago, when these flower fields extended for as far as the eye could see, and an ant could have walked from petal to petal all the way from San Francisco across the Central Valley to the Yosemite foothills without ever touching the ground.

The Central Valley is also home to the unique vernal pool habitat— spring pools and ponds with a hardpan floor that prevent drainage, so instead they slowly evaporate. As they do, a wonderful flora (highlighted by the purple, yellow, and white **downingia**) slowly replaces the now-evaporated water on the higher ground.

Table Mountain, a volcanic mesa rising more than a thousand feet above the surrounding land, is a glorious anomaly—a mixture of foothill and valley flowers plopped down along the eastern edge of the Sacramento Valley. On this hard, volcanic rock, you can find some wonderful vernal pools as well as creeks, cliffs, and wide expanses of grassland.

When

Beginning in late January and February, with the blooming of the **mustard** fields in the orchards, the Central Valley bloom peaks in March with carpets of yellow composites (**goldfields, yellow carpet, blennosperma, tidy tips**). In April, the blues take over, with several tall members of the Brodiaea family (**blue dicks, Ithuriel's spear, ookow**), and the wonderful vernal pool **downingia.** By May, most of the blooming has moved up to the lower mountains.

26) Table Mountain (about 1,100 feet)

FEATURED FLOWER: **Dwarf cliff sedum**. In April and May, these dainty, ground-hugging lanyards paint the table tops lemon-yellow.

DRIVING DIRECTIONS: From SR-70, take the Oroville Dam Boulevard exit east into Oroville. After 1.9 miles, turn left on Washington Avenue, which turns into Table Mountain Boulevard. After about one-and-a-half miles from Oroville Dam Boulevard, turn right on Cherokee Road, which winds up to the Table Mountain plateau. At 6.3 miles on Cherokee, you can park on the left (northwest) side of the road in the large gravel area by the cattle chutes.

WALKING DIRECTIONS: Walk through the gate and wander across the table-top to waterfalls, basalt cliffs, creeks and ponds, and gorgeous masses of wildflowers. Respect the "Private Property" signs and the livestock. Also along Cherokee Road on your way up to the table-top, park carefully from time to time, and check out the great flowers along the road in the grass-lands and open woods.

DESCRIPTION: This fascinating table-top is like an island in time—a haven of wildflowers and fascinating geology rising above the city and the Central Valley a thousand feet below. Although much of it is private grazing land behind fences, the wonderful expanse of North Table Mountain has been made available to lovers of wildflowers and open spaces. Especially in mid-March through April, this is one of the showiest wildflower areas in northern California.

BLOOMING: Late February through May, with the peak blooming in April.

GLORIOUS GARDENS: **Goldfields, dwarf cliff sedum, sky lupine, bird's-eye gilia, volcanic onion, purple owl's-clover, annual poppy, Kellogg's monkeyflower, Douglas violet, meadowfoam, butter-and-eggs, yellow carpet, blue dicks, common yellow monkeyflower.**

SPECIAL FLOWERS NOT IN PROFUSION: **Bitterroot, ookow, red larkspur, bush lupine, toothed downingia, glassy onion, yellow pussy ears, glass lily, foothill saxifrage, elegant brodiaea, spreading larkspur, ground iris, pipevine, Douglas monkeyflower, pansy monkeyflower, hyacinth brodiaea, royal larkspur.**

27) Pleasants Valley Road and Mix Canyon Road (about 50–850 feet)

FEATURED FLOWER: **Mustard**. In February and March, great golden masses cloak the ground under the orchard trees. Although mustard is not a native species here, it still is a beautiful spring feature of these Central Valley grasslands.

DRIVING DIRECTIONS: From Vacaville, drive west on I-80 a couple of miles, then take the Pena Adobe exit, turn left at the stop sign, then after a half-mile, turn right onto Pleasants Valley Road. After about five miles, turn left on Mix Canyon Road, which will climb up the canyon to Mount Vaca.

WALKING DIRECTIONS: Park safely along the roads and explore the edges of the orchards, fields, and woods (being careful of traffic and respecting private property, of course).

DESCRIPTION: In late February, the solid acres of blooming **mustard** under the fruit trees along Pleasants Valley Road is stunning—you may need your sunglasses to look at them! If you come back a few weeks later, it will be even more dazzling with the fruit trees now in bloom canopying the still-gleaming mustard. Although this area is largely naturalized grasslands, it still boasts some dazzling flowers well worth seeing. I have included adjoining Mix Canyon Road with Pleasants Valley Road because of its proximity, although the former actually climbs part way out of the Central Valley. Its mostly shaded canyon adorned with scattered shade-loving native plants offers quite a contrast to the open fields and orchards of Pleasants Valley.

BLOOMING: From February through May, with most flowers in peak bloom from late February through early April.

GLORIOUS GARDENS: **Field mustard, California poppy, harvest brodiaea, golden fairy lantern, red maids, Bermuda sorrel, foothill shooting star, California buttercup, milkmaids.**

SPECIAL FLOWERS NOT IN PROFUSION: **Bush lupine, red larkspur, Chinese houses, mission bells.**

28) Phoenix Park (about 50 feet)

FEATURED FLOWER: **Ithuriel's spear.** In late March through April, many of these purple-flowered "spears" wave with the grass in the spring breeze.

DRIVING DIRECTIONS: From Roseville northwest of Sacramento on I-80, take the Douglas Boulevard exit (Exit 103). Take Douglas Boulevard east and turn on Sunrise heading south. After about six-and-a-half miles, turn left on Sunset, and after 2.75 miles, turn in to Phoenix Park on your right.

WALKING DIRECTIONS: Follow the trails across the grassy fields and to the edges of the vernal pools.

DESCRIPTION: This is a lovely little park in the middle of a residential area highlighted by a connected system of vernal pools with their intriguing **downingia** and an open, grassy field, which is brodiaea (and so, our) heaven!

BLOOMING: Late February through May, with the peak blooming in late March through April.

GLORIOUS GARDENS: **Ithuriel's spear, foothill checkermallow, Johnny-tuck, toothed downingia, blue dicks, meadowfoam.**

SPECIAL FLOWERS NOT IN PROFUSION: **Hyacinth brodiaea, harvest brodiaea, folded downingia, two horned downingia, spotted downingia.**

29) Jepson Prairie Preserve (about 100 feet)

FEATURED FLOWER: **Toothed downingia.** In April, the oh-so-cute, blue, yellow, and white flowers of this species (along with several other similar species) ring the vernal pools and nestle in the hollows between the mounds with their exuberant floral cheer.

DRIVING DIRECTIONS: From I-80 a few miles west of Davis, take SR-113 south (Exit 66a) through Dixon and continue about 10 miles south on SR-113 until the road makes a 90-degree turn to the left. Instead of following the road through the turn, continue straight on the dirt road about three-fourths of a mile until you come to the "Jepson Prairie Preserve" sign on the left.

WALKING DIRECTIONS: You can wander across the fields on the left side of the road behind the sign or on the right side through one of the gates (being careful of the flowers, of course). Be sure to head down to the "shoreline" of Olcott Lake—the large vernal pool to the west.

DESCRIPTION: This is probably the best remaining example of bunchgrass prairie in all the Central Valley. Special features of this preserve are the extensive vernal pools (especially the largest one, Olcott Lake) and mima mounds (see the Jepson Prairie publication in the bibliography for an explanation of the mounds). As the vernal pools evaporate from the shallow perimeter to the deep center, specially adapted plants bloom in rings or patches, mirroring the topography of the pool floor, including several species of the fascinating **downingia**.

BLOOMING: Late February through April, with the peak blooming in mid-March and early April. The several species of vernal pool **downingia** reach their peak in April.

GLORIOUS GARDENS: **Yellow carpet, goldfields, tidy tips, meadowfoam, needle navarretia, butter-and-eggs, Johnny jump-up, fiddleneck.**

SPECIAL FLOWERS NOT IN PROFUSION: **Fragrant fritillary, fringed downingia, toothed downingia, folded downingia, spotted downingia, gold nuggets, Fremont's camas, glass lily.**

FOOTHILLS OF THE SIERRA

Golden hills along the Hite's Cove Trail

FOR MANY PEOPLE, the first thing that comes to mind when they think of the foothills of the Sierra is gold—the gold rush, the Forty-Niners, gold country. For flower lovers, these gradually sloping hills running much of the length of northern and central California between the nearly sea-level Central Valley to the west and the rugged mountains of the Sierra high country to the east may also bring thoughts of gold: but the color, not the metal, and riches for the eye and soul, not for the pocketbook. "Gold fields" describes hillsides of radiant, golden-yellow composites, and "49er" is the narrow, sinuous highway winding slowly among the lush green slopes and amazing wildflower gardens of spring in the foothills. To experience wildflower spring in the Sierra foothills is truly to have found the "mother lode."

Take days and meander along SR-49 from Mariposa north through Angel's Camp, Sutter Creek, Nevada City, and Downieville. Head a little way east up SR-140, SR-120, SR-108, SR-4, and SR-88, and follow your nose and your whim on back-country roads. It is amazing the wildflower displays you can find so close to such foothill towns as Auburn, Placerville, Sonora, Jackson, Nevada City/Grass Valley, and Colfax. Drive to the glorious, impressionistic, floral canvasses of Red Hill and the rare gabbro floral displays of Pine Hill; drive the dirt roads of Camp Nine, Ponderosa Way, Yankee Jim's Road, and Drum Powerhouse Road; get out and hike the wildflower trails along or above the beautiful foothill rivers—the Yuba (Independence Trail, Buttermilk Bend Trail), the American (Codfish Falls Trail), the Mokelumne, the Stanislaus, the Merced (Hite's Cove Trail)—to see, smell, and hear spring in its full glory.

At the extreme southern tip of the Sierra (in the Greenhorn Mountains), drive up SR-178 into the spectacular Kern River Canyon along the rushing river and hillsides solid with spring color.

When

There are a few early bloomers (for example, **western rue-anemone, waterfall buttercup, foothill shooting star**) that may start in late February, but the magnificent spring explosion of floral sunshine won't peak until mid-March and early April. Although this blazing bloom will fade by late April or May, there are some spectacular wildflower treasures that only then come to the fore, notably **Pine Hill flannelbush, bush poppy, blazing star**, and several species of the amazing **clarkia** (especially along Kern River Canyon and Yankee Jim's Road)—a truly glorious way of bidding "farewell to spring."

Northern

30) Buttermilk Bend Trail (about 550 feet)

FEATURED FLOWER: **Lacepod**. In April and May, these tiny, white flowers turn to flying-saucer seedpods.

DRIVING DIRECTIONS: From Grass Valley, drive west on SR-20 past Penn Valley to Pleasant Valley Road. Turn right (north) and drive 9.5 miles through Bridgeport to South Yuba State Park. The Visitors' Center is on the left.

WALKING DIRECTIONS: Drive a few hundred yards across the bridge over the Yuba River, park in the gravel lot on the right, and walk east to the Buttermilk Bend trailhead. Stroll along the easy, mostly level trail along the north bank of the river (about three miles round-trip).

DESCRIPTION: This delightful trail wanders along the grassy hillsides and open woodland along the north side of the Yuba River. The glorious spring wildflower displays rival those of the similar Hite's Cove Trail (p. 49) hours to the south along the south fork of the Merced River, but with its lower elevation, the Buttermilk Bend Trail can actually start blooming a few weeks earlier than its southern counterpart.

BLOOMING: Late February through May, with the peak blooming from mid-March to mid-April.

GLORIOUS GARDENS: **Lacepod, annual poppy, blue dicks, Chinese houses, spreading larkspur, spring vetch, wild cucumber, fiddleneck, white nemophila, popcorn flower, bird's-eye gila.**

SPECIAL FLOWERS NOT IN PROFUSION: **Pipevine, pretty face, harlequin lu-**

pine, ground iris, live forever, foothill saxifrage, elegant clarkia, twining snake lily, harvest brodiaea, wild hyacinth, bush lupine, Ithuriel's spear.

31) Independence Trail (about 3,000 feet)

FEATURED FLOWER: **Showy phlox**. In April and May, these pale pink stars light up the shade along the trail.

DRIVING DIRECTIONS: From Nevada City, drive 5.5 miles north on SR-49 to a parking turnout.

WALKING DIRECTIONS: Walk either the 2.5-mile east trail (on the parking turnout side of the road) or the wheelchair-accessible 2.5-mile west trail (across the road) down to a creek.

DESCRIPTION: These wonderful, gentle trails follow an old flume system across mostly shaded slopes with occasional views of the Yuba River. In places you will be walking on picturesque trestles, bridges, boardwalks, and ramps—all the result of hard work by local volunteers.

BLOOMING: April to June, with peak blooming from mid-April to late May.

GLORIOUS GARDENS: **Pacific sedum, showy phlox, Indian warrior.**

SPECIAL FLOWERS NOT IN PROFUSION: **Fairy lantern, Hartweg's iris, western rue-anemone, California Indian pink, pipevine, twining snake lily, yellow pussy ears.**

32) Drum Powerhouse Road (about 3,000 feet)

FEATURED FLOWER: **Bleeding heart**. In April, the grassy banks along this road are endeared with clusters of these nodding, pink hearts.

DRIVING DIRECTIONS: From I-80 east of Colfax, take the Dutch Flat exit and turn right at the stop sign to head toward Dutch Flat. After 0.4 mile, turn left at the sign to Dutch Flat, and after about one mile, bear right on Main Street through town. One mile beyond town, turn left on Drum Powerhouse Road.

WALKING DIRECTIONS: Park safely off the road from time to time and explore the banks along its edges.

DESCRIPTION: This is a quiet road with little traffic and wonderful displays of some spring flowers you may not find many other places in the foothills. In about six miles the road will end at the powerhouse at the bottom of the American River canyon—an impressive display of roaring water.

BLOOMING: From late March through June, with the peak blooming in April through mid-May.

GLORIOUS GARDENS: **Bleeding heart, fan violet, mountain misery, Pacific sedum, Sierra onion, Hartweg's iris, dwarf phacelia, mountain dogwood, yellow pussy ears, alumroot.**

SPECIAL FLOWERS NOT IN PROFUSION: **Western rue-anemone, grand hound's tongue, yerba santa, bush poppy, white Chinese houses, cobweb thistle, western wallflower, grand collomia, globe gilia, Purdy's brodiaea.**

33) Yankee Jim's Road (about 3,000–2,200 feet)

FEATURED FLOWER: **Williamson's clarkia**. In May, these dazzling, rose-purple–splotched blooms join two other species of clarkia to usher out the spring.

DRIVING DIRECTIONS: Off I-80 near Colfax, take the Canyon Way exit, turn right at the stop sign onto Canyon Way, then after 0.7 mile, turn left on Yankee Jim's Road. In 4.5 miles, you will reach a suspension bridge, which you could cross and continue to Foresthill.

WALKING DIRECTIONS: Explore the banks, flats, and rock gardens along the road.

DESCRIPTION: A dirt road that winds down among spring flowers to a bridge across the North Fork of the American River. The late spring (May to June) display of several species of clarkia is especially dramatic.

BLOOMING: March through June, with the peak blooming from April through May.

GLORIOUS GARDENS: **Williamson's clarkia, common yellow monkeyflower, bilobed clarkia, elegant clarkia, watercress, poison hemlock, live forever, annual poppy, Kellogg's monkeyflower, alumroot, California saxifrage, white Chinese houses, elegant brodiaea, perennial sweet pea, globe gilia, alumroot.**

SPECIAL FLOWERS NOT IN PROFUSION: **Waterfall buttercup, moth mullein, scarlet monkeyflower, Hartweg's iris, mock orange, western rue-anemone.**

34) Ponderosa Way and Codfish Falls (about 1,500 feet)

FEATURED FLOWER: **Bilobed clarkia**. In May, these lovely, red-purple "windmills" bid a fond "farewell to spring."

DRIVING DIRECTIONS: From Auburn, drive about nine miles east on I-80 and take the Weimar Crossing exit. Immediately turn right on Ponderosa Way and drive 5.5 miles to the bridge crossing the American River.

WALKING DIRECTIONS: You can cross the bridge and walk or drive along the dirt road upriver for several miles (a bit of a climb), or you can stay on the north side of the river and take the trail downriver to Codfish Falls.

DESCRIPTION: The grassy banks of the dirt road down to the river are resplendent with spring wildflowers, as are the road on the other side of the bridge and the Codfish Falls trail. The road involves some gradual climbing; the trail is mostly level.

BLOOMING: From March through May, with the peak blooming from late March through late April.

GLORIOUS GARDENS: **Annual poppy, bush lupine, white nemophila, California saxifrage, Pacific sedum, bilobed clarkia.**

SPECIAL FLOWERS NOT IN PROFUSION: **Indian pink, ground iris, grand hound's tongue, fringed woodland star, live forever, foothill lomatium.**

35) Pine Hill Ecological Preserve (to 2,031 feet)

FEATURED FLOWER: **El Dorado mule ears**. In March and April, these rare, large, and showy suns are scattered on the brushy hills.

DRIVING DIRECTIONS: At Cameron Park a few miles west of Placerville on I-80, drive north on Cameron Park Drive for about three miles, then turn right on Green Valley Road. After 1.5 miles, turn left on Ulenkamp Road, which will turn into Pine Hill Road. Stop at the closed gate and park on either side of the road.

WALKING DIRECTIONS: Walk through the pedestrian gate to the right and up the steep hill.

DESCRIPTION: This is a relatively short and steep walk up a paved road with some rare gabbro soil plants and, at the top, some wonderful, open views of the surrounding foothills landscape.

BLOOMING: Mid-March through early June, with the peak blooming in April through mid-May with **El Dorado mule ears** blooming in April and **flannel bush** in May.

GLORIOUS GARDENS: **El Dorado mule ears, Pine Hill flannel bush, spring vetch, foothill shooting star, bush lupine, Sonoma sage, giant-leaf balsamroot, deer brush.**

SPECIAL FLOWERS NOT IN PROFUSION: **Virgin bower, yellow pussy ears, Chinese houses, ground iris, white-margined swertia, wild hyacinth, Bridge's brodiaea, spreading larkspur, pearly everlasting.**

Central and Southern

36) Electra Road (about 1,200 feet)

FEATURED FLOWER: **Spider lupine**. In March and April, the banks along the road are deliciously fragrant with the beautiful blues (and sometimes whites and pinks) of this lovely lupine.

DRIVING DIRECTIONS: From Jackson, drive south on SR-49 about three miles, then turn left on Electra Road, which will continue a little over three miles before ending.

WALKING DIRECTIONS: Pull off the road where it is safe and explore the road edges, especially the steep, often rocky embankment on the left side.

DESCRIPTION: This is a lovely, quiet road along the Mokelumne River with wonderful spring flowers accompanied by several treats for the ear—the rushing of the river, the quacking of ducks, and very likely the squawking of wild turkeys.

BLOOMING: From early March to early June, with the peak blooming from mid-March to mid-April.
GLORIOUS GARDENS: **Annual poppy, spider lupine, bush lupine, live forever, Ithuriel's spear, white nemophila.**
SPECIAL FLOWERS NOT IN PROFUSION: **Purple owl's-clover, moth mullein, globe lily, glassy onion, harlequin lupine, superb mariposa lily.**

37) Camp Nine Road (about 1,300 feet)

FEATURED FLOWER: **Bird's eye gilia.** In March and April, hillsides of these multicolored "eyes" peer up at you with perky cheer.
DRIVING DIRECTIONS: From Angel's Camp, drive east on SR-4 for 4.5 miles to Vallecito; turn right on Parrot's Ferry Road, and after about one mile, turn left on Camp Nine Road. After roughly seven miles, you will reach a bridge that crosses the Stanislaus River, from which point you can continue even farther on either side of the river.
WALKING DIRECTIONS: Pull off the road where it is safe (usually there is very little traffic) and explore both sides of the road.
DESCRIPTION: This is a glorious journey into the heart of the foothills, not only for the wonderful spring flowers and the sweet fragrance hanging in the air (especially of the "California lilac" **buckbrush** and of the various species of **lupine**), but also for the expansive views into the rolling hills and its oak scrub vegetation.
BLOOMING: From early March to early June, with the peak blooming from mid-March to mid-April.
GLORIOUS GARDENS: **Foothill shooting star, buckbrush, fuzzy paintbrush, spider lupine, bush lupine, California saxifrage, foothill lomatium, annual poppy, bird's-eye gilia, sky lupine, Johnny jump-up.**
SPECIAL FLOWERS NOT IN PROFUSION: **Pretty face, clustered broomrape, cobweb thistle, mock orange, redbud.**

38) Red Hill Road (about 1,400 feet)

FEATURED FLOWER: **Five-spot nemophila.** In March and April, these large, bright white bowls with the intense purple spots cluster along fences.
DRIVING DIRECTIONS: From Sonora, drive south and east on SR-49/SR-108 for 5.5 miles to the intersection with SR-120, then drive south on SR-49 for 3.3 miles to Chinese Camp, then turn right on Red Hill Road. After 4.7 miles you will reach the Red Hills trailhead area.
WALKING DIRECTIONS: In the first couple of miles, you can explore the road edges up to the fenced property; after these first couple of miles, the fencing ends and you can drive or walk on several side roads. At the trailhead, there are several trails (but be sure to check the map and know where you are going).
DESCRIPTION: The spring blooming along the road is stunning—like Monet

paintings. In the first two miles, the paintings are "framed" and "under glass" (i.e., behind the fences), but after that you can walk (carefully) across the canvas and get in the "paint"—it is a delicious, sensuous experience.

BLOOMING: Early March to late May, with the peak blooming from mid-March to mid-April.

GLORIOUS GARDENS: **Five-spot nemophila, tidy tips, California poppy, annual poppy, goldfields, cream cups, Fremont's camas, sky lupine, buckbrush, bird's-eye gilia, blue dicks, common yellow monkeyflower.**

SPECIAL FLOWERS NOT IN PROFUSION: **Ithuriel's spear, whiskerbrush, chaparral currant, Douglas monkeyflower, white Chinese houses, glass lily, Williamson's clarkia.**

39) Hite's Cove Trail (about 1,500 feet)

FEATURED FLOWER: **Annual poppy.** In late March into early April, the hillside lining the south fork of the Merced River is ablaze with poppy "fire," so hot you can almost feel the heat from miles away.

DRIVING DIRECTIONS: From Mariposa, drive about 18 miles east on SR-140 toward El Portal through Midpines and down to the Merced River, continuing along the river until you reach the South Fork, coming in from your right. Park here just beyond Savage's Trading Post and the bridge.

WALKING DIRECTIONS: Head up the steep driveway just to the east of the store, and almost immediately turn right onto the marked trail (at first paved). It becomes narrow with a steep drop-off toward the river. You will climb and descend along the sun-beaten east side of the river until, after about two miles, you will reach some large, flat, striated rocks—a perfect place for lunch. With all the flowers along the way, it could be mid-afternoon by the time you reach these rocks.

DESCRIPTION: In a good year, this is one of the great spring wildflower displays anywhere. You could easily spend several hours admiring the flowers in the first half-mile of the trail alone! In some years, the slopes are nearly solid yellow and gold; in others they are mosaics of purples and reds and blues and creams and gold. Interspersed with the open, sun-drenched slopes are shady spots and a few small creeks, so there is great diversity as well as density of flowers.

BLOOMING: Late March through early June, with the peak blooming from late March through mid-April.

GLORIOUS GARDENS: **Annual poppy, purple owl's-clover, bird's-eye gilia, Chinese houses, blue fiesta flower, pretty face, baby blue eyes, mustang clover, spider lupine, blue dicks, goldfields, foothills violet, fiddleneck, yellow carpet, lacepod.**

SPECIAL FLOWERS NOT IN PROFUSION: **Live-forever, twining snake lily, fairy lantern, cream cups, waterfall buttercup, foothill saxifrage, California Indian pink, red maids, bush lupine, harlequin lupine, red bud, western** rue-anemone, cobweb thistle, foothill shooting star, blazing star, fringed woodland star, single-flowered broomrape.

40) Kern River Canyon and Walker Pass (to 5,250 feet)

FEATURED FLOWER: **Speckled clarkia.** In May and June, mile after mile of the grassy slopes along the roaring river and the canyon road are cloaked in pink with thousands and thousands of these lovely "end-of-spring" beauties.

DRIVING DIRECTIONS: From Bakersfield take SR-178 east to Lake Isabella, then continue on up Walker Pass.

WALKING DIRECTIONS: This is a very narrow and winding road with only a few turnouts, so use them carefully. It may be safer to just look at the flowers from the car, but if you want to explore the flowers along the road more closely, use *extreme caution*, walking only near the turnouts.

DESCRIPTION: The road is spectacular, hanging onto the cliff edge up the Kern River Canyon with occasional views of roaring whitewater. There are wonderful flowers along the road (a mixture of Sierra and desert floras), but there are very few safe places to stop and explore. After Lake Isabella, the terrain opens up with wide vistas, and you begin to see more desert terrain and flowers. There are great **Joshua tree** forests before and after Walker Pass.

BLOOMING: March through June, with peak blooming in April and May.

GLORIOUS GARDENS: **Speckled clarkia, elegant clarkia, bush monkey-flower, blue fiesta flower, Ithuriel's spear, bird's-eye gilia, mustang clover, blue dicks, western wallflower, Joshua tree, desert peach, Bigelow's coreopsis, California buckeye, flannelbush, our Lord's candle, golden yarrow, globe gilia, wine-cup clarkia.**

SPECIAL FLOWERS NOT IN PROFUSION: **Kern County larkspur, redbud, Chinese houses, butterfly mariposa lily, gunsight clarkia, Grinnell's penstemon, white keckiella.**

CASCADES

Mount Shasta

AFTER RUNNING FOR OVER 400 MILES along much of the length of southern and central California, the Sierra Nevada begins to taper off north of the Tahoe Basin and eventually is supplanted by the Cascades that then continue up through Oregon and Washington to the Canadian Border. Although the Cascades continue the line of the Sierra, the two ranges are vastly different. While the Sierra range is an upraised block of granite nearly uninterrupted for its entire length, the Cascade range is a necklace of discrete volcanic pearls. And what glorious pearls these are—Mount Baker, Mount Rainier, Mount St. Helens, Mount Adams, Mount Hood, the Three Sisters, Mount Jefferson, and in California, Mount Shasta and Lassen Peak—each rising dramatically above the mostly low surrounding terrain. Lassen Peak (at over 11,000 feet) and especially Mount Shasta (at over 14,000 feet) soar like snow-topped beacons above the high plateau country to the east of the numerous mountain ranges in the northwest corner of the state—beacons whose "light" can be seen for miles in all directions.

The flora of the California Cascades is an interesting mixture of Sierran flowers and others more typical of the Pacific Northwest. A considerable number of species—both low-elevation forest dwellers and high mountain lovers—reach the southernmost extent of their range at Shasta or Lassen, so the Cascades add considerable diversity to the California flora. Come to the California Cascades to find a bit of Washington and Oregon (the volcanoes and the flowers) south of the border.

When

In low-elevation forests around the skirts of Shasta and Lassen, the flowers bloom mostly from May through June, while those in higher-elevation meadows and rocky terrain peak in July and August.

41) Mount Shasta (about 4,000–14,162 feet)

FEATURED FLOWER: **Pink mountain heather**. From July into August, great masses of these dazzling, red, bell-shaped flowers can cover high-altitude open hillsides and rocky areas.

DRIVING DIRECTIONS: From Redding, drive about 62 miles north on I-5 to Mount Shasta (the town). In town take Lake Street east (it turns into Everitt Memorial Highway) for 12.5 miles to Bunny Flat, then travel another two-and-a-half miles past Panther Meadows to the end of the road at the Ski Bowl Trailhead.

You can circle the mountain on I-5 north, U.S. 97 northeast, and dirt roads along the eastern side.

WALKING DIRECTIONS: On the south side of the mountain, stroll through Panther Meadows and hike up the trails at Bunny Flat and the Ski Bowl; on the east side, hike up any of the several trails heading up the mountain from the dirt Forest Service roads.

DESCRIPTION: Mount Shasta is a magnificent, mostly snow-covered volcano rising almost two miles above the surrounding landscape. Despite all the snow cover and five perennial glaciers, there are many lovely wildflower displays in lower-altitude forests, meadows, and seeps, and on rocky ridges and fellfields. You can't just hike to the summit (as with Lassen Peak), as it is a challenging, technical, and dangerous expedition, but there are several delightful trails and cross-country opportunities at lower elevations.

BLOOMING: March into September, with peak blooming on most of the mountain from June into August.

GLORIOUS GARDENS: **Pink mountain heather, pasqueflower, swamp onion, mountain pride, partridge foot, great red paintbrush, twinflower, thimbleberry, leopard lily, creek dogwood, Tolmie's saxifrage, fuchsia, Washington lily, scarlet gilia.**

SPECIAL FLOWERS NOT IN PROFUSION: **White-margined swertia, pygmy lewisia, tofieldia, pitcher plant, round-leaf sundew, dwarf onion, sugar stick, steer's head, queen's cup, three-leaf lewisia, dogbane, western hound's tongue, candyflower, woodland penstemon, western peony, great polemonium.**

42) Lassen National Park (about 5,200–10,457 feet)

FEATURED FLOWER: **Washington lily**. In July and August, these huge, fragrant, glorious white lilies with purple spots occur frequently on chaparral slopes and in forest clearings.

DRIVING DIRECTIONS: SR-89 north of Lake Almanor and south of Burney is the only road through the park. There are three dirt roads that barely enter the park: heading to Butte Lake, to Juniper Lake, and to Warm Valley.

WALKING DIRECTIONS: There are many trails to the numerous lakes and meadows and thermal features, including the relatively easy but dusty trail to the summit of Lassen Peak.

DESCRIPTION: The central and eastern parts of the park consist of a huge, volcanic mudflow plateau dotted with lakes and cinder cones, while the western part is graced by pine and fir forests and meadows and by Lassen Peak itself. Trails take you to lakes, streams, meadows, and rocky ridges, and to a fascinating array of volcanic features, including cinder cones, mud pots, lava flows, and craters. The flora, especially the alpine flora, is more typical of the Cascades than of the Sierra, though especially at lower elevations, the Sierra flora is well represented.

BLOOMING: May into September, with peak blooming in most places in June and July.

GLORIOUS GARDENS: **Davidson's penstemon, mountain pride, Washington lily, yellow pond lily, corn lily, woolly mule ears, pussy paws, western wallflower, fawn lily, Anderson's thistle, scarlet gilia, spreading phlox, pennyroyal, large-leaf lupine, marsh marigold, Lemmon's paintbrush, great red paintbrush, Labrador tea, leopard lily, buckbean, three-leaf lewisia, purple cinquefoil, Torrey's monkeyflower, western dog violet, Sierra onion.**

SPECIAL FLOWERS NOT IN PROFUSION: **Purple fritillary, flat-stemmed onion, steer's head, broad-leaf twayblade, seep-spring arnica, corydalis, bleeding heart, hiker's gentian, alpine gentian, shaggy hawkweed, round-leaf sundew, tofieldia, eupatorium, mountain sorrel, Drummond's anemone, Tolmie's saxifrage, dwarf alpine daisy, porterella, sugarstick, common bladderwort, rock fringe, pasqueflower, Douglas spiraea.**

HIGH SIERRA

The high country of Yosemite

RUNNING FOR ABOUT 400 MILES from northwest to southeast for much of the length of California near the Nevada border, the Sierra Nevada mountain range is certainly one of the most dramatic features of the state's landscape. Gently rising from the Central Valley to its west through rolling foothills, the Sierra gradually reaches its crest at about 9,000 feet in the north and consistently well over 10,000 feet in the south, peaking at 14,494 feet at Mount Whitney. For most of its length, but especially in the south, the eastern side of the crest drops precipitously, most dramatically in the Owens Valley between Bishop and Lone Pine, where it plunges almost two miles practically straight down.

The Sierra boasts some of California's most well-known and celebrated mountain high country—Yosemite National Park, Sequoia/King's Canyon National Park, Mount Whitney, and the Lake Tahoe basin. Above the western foothills, mid-mountain meadows are glorious with spring and early summer wildflower displays, while in mid-to-late summer, open expanses near and above timberline offer endless skies, vast views, and stunning alpine gardens. Trails up the eastern escarpment, such as Onion Valley to Kearsarge Pass, Mosquito Flat to Mono Pass, and the climb to the summit of Mount Whitney, take you across worlds from high desert or Great Basin to high alpine in only a few (labored!) uphill miles. Midsummer in the high Sierra is a wildflower lover's Shangri-La, nirvana, and fountain of youth all wrapped up into one!

When

Usually the mid-mountain Sierra meadows come out from under the snow and start blooming by mid-May (don't miss the amazing **camas lily** fields north of Tahoe), peaking in June and July. The higher elevations usually don't begin blooming until June or early July, peaking from mid-July to August. When the California coasts, the Central Valley, the deserts, the foothills, and the Modoc Plateau are just delicious wildflower memories, it is time to head up to the Sierra (and California's other high mountains) for a couple more months of fresh wildflower delights.

Northern

43) Feather River Canyon (to about 4,000 feet)

FEATURED FLOWER: **Bush monkeyflower**. Individually this shrubby monkeyflower is dazzling, with its scores of large flowers ranging from peach, to salmon, to orange, to buff, to white; but here in the Feather River Canyon in May, the display of these flowers is almost too amazing to believe—over 25 miles of flower-covered cliffs along Route 70!!

DRIVING DIRECTIONS: From south of Chico, take SR-70 east for about 65 miles to Quincy.

WALKING DIRECTIONS: Park carefully from time to time in turnouts and enjoy the gorgeous flower displays, especially on the rock cliffs bordering the road.

DESCRIPTION: A wonderfully scenic drive along the spectacular canyon of the North Fork of the Feather River. The rock cliffs along the road are heavy with flowers, and swimming in the river on a hot day is a delicious bonus.

BLOOMING: From May through July.

GLORIOUS GARDENS: **Bush monkeyflower, red ribbons, globe gilia, woolly sunflower, ookow, deer brush, Chinese houses.**

SPECIAL FLOWERS NOT IN PROFUSION: **Alumroot, foxglove, California buckeye, Hartweg's iris, western wallflower, live forever, mock orange, leopard lily, red larkspur, harlequin lupine.**

44) Butterfly Valley (about 3,400 feet)

FEATURED FLOWER: **California pitcher plant**. From May through July, you will probably find this amazing insect "swallower" with the cobra-like leaves in bloom by the hundreds in the seeps by the road.

DRIVING DIRECTIONS: From Quincy, drive about three-and-a-half miles north on SR-70/SR-89, then turn left on Blackhawk Road. In 1.4 miles the road turns to dirt. At 5.3 miles (from the start), bear right on Bog Road. At 5.8 miles, you will encounter the large pitcher plant seeps on both sides of the road.

WALKING DIRECTIONS: Wander carefully (try to stay out of the wettest areas, as you could do considerable damage) into the edges of the small seep on the left of the road and the large seep on the right.

DESCRIPTION: A short drive through filtered woods to large seep areas with a great variety of interesting and beautiful, wet-environment shrubs and herbs.

BLOOMING: May through July, with the fascinating **pitcher plant** in peak bloom in late May and June.

GLORIOUS GARDENS: **Pitcher plant, starflower, yellow-eyed grass, round-leaf sundew, Labrador tea, mountain dogwood, western azalea, bog asphodel**.

SPECIAL FLOWERS NOT IN PROFUSION: **Showy phlox, red larkspur, Hartweg's iris, Sierra gentian, bear grass**.

45) Sierra Buttes and Lakes Basin (about 5,800–8,587 feet)

FEATURED FLOWER: **Leopard lily**. In July, this tall plant with the showy, orange, recurved flowers is common in wet places throughout the basin.

DRIVING DIRECTIONS: From SR-49 at Bassetts (east of Downieville), drive north on the Gold Lakes Road, or drive south on this road from SR-89 at Graeagle. Off Gold Lakes Road are a few spur roads to various lakes and resorts, to a waterfall, and toward the Sierra Buttes Lookout.

WALKING DIRECTIONS: There are several short trails to and around various lakes and a strenuous trail up to the Lookout tower. Some of the best wildflower areas are along the road to Lower Sardine Lake (especially near the campground), along the west side of Packer Lake, on the ridge above Young American Lake, west of Gold Lake, and between Upper Salmon Lake and Deer Lake.

DESCRIPTION: This is a relatively small area of the northern Sierra, with floral influences from the Cascades to the north. The volcanic crags of the Sierra Buttes tower over the entire area, which is rich in pine forests, glaciated lakes, and flower meadows.

BLOOMING: May through August, with peak blooming from mid-June to mid-July.

GLORIOUS GARDENS: **Labrador tea, alpine shooting star, Sierra rein orchid, Macloskey's violet, monkshood, leopard lily, water-plantain buttercup, mountain spiraea, wandering daisy, Leichtlin's mariposa lily, scarlet gilia, corn lily, great red paintbrush, broad-leaf lupine, arrow-**

leaf senecio, pennyroyal, mountain pride, Sierra onion, Lewis monkey-flower, bluebell, ranger's buttons.

SPECIAL FLOWERS NOT IN PROFUSION: Steer's head, purple fritillary, buck-bean, snow plant, fawn lily, white ladies tresses, dwarf onion, rock fringe, arrowleaf balsamroot, western azalea, dwarf chamaesaracha, Washington lily, tofieldia, yellow pond lily, Sierra primrose, grand collo-mia, flat-stemmed onion, showy polemonium, purple nightshade, eupatorium, hiker's gentian.

46) Sagehen Creek (about 6,200–5,900 feet)

FEATURED FLOWER: **Camas lily.** In early May, Stampede Reservoir seems to extend for acres to the west with the deep blue "waters" of thousands and thousands of this gorgeous lily in full and magnificent bloom.

DRIVING DIRECTIONS: From I-80 just east of Truckee, take the SR-89 North exit and drive about eight miles north on SR-89. Park in the dirt turnout on the right just after the bridge over Sagehen Creek.

WALKING DIRECTIONS: Walk west across SR-89 into the wet meadow and adjoining woods. Return to your car and head east along the trail on the north side of the creek roughly two miles, to the huge meadow just west of Stampede Reservoir.

DESCRIPTION: This is a delightful stroll through a densely flowered, wet meadow (west of SR-89) and an easy, level walk (east of SR-89) along a beaver-dammed creek into a fabulous, lush meadow that boasts probably the most extensive, spectacular display of **camas lily** anywhere in California.

BLOOMING: April through July, with the sensational camas lily display in early May.

GLORIOUS GARDENS: **Camas lily, bull elephant's-head, marsh marigold, bog saxifrage, crimson columbine, star lavender, dwarf phacelia, common yellow monkeyflower, great polemonium, alpine shooting star, water-plantain buttercup, Sierra rein orchid, squaw carpet, bistort, wild rose.**

SPECIAL FLOWERS NOT IN PROFUSION: **Richardson's geranium, Bach's downingia, snow plant, swamp onion, white ladies tresses, northern bog violet, pink paintbrush.**

47) Castle Peak (about 7,200–9,103 feet)

FEATURED FLOWER: **Corn lily.** From July into August, great "forests" of these rather ominous-looking spikes of toxic, greenish-white flowers crowd the seeps on the southern slopes.

DRIVING DIRECTIONS: From Truckee, drive about eight-and-a-half miles west on I-80, exit at Boreal Ridge Road, turn right on the paved spur road, and park along the road where it turns to dirt.

WALKING DIRECTIONS: For the west slope of Castle Peak, hike up the dirt road and along the Pacific Crest Trail and scramble east up toward the ridge. For the east slope, head east on faint trails back behind the rest area, linking up with the major trail toward Summit Lake. After about a mile, turn left at the junction toward Warren Lake and follow the trail all the way up to the ridge. You can scramble west even higher.

DESCRIPTION: This is a rather strenuous but delightful climb through fir and pine forests, wet meadows, rocky slopes, and seeps up to a precipitous, rocky ridge with wonderful subalpine flowers at home in the great diversity of habitats.

BLOOMING: June through September, with the peak blooming in July and August.

GLORIOUS GARDENS: **Corn lily, bull elephant's-head, Copeland's owl's-clover, alpine shooting star, Drummond's anemone, Sierra primrose, pink gilia, grand collomia, Sierra onion, pretty face, great red paintbrush, broad-leaf lupine, Whitney's locoweed.**

SPECIAL FLOWERS NOT IN PROFUSION: **Tiger lily, Leichtlin's mariposa lily, pink wintergreen, one-sided wintergreen, creek dogwood, monkshood.**

48) Lake Tahoe Basin (about 6,230–9,700 feet)

FEATURED FLOWER: **Explorer's gentian.** Clusters of this incredibly dark-blue-purple, tubular flower are found in full bloom in August in several rocky places in the Basin, such as Mount Tallac and Pole Creek.

DRIVING DIRECTIONS: I-80 and U.S. 50, both west from Sacramento, are the main routes to the California part of the Tahoe Basin on the west shore of the lake. You can circle the lake on SR-28, SR-89 south, and U.S. 50, while several paved or dirt roads head west from the lake up toward the Sierra crest.

WALKING DIRECTIONS: The Tahoe Rim Trail encircles the lake mostly well above it, and there are hundreds of miles of short and long trails up into the mountains.

DESCRIPTION: From low-lying meadows to alpine scree slopes, from granite or volcanic cliffs to bogs, from coniferous forest to dry, sandy, sun-beaten slopes, the Tahoe Basin is a wonderland for wildflowers.

BLOOMING: April through September, with a few early spring flowers at lower altitudes blooming in late April, but most flowers are in peak bloom from June through August.

GLORIOUS GARDENS: **Drummond's anemone, Sierra primrose, rock fringe, alpine shooting star, corn lily, bull elephant's-head, Copeland's owl's-clover, fuchsia, Sierra corydalis, blue flax, porterella, seep-spring arnica, eupatorium, mule ears, bladderwort, flat-stemmed onion, Sierra rein orchid, Lewis monkeyflower, glaucous larkspur, pennyroyal, water plantain buttercup, Beckwith violet, Hooker's balsamroot, broad-leaf** lupine, bog saxifrage, explorer's gentian, great red paintbrush, monks-hood.

SPECIAL FLOWERS NOT IN PROFUSION: Sugarstick, yellow-eyed grass, Washington lily, steer's head, fringed grass-of-Parnassus, Tolmie's saxifrage, tofieldia, purple cinquefoil, Gray's lupine, showy polemonium, tiger lily, rosy sedum, bladderwort, duck potato, alpine gentian, alpine gold, swamp onion.

49) Luther Pass and Grass Lake (about 7,500 feet)

FEATURED FLOWER: **Pond lily.** In July, parts of the "lake" seem to be solid leaves and yellow flowers as great masses of this intriguing plant choke the shallows.

DRIVING DIRECTIONS: From the intersection of U.S. 50 and SR-89 in South Lake Tahoe, drive about seven miles south on SR-89 and park in one of the gravel turnouts on your right, next to Grass Lake at Luther Pass.

WALKING DIRECTIONS: Stroll through the woods out onto the spongy ground bordering the lake. As you get closer to open water, the ground will get soggier and springier. Walk softly and carefully, both for your own safety and for minimum impact on the plant life.

DESCRIPTION: The soggy, squishy borders of Grass Lake are home to several fascinating bog plants that you can find in only a few other boggy areas in northern California. Be prepared for warm water between your toes, and don't go too close to the open water.

BLOOMING: June through August, with the peak blooming from mid-June to mid-July.

GLORIOUS GARDENS: **Buckbean, yellow pond lily, fireweed, mountain violet.**

SPECIAL FLOWERS NOT IN PROFUSION: **Purple cinquefoil, white ladies tresses, bladderwort, round-leaf sun sundew, showy penstemon, scarlet gilia.**

50) Carson Pass (about 8,600–10,000 feet)

FEATURED FLOWER: **Western blue flag.** In June and early July, in meadows still wet from melting snow at places like Frog Lake and Meiss Meadows Pond, this lovely iris welcomes in the new flower year and the early hiker.

DRIVING DIRECTIONS: From the intersection of U.S. 50 and SR-89 in South Lake Tahoe, drive south on SR-89 about 11 miles to the intersection with SR-88. Turn right on SR-88 and drive about 10 miles west to the pass and the paved parking lot on the left for the Winnemucca Lake trailhead, or drive slightly further west to the paved parking lot on the right for the Meiss Meadows trailhead (both parking lots charge a small parking fee).

WALKING DIRECTIONS: From the Winnemucca Lake trailhead, hike about a mile, mostly gradually uphill, to Frog Lake and another mile to Winnemucca Lake and above it. From the Meiss Meadows trailhead, hike one-and-a-half miles, mostly uphill, to Meiss Meadows Pond, then cross-country east to approach the summit of Red Lake Peak (10,000 feet).

DESCRIPTION: These two hikes offer some of northern California's prime July through August wildflower gardens—lush seep areas, shoulder-high jungles, grassy meadows where the iris seem to reflect the sky, talus fields, and rocky slopes glowing with carpets of pink, rose, yellow, white, and blue.

BLOOMING: June through August, with the peak blooming from mid-July to mid-August.

GLORIOUS GARDENS: **Deer's tongue (monument plant), broad-leaf lupine, corn lily, western blue flag, great red paintbrush, bull elephant's-head, bluebells, dwarf Sierra onion, low cryptantha, daggerpod, white heather, red heather, Sierra primrose, old man's whiskers, pink gilia, Leichtlin's mariposa lily, Copeland's owl's-clover, narrow-leaf stonecrop, Sierra onion, Lewis monkeyflower, common yellow monkeyflower, alpine shooting star, glaucous larkspur, mountain pride, alpine paintbrush, Pursh's milkvetch, Whitney's locoweed, rabbitbrush, whiskerbrush, arrowleaf senecio.**

SPECIAL FLOWERS NOT IN PROFUSION: **Alpine fireweed, alpine penstemon, alpine buttercup, bush cinquefoil, rosy sedum, alumroot, pretty face, showy penstemon, monkshood, Cusick's veronica.**

Central and Southern

51) Yosemite National Park (from about 1,500–13,141 feet)

FEATURED FLOWER: **Sky pilot.** In July and August, at and near the summits of four of Yosemite's highest peaks, you will be rewarded not only with amazing vistas, but with these gorgeous globes of intensely blue, tubular flowers that seem to be inviting you yet higher, to the sky itself.

DRIVING DIRECTIONS: Yosemite is entered by two paved roads from the west (SR-120 from Manteca and SR-140 from Merced), one from the south (SR-41 from Fresno), and one from the east (the same SR-120, coming from Lee Vining). SR-120 crosses the high country at Tuolumne Meadows; the other routes end up in Yosemite Valley.

WALKING DIRECTIONS: There are many hundreds of miles of trails and almost unlimited backcountry hiking, ranging from foothill slopes to subalpine forests and meadows to high alpine ridges and summits. Some of the best trails and locations for wildflowers are: the Merced River Canyon, Hetch Hetchy, Ahwahnee Meadows, Crane Flat, Cathedral Lakes, Twin Lakes,

Foresta, Wawona, McGurk Meadow, Mount Hoffman, Vogelsang, Gaylor Lakes, Donahue Pass, the Kuna Crest, the Dana Plateau, and Mount Dana. DESCRIPTION: This is one of the most magical parts of the Sierra, with thundering waterfalls, majestic sequoias, lushly flowered meadows, gleaming granite domes, and high alpine ridges and summits. The park is home to over 1,300 species of wildflowers.

BLOOMING: From March through May in the low country, to July through August in the high country. You will find beautiful blooming at some elevation in any month from March through August or even September.

GLORIOUS GARDENS: **Cow parsnip, purple milkweed, dwarf alpine daisy, alpine gold, Lemmon's draba, Davidson's penstemon, California Indian pink, baby blue eyes, mountain dogwood, white heather, swamp laurel, Labrador tea, red heather, snow plant, redbud, Brewer's lupine, Sierra gentian, rock fringe, cushion phlox, mountain spiraea, Lemmon's paintbrush, alpine paintbrush, Lewis monkeyflower, bull elephant's-head, western dog violet, Macloskey's violet, Sierra onion, swamp onion, camas lily, great red paintbrush, alpine tiger lily, corn lily.**

SPECIAL FLOWERS NOT IN PROFUSION: **Eupatorium, orange mountain dandelion, rosy sedum, sugar stick, harlequin lupine, explorer's gentian, alpine gentian, hiker's gentian, Williamson's clarkia, fuchsia, sky pilot, pygmy lewisia, Sierra primrose, alpine columbine, alpine pink columbine hybrid, scarlet monkeyflower, queen's cup, Davidson's fritillary, Washington lily, tofieldia, stream orchid, broad-leaf twayblade, canchalagua, elegant brodiaea.**

52) Mosquito Flat to Mono Pass Trail (about 10,300–11,160 feet)

FEATURED FLOWER: **Alpine columbine.** In July and August, these large, dazzlingly white alpine dwellers cluster among the rocks near and above timberline along the trail toward Mono Pass, outshining even the whitest of the granite.

DRIVING DIRECTIONS: At Tom's Place on U.S. 395 north of Bishop, head west on Rock Creek Road for 10.2 miles to the road's end at Mosquito Flat.

WALKING DIRECTIONS: This is a very-high-elevation trail of about nine-and-a-half miles to Morgan Pass, but for the most part it is nearly level or only slightly ascending.

DESCRIPTION: You walk through a gorgeous valley with a series of crystal lakes nestled in high Sierra granite peaks. The clear blue skies and dazzling white granite are matched only by the magnificent gardens of intensely colored subalpine and alpine flowers.

BLOOMING: July through September, with peak blooming from mid-July to mid-August.

GLORIOUS GARDENS: **Alpine columbine, corn lily, bush cinquefoil, Labrador** tea, wandering daisy, white heather, alpine laurel, red heather, Whit-ney's locoweed, alpine shooting star, brook saxifrage, alpine paint-brush, bull elephant's-head, tiger lily.

SPECIAL FLOWERS NOT IN PROFUSION: Explorer's gentian, dwarf alpine daisy, alpine buttercup, Sierra primrose, alpine gentian, Tolmie's saxi-frage, rosy sedum, cushion phlox, dwarf lewisia, Davidson's penstemon, Eaton's penstemon, Lemmon's paintbrush, lance-leaf stonecrop.

53) Onion Valley and Kearsarge Pass in Kings Canyon National Park (about 9,200–11,823 feet)

FEATURED FLOWER: **Rock fringe**. In July and August, patches of these gor-geous rose-colored hearts huddle around rocks along the upper part of the trail to Kearsarge Pass.

DRIVING DIRECTIONS: From Independence on U.S. 395 south of Bishop, drive west on the Onion Valley Road to its end at Onion Valley.

WALKING DIRECTIONS: Wander through the wet gardens at Onion Valley (9,200 feet), then hike 4.8 miles up the signed trail to Kearsarge Pass (11,823 feet).

DESCRIPTION: At Onion Valley, you'll see (and smell) masses of swamp onion (for which the valley was named) among other wet-garden flowers. The hike to Kearsarge Pass is a strenuous, high-elevation hike of almost 10 miles round-trip with an elevation gain of over 2,500 feet. You'll hike through high-altitude forests of lodgepole, foxtail, and whitebark pine, pass a couple of lakes, then climb above timberline to dazzling rock gar-dens and amazing views west down to Kearsarge Lakes, lying below the dramatic Kearsarge Pinnacles.

BLOOMING: Late June through August, with peak blooming in July and Au-gust.

GLORIOUS GARDENS: **Swamp onion, monkshood, corn lily, Sierra rein or-chid, arrowleaf senecio, glaucous larkspur, bull elephant's-head, rock fringe, fireweed, tiger lily, cow parsnip.**

SPECIAL FLOWERS NOT IN PROFUSION: **Alpine gold, Davidson's penstemon, dwarf alpine daisy, cushion phlox, alpine paintbrush, Whitney's loco-weed, Rothrock's nama.**

NORTHEAST CORNER

Water-plantain buttercup on the Modoc Plateau

EAST OF THE GREAT MOUNTAIN SPINE of the Cascades and Sierra, and north of Susanville and Lassen National Park, lies the little-known "northeast corner" of California. Most of this area is a high plateau of about a mile above sea level with wide expanses of sagebrush scrub and pinyon-juniper woodlands, but also with a considerable number of bodies of water (lakes, ponds, reservoirs) and mixed conifer forests. In the extreme northeast of this area are the Warner Mountains (with Eagle Peak reaching 9,892 feet)—a mountain forest oasis in the middle of the high desert. Key highways are SR-139, SR-299, U.S. 395, and SR-44, but this rectangular area between Susanville, Alturas, Lassen, and Lava Beds is crisscrossed with all sorts of paved and unpaved back roads just waiting to be explored.

With the exception of the Warner Mountains, where you will find many flowers characteristic of the Cascades and even the Sierra, this northeast corner is primarily a place to see flowers typical of the high Great Basin desert of northern Nevada and southeast Oregon.

Perhaps the most entrancing flower display of this area is the masses of bright white **sand lily** that adorn every spring with verve and brilliance, though the spring expanses of bright yellow **water-plantain buttercup** that carpet wet meadows and drying ponds are also dramatic.

When

Spring usually arrives in early to mid-May with giant carpets of pink—**long-leaf phlox** and **big-headed clover**. A week or so later, in somewhat damp openings between the sagebrush, come the amazingly bright white mounds of **sand lily** and the intensely purple **Beckwith violet**, while drier places boast multicolored gardens of yellow "sunflowers" (for example, **mule ears, balsamroot**), deep blue or steely **blue flax**, scarlet **Applegate's paintbrush**, and glistening white **blepharipappus**. You may see occasional yellow "lakes," where the water has been replaced with **water-plantain buttercup** or **tansy-leaf evening primrose**.

Spring comes to the lower Warner Mountains in June, while the summer bloom can extend (at higher altitudes) well into August or even September.

54) Modoc Plateau (about 4,000–4,500 feet)

FEATURED FLOWER: **Sand lily.** Clusters of these bright white lilies lying atop their leaf rosettes form low mounds in openings between the sagebrush in May and June. Although you won't find them in many locations, where they do grow, they may occur in thousands.

DRIVING DIRECTIONS: Within the rectangle from Susanville west to Lassen, north to Lava Beds, east to Alturas and the western edge of the Warner Mountains, and south back to Susanville, is the high desert of the Modoc Plateau. SR-139, SR-299, U.S. 395, and SR-44 will take you to most of the area; back roads will take you almost everywhere else.

WALKING DIRECTIONS: Much of the area is fenced, but lots of flowers decorate the road edges.

DESCRIPTION: Most of the plateau is sagebrush steppe and pine scrub with numerous small lakes and reservoirs. Every now and then you will have great views of the volcanic cones of Lassen Peak and Mount Shasta, heavy with snow most of the year, towering above the horizon to the west.

BLOOMING: May through July, with peak blooming from mid-May through June.

GLORIOUS GARDENS: **Sand lily, water-plantain buttercup, Hooker's balsamroot, arrow-leaf balsamroot, woolly mule ears, blepharipappus, woolly sunflower, bitterbrush, Applegate's paintbrush, blue flax, tansy-leaf evening primrose, big-headed clover, Beckwith's violet, purple fritillary, squaw carpet, common yellow monkeyflower, bull elephant's-head, great red paintbrush, seep-spring arnica, Washington lily, sego lily, Bach's downingia.**

SPECIAL FLOWERS NOT IN PROFUSION: **Showy penstemon, Peregrine thistle, Whitney's locoweed, long-leaf phlox, linear-leaf phacelia, white-margined swertia, western peony, twinberry, Anderson's clover, broad-lipped twayblade, pink gilia, hairy paintbrush.**

55) Warner Mountains (to 9,892 feet)

FEATURED FLOWER: **Heart-leaf arnica**. In May and June, you can find great masses of these delightful, sunny flowers crowding forest clearings, gradually shifting their flower "faces" to follow the sun.

DRIVING DIRECTIONS: There's only one major road across the Warner Mountains (SR-299 between Alturas and Cedarville), but there are several dirt roads giving you access to the range and to a few trailheads.

WALKING DIRECTIONS: The trail along Cedar Creek is a pleasant stroll with easy access to trailheads at both ends (along SR-299). Most of the rest of the wildflower walking will be along back roads.

DESCRIPTION: Though a modest range in size and elevation, the Warner Mountains are nonetheless impressive, rising several thousand feet above the sagebrush steppe and usually holding snow well into June or July. In spring and summer, the cooler temperatures, dense coniferous and aspen forests, and rushing creeks offer respite from the hot high desert below. Here you will find an interesting mix of Great Basin desert and Sierra and Cascade floras.

BLOOMING: From May through August, with the lower slopes reaching their peak in late May and June, and the upper reaches blooming in July and August.

GLORIOUS GARDENS: **Heart-leaf arnica, Anderson's larkspur, Hooker's balsamroot, glaucous larkspur, spreading phlox, eupatorium, camas lily, mountain spiraea, Coulter's daisy, milkmaids, white heather, star lavender, mountain violet, arrow-leaf balsamroot, corn lily, Applegate's paintbrush, woolly sunflower.**

SPECIAL FLOWERS NOT IN PROFUSION: **Showy penstemon, broad-leaf onion, alpine buttercup, bowl clover, one-sided wintergreen, hot-rock penstemon, white-veined wintergreen, purple fritillary, porterella, rosy sedum, Tolmie's saxifrage, dwarf lewisia, fan violet, bitterroot, explorer's gentian, hiker's gentian, Davidson's penstemon, bog wintergreen.**

EAST OF THE SIERRA

The Alabama Hills with evening snow (the flower)

IN THE TAHOE BASIN, the Sierra crests just west of the western shore of Lake Tahoe, leaving the western part of the lake between it and the Nevada border. As this mighty "Range of Light" (the Sierra) heads southeast from Tahoe, it gets even higher and more dramatic and a bit farther from Nevada, leaving more California terrain to its east. And what terrain this is—vast expanses of the Great Basin, and farther to the south, the Mojave Desert and the White and Inyo Mountains.

In the south especially, the eastern escarpment of the Sierra is incredibly dramatic, rising nearly two miles almost vertically from the desert floor. The 60-mile stretch from Bishop south to Lone Pine (Owens Valley at about 4,000 feet) is bordered not only by the Sierra to the west, culminating in Mount Whitney at 14,494 feet, but also by the White Mountains and Inyo Mountains to the east, reaching 14,240 feet at White Mountain. At the far southern tip of the Sierra, the Mojave Desert creeps well up over the feet of the mountains.

This entire area east of the Sierra, seemingly so remote from the rest of California, is a wonderland for flowers in the Great Basin, the Mojave Desert, and the high and dry White Mountains. The startling diversity of biomes and landscapes is reflected in a diverse and dramatic flora, and with all the different environments and the extreme range of elevation, its blooming is spread out over much of the year.

When

Furthest south and at the lowest elevations, in the northern fingers of the Mojave Desert (for example, the Alabama Hills and the California Desert Conservation Area), you can find significant blooming by March and April; in the lower-elevation areas of the Great Basin (for example, Topaz Lake), the bloom will peak in May and June. The flowers will come into their own in the highest elevations in the Carson Range (for example, Freel Peak) and in the White Mountains in July and August.

Northern

56) Freel Peak (to 10,881 feet)

FEATURED FLOWER: **Tolmie's saxifrage**. In July and August near the summit, the stalks of these striking and intricate white flowers form little floral forests around the rocks.

DRIVING DIRECTIONS: From the intersection of U.S. 50 and SR-89 in South Lake Tahoe, drive nine miles south on SR-89 to just beyond Grass Lake. Turn left on a paved road, which will soon turn to dirt and, shortly after that, will be labeled "Forest Service Road 051." After about three-and-a-half miles, just after a small bridge over a creek, park in the large, dirt parking area on your left.

WALKING DIRECTIONS: This is a long, strenuous hike. Walk west and north up the dirt road (not the road you drove in on) and cross a short bridge over a creek shortly after which the road turns to a trail. Within a half-mile or so, you will encounter an intersection where you will take the signed trail heading right (east) toward Star Lake. After about three-and-a-half miles, take the trail to your right marked "Freel Peak—1 mile." This is a switchback trail up the talus to the summit.

DESCRIPTION: The altitude and strenuous trail may result in labored breathing and rest stops, but the views of the Lake Tahoe Basin and the Great Basin to the east and the amazing wildflowers will really take your breath away! You will pass several lovely seep areas on the trail toward Star Lake, but the alpine rock gardens as you switchback up to and above timberline are the floral highlights of this hike.

BLOOMING: July through September, with most flowers in peak bloom from mid-July to mid-August.

GLORIOUS GARDENS: **Glaucous larkspur, Lewis monkeyflower, alpine gold, Davidson's penstemon, Tolmie's saxifrage, Lobb's buckwheat, alpine paintbrush, monkshood, western wallflower, rabbitbrush.**

SPECIAL FLOWERS NOT IN PROFUSION: **Dwarf alpine daisy, Lemmon's draba.**

57) Monitor Pass (to 8,314 feet)

FEATURED FLOWER: **Lemmon's onion**. In May and June, you will see low patches of purple in the grassy meadows from afar, and delicate, intricate, and fragrant onions from up close.

DRIVING DIRECTIONS: From Markleeville southeast of South Lake Tahoe, drive five miles south on SR-89, turn left (east) on SR-89 at the intersection with SR-4, and drive about 17 miles east to Topaz Lake.

WALKING DIRECTIONS: Stroll in the meadows and rocky flats along the road, especially just east and west of the pass.

DESCRIPTION: This drive is an adventure in contrasts, from mid-mountain Sierra meadows, coniferous forests, and aspen groves, to the dry eastern escarpment and the Great Basin desert. Correspondingly, you go from "Sound of Music" meadows of **larkspur, onion, mule ears, lupine**, and **senecio**, to patches of dry-environment flowers more typical of the Great Basin and the deserts of southern California.

BLOOMING: April (in the Great Basin just west of Topaz Lake) through August (with terrific fall color in the aspen groves in October), with the peak blooming east of the pass in May and early June, and west of the pass in late June and July.

GLORIOUS GARDENS: **Lemmon's onion, Anderson's larkspur, pennyroyal, desert peach, blue flax, flat-stemmed onion, water plantain buttercup, checkermallow, showy penstemon**.

SPECIAL FLOWERS NOT IN PROFUSION: **Bridge's penstemon, Fremont's phacelia**.

58) Topaz Lake (about 5,100 feet)

FEATURED FLOWER: **Apricot mallow**. Great clusters of these large, orange, apricot, or reddish desert beauties light up the sagebrush in May.

DRIVING DIRECTIONS: From Gardnerville, Nevada, at the intersection of U.S. 395 and SR-88, drive about 25 miles south on U.S. 395. A couple of miles after you enter California, you will see a "Topaz Lake" sign on your left. Just beyond the sign, park in the dirt turnout (wide shoulder) on the right at the mouth of a draw heading west.

WALKING DIRECTIONS: Wander up the draw and onto the ridge above. Be alert for rattlesnakes, as you are in the Great Basin desert (though I've never seen one here).

DESCRIPTION: You are in a fascinating area of transition here: you are in the westernmost part of the Great Basin desert just to the east of the Carson Range, with the Sierra a bit farther to the west.

BLOOMING: Late March or early April through July, with most flowers in peak bloom in late April and May.

GLORIOUS GARDENS: **Apricot mallow, long-leaf phlox, white-flowered keck-**

iella, **Applegate's paintbrush, rayless daisy, desert peach, prickly phlox, prickly poppy, sego lily.**

SPECIAL FLOWERS NOT IN PROFUSION: **Tufted evening primrose, blazing star, shaggy milkvetch.**

Central and Southern

59) Benton area (about 5,300 feet)

FEATURED FLOWER: **Bigelow's monkeyflower.** In May and June, along SR-120 between Mono Lake and Benton, great patches of this cheery magenta-and-gold monkeyflower brighten the desert flats and your mood, especially when in among the rich, blue lupines.

DRIVING DIRECTIONS: From Lee Vining just west of Mono Lake, drive south on U.S. 395 some 10 miles, then turn left on SR-120 east and continue about 46 miles to Benton. Benton can also be reached by driving roughly 34 miles north on U.S. 6 from Bishop.

WALKING DIRECTIONS: Meander the flats and small hills along the roads to Benton.

DESCRIPTION: SR-120 crosses through pine forests then out into open Great Basin desert flats. Being just north of the upper edge of the Mojave Desert, it will also boast some plants more typical of the Mojave.

BLOOMING: May through July, with peak blooming from May into June.

GLORIOUS GARDENS: **Bigelow's monkeyflower, silver cholla, long-leaf phlox, bird-cage evening primrose.**

SPECIAL FLOWERS NOT IN PROFUSION: **Cushion buckwheat, shaggy milkvetch, rosy penstemon, Mojave prickly pear.**

60) White Mountains (about 4,300–14,246 feet)

FEATURED FLOWER: **Alpine gold.** In July and August, on rocky flats and ridges near and above timberline, this large, golden composite with the sticky, sweetly fragrant leaves forms brilliant clusters that light up the rocks like the first touches of morning sunlight.

DRIVING DIRECTIONS: In California the White Mountains can be accessed by two routes—U.S. 6 heading north from Bishop skirts the western flank, while SR-168 heading east from Big Pine goes over Westgard Pass in the southern portion of the range. From Westgard Pass, White Mountain Road switchbacks north up toward the summit, ending just beyond Patriarch Grove.

WALKING DIRECTIONS: From the end of White Mountain Road, a trail climbs about five miles to the summit. Take it easy—the air is thin up here and you are exposed to wind, cold, and intense sun and ultraviolet radiation. In the lower elevations of the White Mountains, much of the land is private property, but you can wander across some desert flats and into some canyons.

DESCRIPTION: Although only a few miles east of the Sierra Nevada, the flora of the much drier White Mountains is much more "Great Basin desert" in character, especially in the lower elevations. At higher altitudes, much more of the flora is shared with the Sierra. The White Mountain Trail is breathtaking (metaphorically and literally), with fascinating alpine flowers and incredible, expansive views to the west of Owens Valley and the steep eastern escarpment of the Sierra.

BLOOMING: From March through May, at lower elevations in the Desert Scrub Zone, culminating in a July-through-August blooming at upper elevations in the alpine zone above timberline.

GLORIOUS GARDENS: **Tufted evening primrose, wishbone bush, brittlebush, alpine paintbrush, cushion phlox, Anderson's clover, alpine gentian, prickly poppy, showy penstemon, blue flax, rayless daisy, beavertail cactus, Idaho blue-eyed grass, purple sage, notch-leaved phacelia, desert trumpet, annual sunflower, brown-eyed evening primrose, California buckwheat, Whitney's locoweed.**

SPECIAL FLOWERS NOT IN PROFUSION: **Dwarf lewisia, desert aster, apricot mallow, golden cryptantha, blazing star, alpine gold, alpine buttercup, desert plume, scarlet locoweed, Davidson's fritillary, rock nettle, stream orchid, broad-leaf gilia, bitterroot, bush cinquefoil, scarlet monkeyflower, Nevada indigo bush, Kennedy mariposa lily, onion-head buckwheat, Booth's evening primrose, turtleback.**

61) Alabama Hills (about 4,000–5,400 feet)

FEATURED FLOWER: **Sandblossoms.** In a year of good spring rain, in March through May, the sandy flats between the rock formations are in places carpeted nearly solidly with the gorgeous blue-purple and yellow of these bowl-shaped flowers, on such short stems that the sand itself seems to have burst into bloom.

DRIVING DIRECTIONS: From Lone Pine on U.S. 395, drive west on Whitney Portal Road roughly five miles, then turn right onto Movie Road and explore the network of dirt roads that wanders through the Mojave Desert terrain east and below (way below!) Mount Whitney.

WALKING DIRECTIONS: Wander across the flats, down into the canyons, and up the rock formations along the dirt roads.

DESCRIPTION: One of the northernmost portions of the Mojave Desert, these exotic hills with the "movie Western set" rock formations and the stunning backdrop of the Mount Whitney escarpment (rising almost two miles above) boast an amazing array of Mojave Desert wildflowers. In a year of good spring rain, the ground can be carpeted with floral color.

BLOOMING: March through July, with peak blooming from April into May, with some cacti blooming in June and July.

GLORIOUS GARDENS: **Desert dandelion, apricot mallow, evening snow, desert paintbrush, freckled locoweed, scarlet locoweed, sandblossoms, yellow-throat, chia, desert aster, woolly daisy, Pringle's woolly sunflower, yellow peppergrass, desert pincushion, white layia, desert trumpet, yerba santa, California buckwheat, brown-eyed evening primrose.**

SPECIAL FLOWERS NOT IN PROFUSION: **Stream orchid, desert calico, desert plume, golden linanthus, silver cholla, showy gilia, desert five-spot, Bigelow's monkeyflower, purple mat, beavertail cactus, hedgehog cactus, Mojave thistle, desert larkspur, western desert penstemon, yellow eyes, Mojave desert parsley, white golden linanthus, Great Basin gilia, Mojave indigo bush.**

62) California Desert Conservation Area (about 4,000 feet)

FEATURED FLOWER: **Grape soda lupine.** From April into June, thousands of these beautiful, fragrant, blue-flowered shrubs light up the desert landscape under the Joshua trees.

DRIVING DIRECTIONS: From SR-14 just south of where it splits off from U.S. 395 west of Ridgecrest, turn west on SR-178. After eight miles, you will enter the Conservation Area a couple of miles below Walker Pass.

WALKING DIRECTIONS: Wander (safely—this is desert) to your heart's content on the hills and flats on either side of the road.

DESCRIPTION: The road skirts the southeast tip of the Sierra, crossing high desert landscape. You will find wonderful displays of mostly Mojave Desert herbs and shrubs under the **Joshua tree** forests.

BLOOMING: April through June, with peak blooming from May into June.

GLORIOUS GARDENS: **Purple sage, Joshua tree, prickly poppy, grape soda lupine, desert calico, desert penstemon, white layia, purple mat, freckled locoweed, fringed onion, purple sage.**

SPECIAL FLOWERS NOT IN PROFUSION: **Apricot mallow, golden linanthus, sandblossoms.**

SOUTHERN DESERTS

Gorman Hills

MUCH OF SOUTHERN CALIFORNIA east of the coast and the Transverse and Peninsular ranges is desert. The lower, hotter Sonoran Desert covers only a small area, including Anza-Borrego and the eastern half of Joshua Tree; the vast majority is the higher, somewhat less hot Mojave Desert, which reaches all the way up to the Gorman Hills and the Antelope Valley Poppy Reserve west of the Sierra, and even farther up the east side of the Sierra to Death Valley. In southeastern California, especially interesting parts of the Mojave Desert include the large Mojave National Preserve and the Whipple Mountains in the "nose" bordering Nevada. Also interesting floristically is the California Desert Preserve just south of the southern tip of the Sierra at Walker Pass.

The deserts (Sonoran and Mojave) are fascinating for wildflowers. Despite (or perhaps because of) the harsh conditions, there is an amazing number of species that thrive here, including some of the state's most spectacular flowers. There are numerous wildflower books on the cacti alone! Perhaps because of the contrast with the often austere environment, there is something especially striking and endearing about a desert wildflower garden. It almost seems that the flowers are the desert's way of speaking—messengers of mystery and timelessness.

When you think of the desert, you may think of the worst,
Of blistering heat and withering thirst.
You may think of remote and inhospitable lands,
Of slithering snakes and shape-shifting sands,
Of caravans of explorers in search of lost gold,
Of piles of bleached skulls and tales never told.
The desert can swallow man's pride and man's prime,
For it's deeper than thought and older than time.
But if you go to the desert with wide-open arms,
It will speak ancient wisdom and bestow precious charms.
Though the dreams of the Pharaohs lie dead in the tombs,
The dreams of the desert live on in its blooms.

When

The Sonoran Desert blooming can peak as early as February and into March, while the Mojave is later, from March and April into May.

Mojave Desert

63) Gorman Hills (about 4,000 feet)

FEATURED FLOWER: **Bigelow's coreopsis**. In April in good years, this large, bright yellow "sunflower" can paint the hills by the freeway with large gold patches, extending all the way up to the top of the ridge.

DRIVING DIRECTIONS: As I-5 heads from Los Angeles toward Bakersfield, running north through Tejon Pass, it passes some substantial hills to the right of the highway. Exit on the Gorman Post Road to get closer to the hills and to be able to stop and explore.

WALKING DIRECTIONS: Although the hills are private property and are fenced, you can walk a bit along the road to get a closer view of the flowers.

DESCRIPTION: Old-timers will tell you that these famously flowered hills on the edge of the Mojave Desert and the coast ranges have not been as spectacular in recent years (the last great year, they say, was 2003), but perhaps there is hope, as the 2010 and 2011 wildflower seasons seemed to recapture some of the floral splendor of the past. In April, the hills were dazzling impressionistic paintings of gold, yellow, white, blue, and purple, with occasional reddish-purple patches. As more land gets developed and fenced, access becomes more limited, and the flowers must be seen from farther away, but the spring "paintings" are still mesmerizing. (After great controversy about their development, Tejon Ranch currently does allow some access—contact them for information.)

BLOOMING: April through June, with peak blooming in April and May.

GLORIOUS GARDENS: **Goldfields, Bigelow's coreopsis, evening snow, bush lupine, sky lupine, spider lupine, purple owl's-clover, globe gilia, common phacelia, common yellow monkeyflower, California poppy, grape-soda lupine.**
SPECIAL FLOWER NOT IN PROFUSION: **Bladderpod bush.**

64) Antelope Valley California Poppy Reserve and Ripley Desert Woodland State Park (about 2,600–3,000 feet)

FEATURED FLOWER: **California poppy**. In good years, from April into early May, the rolling hills of the Poppy Reserve and the flats in surrounding areas are ablaze with acres and acres of hundreds of thousands of this gorgeous, satiny, orange California state flower.

DRIVING DIRECTIONS: From SR-14 south of Rosamond, drive south on Avenue D (SR-138) for about 15 miles, then turn left on 170th Street at the "Poppy Reserve" sign. After 2.4 miles, turn left at the T intersection (and poppy sign) and drive 2.6 miles to the entrance. For Ripley Desert Woodland State Park, turn right at the T intersection and drive 4.3 miles to the small sign on the right (easy to miss!) and the gap in the fence.

WALKING DIRECTIONS: At the Poppy Reserve, walk the easy trails wandering across the hills, especially the North Poppy Loop Trail, the north and south Antelope trails, and the Lightning Bolt Trail. Along Avenue D and 170th Street, there are many dirt roads you can drive (with an appropriate vehicle), or you may just wander on foot out into the unfenced fields. At Ripley, there are some marked trails across the Joshua tree flats.

DESCRIPTION: Just on the lee (north) side of the big mountains northeast of Los Angeles, the Poppy Reserve and the surrounding fields lie on the flat plain of the northern Mojave Desert (though the Reserve itself consists of gently rolling hills). Ripley State Park is flat. In some years, the Poppy Reserve can be painted almost solid orange; in other years the poppies can be rather sparse, but April and May can still be delightful with the green hills and assorted spring flowers. Even in lean poppy years at the Reserve, the surrounding flats along Avenue D and 170th Street can still be dazzling if not downright astounding! At Ripley State Park, you can find wonderful scenes of poppies blooming against a backdrop of blooming Joshua trees.

BLOOMING: March through May, with the Joshua tree peak blooming from March to April, and the poppies peaking from April to May.

GLORIOUS GARDENS: **California poppy, Joshua tree, sky lupine, desert dandelion, purple owl's-clover, goldfields, stork's bill, sticky sand verbena, yellow peppergrass, tufted evening primrose.**

SPECIAL FLOWERS NOT IN PROFUSION: **Showy gilia, cream cups, early evening primrose, desert star, spectacle pod, desert aster, desert larkspur, sandblossoms, yellow throats, golden linanthus, desert pincushion, desert calico, desert parsley, purple sage.**

65) Death Valley (282 feet below sea level, to 11,049 feet)

FEATURED FLOWER: **Desert gold**. In late February and March, acres of these golden suns bring life and energy to the desert flats, especially between Furnace Creek and Scotty's Castle.

DRIVING DIRECTIONS: There are two paved ways to enter Death Valley from California—one from Lone Pine or Olancha or Ridgecrest east over the Panamint Range at Townes Pass and into Stovepipe Wells, the other from Baker north through Shoshone and Death Valley Junction. There is also a northern partly paved and partly rough dirt way from Big Pine via the Eureka Dunes to Scotty's Castle. Within the park there is one main route (SR-190) from Scotty's Castle to Furnace Creek and then SR-178 over Salisbury Pass, but the real fun (if you're careful) is on the dirt roads and walks into the various canyons, especially Titus, Golden, Echo, and Wildrose.

WALKING DIRECTIONS: You can wander to your heart's content (carefully provisioned, of course) on the desert flats along SR-190 and along the numerous dirt side roads toward and into the many canyons, in the Ubehebe Crater area, at Zabriskie Point, and at Dante's View. For a unique experience you can hike the strenuous seven-mile (one-way) trail with over 2,900 feet of climbing up Telescope Peak, high up to the bristlecone pines, about two vertical miles above Badwater—the lowest spot in the United States

DESCRIPTION: In good rain years (such as 1998), the swaths of wildflower colors (especially desert gold) on the valley floors and alluvial fans (for example, just north of Furnace Creek) are so extensive and dazzling that you can see them from 10 miles away as you come over the Panamint Range from the west!

BLOOMING: February through April at the lower elevations on the valley floors and alluvial fans, April into June at the higher mountain elevations. In exceptional rain years, the blooming can begin as early as December.

GLORIOUS GARDENS: **Desert gold, sticky sand verbena, creosote bush, brown-eyed evening primrose, notch-leaf phacelia, caltha-leaf phacelia, Bigelow's monkeyflower, desert poppy, brittlebush, desert dandelion, showy gilia, desert aster, common phacelia, desert trumpet, desert chicory, lesser mohavea.**

SPECIAL FLOWERS NOT IN PROFUSION: **Desert five-spot, rock nettle, Death Valley goldeneye, gravel ghost, apricot mallow, beavertail cactus, broad-leaf gilia, Death Valley sage, Layne's locoweed, Mojave indigo bush, Arizona lupine, datura, bladdersage, Kennedy's mariposa lily, stream orchid, desert larkspur, windmills, rock pea, turtleback, desert star, Coulter's lupine, yellow eyes, beehive cactus, scented pentstemon, Panamint daisy, rayless goldenhead, weak-stem mariposa lily, desert marigold.**

Sonoran Desert

66) Joshua Tree National Park
(about 1,200–6,000 feet)

FEATURED FLOWER: **Canterbury bells**. From February into April, gravel flats and roadsides "ring" with the dark, rich blue tones of these gorgeous bells.

DRIVING DIRECTIONS: You can enter the park from the south from I-10 east of Palm Springs at Cottonwood Spring, or from the north from SR-62 at Joshua Tree or at Twenty-nine Palms. There is one major paved road cutting across the park from north to south, with a side road in the north through the Hidden Valley area.

WALKING DIRECTIONS: You can wander at will along the roads, and there are several short and a few longer hikes.

DESCRIPTION: The western half of the park, which is above 3,000 feet, is part of the higher, colder Mojave Desert epitomized by Joshua tree. The eastern half of the park, which is below 3,000 feet, is part of the hotter Sonoran Desert epitomized by creosote bush.

BLOOMING: February through June, with peak blooming from March through April, though higher elevations usually peak in June.

GLORIOUS GARDENS: **Desert senna, desert willow, bladdersage, creosote bush, Joshua tree, white rhatany, apricot mallow, canterbury bells, brittlebush, chuparosa, desert aster, beavertail cactus, desert larkspur, notch-leaf phacelia, ocotillo, sticky sand verbena, bladderpod bush, desert gold, desert trumpet, bird-cage evening primrose, brown-eyed evening primrose, white tackstem, barrel cactus.**

SPECIAL FLOWERS NOT IN PROFUSION: **Parry's nolina, desert plume, Arizona lupine, windmills, California four o'clock, early evening primrose, rock pea, yellowhead, sand blazing star, desert star, desert lily, spectacle pod, Coulter's lupine, amsonia, beehive cactus.**

67) Anza-Borrego Desert State Park
(about 150–6,200 feet)

FEATURED FLOWER: **Chuparosa**. From late February into April, these lovely red shrubs decorate the desert floor; sometimes teaming up with other plants, sometimes all by themselves.

DRIVING DIRECTIONS: This is a large area about 100 miles northeast of San Diego. The two major centers are Borrego Springs in the north, reached by County Road S22 from west or east, and Ocotillo Wells in the east on SR-78 from the west or east. Most of the roads to the trailheads are dirt (sand), which you should drive with caution and preferably in a four-wheel drive vehicle, though many of them are accessible to a regular passenger car (check conditions with the Visitors' Center before trying).

WALKING DIRECTIONS: There are numerous trails, some of them long and arduous, but many are relatively short and easy (with proper preparation for the weather conditions). Water and sun protection are vital. Especially wonderful trails for the wildflowers include Coyote Canyon, Hellhole Canyon, Henderson Canyon, Glorietta Canyon, Desert Palm Canyon, and Elephant Tree.

DESCRIPTION: This large area in the rain shadow east of the coastal range and just north of the Mexican border is a wonderland of open desert floor, washes and canyons, springs, and palm oases. In great years, the flowers are so dense and varied that they can almost completely cover the wide expanses of sand. In good years, the sand is quite apparent but so, too, are the showy clusters of scores and scores of species of desert flowers. In late February and early March, when the Mojave Desert to the north is just beginning to stir florally, Anza-Borrego can be swarming with flowers and flower-lovers alike.

BLOOMING: Late February through May, with most flowers in peak bloom from March through April.

GLORIOUS GARDENS: **Brown-eyed evening primrose, bird-cage evening primrose, Bigelow's monkeyflower, common phacelia, desert sand verbena, silver cholla, barrel cactus, beavertail cactus, brittlebush, desert dandelion, California sun cup, chuparosa, ocotillo, manroot, wishbone bush, spectacle pod, Wallace's woolly daisy, bladderpod bush, baby blue eyes, notch-leaf phacelia, creosote bush, desert gold, desert trumpet, banana yucca, desert willow, goldfields.**

SPECIAL FLOWERS NOT IN PROFUSION: **Desert lily, wild canterbury bells, Arizona lupine, whispering bells, desert star, windmills, turtleback, rock pea, apache plume, sand blazing star, alkali heliotrope, fishhook cactus, Engelmann's hedgehog cactus, yellowhead, Parry's nolina.**

*In the motion of the very leaves of Spring, in the blue air,
there is then found a secret correspondence with our heart.*

PERCY BYSSHE SHELLEY, "ON LOVE," 1818

*The force that through the green fuse drives the flower
drives my green age.*

DYLAN THOMAS, "THE FORCE THAT THROUGH THE GREEN FUSE
DRIVES THE FLOWER," 1934

LATE JANUARY–FEBRUARY

Mustard fields along Pleasants Valley Road

ALTHOUGH THERE ARE A FEW non-natives and garden escapees as well as a few natives that (especially in years of good winter rain) may be in bloom between November and January, the first significant blooming of native wildflowers in California occurs most years in late January and February. While the peak of the spring explosion of flowers along the coast and in the coast ranges, in the Central Valley, and in the Mojave Desert is still a few weeks away, late January and February bring us some lovely early bloomers in many of these low-elevation locations—delicious appetizers for the main course to follow. In the Sonoran Desert in the far south of the state (especially in Anza-Borrego Desert State Park), however, the meal can be well into the entrée course by late February, and what a feast it can be! If you hear it's a great flower year in Anza-Borrego, you might just want to take an extended leave from your "normal" life and take up temporary residence with the flowers in the desert.

Highlights

Beaches and Bluffs Along the Coast

Baby blue eyes at Manchester Beach
White baby blue eyes at Bodega Head

Footsteps of spring and **Douglas iris** at Salt Point
Giant trillium north of Stinson Beach
Foothills shooting star, coast sun cup, and **Indian warrior** at China Camp
Bush poppy at Torrey Pines
Mustard fields north of Jenner

Coast Ranges

Bush monkeyflower and **Fremont's camas** on Mount Tamalpais
Slink pod in Muir Woods
Ground pink, Padre's shooting star, and **chocolate lily** on the Santa Rosa Plateau
Mustard fields in Napa Valley orchards

Central Valley

Mustard fields along Pleasants Valley Road

Deserts

Ocotillo, barrel cactus, Canterbury bells, desert lily, chuparosa, and **sticky sand verbena** at Anza-Borrego
Desert gold at Death Valley

Flowers

BABY BLUE EYES
Nemophila menziesii

Borage family (previously included in Waterleaf family)

DESCRIPTION: 4–12 inches. Black-spotted, sky-blue or pale blue (for the white variety, see p. 123), bowl-shaped flowers (to one-and-a-half inches wide), usually with white centers. Pinnately lobed, fleshy leaves.

Baby blue eyes

NOTE: These lovely, cheery, blue flowers usually grow in open, grassy, sun-warmed fields and meadows or sandy flats. Not uncommonly in bloom in some places before late January.

HABITAT: Grows in open, grassy fields and meadows, and sandy flats (to 6,200 feet); found in much of California.

WHERE AND WHEN:

San Gabriel Mountains (February–June)

Anza-Borrego (February–April)

Manchester Beach (February–May)

SR-58 (February–April)

Hite's Cove Trail (March–April)

Six Rivers National Forest (May–June)

BLUE DICKS
Dichelostemma capitatum

Brodiaea family (previously included in Lily family)

DESCRIPTION: 1–3 feet. Stems terminate in a densely flowered umbel of up to 15 blue-purple or pink-purple, six-tepaled flowers subtended by two to four dark, metallic purple bracts. Long, grasslike leaves.

NOTE: Because the stems are rather weak, the plants will wave in a breeze, and the umbels of flowers will often bend over. Not uncommonly in bloom in some places before late January.

HABITAT: Found in grasslands, woodlands, scrub, and deserts (to 7,500 feet); in much of California.

WHERE AND WHEN:

Santa Rosa Plateau (February–May)

Nipomo-Guadalupe Dunes (February–June)

Phoenix Park (February–April)

Blue dicks

Wind Wolves Preserve (February–April)
Buttermilk Bend Trail (March–April)
Table Mountain (March–April)

CANTERBURY BELLS or DESERT BELLS or DESERT BLUEBELLS
Phacelia campanularia

Borage family (previously included in Waterleaf family)

DESCRIPTION: 0.5–2 feet. Stout, glandular-hairy stem with deep blue, funnel-shaped flowers (to one-and-a-half inches across) scattered along it and in terminal, coiled cymes. Broad, dark green, distinctly veined, toothed leaves. Endemic to California.

NOTE: These deep-blue trumpet flowers jazz up the desert with soulful, floral music, but it's probably better to just look and listen—the hairs on the plant can be quite irritating to touch.

HABITAT: Prefers sandy or gravelly flats (to 5,200 feet); found in the Mojave and Sonoran deserts.

WHERE AND WHEN:

Anza-Borrego (February–March)
Joshua Tree (February–April)

Canterbury bells

Mojave National Preserve (February–April)
Coachella Valley (February–April)
San Felipe Valley (February–April)
Jacumba area (March–May)

HOUND'S TONGUE, GRAND

Borage family

Cynoglossum grande

DESCRIPTION: 1–3 feet. Blue, pinwheel-like flowers (to one-half inch in diameter) with raised, toothed, white rim around the throat. Large, broad, dark-green leaves with long petioles.

NOTE: Like its close relative, stickseed (*Hackelia* genus), hound's tongue has prickly fruits that are as interesting and picturesque as the flowers.

HABITAT: Grows in forest openings and edges (to 5,000 feet); found in the northwest mountains, coast ranges, foothills, Cascades, and northern Sierra.

WHERE AND WHEN:
Muir Woods (February–April)
Pinnacles (February–April)
Santa Lucia Range (March–May)

Grand hound's tongue

Drum Powerhouse Road (March–May)
Trinity Alps (March–May)
Six Rivers National Forest (May–June)

IRIS, DOUGLAS   *Iris douglasiana*
Iris family

DESCRIPTION: 0.5–3 feet. Two or three flowers (to three inches in diameter) at the top of the stem. Three tonguelike, spreading, purple sepals with yellow and white central area. Three narrower, erect petals, and three erect, feathery pistils.

Douglas iris

NOTE: These large, stunning flowers range in color from deep blue-purple to red-purple to creamy yellow. The small, nipplelike bumps at the top of the ovary are a distinguishing characteristic.

HABITAT: Grows in grasslands, woodlands, bluffs, and pastures (to 3,300 feet) of the coast and coast ranges, northeast corner, and Transverse Ranges.

WHERE AND WHEN:
Santa Lucia Range (February–April)
Salt Point (February–April)
Ring Mountain (February–April)
north of Stinson Beach (February–May)
Canada Honda Creek (March–April)
Warner Mountains (April–June)

NIGHTSHADE, PARISH'S PURPLE   *Solanum parishii*
Nightshade family

DESCRIPTION: 1–3.5 feet. Subshrub with smooth, hairless, angled, or ribbed stems with many tonguelike leaves and umbel-like clusters of hanging, saucer-shaped, blue-purple flowers (up to one inch across) with a yellow "corncob" in center. Pair of green spots on a yellow field at the base of each petal.

NOTE: Occasionally you will find pure white flowers—apparently a "whiter shade of purple!"

HABITAT: Appears in chaparral and woodlands (to 6,500 feet) across much of California (except the Central Valley and deserts).

WHERE AND WHEN:
Torrey Pines (February–May)
Santa Rosa Plateau
    (February–May)
Mount Sanhedrin (March–
    May)
Palomar Mountain (March–
    May)
Agua Tibia Mountains
    (March–May)
Bear Valley (March–May)

Parish's purple nightshade

PHACELIA, COMMON or WILD HELIOTROPE   *Phacelia distans*
Borage family (previously included in Waterleaf family)

DESCRIPTION: 0.5–3 feet. Branching stiff and hairy stems, often tangled in

shrubs. Deeply divided leaves with toothed or scalloped segments. Coils of many light-blue or violet, shallow, bell-shaped flowers (to one-half inch across) with whitish throats with purple markings. Five long, protruding stamens.

NOTE: Of all the *Phacelia* species in California, this is probably the most common and widespread.

HABITAT: Found in clay or rocky flats and slopes (to 7,000 feet) of the coast and coast ranges, the Central Valley, east of the Sierra, the Transverse Ranges, and in the Mojave Desert and Sonoran Desert.

Common phacelia

WHERE AND WHEN:
Anza-Borrego (February–April)
Torrey Pines (February–April)
Death Valley (March–May)
Fort Bragg area (March–June)
Edgewood Natural Preserve (March–June)
Santa Monica Mountains (March–June)

PHACELIA, LARGE-FLOWERED   *Phacelia grandiflora*
Borage family (previously included in Waterleaf family)
DESCRIPTION: 1–3 feet. Sticky, hairy plant with broad, coarsely toothed leaves and clusters of large (up to 2 inches), shallow, bowl-shaped, pale blue or violet flowers with dark purple streaks. Glandular hairs can cause rashes. Especially abundant after fires.

Large-flowered phacelia

NOTE: Many of the phacelias dazzle with their rich blue flowers; this species is a bit paler in color but stunning in size.

HABITAT: Grows in woodlands, chaparral, and disturbed places (to 3,000 feet) on the south coast and coast ranges, and the Transverse Ranges.

WHERE AND WHEN:
San Gabriel Mountains
   (February–June)
Santa Monica Mountains
   (February–June)
Santa Ynez Mountains (March–
   June)
Channel Islands (March–June)
Torrey Pines (May–June)
Otay Mountains (May–June)

PHACELIA, NOTCH-LEAF   *Phacelia crenulata*
Borage family (previously included in Waterleaf family)
DESCRIPTION: 4–20 inches. Glandular-hairy stem with many coiled clusters of bowl-shaped or funnel-shaped, violet or blue-purple flowers (to one-half inch). White at throat. Deeply pinnately lobed leaves.
NOTE: Most *Phacelia* species are hairy and have long-protruding reproductive parts, giving the plants a rather fuzzy appearance. In many species

(including this one), touching the hairs may be a "rash" act!

HABITAT: Grows on sandy or gravelly flats and slopes, in washes (to 7,200 feet); found in the northeast corner, east of the Sierra, the Mojave Desert, and the Sonoran Desert.

WHERE AND WHEN:
Anza-Borrego (February–April)
Death Valley (March–April)
Joshua Tree (March–April)
Algodones Dunes (March–April)
White Mountains (March–April)
Warner Mountains (May–June)

Notch-leaf phacelia

WILD HOLLYHOCK
Sidalcea malviflora

Mallow family

DESCRIPTION: 0.5–2 feet. Several open, bowl-shaped flowers (to 1.5 inches) along and at the tip of the stem. Five separate, overlapping pink petals with darker red-purple and white veins.

NOTE: Unlike most plants, many of those in the Mallow family have both male (white froth below) and female (scarlet or pink thread above) parts on the same central column. Not uncommonly in bloom in some places before late January.

HABITAT: Grows on grassy bluffs; scrubby slopes; forest openings (to 7,500 feet); found in much of California (except northeast corner and deserts).

WHERE AND WHEN:
China Camp State Park (February–May)

Checkerbloom

Anza-Borrego (February–May)
Santa Rosa Plateau (February–July)
San Bruno Mountain (March–May)
Santa Monica Mountains (March–June)
Salt Point (May–June)

CHUPAROSA or BELOPERONE *Justicia californica*
Acanthus family

DESCRIPTION: 2–7 feet. Shrub with tangle of stiff branches and many red, tubular, two-lipped flowers. Hoodlike upper lip and tonguelike lower lip. Pairs of opposite leaves usually drop off by flowering time.

NOTE: *Chuparosa* means "it sucks the rose," in reference to the copious and accessible (mostly to hummingbirds) nectar.

HABITAT: Grows on sandy or rocky flats, and in washes (to 2,600 feet); can be seen in the Peninsular Ranges and the Sonoran Desert.

WHERE AND WHEN:
*Elephant Tree Trail in Anza-
    Borrego* (February–April)
*Borrego-Palm Canyon in
    Anza-Borrego* (February–
    April)
*Henderson Canyon in Anza-
    Borrego* (February–April)
Joshua Tree (February–April)
San Diego River (March–
    May)
29 Palms area (March–May)

Chuparosa or Beloperone

CURRANT, CHAPARRAL *Ribes malvaceum*
Gooseberry family

DESCRIPTION: 3–6 feet. Shrub with somewhat crinkly, three-to five-lobed hairy leaves, and clusters of 10 to 25 rose-pink, tubular flowers. Smooth, dark-purple-to-black berries.

NOTE: The fruits look tasty, but looks can be deceiving—these are extremely bitter.

HABITAT: Grows in chaparral and woodlands (to 5,000 feet); found in the coast ranges, foothills, Transverse Ranges, and Peninsular Ranges.

WHERE AND WHEN:

Santa Monica Mountains
(January–March)

Placerita Canyon Natural
Area (January–March)

Point Magu State Park
(January–March)

Santa Rosa Plateau
(January–March)

Red Hill Road (March–May)

Bear Valley (March–May)

Chapparal currant

CURRANT, RED-FLOWERING *Ribes sanguineum*

Gooseberry family

DESCRIPTION: 2–10 feet. Shrub with hanging clusters of 10 to 20 star-shaped, blood-red, pink, or white fragrant flowers (to one-half inch across). Blue-black, hairy, tasteless berries. Broad, crinkly leaves with shallow lobes.

NOTE: *Sanguine* may refer to the (bloody) color of the blossoms, but per-

Red-flowering currant

haps it is also because seeing (and smelling) these beauties is likely to create a cheerful and optimistic mood!

HABITAT: Grows on shrubby slopes and forest edges (to 7,200 feet); found in the northwest mountains, coast, and coast ranges.

WHERE AND WHEN:
Edgewood Preserve (February–April)
Santa Cruz Mountains (February–April)
Santa Ynez Mountains (March–May)
Santa Lucia Range (March–April)
Kruse Rhododendron State Reserve (March–April)
Trinity Alps (June–July)

GOOSEBERRY, FUCHSIA-FLOWERED   *Ribes speciosum*
Gooseberry family

DESCRIPTION: 4–8 feet. Shrub with broad, dark green, leathery, shiny leaves and triple spines in leaf axils. One to four hanging, narrowly tubular flowers (to three-fourths of an inch in diameter) with bright scarlet sepals and petals. Long-protruding stamens.

NOTE: With the intensely red flowers and fruits and the glossy green leaves, this plant is as stunning to plant lovers as it is alluring to hummingbirds.

HABITAT: Grows among coastal scrub and chaparral (to 1,700 feet); seen on the central and south coast and coast ranges, Transverse Ranges, and Peninsular Ranges.

WHERE AND WHEN:
Santa Monica Mountains
  (February–April)
Santa Ana Mountains
  (February–April)
Montana del Oro (February–April)
Eaton Canyon (February–April)
Figueroa Mountain (February–May)
Cachuma Lake Recreational Area
  (February–May)

Fuchsia-flowered gooseberry

Fuchsia-flowered
gooseberry

INDIAN WARRIOR   *Pedicularis densiflora*
Broomrape family (previously included in Snapdragon family)
DESCRIPTION: 0.5–2 feet. Dense spike of wine-red or scarlet, two-lipped, tubular flowers (to one-and-a-half inches long). Upper lip is a stout beak, lower lip is three small lobes halfway back on the flower tube. Partial parasite.

NOTE: The array of flowers can range in color from crimson, to magenta, to wine red, to rust.

HABITAT: Grows in shrubby forest openings or edges and grasslands (to 6,000 feet); seen in the northwest mountains, coast, coast ranges, foothills, Cascades, Transverse Ranges, and Peninsular Ranges.

WHERE AND WHEN:
China Camp (February–March)

Indian warrior

Santa Monica Mountains (February–April)
San Gabriel Mountains (March–June)
Pinnacles (March–April)
Independence Trail (March–April)
Trinity Alps (March–June)

LUPINE, ARIZONA
Pea family

Lupinus arizonicus

DESCRIPTION: 4–20 inches. Branching, hairy stem with leaves well up the plant. Raceme up to 10 inches of spiraling or whorls of pink pea flowers (to one-half-inch broad).

Red-spotted, yellow or white patch on banner, becoming magenta with age. Six to 10 broad leaflets.

NOTE: The pinkish color of the banner and wings is unusual for a lupine, blue or blue-purple being much more common.

HABITAT: Grows in sandy flats and washes (to 3,600 feet); found in the Mojave Desert and Sonoran Desert.

WHERE AND WHEN:
Anza-Borrego (February–
    April)
Joshua Tree (March–April)
near Indio (March–April)
Death Valley (March–April)
Coachella Valley (March–
    April)

Arizona lupine

Mojave National Preserve (March–May)

MORNING GLORY, BEACH
Morning-glory family

Calystegia soldanella

DESCRIPTION: 1–2 feet. Large (to 2 inches), trumpet-shaped flowers along trailing stem. Five pink petal lobes with white streaks and white throat. Broad, fleshy, kidney-shaped leaves.

NOTE: The stem trails along the sand, so these large, showy flowers and the broad, fleshy leaves leave quite a track of "footprints" across beaches and dunes.

HABITAT: Thrives on beaches and dunes (to 200 feet); found on the coast.

Beach morning glory

WHERE AND WHEN:
Nipomo-Guadalupe Dunes (February–June)
Channel Islands (February–July)
Dunes of Arcata (March–July)
Manchester Beach (March–July)
Santa Monica Mountains (April–August)
Humboldt Lagoon State Park (June–July)

OCOTILLO
Fouquieria splendens
Ocotillo family

DESCRIPTION: 6–30 feet. Thorny shrub with canelike stems, clusters of oval leaves, and brushlike clusters of scarlet, tubular flowers (to one-half inch wide) with long, protruding reproductive parts.

NOTE: The stems are leafless most of the year; the deciduous leaves appearing only with sufficient rain, which can happen several times a year. The flowers are truly "splendens."

HABITAT: Grows on gravelly or rocky flats and slopes (to 2,300 feet); seen in the Mojave Desert and Sonoran Desert.

WHERE AND WHEN:
Anza-Borrego (February–June)
Joshua Tree (March–May)
Chuckwalla Mountains
(March–May)
Turtle Mountains (March–May)

Ocotillo

Algodones Dunes (March–May)
Chocolate Mountains (March–June)

PAINTBRUSH, COAST
Castilleja affinis

Broomrape family (previously included in Snapdragon family)

DESCRIPTION: 0.5–2 feet. Usually softly hairy plant with bright red (sometimes yellow) bracts with four to six narrow lobes. Narrow, dark-green leaves, unlobed or with two to six short, very narrow lobes.

NOTE: "Narrow" is the key word here, as the bracts and leaves and their lobes, if any, are much longer than they are wide.

HABITAT: Flourishes in bluffs, grasslands, and chaparral (to 4,000 feet); seen along the coast and coast ranges, foothills, Transverse Ranges, and Peninsular Ranges.

WHERE AND WHEN:
Torrey Pines (February–May)
Santa Monica Mountains
    (February–May)
Santa Ana Mountains
    (February–May)
Figueroa Mountain
    (February–May)

Coast paintbrush

Nipomo-Guadalupe Dunes
    (February–May)
Mendocino area (March–June)

PHLOX, CALIFORNIA PRICKLY
Linanthus californicus or
Leptodactylon californicum

Phlox family

DESCRIPTION: 1–3 feet. Shrub with prickly leaves, and nearly flat, pinwheel-shaped flowers with five petal lobes flaring out of a long flower tube. The rose-pink flowers (to 1.5 inches across) have white centers. Delicately fragrant.

NOTE: At first the leaves are palmately lobed with sharp points, but later these fall off, leaving clusters of smaller, needlelike leaves that are *really* prickly!

HABITAT: Grows among scrub, woodlands, and along the coast (to 5,000 feet); found on the south coast and coast ranges, Transverse Ranges, and Peninsular Ranges.

WHERE AND WHEN:
Santa Monica Mountains
(February–May)
Cuyama Valley (February–June)
San Gabriel Mountains
(February–June)
SR-58 (February–May)
Point Magu State Park
(February–June)
Nipomo-Guadalupe Dunes
(March–June)

California prickly phlox

PINK, GROUND or FRINGED LINANTHUS *Linanthus dianthiflorus*
Phlox family

DESCRIPTION: 2–5 inches. Prostrate plant with delicate, branching stem with one or a few showy terminal, shallow bowl-shaped flowers (to 1 inch). Five fringe-toothed petal lobes, pink or lavender toward the tip and white toward the base. Yellow flower tube with dark purple spots. Sparse, threadlike leaves. Endemic to California.

NOTE: These exquisite flowers usually form extensive, densely flowered colonies.

Ground pink or
Fringed linanthus

HABITAT: Thrives in grasslands and coastal scrub (to 4,200 feet); found along the south coast and the coast ranges, Transverse Ranges, and Peninsular Ranges.

WHERE AND WHEN:
Santa Rosa Plateau (February–April)
Torrey Pines (February–April)
Santa Monica Mountains (February–April)
Otay Mountains (February–April)
Malibu Creek State Park (February–April)
Point Magu State Park (February–April)

RED MAIDS   *Calandrinia ciliata*
Miner's lettuce family (previously included in Purslane family)

DESCRIPTION: 2–24 inches. Bright half-inch flowers with five separate, silky, red or red-purple petals and orange anthers. Flowers can carpet large areas.

NOTE: You may notice these flowers in the afternoon where you didn't in the early morning—they open only in bright sunlight.

HABITAT: Flourishes in grassy fields, bluffs, and disturbed places (to 6,000 feet); found in much of California.

WHERE AND WHEN:
Pleasants Valley Road
   (February–May)
Carrizo Plain (February–
   May)
Big Sur (February–May)
San Bernardino Mountains
   (March–May)
Bear Valley (April–May)
Lassen National Park (May–
   June)

Red maids

SHOOTING STAR, FOOTHILL or MOSQUITO BILLS or HENDERSON'S SHOOTING STAR   *Dodecatheon hendersonii*
Primrose family

DESCRIPTION: 5–16 inches. Umbels of a few inside-out flowers hanging upside-down at the tips of arching pedicels. Five (sometimes four) pink or magenta petal lobes yellow and white just above the "snout."

Foothill shooting star

NOTE: How lucky we are that this lovely flower brings its message of vernal joy to so much of California's spring.
HABITAT: Open woods, brushy slopes, grasslands, wet meadows (to 5,000 feet); found in northwest mountains, coast, coast ranges, Central Valley, foothills, Transverse Ranges.
WHERE AND WHEN:
Mix Canyon Road (January–April)
San Bernardino Mountains (February–March)
Hite's Cove Trail (February–March)
Santa Ynez Mountains (February–March)
China Camp (February–April)
Trinity Alps (February–June)

SHOOTING STAR, PADRE'S   *Dodecatheon clevelandii*
Primrose family
DESCRIPTION: 1–2 feet. Slightly sticky, thick, leafless stem with one to 16 five-petaled flowers hanging from arching pedicels. Five (sometimes four) magenta or pink (sometimes white) petals with white and yellow bands above maroon anther tubes. Light-colored anthers. Broad, thick, basal leaves.
NOTE: These lovely flowers deserve a close sniff, for they have a delicate, pleasant aroma.
HABITAT: Grassy fields (to 2,500 feet); central and southern coast and coast ranges, Central Valley, foothills, Transverse Ranges, Peninsular Ranges
WHERE AND WHEN:
Santa Rosa Plateau (February–April)
Figueroa Mountain (February–April)
Torrey Pines (February–April)
Channel Islands (February–April)
SR-58 (February–April)
Greenhorn Range (March–May)

Padre's shooting star

SORREL, REDWOOD   *Oxalis oregana*
Wood Sorrel family

DESCRIPTION: 2–12 inches. Solitary flower (to one inch) at tip of slender stalk. Five separate, pink or white petals; three clover-like, rather heart-shaped leaflets.

NOTE: Both the genus names *Oxalis* and *Oxyria* (mountain sorrel, p. 491)

Redwood sorrel

are from the Greek word meaning "acid," in reference to the tart taste of the leaves, which contain oxalic acid.

HABITAT: Moist forest shade (to 3,300 feet); north and central coast and coast ranges

WHERE AND WHEN:

Muir Woods (February–September)
Big Basin Redwoods State Park (February–September)
Big Sur (March–May)
Salt Point (March–May)
Redwood National Park (March–June)
Mount Tamalpais (March–June)

VERBENA, MAGENTA or RED SAND VERBENA or BEACH PANCAKE   *Abronia maritima*

Four o'clock family

DESCRIPTION: 1–6 feet. Prostrate, spreading, glandular-hairy plant with thick, elliptical or round, succulent leaves and round heads of many small, tubular, wine-red or rose-violet flowers on short, erect stems. CNPS Rare and Endangered List—endangered.

NOTE: The alternate common name "beach pancake" refers to the thick, roundish leaves. The color of the flowers is startling—almost fluorescent.

HABITAT: Coastal dunes (to 350 feet); central and southern coast.

WHERE AND WHEN:

Nipomo-Guadalupe Dunes (February–October)
Channel Islands (February–October)
Point Magu State Park (February–October)
Point Dume (March–November)
Torrey Pines (March–November)
Morro Bay (March–November)

Magenta verbena

VERBENA, STICKY SAND or
DESERT SAND VERBENA   *Abronia villosa*
Four o'clock family

DESCRIPTION: 1–3 feet. Glandular-hairy, prostrate plant with spreading stem. Spherical clusters of 15–30 pink or magenta, starfish-like flowers with usually five heart-shaped lobes. Large, round, fleshy leaves.

NOTE: After a good soaking rain, it is amazing how quickly these plants can spread and bloom, carpeting great expanses of sand with their dazzling color and sweet aroma.

HABITAT: Sandy flats, dunes, desert scrub, coastal sagebrush scrub (to 5,500 feet); found on the south coast, Mojave Desert, Sonoran Desert.

WHERE AND WHEN:
Coachella Valley (February–May)
Joshua Tree (February–May)
Death Valley (February–May)
Antelope Valley (February–May)
Anza-Borrego (February–June)
Mojave National Preserve (February–June)

Sticky sand verbena

WINDMILLS or TRAILING FOUR O'CLOCK   *Allionia incarnata*
Four o'clock family

DESCRIPTION: 1–2 inches. Sticky-hairy plant with trailing stem and broad, somewhat wavy-edged leaves. Apparently solitary, saucer-shaped, pink-purple flowers at the tips of slender pedicels.

NOTE: These flowers are quite deceptive—what appears to be a single flower with nine heart-shaped petals is actually three flowers clustered together.

HABITAT: Desert scrub (to 5,000 feet); found in the Mojave Desert, Sonoran Desert.

WHERE AND WHEN:
Anza-Borrego (February–May)
Mojave National Preserve (March–May)
Death Valley (April–May)

Joshua Tree (April–May)
Eureka Dunes (April–July)
Chocolate Mountains (April–July)

Windmills

WISHBONE BUSH, CALIFORNIA or CALIFORNIA FOUR O'CLOCK *Mirabilis laevis* var. *crassifolia* or *M. californica*

Four-o'clock family

DESCRIPTION: 1–3 feet. Low, bushy, sticky-hairy plant with trailing, forked stems and oval or heart-shaped leaves. Five pink-purple, petal-like sepals that are two-parted at tip.

NOTE: The trailing stems sometimes lean on a neighbor for support. They are also "supported" by fire—they can occur in tremendous numbers following a blaze.

HABITAT: Chaparral, washes, dunes, burn areas (to 3,000 feet); common on the central and south coast and coast ranges, Transverse Ranges, Peninsular Ranges, Mojave Desert.

WHERE AND WHEN:
Torrey Pines (February–March)
Joshua Tree (February–March)

California wishbone bush

Carrizo Plain (February–March)
Santa Monica Mountains (March–May)
San Gabriel Mountains (March–May)
Santa Lucia Mountains (March–June)

BLADDERPOD BUSH   *Peritome arborea* or *Isomeris arborea*
Cleome family (previously included in Caper family)
DESCRIPTION: 2–10 feet. Much-branched shrub with blue-green leaves, usually with three leaflets. Terminal racemes of many bright yellow, four-petaled flowers (to two inches). Large, pendant, smooth, green, pointed pods.

NOTE: A dazzling shrub, especially when the flowers and the fruits are on the plant at the same time. In bloom in many places for most of the year.

HABITAT: Coastal bluffs, desert flats and washes (to 4,300 feet); grows on the central and south coast, Transverse Ranges, Mojave Desert, Sonoran Desert.

WHERE AND WHEN:
Joshua Tree (all year)
Carrizo Plain (all year)
Mojave National Preserve (all
    year)
Channel Islands (all year)
Santa Monica Mountains (all
    year)
Torrey Pines (all year)

Bladderpod bush

BRITTLEBUSH or INCIENSO   *Encelia farinosa*
Aster family
DESCRIPTION: 1–5 feet. Much-branched, dome-shaped shrub thick with broad, egg-shaped, blue-green leaves and many flower heads (to 1.5 inches) with 11–21 yellow, three-lobed ray flowers.

NOTE: Resin from this plant was burned as incense, hence the alternative common name.

HABITAT: Coastal scrub, rocky desert slopes (to 3,300 feet); found on south coast and coast ranges, Mojave Desert, Sonoran Desert.

WHERE AND WHEN:
Anza-Borrego (January–May)

Brittlebush

Torrey Pines (March–May)
Joshua Tree (March–May)
San Bernardino Valley (March–May)
Death Valley (March–May)
Santa Rosa Plateau (March–May)

BUTTERCUP, CALIFORNIA

Ranunculus californicus

Buttercup family

DESCRIPTION: 1–2.5 feet. Stem branches terminate in one or a few flowers

California buttercup

(to one inch) with seven to 22 bright yellow, waxy petals. A few broad, compound leaves with three-to five-toothed leaflets.

NOTE: The photo shows a prostrate variety with thick, wedge-shaped leaflets (sometimes called California coast buttercup), which occurs on bluffs along the coast.

HABITAT: Grassy fields, woodlands, wet meadows (to 7,500 feet); found in much of California (except deserts and eastern edge).

WHERE AND WHEN:
Salt Point (February–April)
Santa Monica Mountains (February–April)
Mix Canyon Road (February–May)
Edgewood Preserve (February–May)
Channel Islands (February–May)
Santa Ana Mountains (March–April)

CACTUS, BARREL or BISNAGA   *Ferocactus cylindraceus*
Cactus family

DESCRIPTION: 1–9 feet. Cylindrical, barrel-like stem (usually single but sometimes in clumps of several stems) heavily armed with intermeshed, long, flat, reddish or golden spines. Large yellow flowers (to two inches) in a ring on the top of the barrel.

NOTE: *Bisnaga* probably derives from an Aztec word meaning "vicinity of thorns." And how!

HABITAT: Sandy or gravelly slopes, rocky places (to 5,000 feet); found in Mojave Desert, Sonoran Desert.

WHERE AND WHEN:
Anza-Borrego (February–
    May)
Joshua Tree (March–May)
Jacumba area (April–May)
Chocolate Mountains (April–
    May)
San Felipe Valley (April–
    May)
Mojave National Preserve   Barrel cactus
    (April–June)

CREOSOTE BUSH   *Larrea tridentata*
Caltrop family

DESCRIPTION: 2–7 feet. Shrub with gray, resinous, brittle branches and tiny, rough, sticky leaves. Scattered flowers (to one inch) with five narrow, widely separate, twisted petals.

NOTE: This widespread desert shrub can dominate acres of desert floor,

Creosote bush

filling the air with a pungent aroma after rains and filling its branches with white, cotton-ball fruits after pollination.

HABITAT: Desert scrub (to 3,300 feet); found on south coast, San Joaquin Valley, east of the Sierra, Mojave Desert, Sonoran Desert.

WHERE AND WHEN:

Anza-Borrego (February–May)
Joshua Tree (March–May)
Death Valley (March–May)
Mojave National Preserve (April–May)
Alabama Hills (April–May)
Vallecito Stage Station (April–May)

DANDELION, DESERT   *Malacothrix glabrata*

Aster family

DESCRIPTION: 4–16 inches. Many broad, yellow flower heads (to 1.5 inches), often with rosy spot at the center. Ray flowers only: bright yellow when first open, then becoming pale yellow or cream. Leaves with long, narrow, threadlike lobes.

NOTE: These large, colorful flowers often form great masses across the desert floor.

HABITAT: Sandy or clay flats, desert scrub (to 6,500 feet); found in northeast corner, south coast ranges, San Joaquin Valley, east of the Sierra, Mojave Desert, Sonoran Desert.

WHERE AND WHEN:

Anza-Borrego (February–April)

Alabama Hills (March–
April)
Antelope Valley (March–
April)
Death Valley (March–May)
Temblor Range (March–May)
Doyle area (April–June)

Desert dandelion

DESERT GOLD or DESERT SUNFLOWER   *Geraea canescens*
Aster family

DESCRIPTION: 0.5–2 feet. Stout, short-haired stem with terminal flower head (to 2 inches across) and perhaps one or a few others out of leaf axils. Ten to 21 bright yellow rays around orange disk. Broad, diamond-shaped leaves.

NOTE: Desert gold can occur in great masses on desert floors, creating wide swaths of gold visible from miles away (the photo on the next page is of Death Valley).

HABITAT: Sandy or gravelly flats (to 4,200 feet); found in Mojave Desert, Sonoran Desert.

WHERE AND WHEN:

Algodones Dunes (January–April)
Death Valley (February–April)
Joshua Tree (February–April)
Barstow area (February–April)
Anza-Borrego (February–April)
Ocotillo (February–April)

Desert gold

DESERT TRUMPET   *Eriogonum inflatum*
Buckwheat family

DESCRIPTION: 2–5 feet. Much-branched, smooth, blue-green stems that become ribbed and rough with age. Tiny yellow flowers with reddish midribs on the six petal-like sepals.

NOTE: The hollow swellings at the nodes, to which the species name refers, are sometimes used by wasps as protected "nests" for their eggs.

HABITAT: Sandy or gravelly flats (to 6,500 feet); found in northeast corner, central coast ranges, east of the Sierra, Mojave Desert, Sonoran Desert.

WHERE AND WHEN:

Anza-Borrego (February–
    April)
Alabama Hills (March–April)
Death Valley (March–April)
Carrizo Plain (March–May)
White Mountains (March–May,
    September–October)
Joshua Tree (March–July,
    September–October)

Desert trumpet

EVENING PRIMROSE, EARLY or
YELLOW DESERT EVENING PRIMROSE   *Oenothera primiveris*

Evening primrose family

DESCRIPTION: 1–15 inches. Often stemless with a basal rosette of narrow, pinnately lobed leaves. Open, pinwheel-like flowers rest on or slightly above the leaves. Four heart-shaped yellow or cream petals.

Early evening
primrose

NOTE: As with many species of evening primrose, the flowers fade reddish or orange. Like many *Oenothera* species, it blooms in the evening and into the next morning.

HABITAT: Sandy flats, edges of dunes (to 4,600 feet); found in the Mojave Desert, Sonoran Desert.

WHERE AND WHEN:

Anza-Borrego (February–March)
Red Rock Canyon (February–March)
Joshua Tree (February–March)
Boron area (February–March)
Antelope Valley (February–March)
Inyokern area (February–March)

FIDDLENECK, COMMON   *A. menziesii* var. *intermedia* or
                          Amsinckia intermedia

Borage family

DESCRIPTION: 1–3 feet. Many tiny, funnel-shaped flowers along one side of the upper stem and in the tightly coiled raceme. Yellow-orange petal lobes with darker orange or red splotches.

NOTE: The red blotches on the orange petals give this common flower a touch of intensity and intrigue.

HABITAT: Grasslands, open woods, orchards, disturbed places (to 5,000 feet); found in much of California.

WHERE AND WHEN:
Jepson Prairie Preserve
(February–April)
Anza-Borrego (February–
April)
Channel Islands (February–
April)
Hite's Cove Trail (April–May)
MacKerricher State Park
(March–June)
Edgewood Preserve (March–
June)

Common fiddleneck

FOOTSTEPS OF SPRING or YELLOW MATS   *Sanicula arctopoides*
Carrot family
DESCRIPTION: 1–4 inches. Matted rosette up to 1 foot across of deeply di-

vided, sharp-tipped, yellow-green leaves. One to several small, spherical umbels of tiny, yellow flowers nestled in a bed of leaves.

NOTE: This early bloomer forms a series of yellow-green "steps" across grassy fields and bluffs.

HABITAT: Bluffs, dunes (to 800 feet); found on the coast.

WHERE AND WHEN:
Salt Point (February–March)
San Bruno Mountain
(February–March)
Point Reyes (February–
March)
Monterey Peninsula
(February–March)

Footsteps of spring

Santa Lucia Range (February–March)
Toro Park (March–April)

GOLDENEYE, DEATH VALLEY

Bahiopsis reticulata or
Viguiera reticulata

Aster family

DESCRIPTION: 1.5–4 feet. Evergreen shrub with broad, white-hairy, conspicuously veined leaves and branching racemes of bright yellow flower heads. Ten to 15 narrow, separated rays surrounding yellow or orange disk.

NOTE: Evergreen isn't really forever green, so you will often find old, dried leaves still on the plant along with the live ones.

HABITAT: Dry slopes, rocky places (to 5,000 feet); found in Mojave Desert—only in Death Valley, Mojave National Preserve, and vicinity.

WHERE AND WHEN:
Titus Canyon in Death Valley
    (February–June)
Clark Mountains in Mojave
    National Preserve
    (February–June)
Wildrose Canyon in Death
    Valley (February–June)
near Little Lake (February–
    June)

Death Valley goldeneye

Dedeckera Canyon in Death Valley (February–June)
Last Chance Mountains in Death Valley (February–June)

GOLDFIELDS, COMMON or
CALIFORNIA GOLDFIELDS *Lasthenia californica* or *L. chrysostoma*
Aster family

DESCRIPTION: 2–10 inches. Slender stems with small flower heads of five to 15 golden yellow rays around a yellow-orange disk. Opposite pairs of linear leaves.

NOTE: These plants often paint whole hillsides and fields with gold (as in the photo at the Carizzo Plain). Not uncommonly in bloom in some places before late January.

Common
goldfields

Common goldfields

HABITAT: Dry hillsides, bluffs, forest openings (to 4,000 feet); found in much of California.

WHERE AND WHEN:

Anza-Borrego (February–April)
Santa Rosa Plateau (February–June)
Bear Valley (March–April)
Table Mountain (March–April)
Carrizo Plain (March–April)
Antelope Valley (March–April)

LOMATIUM, FOOTHILL or HOG FENNEL   *Lomatium utriculatum*

Carrot family

DESCRIPTION: 4–20 inches. Flat-topped, five-to 20-rayed umbel with tiny, yellow flowers. Finely dissected leaves with long, threadlike segments.

NOTE: Early in the blooming, the delicate umbels of flowers are nestled in the leaves; later the flower stem elongates, lifting the umbels (now less delicate balls) well above the leaves. Not uncommonly in bloom in some places before late January.

HABITAT: Grasslands, forest edges (to 5,500 feet); found in much of California.

WHERE AND WHEN:

Ponderosa Way (February–March)

Bodega Bay (February–March)

Carrizo Plain (February–May)

Mount Diablo (February–May)

Santa Rosa Plateau (February–May)

White Mountains (April–June)

Foothill lomatium

MONKEYFLOWER, BUSH or STICKY MONKEYFLOWER

Mimulus aurantiacus

Lopseed family (previously included in Snapdragon family)

DESCRIPTION: 2–4 feet. Shrub with sticky stems and sticky, pointed, glossy leaves and many two-lipped, yellow, orange, buff, apricot, cream, vermilion, red, or white flowers (to 1.5 inches).

NOTE: The only California *Mimulus* species that is a shrub and the only one with flowers with such a wide color range.

HABITAT: Scrubby slopes, rocky places, canyons, woodlands (to 7,500 feet); found in much of California.

WHERE AND WHEN:

Anza-Borrego (February–March)

Mount Tamalpais (February–April)

Kern River Canyon (March–April)

Bush monkeyflower

Bush monkeyflower

Santa Monica Mountains
(March–June)
San Gabriel Mountains
(March–July)
Feather River Canyon (May–
June)

POPPY, BUSH

Dendromecon rigida

Poppy family

DESCRIPTION: 3–9 feet. Shrub with branching, woody stems with many showy (to 2 inches), satiny, yellow or orangish, four-petaled flowers. Clus-

Bush poppy

ter of many stamens. Dark-green oval leaves.

NOTE: With all the "blankets" of golden poppies in California, it is a bit of a surprise to see poppy flowers held up so far off the ground on this shrub.

HABITAT: Dry slopes, washes (to 6,000 feet); found in northwest mountains, coast and coast ranges, foothills, Transverse Ranges, Sonoran Desert.

WHERE AND WHEN:

Torrey Pines (February–
April)
Anza-Borrego (February–
April)

San Gabriel Mountains (February–June)
SR-193 north of Placerville (April–May)
Trinity Alps (April–May)
Mount Tamalpais (April–May)

POPPY, CALIFORNIA   *Eschscholzia californica*
Poppy family

DESCRIPTION: 6–24 inches. Solitary, bowl-shaped flower (to 2.5 inches) at tip of stem. Four bright orange (sometimes yellow, especially near the coast) petals with a flat pink rim beneath.

NOTE: Standing in a field of poppies lit up by the sun, you can begin to feel what early settlers in California must have felt before so many of the flower fields were re-placed with development. Not uncommonly in bloom in some places before late January.

HABITAT: Grasslands (to 6,500 feet); found in much of California.

WHERE AND WHEN:

Anza-Borrego (February–April)

Santa Rosa Plateau (February–July)

Mount Tamalpais (February–July)

Antelope Valley (March–April)

Lake Elsinore area (March–April)

Merced River Canyon (March–April)

California poppy

ROCK PEA, DESERT or SHRUBBY DEERVETCH or DESERT LOTUS   *Lotus rigidus*
Pea family

DESCRIPTION: 1–5 feet. Shrublike, perennial plant with tangled, rigid branches and small leaves with three to four narrow leaflets. Terminal clusters of yellow pea flowers (to one-half inch) that turn red with age.

NOTE: Death and resurrection—in midsummer the flowers are gone

Desert rock pea

and the leaves have dropped, leaving an apparently dead, twiggy "skeleton," but with the rains the leaves will return and the plant will be "reborn." **HABITAT:** Washes, rocky slopes (to 5,000 feet); found in Peninsular Ranges, Mojave Desert, Sonoran Desert.

WHERE AND WHEN:
Yaqui Well (January–May)
Vallecito Stage Station
   (January–May)
Death Valley (March–May)
Joshua Tree (March–May)
Mojave National Preserve
   (March–May)
Anza-Borrego (April–May)

SUN CUP, COAST or GOLDEN EGGS   *Camissonia ovata*
Evening primrose family

DESCRIPTION: Stemless. Bright yellow, flat or shallow bowl-shaped, four-petaled flowers (to 2 inches) nestled in a bed of broad, dark-green deeply veined leaves. Day bloomer.

NOTE: Without a stem and with an inferior ovary on or under the ground, this plant doesn't have far to go to plant its seeds!

HABITAT: Grasslands (to 1,700 feet); found on north and central coast and coast ranges.

WHERE AND WHEN:
China Camp (February–April)
San Simeon coast (February–April)

Coast sun cup

Point Reyes (February–April)
Ring Mountain (February–April)
San Bruno Mountain (February–April)
Salt Point (February–April)

SUNFLOWER, ANNUAL or
COMMON SUNFLOWER   *Helianthus annuus*
Aster family

DESCRIPTION: 2–7 feet. Stout, roughly hairy stem with many dark-green broadly oval, often wavy-edged leaves. Showy (to 4 inches) flower heads with 15 or more long, narrow, pointed yellow rays surrounding reddish-brown or purplish disk.

NOTE: It is difficult to believe, but the species name does not lie—this is an annual, so all those feet of growth happen in one growing season!

HABITAT: Dry flats, meadows, roadsides and other disturbed places (to 6,200 feet); found in much of California.

WHERE AND WHEN:

Santa Monica Mountains (February–October)
Point Loma (February–October)
White Mountains (May–August)
Yosemite Valley (May–August)

Annual sunflower

Just north of Bishop (June–August)
Santa Cruz Mountains (July–October)

TURTLEBACK or DESERT VELVET   *Psathyrotes ramosissima*
Aster family

DESCRIPTION: 2–6 inches. Prostrate shrub with white woolly stems and many broad, velvety, deeply veined, gray-green leaves. A few small flower heads just above the leaves with 16–32 yellow disk flowers (no rays). Strong, resinous odor.

NOTE: The flower heads are small and inconspicuous, but this is quite a

showy plant with its dramatic mass of leaves—like a gathering of turtles on the desert floor.

HABITAT: Sandy flats, desert scrub (to 3,300 feet); found east of the Sierra, Mojave Desert, Sonoran Desert.

WHERE AND WHEN:

Ocotillo Wells (January–April)

along Imperial Highway S2 (February–April)

Baker area (February–April)

Anza-Borrego (February–April)

Death Valley (March–April)

White Mountains (March–May)

Turtleback

VIOLET, GOLDEN or JOHNNY JUMP-UP or YELLOW PANSY

Viola pedunculata

Violet family

DESCRIPTION: 4–12 inches. Branching stem with several showy flowers (to 2 inches). Five broad, rounded, golden-yellow petals, the lower ones with

purple splotches or lines at the base. Broad, toothed, deeply veined leaves.

NOTE: The distinguishing characteristic of this golden violet is the broad, rounded petals that are all about the same size and shape. Not uncommonly in bloom in some places before late January.

HABITAT: Grasslands, chaparral, woodlands (to 3,300 feet); found on central and south coast and coast ranges, foothills, Transverse Ranges, Peninsular Ranges.

WHERE AND WHEN:

Santa Monica Mountains (February–April)

Golden violet

Santa Rosa Plateau (February–April)
Pinnacles (February–April)
Torrey Pines (March–May)
Camp Nine Road (April–May)
San Bruno Mountain (April–May)

WALLFLOWER, WESTERN or
SAND DUNE WALLFLOWER
Erysimum capitatum
Mustard family

DESCRIPTION: 0.5–3 feet. Cylindrical or nearly spherical inflorescence of many four-petaled, fragrant yellow or orange flowers (to 1 inch). Narrow, smooth-edged or toothed leaves.

Western wallflower

NOTE: Wallflower is tenacious—it is one of the first bloomers of spring in the higher elevations, it is widely distributed across the United States, and it occurs in practically any dry place from sea level to above timberline.
HABITAT: Grasslands, rocky slopes and ridges, sandy flats, forest openings (to 13,000 feet); found in much of California (except Central Valley).
WHERE AND WHEN:
Anza-Borrego (February–April)
Santa Monica Mountains (February–May)
Mount Diablo (March–May)
Bear Valley (March–June)
Carrizo Plain (March–July)
Freel Peak (July)

YARROW, GOLDEN   *Eriophyllum confertiflorum*
Aster family

DESCRIPTION: 0.5–2 feet. Shrub with clusters of golden yellow flower heads with four to six rays and many disk flowers. Deeply lobed leaves with narrow segments. Stems and leaves are white woolly (early), wool-less (later).

Golden yarrow

NOTE: Although the flower heads are small, their very bright yellow color reflects a dazzling light that stands out from all its spring neighbors.

HABITAT: Grasslands, chaparral (to 10,000 feet); found in coast ranges, foothills, Sierra, Transverse Ranges, Peninsular Ranges, Mojave Desert, Sonoran Desert.

WHERE AND WHEN:

Santa Rosa Plateau (February–June)

Kern River Canyon (February–July)

Channel Islands (February–July)

Mount Hamilton Range (February–July)

Santa Monica Mountains (February–July)

Santa Cruz Mountains (March–November)

YELLOW CARPET or BLENNOSPERMA   *Blennosperma nanum*
Aster family

DESCRIPTION: 1–6 inches. Dwarf plant bearing numerous pale yellow flower heads. Usually seven to 10 separated, blunt-tipped rays, but sometimes more. Usually forms extensive carpets.

NOTE: Resembling goldfields (p. 112), but the back of the yellow rays and of the green phyllaries are edged or tinged with brownish-purple, and the anthers are tipped with tiny, white, gooey pollen balls. Not uncommonly in bloom in some places before late January.

HABITAT: Grasslands (to 5,200 feet); found on central and south coast and coast ranges, Central Valley, foothills.

WHERE AND WHEN:

Jepson Prairie Preserve (February–April)

Santa Rosa Plateau (February–April)

Channel Islands (February–
    April)
Table Mountain (March–
    April)
Hite's Cove Trail (March–
    April)
Carrizo Plain (March–April)

Yellow carpet

YELLOW HEAD or YELLOW DOME   *Trichoptilium incisum*
Aster family

DESCRIPTION: 2–10 inches. Single spherical flower head (to 0.5 inch) at the tip of a slender, often reddish stem. Many tiny, yellow disk flowers (no ray flowers). Hairy, toothed, mostly basal leaves.

NOTE: The leaves, stems, and phyllaries are all covered with a mat of soft, felty, white hairs. Only the flowers are "unclothed."

HABITAT: Sandy or gravelly flats and slopes (to 3,300 feet); found in Mojave Desert, Sonoran Desert.

WHERE AND WHEN:

Anza-Borrego (January–May, October)
Joshua Tree (February–April)
Sheephole Mountains (February–April)
Old Woman Mountains (February–April)
Chocolate Mountains (February–April)
Ocotillo Wells (March–May)

Yellow head

BABY BLUE EYES, WHITE *Nemophila menziesii* var. *atomaria*
Borage family (previously included in Waterleaf family)
DESCRIPTION: 4–12 inches. A variation on the much more common blue-flowered type of this species (see p. 83) with white instead of blue petals. Black spots and lines radiating out from center of corolla.
NOTE: Occasionally in a patch of these flowers, you will find one or a few with a faint blue tinge on the petals.
HABITAT: Grassy slopes, coastal bluffs (to 5,000 feet); found on north and central coast and coast ranges.
WHERE AND WHEN:
Bodega Head (February–April)
Fort Ross area (February–April)
Point Reyes (February–April)
south of Dos Rios (February–April)
Henry Coe State Park (February–April)
south of Ukiah (February–April)

White baby
blue eyes

BLACKBERRY, CALIFORNIA · *Rubus ursinus*

Rose family

DESCRIPTION: 1–10 feet. Vine with many soft white or pink, five-petaled, flowers (to 2 inches). Petals usually rather crinkly. Large, dark-green, toothed, deeply veined leaves. Prickles.

NOTE: It is certainly worth braving the thorns for the delicious, juicy fruit, especially on a sunny, berry-warming day.

HABITAT: Stream banks, shrubby slopes (to 4,500 feet); found in much of California.

WHERE AND WHEN:

Anza-Borrego (February–April)

Nipomo-Guadalupe Dunes (February–May)

Santa Monica Mountains (February–June)

Muir Woods (March–May)

Santa Cruz Mountains (March–August)

Hetch Hetchy in Yosemite (April–July)

California blackberry

BLAZING STAR, SAND or
WHITEBRACT BLAZING STAR   *Mentzelia involucrata*

Loasa family

DESCRIPTION: 4–16 inches. White stems with glossy green, hairy, toothed leaves and many bowl-shaped, pearly or creamy flowers (to 2.5 inches), sometimes with fine orange or reddish veins.

Sand blazing star

NOTE: The stiff hairs feel sandpapery to the touch—a bit like being licked by a desert cat.

HABITAT: Gravelly flats and slopes, washes, canyons, desert scrub (to 3,000 feet); found in the Mojave Desert, Sonoran Desert.

WHERE AND WHEN:

Red Rock Canyon (February–April)

Joshua Tree (February–April)

Sheephole Mountains (February–April)

Anza-Borrego (February–April)

Whipple Mountains (February–April)

Mojave National Preserve (February–May)

CAMAS, FREMONT'S or CHAPARRAL STAR LILY
Toxicoscordion fremontii or *Zigadenus fremontii*

Trillium family (previously included in Lily family)

DESCRIPTION: 1–1.5 feet. Densely flowered, cylindrical or conical raceme on fleshy stalk. Six pointed tepals with yellow-green gland at base.

NOTE: Although it doesn't have the warnings in the names as does its close kin *Z. venenosus* (p. 454), this species is also highly toxic to livestock and poisonous to humans.

HABITAT: Grassy fields, rock outcrops, woodlands (to 3,500 feet); found in

northwest mountains, coast, coast
ranges, Sacramento Valley, Transverse Ranges.

WHERE AND WHEN:

Mount Tamalpais (February–
April)

Laguna Coast Wilderness Park
(February–April)

Channel Islands (March–April)

Santa Ana Mountains (March–
April)

Salt Point (March–April)

Bear Valley (April–May)

Fremont's camas

COLTSFOOT   *Petasites frigidus*
Aster family

DESCRIPTION: 1–2 feet. Loose umbel of many small flower heads at tip of
stout stem. Creamy white rays (turning pink or red) surrounding whitish
or pink disk flowers. Broad, maple-like leaves.

NOTE: These early blooming plants often grow in seeps and boggy places
that are indeed "*frigidus,*" at least at night.

HABITAT: Seeps, wet forest openings, swamps (to 3,500 feet); found in
northwest mountains, north and central coast and coast ranges.

Coltsfoot

WHERE AND WHEN:
North of Stinson Beach (February–March)
Big Sur (February–March)
Trinity Alps (March–April)
Salt Point (March–April)
Big Basin State Park (March–May)
Yolla Bolly-Middle Eel Wilderness (March–May)

COW PARSNIP   *Heracleum maximum* or *H. lanatum*
Carrot family
DESCRIPTION: 3–8 feet. Stout, hollow, hairy, branching stem with large, flat-topped umbels of 13–25 umbellets of tiny white flowers. Very large maple-like leaves.
NOTE: This "Hercules" plant is large in every way except for the tiny flowers. Be careful of touching the sap—it can create extreme photosensitivity.
HABITAT: Moist grasslands, coastal bluffs, stream banks, wet meadows, woodlands (to 9,000 feet); found in much of California (except deserts).
WHERE AND WHEN:
North of Stinson Beach (February–April)
Big Sur (April–May)

Cow parsnip

Trinity Alps (April–July)
Onion Valley (June–July)
Lassen National Park (June–July)
San Bernardino Mountains (June–August)

CUCUMBER, WILD or CALIFORNIA MANROOT   *Marah fabaceus*
Gourd family

DESCRIPTION: 1–20 feet. Decumbent or climbing vine with ribbed stems and spiraling tendrils, and broad, lobed leaves with angled segments. Small, flat, star-shaped, creamy white or yellowish flowers.

Wild cucumber

NOTE: The cylindrical or roundish fruits are impressive (and maybe even a little intimidating), being covered with porcupine-like prickles.

HABITAT: Grasslands, scrubby slopes, canyons, stream banks (to 5,200 feet); found in much of California.

WHERE AND WHEN:
Buttermilk Bend Trail (February–March)
Mount Tamalpais (February–April)
Bodega Head (February–April)
Santa Lucia Range (February–April)
Carrizo Plain (February–May)
Santa Cruz Mountains (March–April)

DESERT STAR, MOJAVE   *Monoptilon bellioides*
Aster family

DESCRIPTION: 1–3 inches. Prostrate plant with spreading stem creating mats several inches across. Flower heads nearly on the ground. Twelve to 20 bright white, overlapping rays surround yellow disk. Narrowly spoon-shaped, white-hairy leaves.

Mojave desert star

NOTE: The sand, the white-hairy leaves, and the soft white rays together create a delicate, soothing, desert tableau.

HABITAT: Sandy flats, washes (to 4,000 feet); found in the Mojave Desert, Sonoran Desert.

WHERE AND WHEN:

Antelope Valley (February–April)

Mojave National Preserve (February–April)

Anza-Borrego (February–April)

Death Valley (February–May)

Coachella Valley (March–April)

Joshua Tree (March–April)

EVENING PRIMROSE, BIRD-CAGE or DUNE PRIMROSE or BASKET EVENING PRIMROSE　　　　　　*Oenothera deltoides*

Evening Primrose family

DESCRIPTION: 0.5–2 feet. Several large (to 3 inches), four-petaled, white flowers aging pink or lavender. Stems eventually peel. Flowers open in late afternoon. Narrow, smooth-edged or sawtoothed leaves.

NOTE: The common name (bird-cage or basket) refers to the bizarre shape of the mature plants, whose outer stems curve inward to form a "cage."

HABITAT: Sandy flats, dunes (to 5,900 feet); found in northeast corner, east of the Sierra, central and south coast ranges, San Joaquin Valley, Mojave Desert, Sonoran Desert.

WHERE AND WHEN:

Anza-Borrego (February–March)

Bird-cage evening primrose

Joshua Tree (March–April)
Red Rock Canyon (March–May)
Carrizo Plain (March–May)
Doyle area (May–June)
Benton area (May–June)

EVENING PRIMROSE, BOOTH'S or WOODY BOTTLE-WASHER or SHREDDING EVENING PRIMROSE   *Camissonia boothii*

Evening Primrose family

DESCRIPTION: 4–16 inches. Dense-flowered cluster of white, four-petaled flowers (to 0.5 inches) aging red or pink. Tonguelike, bright green leaves usually with reddish spots, both in basal cluster and up the stem, sometimes withering by blooming time.

NOTE: The "bark" of the stems eventually peels (hence "shredding").

HABITAT: Open, sandy or gravelly flats, washes (to 7,900 feet); found in the northeast corner, central coast and coast ranges, southern Sierra, east of the Sierra, Mojave Desert, Sonoran Desert.

WHERE AND WHEN:

Anza-Borrego (February–April)
Alabama Hills (March–April)
Susanville area (April–June)
White Mountains (April–June)
SR-58 (April–June)
Greenhorn Mountains (April–June)

Booth's evening primrose

EVENING PRIMROSE, BROWN-EYED *Camissonia claviformis*

Evening Primrose family

DESCRIPTION: 4–20 inches. Softly hairy stem rising above broad, mostly

Brown-eyed evening primrose

basal, pinnately lobed or toothed, often purple-spotted leaves. Twenty to 40 bowl-shaped, four-petaled flowers (to 0.5 inches) nod in clusters in bud, then spread out in bloom. Brown-purple "eye" in center of flower.

NOTE: The petals can be white or yellow, both of which offer striking contrast to the brown-purple "eye."

HABITAT: Sandy or rocky flats, slopes, washes (to 6,600 feet); found in the northeast corner, east of the Sierra, Mojave Desert, Sonoran Desert.

WHERE AND WHEN:
Mojave National Preserve (February–April)

Joshua Tree (February–April)
Anza-Borrego (February–April)
Alabama Hills (March–April)
Eagleville area (April–May)
White Mountains (April–May)

IRIS, BOWL-TUBED or GROUND IRIS   *Iris macrosiphon*
Iris family

DESCRIPTION: 0.5–1 foot. One or two flowers (to 3 inches) with three tonguelike, spreading, white or yellowish or blue sepals with conspicuous veins; three similar, erect petals without noticeable veins.

NOTE: The most distinctive feature of this species is the long flower tube above the ovary with an enlargement just below the flower.

HABITAT: Grasslands, edges of woods (to 3,000 feet); found on north and central coast and coast ranges, foothills.

WHERE AND WHEN:

China Camp (February–May)

Buttermilk Bend Trail (February–April)

Pine Hill Preserve (March–April)

Mount Tamalpais (March–April)

Santa Cruz Mountains (March–June)

Ponderosa Way (April–May)

Bowl-tubed iris

LACEPOD or FRINGEPOD   *Thysanocarpus curvipes*
Mustard family

DESCRIPTION: 8–20 inches. Loose raceme of tiny, four-petaled, white flowers (often with purplish tinge) at ends of short pedicels. Flat, round seedpods with spoked membrane often turning pink with age.

NOTE: These flying-saucer seedpods are larger and more attention-grabbing than are the inconspicuous flowers, a common occurrence in the Mustard family.

HABITAT: Grasslands (to 5,000 feet); found in much of California.

WHERE AND WHEN:
Santa Monica Mountains
(February–April)
Hite's Cove Trail (March–April)
Buttermilk Bend Trail (March–
April)
Death Valley (March–April)
Carrizo Plain (March–May)
Trinity Alps (April–May)

Lacepod

LILY, DESERT

Hesperocallis undulata

Agave family (previously included in Lily family)

DESCRIPTION: 1–30 inches. Stout stem with long, wavy-edged, basal leaves and a few alternating stem leaves. Raceme of many funnel-shaped, six-

tepaled, white flowers (to 2.5 inches). Tepals have greenish mid-vein, especially pronounced on the underside.

NOTE: "Undulata" is a perfect description of the wavy, undulating leaves.

HABITAT: Sandy flats, dunes (to 2,600 feet); found in the Mojave Desert, Sonoran Desert.

WHERE AND WHEN:
Mojave National Preserve
(February–March)
Desert Lily Preserve
(February–March)
Anza-Borrego (February–
March)
Ocotillo Wells (February–
March)

Desert lily

Joshua Tree (February–March)
Sweeney Pass (February–March)

MANROOT, CUCAMONGA   *Marah macrocarpus*
Gourd family

DESCRIPTION: 1–25 feet. Sprawling vine with large, fleshy, compound leaves with five to seven triangular lobes. Raceme of many small, shallowly cup-shaped, white flowers. Large, heavy, oblong fruit covered with stiff spines.

NOTE: The amazingly large, tuberous (bitter) root can weigh more than 100 pounds!

HABITAT: Shrubby slopes, washes (to 3,000 feet); found on south coast and coast ranges, Transverse Ranges, Peninsular Ranges, Sonoran Desert.

WHERE AND WHEN:
Anza-Borrego (January–March)
Santa Ynez Mountains (January–April)
Torrey Pines (January–April)
San Gabriel Mountains (February–April)
Santa Rosa Plateau (February–April)
Santa Monica Mountains (February–April)

Cucamonga manroot

MANZANITA, HOARY   *Arctostaphylos canescens*
Heath family

DESCRIPTION: 1–6 feet. Shrub with softly hairy stems and clusters of bright white or pink, hanging, urn-shaped flowers. Oval leaves with sharp-pointed tips and edges fringed with hairs. Hairy, red berries.

NOTE: The short white hairs along the edges of the leaves bring a softness to this otherwise crisp, stiff foliage.

HABITAT: Forest openings, brushy slopes, ridges (to 5,000 feet); found in northwest mountains, north and central coast and coast ranges.

WHERE AND WHEN:
Santa Cruz Mountains (February–April)

Mount Tamalpais (February–
    May)
west of Elk Creek (February–
    May)
Fort Ross area (February–
    May)
Mount Hood (February–
    May)
Gabilan Range (April–June)

Hoary manzanita

MILKMAIDS or CALIFORNIA TOOTHWORT   *Cardamine californica*
Mustard family
DESCRIPTION: 0.5–2 feet. Several creamy white (sometimes pink), four-pet-aled, half-inch flowers in loose raceme. Pinnately compound leaves with

irregular, toothed lobes.
NOTE: Wherever it is growing, this is one of the first wild-flowers of spring, ushering in the blooming season with a milky or rosy sip of bright cheer. Not uncommonly in bloom in some places before late January.
HABITAT: Open woods, grass-lands, canyons, roadsides and other disturbed places (to 6,000 feet); found in much of California (except deserts).
WHERE AND WHEN:
Nipomo-Guadalupe Dunes
    (January–April)
Channel Islands (February–
    March)

Milkmaids

Santa Rosa Plateau (February–April)
Salt Point (February–May)
Mix Canyon Road (February–May)
Warner Mountains (March–April)

MINER'S LETTUCE   *Claytonia perfoliata*

Miner's Lettuce family (previously included in Purslane family)

DESCRIPTION: 1–16 inches. Many stems with short raceme of five to 40 tiny, five-petaled, white or pink flowers just above large, fleshy, round, shield-like leaf completely surrounding stem.

NOTE: *Perfoliata* (meaning "through leaf") points to this plant's most conspicuous feature—the large stem leaf (actually two leaves fused together) speared by the stem. Not uncommonly in bloom in some places before late January.

HABITAT: Moist shade around trees, disturbed places (to 7,500 feet); found in much of California.

Miner's lettuce

WHERE AND WHEN:
Salt Point (February–April)
Anza-Borrego (February–April)
Channel Islands (February–April)
San Gabriel Mountains (February–May)
Yosemite Valley (February–May)
Mount Diablo (February–May)

MORNING GLORY, PURPLE or WESTERN MORNING GLORY   *Calystegia purpurata*

Morning-glory family

DESCRIPTION: 1–15 feet. Decumbent or climbing stem with cluster of one to five funnel-shaped flowers (to 2 inches). White, cream-colored, or pink corolla often with purple stripes or splotches. Dark-green leaves with angled segments.

NOTE: This beautiful flower can be in the grass practically directly on the

ground or can be over your head—the plant is a tenacious climber and twiner.

HABITAT: Coastal scrub (to 1,000 feet); found on coast, coast ranges, Central Valley, Transverse Ranges.

WHERE AND WHEN:
north of Stinson Beach (February–May)
Edgewood Preserve (April–June)
Bodega Head (May–June)
Big Sur (May–June)
Jenner-Fort Ross area (May–June)
Salt Point (May–June)

Purple morning glory

POPPY, PRICKLY   *Argemone munita*
Poppy family

DESCRIPTION: 2–5 feet. Several large (to 3 inches) bowl-shaped flowers along stem. Six white, crinkly petals surrounding dense cluster of 150–

250 yellow stamens and one large, black-purple, spherical stigma. Pinnately lobed, prickly leaves.

NOTE: Scores of yellow male worshippers paying homage to an adored purple queen!

HABITAT: Dry, open flats; sagebrush scrub (4,000–8,500 feet); found in northwest mountains, central and south coast ranges, east of the Sierra, northeast corner, Transverse Ranges, Mojave Desert, Sonoran Desert.

WHERE AND WHEN:
Ocotillo area (February–April)
Topaz Lake (May–June)

Prickly poppy

Santa Lucia Range (May–June)
Modoc Plateau (May–July)
east of Monitor Pass (June–July)
San Gabriel Mountains (June–August)

RUE-ANEMONE, WESTERN FALSE

Enemion occidentale or
Isopyrum occidentale

Buttercup family

DESCRIPTION: 3–10 inches. Nearly flat, white or pink flowers (to three-fourths of an inch). Five (sometimes four or six) petal-like sepals with cluster of many yellow stamens at center.

NOTE: In April in the foothills when so many flowers are just reaching the peak of their bloom, this plant will already be in beautiful fruit.

HABITAT: Shady slopes (to 5,000 feet); found in north and central coast ranges, foothills, Transverse Ranges.

WHERE AND WHEN:

Hite's Cove Trail (February–March)

Big Basin Redwood State Park (March–April)

Santa Lucia Range (March–April)

Greenhorn Range (March–April)

Yankee Jim Road (March–April)

Quarry Trail (March–April)

Western false rue-anemone

SAXIFRAGE, FOOTHILL or
CALIFORNIA SAXIFRAGE

Saxifraga californica

Saxifrage family

DESCRIPTION: 4–12 inches. Slender, branching, leafless stem with several loose, candelabra-like racemes of tiny, bright white flowers with five separate petals.

NOTE: With such small flowers, the ovaries are tiny and inconspicuous, but

Foothill saxifrage

when the plant goes to fruit, the two-branched, beaked pistils typical of the *Saxifraga* genus are quite noticeable.

HABITAT: Moist, grassy, shady flats and slopes (to 7,500 feet); found in much of California (except deserts and eastern edge).

WHERE AND WHEN:
Hite's Cove Trail (February–March)
Santa Ana Mountains (February–March)
Mount Tamalpais (February–March)
Table Mountain (February–April)
San Gabriel Mountains (February–April)
Channel Islands (February–April)

SPECTACLE POD or SHIELDPOD   *Dithyrea californica*
Mustard family

DESCRIPTION: 4–12 inches. Stem rising above rosette of broad, toothed leaves with smaller stem leaves. Extended raceme of small, four-petaled, white (sometimes pale lavender) trumpetlike flowers (to 0.5 inches). Pairs of flat, round, hairy fruits.

NOTE: The odd fruits do resemble a pair of spectacles—perhaps someone looking at you with wide-eyed amazement.

HABITAT: Sandy flats, dunes, washes, desert scrub (to 4,600 feet); found in the Mojave Desert, Sonoran Desert.

WHERE AND WHEN:
Anza-Borrego (February–May)
Yaqui Well (March–April)
Antelope Valley (March–May)
Mojave National Preserve (March–May)
Red Rock Canyon (March–May)
Joshua Tree (March–May)

Spectacle pod

STRAWBERRY, BEACH   *Fragaria chiloensis*
Rose family

DESCRIPTION: 2–8 inches. One or a few mostly flat, bright white, five-petaled flowers (to 1.5 inches) rise slightly above dark green, shiny, toothed leaves. Plants spread by runners.

Beach strawberry

NOTE: Although the small berries are not as tasty as those of some other strawberry species, you still may not get to taste (or see) them, for they are eagerly sought by all sorts of other two-legged and four-legged critters.

HABITAT: Beaches, bluffs, dunes, grassy fields (to 700 feet); found on the coast.

WHERE AND WHEN:

Nipomo-Guadalupe Dunes (February–May)
Monterey Peninsula (February–May)
Manchester Beach (March–May)
Bodega Head (March–May)
Salt Point (March–May)
Stinson Beach (March–May)

STRAWBERRY, CALIFORNIA or
WOOD STRAWBERRY   *Fragaria vesca*
Rose family

DESCRIPTION: 1–10 inches. Plants spreading on long runners. Bright white flowers (to 0.5 inches) with cluster of many reproductive parts. Long-petioled leaves with three toothed leaflets with silky hairs on underside.

NOTE: The fruits are small but very tasty—just leave a few for the seed-spreading wild creatures!

HABITAT: Grasslands, forest openings (to 6,600 feet); found in northwest mountains, north and central coast and coast ranges, foothills, Cascades, Sierra, Transverse Ranges, Peninsular Ranges.

WHERE AND WHEN:

San Bruno Mountain (February–May)
Mount Tamalpais (February–May)
Salt Point (March–April)
San Jacinto Mountains (March–April)
San Bernardino Mountains (March–April)
Palomar Mount State Park (April–June)

California strawberry

TRILLIUM, GIANT   *Trillium chloropetalum*
Trillium family (previously included in Lily family)

DESCRIPTION: 0.5–2 feet. Single large flower directly atop three very large, broad, pointed leaves that whorl around the tip of the stem. Three narrow, erect, white, yellowish, or purple petals (to 4 inches long).

NOTE: The giant leaves often have large, dark brown or dark green splotches.

HABITAT: Redwood forests, scrubby slopes, moist canyon banks (to 4,500 feet); found in northwest mountains, north and central coast, and coast ranges.

WHERE AND WHEN:
Mount Diablo (February–
    April)
north of Stinson Beach
    (February–June)
Santa Lucia Range (March–
    April)
San Bruno Mountain
    (March–June)
Six Rivers National Forest
    (May–June)
Trinity Alps (May–June)

Giant trillium

TRILLIUM, WESTERN or WESTERN WAKE-ROBIN   *Trillium ovatum*
Trillium family (previously included in Lily family)

DESCRIPTION: 0.5–2 feet. Solitary, three-petaled, bright white (aging pink or purple) flower above three spreading, leaflike sepals. Tonguelike petals. One whorl of three broad, pointed, conspicuously veined leaves.

NOTE: These flowers are lovely whether fresh in bloom or withering—the bright white or pale pink petals age to lush purple.

HABITAT: Forest shade, brush (to 6,600 feet); found in northwest mountains, north and central coast and coast ranges, Cascades.

WHERE AND WHEN:
Santa Lucia Range (February–March)
north of Stinson Beach (February–April)
Mount Tamalpais (February–April)
Redwood National Park (March–April)
Six Rivers National Forest (May–June)
Trinity Alps (June–July)

Western trillium

VIRGIN BOWER or
PIPESTEM CLEMATIS

Clematis lasiantha

Buttercup family

DESCRIPTION: 6–15 feet. Vine with many erect, creamy flowers (to three-fourths of an inch). Four petal-like sepals with dense cluster of five to 100 stamens and 75–100 pistils. Compound leaves with three to five leaflets, each more-or-less three-lobed.

Virgin bower

NOTE: The shaggy, Dr. Seuss-like fruit is unmistakable and fascinating.

HABITAT: Chaparral, woodlands (to 6,000 feet); found in coast ranges, foothills, Transverse Ranges, Sonoran Desert.

WHERE AND WHEN:

Anza-Borrego (February–April)

Santa Rosa Plateau (February–May)

Santa Monica Mountains (February–May)

Pinnacles (March–May)

Mount Tamalpais (March–June)

Pine Hill Preserve (March–June)

Virgin bower

WISHBONE BUSH   *Mirabilis laevis* var. *villosa* or *Mirabilis bigelovii*
Four o'clock family

DESCRIPTION: 1–3 feet. Shrub with glandular-hairy, two-branched (i.e., "wishbone") stem with clusters of funnel-shaped flowers (to 1 inch), each two-lobed. Five petal-like, white or pink sepals. Opposite pairs of sticky-hairy leaves.

NOTE: This plant is usually open only in mornings, evenings, and cloudy days—it closes in sunny heat.

HABITAT: Sandy or rocky flats and slopes, washes (to 7,500 feet); found in the northeast corner, south coast, east of the Sierra, Mojave Desert, Sonoran Desert.

WHERE AND WHEN:
Anza-Borrego (February–
    April)
Point Magu (February–
    April)
Joshua Tree (March–
    April)

Wishbone bush

Susanville area (March–April)
Alabama Hills (March–May)
White Mountains (March–June)

WOODLAND STAR, FRINGED or
SAN FRANCISCO WOODLAND STAR   *Lithophragma affine*

Saxifrage family

DESCRIPTION: 0.5–2 feet. Slender stem with long raceme of three to 15 white, star-shaped flowers. Five petals deeply three- to five-lobed.

NOTE: These bright white flowers with the lobed petals look like snowflakes blown onto the stems during a storm. Not uncommonly in bloom in some places before late January.

HABITAT: Grasslands, forest openings (to 6,600 feet); found in northwest mountains, coast, coast ranges, Sierra foothills, Transverse Ranges, Peninsular Ranges.

WHERE AND WHEN:
Santa Rosa Plateau
  (February–June)
Torrey Pines (March–April)
Hite's Cove Trail (March–
  April)
Santa Cruz Mountains
  (March–May)
Fort Ross area (March–May)
Mount Tamalpais (March–
  May)

Fringed woodland star

LILY, CHOCOLATE   *Fritillaria biflora*

Lily family

DESCRIPTION: 0.5–1.5 feet. One to seven bell-shaped, nodding flowers (to 1.5 inches) with six dark-brown (occasionally yellowish-green) tepals marked with green and purple inside. Bright yellow anthers. Three to seven narrow leaves form rosette on lower stem just above the ground. Plants often form dense colonies.

NOTE: This amazingly chocolaty dessert is a long time in the making—taking four or five years to develop a mature bulb.

HABITAT: Grassy fields, bluffs (to 4,000 feet); found on the coast and coast ranges, Transverse Ranges, Peninsular Ranges.

WHERE AND WHEN:
Santa Rosa Plateau
  (February–March)
Figueroa Mountain
  (February–March)
Point Loma (February–April)
Santa Monica Mountains
  (February–April)
San Simeon area (March–April)
Montana del Oro State Park
  (March–April)

Chocolate lily

PEONY, CALIFORNIA
Peony family

Paeonia californica

DESCRIPTION: 1–2 feet. Subshrub heavy with large, twice-pinnately divided leaves and hanging, red-maroon flowers (to 1.5 inches) with five or six cupped petals partly concealing many yellow stamens. California endemic.

NOTE: Just like its northern cousin, Western peony (p. 417), this plant is one of the first to bloom in the new year. Its flowers tend to be chocolatier than those of its lighter maroon relative.

HABITAT: Coastal scrub (to 5,000 feet); found on the south coast and coast ranges, Transverse Ranges, Peninsular Ranges.

WHERE AND WHEN:
Santa Monica Mountains
  (January–April)
Cachuma Lake Rec. Area
  (January–April)
San Gabriel Mountains
  (January–April)

California peony

Santa Ana Mountains (January–April)
Santa Rosa Plateau (February–April)
Point Magu State Park (February–April)

PIPEVINE or DUTCHMAN'S PIPE — *Aristolochia californica*
Pipevine family

DESCRIPTION: 2–12 feet. Woody, climbing vine with showy, pipe-shaped flowers (to 2.5 inches) hanging from long, slender pedicels. Three papery,

greenish or brownish sepals fused into swollen, curved tube with red stripes. No petals. California endemic.

NOTE: The climbing vine often hangs all over some shrub or small tree, nearly covering it with the bizarre flowers.

HABITAT: Brushy slopes, woodlands, stream banks (to 1,500 feet); found in northwest mountains, coast, coast ranges, Central Valley, foothills.

WHERE AND WHEN:
Buttermilk Bend Trail
    (February–March)
Table Mountain (February–
    March)
Mount Tamalpais (February–
    March)
Santa Lucia Range
    (February–March)
Pinnacles (March–April)
Sutter Buttes (March–May)

Dutchman's pipe

SLINK POD or FETID ADDER'S TONGUE — *Scoliopus bigelovii*
Lily family

DESCRIPTION: 4–8 inches. Broad, shiny green leaves with conspicuous mottling. Two to 12 slender, brownish stems, each with a delicate (to 1 inch) flower with three narrow, widely separate, pale green (sometimes almost white) petals with dramatic dark maroon or black stripes. California endemic.

NOTE: The flower stems wilt when the flowers go to seed, creating a "snaky" tangle of seedpod-bearing stems lying on the leaves.

Slink pod

HABITAT: Coastal forests (to 3,600 feet); found in northwest mountains, north and central coast ranges.

WHERE AND WHEN:

Muir Woods (February–March)

Pulgas Ridge (February–March)

Orr Spring Road (February–March)

Huddard Park (February–March)

Pocket Canyon (February–March)

Hendy Woods (February–March)

NON-NATIVE BOUQUETS

First Bouquet

Common borage

Common Borage
Borago officinalis
Borage Family

DESCRIPTION: Rough hairy plant with bright blue, star-shaped, often nodding flowers.

EXAMPLE OF LOCATION: North of Stinson Beach.

Periwinkle

Periwinkle
Vinca major
Dogbane Family

DESCRIPTION: Large, blue-purple or lavender, pinwheel flowers on bed of broad, dark-green leaves.

EXAMPLE OF LOCATION: Pleasants Valley Road.

(First bouquet, continued)

**Persian Speedwell or
Birdeye Speedwell**
Veronica persica
Plantain Family (previously included in
Snapdragon family)

DESCRIPTION: Prostrate plant with tiny,
blue, four-petaled flowers with white
center and purple veins; broad, scalloped leaves.

EXAMPLE OF LOCATION: Roadside near
Rough and Ready.

Persian speedwell

Hottentot Fig or Ice Plant
Carpobrotus edulis
Fig-marigold Family

DESCRIPTION: Dense mats of succulent,
three-sided leaves cradling large, yellow,
fringelike flowers that turn pink with
age.

EXAMPLE OF LOCATION: *Torrey Pines*

Hottentot fig

Second Bouquet

Common geranium

Common Geranium
Pelargonium zonale
Geranium Family

DESCRIPTION: Clusters of five-petaled pink flowers with dark, red stripes; hairy, beaked fruits.

EXAMPLE OF LOCATION: North of Stinson Beach.

Wild radish

Radish, Wild
Raphanus sativus
Mustard Family

DESCRIPTION: Clawed, pink-purple (sometimes whitish or pale yellow) petals with dark purple veins.

EXAMPLE OF LOCATION: Napa area.

(Second bouquet, continued)

Sea Rocket
Cakile maritima
Mustard Family

DESCRIPTION: Clusters of small, four-petaled, half-inch purple flowers along fleshy, usually prostrate stem.

EXAMPLE OF LOCATION: *Channel Islands.*

Sea rocket

Third Bouquet

Stork's Bill, Redstem or Redstem Filaree
Erodium cicutarium
Geranium Family

DESCRIPTION: Small, five-petaled, pink or red-purple flowers. Long, beaklike seedpod. Not uncommonly in bloom in some places before late January.

EXAMPLE OF LOCATION: *San Gabriel Mountains.*

Redstem storksbill

(Third bouquet, continued)

Field mustard

Field Mustard
Brassica rapa/B. campestris
Mustard Family

DESCRIPTION: Four-petaled, bright yellow flowers and long, cylindrical seedpods.

EXAMPLE OF LOCATION: Orchards near Vacaville.

Fourth Bouquet

Bermuda sorrel

Bermuda Sorrel or Bermuda Buttercup
Oxalis pes-caprae
Wood Sorrel Family

DESCRIPTION: Bright yellow, funnel-shaped flowers on leafless stem above cloverlike leaves.

EXAMPLE OF LOCATION: Pleasants Valley Road.

(Fourth bouquet, continued)

Sowthistle

Sowthistle
Sonchus oleraceus
Aster Family

DESCRIPTION: Small, yellow flower heads with ray flowers only; milky sap. Not uncommonly in bloom in some places before late January.

EXAMPLE OF LOCATION: *Malibu Lagoon State Park.*

Calla lily

Calla Lily
Zantedeschia aethiopica
Arum Family

DESCRIPTION: Enormous, creamy white, funnel-shaped flowers; large, smooth, wavy-edged leaves.

EXAMPLE OF LOCATION: North of Stinson Beach.

(Fourth bouquet, continued)

Sacred datura

Sacred Datura or Jimsonweed
Datura wrightii
Nightshade Family

DESCRIPTION: Huge, funnel-shaped flowers; large, triangular, dark-green leaves

EXAMPLE OF LOCATION: *Santa Monica Mountains*

MARCH

Ground pink on the Santa Rosa Plateau

WHAT A MARVELOUS TIME to be out and about in the lower elevations of California. Spring and its flowers are exploding all around you. The broad, open fields of the Central Valley (or at least the small, wild remnants and ecological preserves that survive), the beaches, the coast ranges, and the southern deserts are already in splendid bloom, while the rolling, green foothills are filled with rushing water and the beginnings of another spectacular wildflower season. And in the small band of cold desert east of the Sierra, especially in the Topaz Lake area, the Great Basin flowers, too, are starting to make a splash. Practically anywhere in California below the altitude of about 3,000 feet in the north and about 5,000 feet in the south is alive with the hues and buzz of wildflower spring.

Highlights

Beaches and Bluffs Along the Coast

Parish's purple nightshade, southern sun cup, stinging lupine, and **sea dahlia** at Torrey Pines
Dune wallflower, silver dune lupine, and **magenta sand verbena** at Nipomo-Guadalupe Dunes

Coast Ranges

Adobe lily and **large blue-eyed Mary** at Bear Valley
Rose rock cress, mission bells, Franciscan wallflower, and **San Bruno manzanita** on San Bruno Mountain
Hillside daisy, blue dicks, fiddleneck, and **purple owl's-clover** at Wind Wolves Natural Preserve
Goldfields and **hillside daisy** on the Carrizo Plain and in the Temblor Range
Padre's shooting star and **Lindley's blazing star** on SR58
Giant coreopsis at the base of the Santa Monica Mountains
Chocolate lily, padre's shooting star, and **ground pink** on the Santa Rosa Plateau

Central Valley

Meadow foam, tidy tips, and perhaps **fragrant fritillary** at Jepson Prairie Preserve
Goldfields, Douglas violet, Kellogg's monkeyflower, bird's-eye gilia, sky lupine, dwarf cliff sedum, and **volcanic onion** on Table Mountain

Foothills

Pipevine and **spreading larkspur** along Buttermilk Bend Trail
The rare **El Dorado mule ears** at Pine Hill Preserve
Cream cups, bird's-eye gilia, five-spot nemophila, and **sky lupine** along
Red Hill Road

East of the Sierra

Long-leaf phlox at Topaz Lake

Deserts

Bigelow's monkeyflower, Arizona lupine, desert dandelion, desert lily,
and **wishbone bush** at Anza-Borrego
Desert gold and **Death Valley sage** at Death Valley

Flowers

ASTER, DESERT or MOJAVE ASTER   *Xylorhiza tortifolia*
Aster family

DESCRIPTION: 1–1.5 feet. Subshrub thick with narrow, wavy-edged leaves
and leafless stems tipped with a single large flower head. Twenty-five to 60
long, violet rays surround yellow
or orange disk.

NOTE: The many unusually large
(to 2.5 inches) flower heads and
the violet and yellow contrasting
colors create a dazzling desert
spectacle. With sufficient rains, it
can bloom all over again in the
fall.

HABITAT: Sandy or gravelly flats
and slopes, canyons (to 6,600
feet); found east of the Sierra; the
Mojave Desert, Sonoran Desert.

WHERE AND WHEN:
Alabama Hills (March–May)
Anza-Borrego (March–May)
Red Rock Canyon (March–May)
Death Valley (March–May)
Antelope Valley (March–May)
Mojave National Preserve
    (March–May, October)

Desert aster

BLADDER SAGE or PAPERBAG BUSH *Salazaria mexicana*

Mint family

DESCRIPTION: 2–4 feet. Shrub with interlaced branches becoming spinelike and opposite pairs of two-lipped flowers (to 1 inch) along upper stems. Upper flower lip white or violet, lower lip velvety blue-purple.

Bladder sage

NOTE: The common names refer to the reddish-purple calyx, which becomes bladderlike in fruit, especially striking when the colorful flowers are also still attached.

HABITAT: Sandy or gravelly slopes, washes, desert scrub, woodlands (to 6,000 feet); found east of the Sierra, Transverse Ranges, Mojave Desert, Sonoran Desert.

WHERE AND WHEN:

San Bernardino Mountains (March–April)

Alabama Hills (March–April)

Antelope Valley (March–April)

Joshua Tree (March–May)

Death Valley (March–May)

Mojave National Preserve (March–June)

BLUE BLOSSOM *Ceanothus thyrsiflorus*

Buckbrush family

DESCRIPTION: 3–20 feet. Prostrate or erect shrub or small tree with cylindrical clusters of scores of tiny blue or lavender flowers at tips of branches. Five clawed petals. Dark green, oval, evergreen leaves with prominent veins.

NOTE: As the family name suggests, these delightful pale blue blossoms are also deliciously fragrant.

HABITAT: Brushy slopes, woodlands, canyons (to 2,000 feet); found in northwest mountains, coast, coast ranges.

WHERE AND WHEN:

South of Elk along SR-1 (March–May)

Monterey Peninsula (March–May)

Santa Lucia Range (March–May)

San Bruno Mountain
(March–May)
Salt Point (March–June)
Mount Tamalpais (April–
June)

Blue blossom

BLUE-EYED GRASS, WESTERN   *Sisyrinchium bellum*

Iris family

DESCRIPTION: 4–16 inches. Flattened stem bearing several star-shaped, half-inch flowers. Six blue-purple tepals with darker purple veins and a dark purple splotch at the base. Yellow patch in throat.

NOTE: The yellow patch in the center is very attractive to pollinators, apparently deceptively like a promised sip of nectar.

HABITAT: Grasslands, bluffs, woodlands (to 3,000 feet); found in much of California.

WHERE AND WHEN:

Santa Rosa Plateau (March–
May)
Santa Monica Mountains
(March–June)
Ring Mountain (April–May)
Big Sur (April–May)
Edgewood Preserve (April–
June)
Salt Point (April–June)

Western blue-eyed grass

BLUE-EYED MARY, LARGE or
SPINSTER'S BLUE-EYED MARY   *Collinsia sparsiflora*

Plantain family (previously included in Snapdragon family)

DESCRIPTION: 2–10 inches. A few two-lipped (to 0.5 inches) flowers with four visible petal lobes, blue-purple or lavender; the upper two with white at the base with purple spots. Fifth petal lobe folded between the other two of the lower lip.

Blue-eyed Mary

NOTE: Depending on how you look at it, this Mary is blue-eyed or white-eyed.

HABITAT: Grasslands (to 5,000 feet); found in much of California (except deserts and eastern edge).

WHERE AND WHEN:
Bear Valley (March–April)
Santa Lucia Range (March–April)
Table Mountain (March–April)
Mount Tamalpais (March–April)
Carrizo Plain (March–April)
San Bernardino Mountains (March–May)

BROOMRAPE, SINGLE-FLOWERED or
NAKED BROOMRAPE   *Orobanche uniflora*

Broomrape family

DESCRIPTION: 2–6 inches. Usually solitary tubular, two-lipped flower (to 1 inch) at tip of slender, sticky, yellowish pedicel. Purple, pink, or straw-yellow petal lobes with dark purple veins. No green leaves—a parasite.

NOTE: *Orobanche* means "vetch strangler"—a rather graphic reference to the plant's parasitizing lifestyle.

HABITAT: Moist, grassy or rocky places (to 8,500 feet); found in much of California.

WHERE AND WHEN:
Hite's Cove Trail (March–April)
San Bernardino Mountains (March–April)
Santa Monica Mountains (March–May)
Table Mountain (March–July)
Trinity Alps (April–June)
Warner Mountains (June–July)

Single-flowered broomrape

CANTERBURY BELLS, WILD or
CALIFORNIA BLUEBELLS   *Phacelia minor*
Borage family (previously included in Waterleaf family)

DESCRIPTION: 8–24 inches. Stiffly hairy stem with several long and broad-tubed, blue-purple, vase-shaped flowers (to 1.5 inches) in loose raceme. Oval, irregularly toothed leaves along stem.

NOTE: These large, gorgeous, intensely colored flowers with the long and broad tubes often are among the "pioneers" in burn areas in the mountains.

HABITAT: Sandy or gravelly flats, open slopes, burn areas (to 5,200 feet); found on south coast and coast ranges, Transverse Ranges, Peninsular Ranges, Sonoran Desert.

WHERE AND WHEN:

Anza-Borrego (March–April)
Palomar Mountain (March–
   May)
Santa Monica Mountains
   (March–May)

Wild Canterbury bells

Santa Rosa Plateau (March–June)
Santa Ana Mountains (March–June)
San Gabriel Mountains (March–June)

CHIA   *Salvia columbariae*
Mint family

DESCRIPTION: 4–20 inches. Square stem with a terminal whorl of delicately blue, two-lipped flowers (to 0.5 inches) and usually one or two additional whorls at intervals below it. Dark red-purple, spiky sepals. Basal rosette of crinkly, pinnately lobed leaves.

NOTE: The two-lipped flowers are rather comical, resembling some kind of cartoon character with a squat body and large ears.

HABITAT: Sandy or gravelly flats, sagebrush scrub (to 7,000 feet); found in much of California (except Cascades).

WHERE AND WHEN:
Alabama Hills (March–April)
Mayacmas Range (March–April)
Carrizo Plain (March–April)
Edgewood Preserve (March–April)
Nipomo-Guadalupe Dunes (March–June)
Mount Diablo (April–June)

Chia

CHINESE HOUSES or CHINESE PAGODAS   *Collinsia heterophylla*
Plantain family (previously included in Snapdragon family)

DESCRIPTION: 4–24 inches. Whorls of two-lipped flowers (to 1 inch). Two visible petal lobes of lower lip are blue-purple or red-purple, two lobes of upper lip are white with purple spots and lines and purple tips.

NOTE: The third petal lobe of the lower lip is neatly folded and hidden beneath and between the other two lower lobes.

HABITAT: Shady places (to 5,000 feet); found in much of California (except northeast corner, deserts, and eastern edge).

WHERE AND WHEN:
Hite's Cove trail (March–April)
King's Canyon/Sequoia (March–April)
Torrey Pines (March–April)
Feather River Canyon (April–May)
Pinnacles (April–May)
Mix Canyon Road (April–May)

Chinese houses

FIESTA FLOWER, BLUE   *Pholistoma auritum*
Borage family (previously included in Waterleaf family)

DESCRIPTION: 1–4 feet. Tall, weak, branching stem with bowl-shaped, blue flowers (to 1.5 inches) at tips. Long, pinnately lobed, clasping, dandelion-like leaves.

Blue fiesta flower

NOTE: The stems and the leaves are covered with velcro-like, reversed prickles that cling to other plants [caterpillar phacelia (*Phacelia cicutaria*) in the photo] for support.

HABITAT: Bluffs, woodlands (to 6,200 feet); found on central and southern coast and coast ranges, San Joaquin Valley, central and southern foothills, southern Sierra, Transverse Ranges, Peninsular Ranges, Sonoran Desert.

WHERE AND WHEN:

Hite's Cove trail (March–April)
Kern River Canyon (March–April)
Pinnacles (March–April)
Channel Islands (March–April)
Santa Monica Mountains (March–May)
San Bruno Mountain (March–June)

GILIA, GLOBE or BLUE FIELD GILIA   *Gilia capitata*

Phlox family

DESCRIPTION: 0.5–2 feet. Round, terminal cluster of 50–100 small, pale blue, tubular flowers. Scattered leaves with very narrow, needlelike segments.

NOTE: Whether pale blue or even almost white, these flowers attract a wide variety of pollinators—bees, butterflies, wasps, flies.

HABITAT: Sandy or rocky flats (to 7,000 feet); found in much of California.

WHERE AND WHEN:

Hite's Cove Trail (March–April)
Gorman Hills (March–April)
Ring Mountain (March–April)
Kern R. Canyon (April–May)
Santa Monica Mountains (April–May)
Trinity Alps (June–July)

Globe gilia

HOUND'S TONGUE, WESTERN *Cynoglossum occidentale*
Borage family

DESCRIPTION: 0.5–2 feet. Clusters of a few small, pale blue, pinwheel-like flowers held above the leaves on pedicels out of the leaf axils. Raised yellow or white rim around throat. Tonguelike stem leaves are sessile (in contrast to the petioled leaves of grand hound's tongue, p. 85).

NOTE: The broad, dark-green leaves are a perfect background on which to display the delicate, pale blue flowers.

HABITAT: Open woods (1,000–7,000 feet); found in northwest mountains, north coast ranges, Cascades, Sierra, northeast corner.

WHERE AND WHEN:
Jenner-Fort Ross area
　(March–April)
Muir Woods (March–April)
Greenhorn Range (March–May)
Trinity Alps (May–June)
Mount Shasta (May–July)
Lassen National Park (May–July)

Western hound's tongue

HYACINTH, WILD or OOKOW or
MANY-FLOWERED BRODIAEA *Dichelostemma multiflorum*
Brodiaea family (previously included in Lily family)

DESCRIPTION: 1–2 feet. Tight umbel of 10–35 lavender or pink, star-shaped flowers (to 0.5 inches). Six flaring tepals (often with dark mid-veins) above pinched calyx.

NOTE: The many small flowers crowded in the umbel, the decidedly pinched tube, and the pale pink or lavender color of the tepals help distinguish this species from its many close relatives.

HABITAT: Grassland; forest openings (to 5,000 feet); found in northwest mountains, north coast ranges, foothills, Sierra, northeast corner.

WHERE AND WHEN:
Table Mountain (March–April)
Trinity Alps (March–April)
Drum Powerhouse Road (March–April)

Pine Hill Preserve (March–
   April)
Feather River Canyon (May–
   June)
Warner Mountains (May–
   June)

Ookow

ITHURIEL'S SPEAR or WALLY BASKET or GRASSNUT *Triteleia laxa*
Brodiaea family (previously included in Lily family)
DESCRIPTION: 1–3 feet. Terminal, loose umbel of five to 50 funnel-shaped,
pale violet, six-tepaled flowers (to 1.5 inches). Non-shiny tepals with dark
purple mid-veins.
NOTE: This is an especially striking and satisfying plant for the delicious
contrast between its violet flowers and the lush green grass of its habitat.
HABITAT: Grassland, forest openings (to 5,000 feet); found in much of California.

Ithuriel's spear

Phoenix Park (March–April)
Kern River Canyon (March–April)
King's Canyon/Sequoia (April–May)
Mount Diablo (April–May)
Table Mountain (April–May)
Santa Lucia Range (April–May)

LARKSPUR, DESERT   *Delphinium parishii*
Buttercup family

DESCRIPTION: 0.5–2 feet. Six to 75 pale blue (sepals) flowers (to 1 inch) spread along stem. Two small, lower petals blue and usually hairy; two upper petals white.

NOTE: This is the only desert larkspur, but it occurs in both California southern deserts, bringing its lovely shade of blue to all but the southern-most part of the Sonoran Desert.

HABITAT: Sandy flats, desert scrub (to 8,200 feet); found east of the Sierra, Transverse Ranges, Mojave Desert, Sonoran Desert.

WHERE AND WHEN:
Anza-Borrego (March–April)
Antelope Valley (March–May)
Death Valley (March–June)
Alabama Hills (April–May)
Joshua Tree National Park
   (April–June)
Mojave National Preserve
   (April–June)

Desert larkspur

LARKSPUR, SPREADING or
ZIG-ZAG LARKSPUR   *Delphinium patens*
Buttercup family

DESCRIPTION: 6–20 inches. Slender, wiry, branching stem with loosely arranged, spurred, dark blue flowers. Long nectar spur (sepal) usually mostly straight. Small, upper two petals white and blue, lower two blue.

NOTE: The common names refer to the somewhat zig-zagging stem and the loose raceme of flowers.

Grasslands, open woods (to 9,200 feet); found in coast ranges, Central Valley, foothills, Transverse Ranges, Peninsular Ranges.

WHERE AND WHEN:
Buttermilk Bend Trail (March–April)
Carrizo Plain (March–April)
Table Mountain (March–April)
Pine Hill Preserve (March–April)
Santa Monica Mountains (March–May)
San Gabriel Mountains (April–May)

Spreading larkspur

LOCOWEED, LAYNE'S or LAYNE'S MILKVETCH   *Astragalus layneae*
Pea family

DESCRIPTION: 1–10 inches. 10–45 pea flowers (to three-fourths of an inch) arranged loosely along stem, more crowded at tip. Wings and keel white

with purple tip, banner mostly purple or lilac. Pinnately compound leaves with 11–23 white-hairy, oval leaflets.

NOTE: The white and purple coloring of the petals is unusual, but the most distinctive characteristic of this locoweed is the strongly incurved seedpod, which usually forms at least half of a circle.

HABITAT: Sandy flats, washes (1,000–5,000 feet); found east of the Sierra, Mojave Desert.

Layne's locoweed

WHERE AND WHEN:
Death Valley (March–May)
Rand Mountains (March–May)
Twenty-Nine Palms (March–May)
Indian Wells Valley (March–May)
Mojave National Preserve (March–May)
Randsburg area (March–May)

LUPINE, ARROYO
Lupinus succulentus
Pea family

DESCRIPTION: 0.5–3 feet. Stout stem bearing long raceme (to 6 inches) of distinct whorls of blue-purple flowers. Black-spotted, white patch on banner aging magenta. Seven to nine broad leaflets with smooth, hairless upper surface.

NOTE: The banner is sharply bent back, so the color is visible from the sides as well as from straight on.

HABITAT: Grasslands, road banks (to 2,500 feet); found in northwest mountains, coast and coast ranges, Central Valley, Transverse Ranges, Peninsular Ranges.

WHERE AND WHEN:
Wind Wolves Preserve
    (March–April)
Point Loma (March–April)
Cuyama Valley (March–May)
Mount Diablo (March–May)
Channel Islands (March–May)
Bear Valley (April–May)

Arroyo lupine

LUPINE, BUSH or SILVER LUPINE
Lupinus albifrons
Pea family

DESCRIPTION: 2–5 feet. Bushy shrub with long racemes of many whorls or near whorls of blue-purple pea flowers with white or yellow patch on banner.

NOTE: Walking past this showy bush on a hot spring day will delight your nose (with a sweet, grapelike fragrance) as well as your eyes.

HABITAT: Cliffs, rock outcrops, sandy or grassy banks (to 6,500 feet); found

in northwest mountains, coast and coast ranges, foothills, Mojave Desert.
WHERE AND WHEN:
Buttermilk Bend Trail (March–April)
Hite's Cove Trail (March–April)
Camp Nine Road (March–April)
Anza-Borrego (March–April)
Carrizo Plain (March–May)
Nipomo-Guadalupe Dunes (March–May)

Bush lupine

LUPINE, COULTER'S   *Lupinus sparsiflorus*
Pea family
DESCRIPTION: 8–16 inches. Blue pea flowers (to 0.5 inches) spiral gracefully up the stem. Banner notched at top with white patch becoming magenta with age. Red-spotted, yellow splotch at base of white patch. Hairy leaves with seven to 11 narrow, pointed, widely separated leaflets.

NOTE: Although the flowers can sometimes appear almost whorled, more often they are noticeably spiraling up the stem.
HABITAT: Sandy flats, washes (to 4,300 feet); found in the central and south coast ranges, Transverse Ranges, Peninsular Ranges, Mojave Desert, Sonoran Desert.
WHERE AND WHEN:
Death Valley (March–April)
Whipple Mountains (March–April)
Joshua Tree (March–April)
San Bernardino Mountains (March–May)
Santa Lucia Range (March–May)
Granite Mountains in Mojave National Preserve (March–May)

Coulter's lupine

LUPINE, DOUGLAS or SKY LUPINE

Lupinus nanus

Pea family

DESCRIPTION: 0.5–1.5 feet. Raceme of several whorls of dark blue, pea flowers. Banner is low and rounded with a central, black-spotted, white patch that turns rosy with age.

Sky lupine

NOTE: This delightful white and blue lupine often carpets large areas, notably Table Mountain and Wind Wolves Preserve, usually in late March or early April.

HABITAT: Grassland (to 3,500 feet); found in much of California (except northeast corner, desert, and eastern edge).

WHERE AND WHEN:

Camp Nine Road (March–
　April)
Wind Wolves Preserve (March–
　April)
Table Mountain (March–May)
Carrizo Plain (March–May)
Santa Monica Mountains
　(April–May)
Hite's Cove Trail (April–May)

LUPINE, SILVER DUNE or BEACH BLUE LUPINE

Lupinus chamissonis

Pea family

DESCRIPTION: 2–6 feet. Shrub thick with silvery-hairy leaves with five to nine broad leaflets and long (to 8 inches) raceme of more or less whorled, pea flowers. Petals light blue or violet with yellow patch on banner. Back of banner densely hairy. California endemic.

NOTE: This species resembles bush lupine (p. 170) in its silvery-hairy, bushy appearance, but it differs in its much more limited distribution and in the hairy back of the banner.

HABITAT: Dunes (to 35 feet); found on coast.

WHERE AND WHEN:

Nipomo-Guadalupe Dunes (March–July)
Bodega Head (March–July)
San Francisco Bay area (March–July)
Lompoc area (March–July)
Point Reyes (March–July)
San Bruno Mountain (May–July)

Silver dune lupine

LUPINE, SPIDER or BENTHAM LUPINE   *Lupinus benthamii*
Pea family

DESCRIPTION: 1–3 feet. Pea flowers more or less whorled on upper two to 10 inches of hairy stem. Bright blue flowers with white patch on banner turning magenta with age. California endemic.

NOTE: The main distinguishing characteristic is its long, extremely narrow leaflets reminiscent of some graceful, green, long-legged spider.

HABITAT: Grasslands, roadbanks, rocky places (to 3,800 feet); found in central and south coast ranges, Central Valley, foothills.

WHERE AND WHEN:
Hite's Cove Trail (March–April)

Spider lupine

Gorman (March–April)
Electra Road (March–April)
Red Hill Road (March–April)
Santa Lucia Range (March–April)
Cuyama Valley (March–May)

PHACELIA, CALIFORNIA COAST   *Phacelia californica*

Borage family (previously included in Waterleaf family)

DESCRIPTION: 1–3 feet. Decumbent or erect, hairy stems bearing densely flowered coils of pale blue or white, bowl-shaped, papery flowers with long-protruding stamens.

Crinkly, deeply veined, smooth-edged, silvery-hairy leaves. California endemic.

NOTE: The coiled arrangement of the flowers is called a "cyme"—a bit like a floral "caterpillar" cozily curled up.

HABITAT: Coastal bluffs, rocky places, woodlands (to 3,300 feet); found on north and central coast and coast ranges.

WHERE AND WHEN:

Point Reyes (March–May)
Figueroa Mountain (March–
   May)
San Bruno Mountain
   (March–September)
Salt Point (April–July)
Santa Cruz Mountains
   (April–September)

California coast phacelia

PHACELIA, CALTHA-LEAF or
CALTHALEAF SCORPIONWEED   *Phacelia calthifolia*

Borage family (previously included in Waterleaf family)

DESCRIPTION: 4–18 inches. Spreading or erect, slender, glandular-hairy stem with coiled cluster of many violet or purple, funnel-shaped or bowl-shaped flowers (to 0.5 inches). Round, scalloped, deeply veined, basal leaves with sticky glands.

NOTE: "Caltha-leaf" refers to the similarity in shape of these leaves to those of the *Caltha* genus (marsh marigold, p. 402).

HABITAT: Sandy flats, desert scrub (to 3,300 feet); found in Mojave Desert.

WHERE AND WHEN:
Titus Canyon in Death Valley
(March–April)
south of Shoshone (March–
April)
*Wildrose Canyon in Death
Valley* (March–April)
Ludlow area (March–April)
Saline Valley in Death Valley
(March–April)
east of Tecopa (March–April)

Caltha-leaf phacelia

PHACELIA, PARRY'S

Phacelia parryi

Borage family (previously included in Waterleaf family)
DESCRIPTION: 0.5–2 feet. Stiff-hairy, sticky stems with many broad, irregularly toothed leaves and several, shallowly bowl-shaped, dark blue-purple flowers (to three-fourths inch) with white or pale violet throats.

NOTE: The rich, saturated blue-purple color of the flowers is similar to that of its desert kin wild canterbury bells (p. 162), but Parry's phacelia has smaller flowers with much smaller tubes and with white at the throat.

HABITAT: Coastal scrub, chaparral, burn areas (to 8,000 feet); found on south coast and coast ranges, Transverse Ranges, Peninsular Ranges, Mojave Desert, Sonoran Desert.

WHERE AND WHEN:
Santa Monica Mountains
(March–June)

Parry's phacelia

Santa Ana Mountains (March–June)
Torrey Pines (March–June)
Aqua Tibia Mountains (March–June)
Cuyamaca Mountains (March–June)
Point Magu State Park (March–June)

PHACELIA, TANSY-LEAF or LACY PHACELIA *Phacelia tanacetifolia*

Borage family (previously included in Waterleaf family)

DESCRIPTION: 0.5–3.5 feet. Stiff-hairy stem with many fernlike leaves and caterpillar-like coils of pale blue, shallow bowl-shaped flowers (to 0.5 inches). Fingerlike, hairy sepals.

NOTE: Most *Phacelia* species have pinnately compound leaves, but as the common and species names suggest, the leaves of this species are deeply divided into tiny, tansylike segments.

HABITAT: Grasslands, sandy or gravelly slopes (to 6,000 feet); found in coast ranges, Central Valley, foothills, Transverse Ranges, Peninsular Ranges, Mojave Desert.

WHERE AND WHEN:

Wind Wolves Preserve
    (March–April)
Santa Ana Mountains
    (March–May)
Cuyama Valley (March–
    May)
SR-58 (March–May)
west of Pinnacles (March–
    May)
Red Rock Canyon (March–May)

Tansy-leaf phacelia

SAGE, DEATH VALLEY or WOOLLY SAGE   *Salvia funerea*

Mint family

DESCRIPTION: 2–4 feet. Densely branched shrub covered with white-woolly hairs. Numerous violet, two-lipped flowers in clusters of three or four in leaf axils. Broad leaves with several spine-tipped lobes. CNPS Rare and Endangered List—limited distribution.

NOTE: This shrub is so densely white-woolly that it is a bit of a shock to see

its many violet flowers—such flashes of colorful life on such a ghostly canvas!

HABITAT: Dry washes, canyons (to 1,000 feet); found in Mojave Desert.

WHERE AND WHEN:
Titus Canyon in Death Valley
    (March–June)
Granite Mountains (March–
    June)
Echo Canyon in Death Valley
    (March–June)
Bristol Mountains (March–
    June)
*Dedeckera Canyon in Death
    Valley* (March–June)
Mosaic Canyon in Death Valley
    (March–June)

Death Valley sage

SAGE, CREEPING or SONOMA SAGE   *Salvia sonomensis*
Mint family

DESCRIPTION: 6–16 inches. Erect, square stem rises above mat-forming leaves. Four to six separated whorls of small, tubular, two-lipped, pale blue flowers. Petal lobes ragged.

NOTE: Crush these leaves for a strong, not altogether pleasant, somewhat acrid aroma. On a hot day, just being in the vicinity of the plants might be an olfactory overload!

HABITAT: Woodlands, chaparral (to 6,500 feet); found in northwest mountains, coast ranges, south coast, foothills, Peninsular Ranges.

WHERE AND WHEN:
Pine Hill Preserve (March–
    April)
San Ysidro Mountains
    (March–April)
Santa Lucia Range (March–
    May)

Sonoma sage

Yuba River Canyon (April–May)
Treplett Mountain (May–June)
Trinity Alps (May–June)

SANDBLOSSOMS   *Linanthus parryae*
Phlox family

DESCRIPTION: 1–4 inches. Cluster of funnel-shaped, deep blue (sometimes pale lavender or even white) flowers (to 1 inch) at tip of very short stem. Deep purple, feltlike throat with yellow anthers and white, threadlike stigma. California endemic.

NOTE: When you see a carpet of these lovely flowers, you might almost think the sand (or gravel) itself is blooming.

HABITAT: Sandy or gravelly flats (to 6,500 feet); found in south and central coast ranges, San Joaquin Valley, foothills, east of the Sierra, Mojave Desert.

Sandblossoms

WHERE AND WHEN:
Death Valley (March–May)
Antelope Valley (March–May)
Alabama Hills (March–May)
Greenhorn Range (March–May)
Aberdeen area (March–May)
San Emigdio Range (March–May)

Sandblossoms

VIOLET, WESTERN DOG or EARLY BLUE VIOLET   *Viola adunca*
Violet family

DESCRIPTION: 2–6 inches. One or several peduncles each with a terminal violet or blue flower (to three-fourths inch). Center petal lobe of lower lip has purple-streaked white patch.

NOTE: A rose is rose, a peach (the fruit) is peach, a salmon (the fish) is salmon—at last, here is a violet that is (pretty much) violet.

HABITAT: Moist meadows, stream banks, forest edges (to 11,000 feet); found in much of California (except northeast corner, deserts, and eastern edge).

WHERE AND WHEN:
San Bruno Mountain (March–April)
San Jacinto Mountains (March–May)
Bodega Bay (March–May)
Santa Lucia Range (March–May)
Trinity Alps (June–July)
Hope Valley near Carson Pass (June)

Western dog
violet

YELLOW THROATS or FREMONT'S PHACELIA   *Phacelia fremontii*
Borage family (previously included in Waterleaf family)

DESCRIPTION: 2–20 inches. Caterpillar-like coil of several lavender or violet, funnel-shaped flowers (to three-fourths inch) at tip of short, stem. White patch at center of flower with yellow throat.

NOTE: In wet years, these multicolored beauties can carpet large areas of desert floors. They don't smell as delicious as they look (unless you like *eau de skunk*).

HABITAT: Sandy or gravelly flats, desert scrub, grasslands (to 7,000 feet); found in south coast ranges, San Joaquin Valley, Transverse Ranges, east of the Sierra, Mojave Desert.

WHERE AND WHEN:
Antelope Valley (March–April)

Red Rock Canyon (March–April)
Death Valley (March–May)
Carrizo Plain (March–June)
Alabama Hills (April–May)
Mojave National Preserve (April–May)

Yellow throats

YERBA SANTA, THICK-LEAVED · *Eriodictyon crassifolium*

Borage family (previously included in Waterleaf family)

DESCRIPTION: 3–12 feet. White-hairy shrub thick with broad, toothed, somewhat crinkly, felty, gray-green leaves and clusters of pale violet, bell-shaped flowers. California endemic.

NOTE: Unlike its more northern cousin *E. californicum*, (p. 414), the upper surface of the leaves of this yerba santa is densely hairy and crinkly rather than smooth and shiny green.

HABITAT: Dry slopes, washes (to 8,200 feet); found on south coast and coast ranges, Transverse Ranges, Peninsular Ranges, Mojave Desert, Sonoran Desert.

WHERE AND WHEN:

Santa Monica Mountains (March–May)

Joshua Tree (March–May)

Thick-leaved yerba santa

Torrey Pines (March–May)
Wind Wolves Preserve (March–May)
Santa Rosa Plateau (March–May)
Cuyama Valley (March–May)

BEAVERTAIL or BEAVERTAIL CACTUS   *Opuntia basilaris*
Cactus family

DESCRIPTION: 0.5–1.5 feet. Clump of spineless pads with numerous showy, magenta, bowl-shaped flowers (to 3 inches). Many satiny, overlapping pet-

als cradling cluster of scores of magenta stamens and a much-branched, white stigma.

NOTE: Although the pads are technically spineless, the little bristles in the eyespots can still hurt if you touch them.

HABITAT: Dry flats and slopes, sagebrush scrub (to 7,200 feet); found in San Joaquin Valley, southern foothills, east of the Sierra, Transverse Ranges, Peninsular Ranges, Mojave Desert, Sonoran Desert.

WHERE AND WHEN:

Death Valley (March–April)

Anza-Borrego (March–April)

Alabama Hills (March–May)

Beavertail cactus

Joshua Tree (March–May)

Coachella Valley (March–May)

Mojave National Preserve (March–June)

BLEEDING HEART, PACIFIC   *Dicentra formosa*
Poppy family

DESCRIPTION: 8–18 inches. Clusters of four or more, pink or rose-purple, flattened, heart-shaped flowers (to 1 inch) nod from tips of arching stems. Four united petals, the outer two with small, flaring tips. California endemic.

NOTE: If these graceful flowers are any indication, being called a "bleeding heart" is quite a compliment!

HABITAT: Moist, forest shade; meadows (to 10,000 feet); found in northwest mountains, coast, coast ranges, foothills, Cascades, Sierra.

WHERE AND WHEN:
Redwood National Park
(March–June)
Santa Lucia Range (March–
June)
Drum Powerhouse Road
(March–June)
Trinity Alps (April–July)
King's Canyon/Sequoia
(June–July)
Lassen National Park (June–
August)

Pacific bleeding heart

BUTTER-AND-EGGS, ROSY or
PINK BUTTER-AND-EGGS *Triphysaria eriantha* subsp. *rosea*
Broomrape family (previously included in Snapdragon family)
DESCRIPTION: 4–15 inches. Spike of many, long-tubular, two-lipped flow-
ers. Very similar to Johnny tuck (p. 208) except the flowers are white turn-
ing rose-purple instead of yellow. California endemic.
NOTE: Being a rosy subspecies of Johnny tuck, perhaps we could call this
plant "blushing Johnny."
HABITAT: Grassy fields, bluffs (to 300 feet); found on coast.
WHERE AND WHEN:
Sea Ranch (March–April)
Humboldt Bay (March–April)

Rosy butter-and-
eggs

Point Reyes (March–April)
near Santa Cruz (April–May)
Salt Point (April–June)
Mendocino Headlands State Park (May–June)

CANDY FLOWER or SIBERIAN
SPRING BEAUTY   *Claytonia sibirica*
Miner's lettuce family (previously included in Purslane family)
DESCRIPTION: 0.5–2 feet. Branching stem with loose inflorescence of 10–20 more or less flat flowers (to three-fourths inch). Five separate, notched, white petals with narrow, pink stripes.
NOTE: Like miner's lettuce (p. 136), another *Claytonia* species, candy flower has interesting and distinctive stem leaves, but in this case they don't fuse around the stem, but rather abut it.
HABITAT: Moist, shady woodlands; stream banks, marshes (to 7,500 feet); found in northwest mountains, northern and central coast and coast ranges, Cascades, Transverse Ranges.
WHERE AND WHEN:
Point Reyes (March–July)
Yolla Bolly-Middle Eel Wilderness (March–July)
Bodega Bay (March–August)
Mount Shasta (March–September)
San Bernardino Mountains (April–July)
Trinity Alps (April–July)

Candy flower

DAISY, SEASIDE or SEASIDE FLEABANE   *Erigeron glaucus*
Aster family
DESCRIPTION: 4–16 inches. Solitary flower head (to 1 inch) atop stem with a few leaves, crowded with up to 150 very narrow, pink, violet or white rays surrounding a disk densely packed with a hundred or so yellow disk flowers.

Seaside daisy

NOTE: Unlike most composites, the rays in this daisy seem secondary, as the large yellow disk is much broader than the rays are long.

HABITAT: Bluffs, dunes, beaches (to 70 feet); found on the coast.

WHERE AND WHEN:

Salt Point (March–June)
Nipomo-Guadalupe Dunes (March–June)
Manchester Beach (March–July)
Big Sur (March–July)
Channel Islands (March–July)
Stinson Beach (April–June)

FIVE-SPOT, DESERT   *Eremalche rotundifolia*
Mallow family

DESCRIPTION: 3–24 inches. Bristly-hairy plant with broad, round, dark green, toothed leaves and many pink, globe-shaped flowers (to 1.5 inches). Inside of flower with dark red-purple, basal splotches.

NOTE: These gorgeous flowers form almost completely closed globes, so you (and the pollinator) have to peer in the opening at the top to see the amazing red splotches within.

HABITAT: Sandy or gravelly flats and slopes, rocky places (to 4,000 feet); found east of the Sierra, Mojave Desert, Sonoran Desert.

WHERE AND WHEN:

Death Valley (March–April)
Anza-Borrego (March–April)
Alabama Hills (March–April)
Red Rock Canyon State Park (March–April)
Mojave National Preserve (March–April)
Joshua Tree (April–May)

Desert five-spot

GILIA, BIRD'S-EYE

Gilia tricolor

Phlox family

DESCRIPTION: 4–12 inches. Flat or shallow bowl-shaped flowers (to 0.5 inches) with narrow, yellow tube with purple lines at throat. Five overlapping, rounded petal lobes white with pink or violet tips.

NOTE: When the sun strikes a slope of these flowers in the morning or after a storm, and the blossoms open, the slope seems filled with thousands of multicolored eyes greeting you in beauty.

HABITAT: Grasslands (to 4,000 feet); found in coast ranges, Central Valley, foothills, east of the Sierra, Transverse Ranges.

WHERE AND WHEN:

Hite's Cove Trail (March–April)

Haiwee Reservoir (March–April)

Bird's-eye gilia

Kern River Canyon (March–May)
Bear Valley (March–May)
San Bernardino Mountains (April–May)
Table Mountain (April–May)

GILIA, BROAD-LEAF
Phlox family

Aliciella latifolia or *Gilia latifolia*

DESCRIPTION: 4–12 inches. Glandular-hairy, strong-scented plant with cluster of tubular flowers (to 0.5 inches) above very large, basal, toothed, deeply veined, hollylike (although huge) leaves. Flower tube white, flaring lobes pink.

NOTE: The flowers look even tinier against their backdrop of unusually large, showy leaves.

HABITAT: Rocky flats and slopes, washes (to 6,000 feet); found east of the Sierra, Mojave Desert, Sonoran Desert.

WHERE AND WHEN:
Alabama Hills (March–April)
El Paso Mountains (March–April)
Indio Hills (March–April)
Death Valley (March–May)
White Mountains (March–May)
Ocotillo Wells (March–May)

Broad-leaf gilia

HEDGENETTLE, CALIFORNIA
Mint family

Stachys bullata

DESCRIPTION: 1–3 feet. Stout, square stem with numerous, widely spaced whorls of about six two-lipped, pink flowers with white patch near base of petal lobes. Two lobes of upper lip form canopy. California endemic.

NOTE: Check out the exquisite, four-parted ovary cradled by the bristly-hairy calyx (as shown in the photo)—it looks like a clutch of precious green bird eggs nestled in a green nest.

HABITAT: Woodlands (to 1,800 feet); found on coast, in coast ranges, Transverse Ranges, Peninsular Ranges.

WHERE AND WHEN:
Santa Monica Mountains (March–May)
Point Lobos (March–May)

Santa Lucia Range (March–
   May)
Figueroa Mountain (March–
   August)
Fort Ross area (April–
   September)
San Bruno Mountain (April–
   September)

California hedgenettle

INDIAN PINK, CALIFORNIA   *Silene laciniata* subsp. *californica* or *S. californica*

Pink family

DESCRIPTION: 0.5–1.5 feet. Several large, pinwheel-like, scarlet flowers with five separate petals. Each petal four-lobed with usually the inner two lobes

broader and longer than the outer two lobes.

NOTE: To find clusters of these brilliant, scarlet flowers in open woods contrasting with the shade and the greenery is always a surprise and a de-light.

HABITAT: Woodlands (to 5,000 feet); found in north-west mountains, north and central coast ranges, foot-hills, Cascades, Sierra, Trans-verse Ranges.

WHERE AND WHEN:
Hite's Cove Trail (March–
April)

California Indian pink

King's Canyon/Sequoia (March–April)
Traverse Creek Botanical Area (March–April)
Santa Lucia Range (March–May)
Trinity Alps (March–May)
Ring Mountain (May–June)

LARKSPUR, RED or CANYON LARKSPUR   *Delphimium nudicaule*
Buttercup family

DESCRIPTION: 0.5–4 feet. Long-tubular, bright scarlet or orange-red flowers (to 1.5 inches) with long nectar spur on slender pedicels that are scattered along the upper stem.

NOTE: With all the deeply blue delphiniums, it is a bit of a shock to see these flaming red flowers.

HABITAT: Rocky slopes and flats, brushy slopes, open woods (to 6,500 feet); found in northwest mountains, north and central coast and coast ranges, foothills, Cascades, Sierra, northeast corner, Transverse Ranges.

WHERE AND WHEN:
Table Mountain (March–April)
Jenner area (March–April)
Santa Lucia Range (April–May)
Feather River Canyon (April–May)
Trinity Alps (April–June)
San Gabriel Mountains (May–July)

Red larkspur

LILY, ADOBE   *Fritillaria pluriflora*
Lily family

DESCRIPTION: 4–20 inches. One or several large (to 2.5 inches), showy, pink or rose (occasionally white), six-tepaled flowers mostly nodding off thick stalk. Three to 10 broad, fleshy, usually wavy-edged leaves clustered near the ground. California endemic. CNPS Rare and Endangered List—endangered.

NOTE: This rare plant is anything but rare in Bear Valley—in a good year you will find (for a short couple of weeks) thousands of these spectacular blooms creating a pink swath across southern parts of the valley.

HABITAT: Dry grasslands (to 1,800 feet); found in north coast ranges, Central Valley, foothills.

WHERE AND WHEN:
Bear Valley (March)
near Elk Creek (March)
Vina Plains Preserve
(March)
Dye Creek Preserve (March)
Success Lake (March)
East Park Reservoir (March)

Adobe lily

LOCOWEED, SCARLET   *Astragalus coccineus*
Pea family

DESCRIPTION: 1–2 feet. Forms nearly stemless clumps a foot or so across with scarlet pea flowers (to 2 inches). Banner streaked with white. Pinnately compound, white-hairy leaves with seven to 15 tiny, oval leaflets. White, fuzzy seedpods.

NOTE: At peak blooming, the dazzling scarlet flowers usually almost completely cover the plant, creating a crimson beacon visible far out "to desert."

Scarlet locoweed

HABITAT: Gravelly flats and slopes, sagebrush scrub (2,500–8,000 feet); found east of the Sierra, Transverse Ranges, Peninsular Ranges, Mojave Desert, Sonoran Desert.

WHERE AND WHEN:

Anza-Borrego (March–April)

Joshua Tree (March–April)

Jacumba area (March–May)

Alabama Hills (April–May)

Death Valley (April–May)

White Mountains (April–July)

LUPINE, HARLEQUIN   *Lupinus stiversii*
Pea family

DESCRIPTION: 4–20 inches. Short raceme dense with spectacularly multi-colored pea flowers. Yellow banner, pink wings, and white keel (hidden inside wings). Palmately compound leaves with six to nine broad leaflets. California endemic.

NOTE: This is the perfect flower for the "lupine novice," for the three types of pea petals are color-coded for easy differentiation.

HABITAT: Grassy flats, rock ledges (to 4,600 feet); found in central and south coast ranges, foothills, Sierra, Transverse Ranges.

WHERE AND WHEN:

Hite's Cove Trail (March–April)

Santa Lucia Range (March–April)

Electra Road (March–April)

Feather River Canyon (April–May)

Buttermilk Bend Trail (April–May)

Monterey Peninsula (April–May)

Harlequin lupine

LUPINE, STINGING

Lupinus hirsutissimus

Pea family

DESCRIPTION: 0.5–3 feet. Rigid stem with several, large, long-petioled leaves with five to eight broad, rounded leaflets. Long (to 8 inches) raceme with showy, pink or magenta flowers (to three-fourths inch) with yellow patch on banner aging purple. Entire plant (except petals) covered with stiff silvery or yellowish hairs.

Stinging lupine

NOTE: The common name gives fair warning—touching the hairs can be a painful experience.

HABITAT: Dry, rocky places; burn areas (to 4,600 feet); found on central and south coast and coast ranges, central foothills, Transverse Ranges, Peninsular Ranges.

WHERE AND WHEN:
Torrey Pines (March–April)
San Gabriel Mountains (March–April)
Santa Monica Mountains (March–April)
San Felipe Valley (March–April)
Channel Islands (March–May)
Santa Rosa Plateau (March–May)

MILKWEED, CLIMBING or FRINGED TWINEVINE

Funastrum cynanchoides or *Sarcostemma cynanchoides*

Dogbane family (previously included in Milkweed family)

DESCRIPTION: 1–4 feet. Twining stems with narrow, arrow-shaped leaves and dense, umbel-like clusters of pink, star-shaped flowers (to 0.5 inches). Ring of tissue at base of petal lobes with saclike, white filament column appendages within.

NOTE: The aggressively twining stems often interweave, forming thick, braided "ropes."

HABITAT: Sandy or rocky flats, canyons, ditches (to 5,000 feet); found on south coast and coast ranges, Transverse Ranges, Peninsular Ranges, Mojave Desert, Sonoran Desert.

Mojave National Preserve
(March–May)
San Gabriel Mountains
(March–May)
along Imperial Highway S2
(March–May)
Gabilan Range (March–May)
Torrey Pines (March–May)
Pinyon Mountain (March–
June)

Climbing milkweed

MINT, CRISP DUNE   *Monardella crispa*
Mint family

DESCRIPTION: 4–20 inches. Low, tufted, often mounding plant with fleshy, tonguelike leaves with crisped edges. Heads (to 1.5 inches) above woolly calyx with many closely packed, rose-purple, tubular flowers with long-protruding reproductive parts. California endemic. CNPS Rare and Endangered List—endangered.

NOTE: As if to be sure you know its whereabouts and don't step on it, this endangered plant announces its presence from a distance with a sweet, minty fragrance.

HABITAT: Dunes (to 350 feet); found on central coast.

Crisp dune mint

Nipomo-Guadalupe Dunes (March–October)
Vandenburg Air Force Base (March–October)

MONKEYFLOWER, BIGELOW'S — *Mimulus bigelovii*

Lopseed family (previously included in Snapdragon family)

DESCRIPTION: 1–12 inches. Branching stem thick with two-lipped, rose or

magenta flowers (to 1 inch). At throat, two golden ridges margined with purple and two lateral dark-purple patches.

NOTE: The deep-magenta flowers are particularly striking when the plants form extensive patches on otherwise rather bare, rocky desert terrain.

HABITAT: Rocky desert flats and slopes, washes (to 7,500 feet); found east of the Sierra, Peninsular Ranges, Mojave Desert, Sonoran Desert.

WHERE AND WHEN:
Anza-Borrego (March–April)
San Jacinto Mountains (March–April)
Joshua Tree (March–April)
Buckhorn Dry Lake (March–April)
Death Valley (March–May)
near Benton (May–June)

Bigelow's monkeyflower

MONKEYFLOWER, DOUGLAS or CHINLESS MONKEYFLOWER or PURPLE MOUSE EARS — *Mimulus douglasii*

Lopseed family (previously included in Snapdragon family)

DESCRIPTION: 2–3 inches. Dwarf plant with two-lipped flowers at tips of stems. Two petal lobes of upper lip are solid rose or magenta; three lobes of lower lip are truncated and have two golden yellow spots.

NOTE: The reason for the "chinless" name is obvious, as the lower lip is almost nonexistent.

HABITAT: Bare, gravelly flats (to 4,000 feet); found in northwest mountains, coast ranges, Sacramento Valley, foothills.

WHERE AND WHEN:
Greenhorn Range (March–
    April)
Red Hill Road (March–April)
Santa Lucia Range (March–
    April)
Table Mountain (March–
    May)
Bishop Creek trail in Yosemite
    (April–May)
Sutter Buttes (April–May)

Douglas monkeyflower

MONKEYFLOWER, KELLOGG'S   *Mimulus kelloggii*
Lopseed family (previously included in Snapdragon family)
DESCRIPTION: 2–12 inches. Several two-lipped flowers (to 1 inch) in leaf
axils. Velvety, deep rose-purple petal lobes with two yellow spots on middle lobe of lower lip. Yellow
throat with small red spots.
California endemic.

NOTE: Of all the reddish monkeyflowers in California, this
may be the richest, most velvety, most striking red-purple.

HABITAT: Grassy fields (to
3,000 feet); found in northwest mountains, north and
central coast ranges, foothills.

WHERE AND WHEN:
El Portal west of Yosemite
    (March–May)
Bartlett Springs Road
    (March–May)
Greenhorn Range (March–
    May)
Table Mountain (April–May)
Traverse Creek Botanical
    Area (April–May)
Hite's Cove Trail (April–May)

Kellogg's monkeyflower

Volcanic onion

ONION, VOLCANIC or CRATER ONION or
CASCADE ONION   *Allium cratericola*
Onion family (previously included in Lily family)

DESCRIPTION: 1–5 inches. Ball-shaped umbel of 20–30 tightly packed, pink or white flowers on or nearly on the ground. Six pointed tepals with dark rose mid-veins. One or two grasslike leaves much longer than flower stalk. California endemic.

NOTE: This lovely and diminutive onion often "erupts" over barren basalt outcrops, such as on Table Mountain.

HABITAT: Open volcanic soil, serpentine, or granite (to 2,500 feet); found in northwest mountains, coast ranges, foothills, Transverse Ranges, Peninsular Ranges.

WHERE AND WHEN:
Table Mountain (March–April)
Pinnacles (March–April)
Greenhorn Range (March–April)
San Jacinto Mountains (March–May)
SR-36 west of Red Bluff (March–April)
Bear Valley/Walker Ridge (April–May)

OWL'S CLOVER, PURPLE   *Castilleja exserta*
Broomrape family (previously included in Snapdragon family)

DESCRIPTION: 4–16 inches. Upper stem dense with "paintbrush" of pink-purple bracts cradling flowers. Three petals of lower lip deep red-purple, and two petals of upper lip red-purple beak with hairy cap.

NOTE: *En masse*, these plants create hillsides of gorgeous purple; individually they intrigue with their whimsical spike-hairdo characters looking out from their perches on the purple "tree."

HABITAT: Grasslands (to 5,200 feet); found in much of low- to mid-elevation California.

WHERE AND WHEN:

Hite's Cove trail (March–April)

Wind Wolves (March–April)

Table Mountain (March–April)

Nipomo-Guadalupe Dunes (March–May)

Anza-Borrego (April–May)

Bear Valley (April–May)

Purple owl's clover

PAINTBRUSH, FUZZY or WOOLLY PAINTBRUSH *Castilleja foliolosa*

Broomrape family (previously included in Snapdragon family)

DESCRIPTION: 1–2 feet. Red-orange bracts sometimes unlobed, sometimes three-to five-lobed. Plant covered with feltlike white or gray hairs.

NOTE: Many paintbrush species look quite similar, but this one (as the common name and species name indicate) is distinctive with its fuzzy-hairy stems and bracts.

HABITAT: Rocky slopes, chaparral, forest edges (to 5,000 feet); found on coast and coast ranges, foothills, Transverse Ranges, Mojave Desert.

Fuzzy paintbrush

WHERE AND WHEN:
Camp Nine Road (March–April)
Torrey Pines (March–April)
Anza-Borrego (March–April)
Mount Diablo (March–April)
San Bernardino Mountains (March–May)
Big Basin Redwoods State Park (March–May)

PENSTEMON, CLIMBING or HEART-LEAF PENSTEMON
Keckiella cordifolia or *Penstemon cordifolius*
Plantain family (previously included in Snapdragon family)
DESCRIPTION: 3–10 feet. Vinelike climber with opposite pairs of broad, heart-shaped leaves and clusters of orange-red, two-lipped, tubular flowers. Long reproductive parts canopied by upper lip. Staminode (sterile stamen) densely yellow-hairy.

NOTE: The climbing stem can lift these striking red flowers well over your head.

HABITAT: Chaparral, woodlands (to 4,000 feet); found on south coast and in coast ranges, Transverse Ranges, Peninsular Ranges.

WHERE AND WHEN:
Channel Islands (March–July)
San Gabriel Mountains (March–August)
Santa Monica Mountains (March–August)
Santa Ynez Mountains (March–August)
Santa Rosa Plateau (April–May)
Palomar Mountain (April–July)

Climbing penstemon

PENSTEMON, EATON or EATON FIRECRACKER *Penstemon eatonii*
Plantain family (previously included in Snapdragon family)
DESCRIPTION: 1.5–3 feet. Stout stem with opposite pairs of broad, pointed leathery leaves and pairs or small clusters of long-tubular, scarlet, two-lipped flowers (to 1.5 inches) with barely spreading petal lobes.
NOTE: Most penstemons have long flower tubes with small, flaring petal

lobes; this species has a "neck" with barely any "face" at all.

HABITAT: Sagebrush scrub, woodlands (5,000–9,200 feet); found in southern Sierra, Transverse Ranges, Mojave Desert, Sonoran Desert.

WHERE AND WHEN:

Anza-Borrego (March–May)
Mojave National Preserve (March–May)
Joshua Tree (March–May)
Greenhorn Range (March–July)
San Bernardino Mountains (April–July)
Mosquito Flat trail (April–July)

Eaton penstemon

PHLOX, LONG–LEAF   *Phlox longifolia*
Phlox family

DESCRIPTION: 4–16 inches. Woody base. Several slender pedicels arising from leaf axils bearing clusters of star-shaped flowers. Five pink or white, wedge-shaped petal lobes flaring from narrow tube.

Long-leaf phlox

NOTE: As with many species of *Phlox*, the flowers tend to get pinker or more purple after pollination, so you'll often see a range of colors on adjacent plants or sometimes even on the same plant.

HABITAT: Sagebrush scrub (4,000–8,000 feet); found east of the Sierra, northeast corner, north coast ranges, Mojave Desert, Sonoran Desert.

WHERE AND WHEN:
Topaz Lake (March–April)
Panamint Mountains (March–June)
Lake Crowley area (March–June)
Antelope Mountain (March–June)
White Mountains (March–June)
Modoc Plateau (April–June)

PINK, SOUTHERN or FRINGED INDIAN PINK   *Silene laciniata* subsp. *laciniata*

Pink family

DESCRIPTION: 0.5–2 feet. Sticky-hairy stem (often reclining) with pairs of opposite narrow leaves. Scarlet, five-petaled flowers (to three-fourths inch) with each flaring petal deeply lobed into four nearly equal, narrow segments.

NOTE: The species name *laciniata* means "torn," in reference to the fringed petals—if torn, most carefully and symmetrically so!

Southern pink

HABITAT: Chaparral, canyons, oak woodlands (to 4,000 feet); found on south coast and coast ranges, Transverse Ranges, Peninsular Ranges.

WHERE AND WHEN:
Santa Monica Mountains (March–July)
Santa Ynez Mountains (March–July)
Point Loma (March–July)
Channel Islands (March–July)
Wind Wolves Preserve (March–July)
Santa Rosa Plateau (March–July)

PURPLE MAT
Nama demissum

Borage family (previously included in Waterleaf family)

DESCRIPTION: 1–6 inches. Prostrate plant with spreading stems and clusters of red-purple or pink, bowl-shaped flowers (to 0.5 inches). Yellow flower tube with surrounding white ring before pink or purple petal lobes. Narrow, sticky-hairy leaves.

NOTE: In years of good rain, the stems can spread out a couple feet or more with dense, ground-hugging clusters of flowers.

HABITAT: Sandy or gravelly flats, washes (to 5,200 feet); found in south coast ranges, east of the Sierra, Transverse Ranges, Peninsular Ranges, Mojave Desert, Sonoran Desert.

WHERE AND WHEN:
Death Valley (March–April)
White Mountains (March–April)
Joshua Tree (March–April)
Anza-Borrego (March–April)
Alabama Hills (March–April)
Sawmill Pass Trail (March–May)

Purple mat

REDBUD, WESTERN
Cercis occidentalis

Pea family

DESCRIPTION: 7–20 feet. Shrub or small tree with many loose racemes of three to six pink or magenta pea flowers.

NOTE: This shrub is a spectacular component of the early spring blossoming, even more so because the flowers are in full bloom before the leaves appear, displaying the pink or magenta flowers in their full, unobstructed glory.

HABITAT: Shrubby slopes, canyons and ravines, woodlands, stream banks (to 4,000 feet); found in northwest mountains, coast ranges, Central Valley, foothills, northeast corner, Peninsular Ranges.

WHERE AND WHEN:
Hite's Cove trail (March–April)
Bear Valley (March–April)

Camp Nine Road (March–
    April)
King's Canyon/Sequoia
    (March–April)
San Joaquin Valley (March–
    April)
Mix Canyon (March–May)

Western redbud

ROCK CRESS, ROSE or COAST ROCK CRESS *Arabis blepharophylla*
Mustard family
DESCRIPTION: 2–8 inches. One or a few stems rise above a basal rosette of tonguelike leaves. Clusters of intensely rose-purple, four-petalled flowers with spoon-shaped petals. Long, cylindrical seed pods. California endemic. CNPS Rare and Endangered List—limited distribution.
NOTE: This is one of several uncommon or rare plants found on San Bruno

Mountain just south of San Francisco (p. 27).
HABITAT: Rocky outcrops, grassy slopes (to 1,700 feet); found on north and central coast and coast ranges.
WHERE AND WHEN:
San Bruno Mountain
    (March–April)
Bodega Head (March–April)
Mount Tamalpais (March–
    April)
Point Reyes (March–April)
Santa Lucia Range (March–
    April)
Santa Cruz area (March–
    May)

Rose rock cress

SAGE, HUMMINGBIRD or CRIMSON PITCHER SAGE
Salvia spathacea
Mint family

DESCRIPTION: 1–2.5 feet. Stout, white-woolly stem with opposite pairs of crinkly, white-woolly, toothed leaves and widely separated whorls of crimson, two-lipped flowers (to 1.5 inches) subtended by purplish bracts. California endemic.

NOTE: With the red, long-tubular flowers that produce copious nectar, these flowers are indeed hummingbird (and human) seducers.

HABITAT: Coastal scrub, chaparral, oak woodlands (to 2,500 feet); found on central and south coast and coast ranges, Central Valley, Transverse Ranges.

WHERE AND WHEN:
Santa Monica Mountains (March–May)
Santa Lucia Range (March–May)
Point Magu State Park (March–May)
Cachuma Lake Recreational Area (March–June)
Montana del Oro (March–June)
Mount Diablo (April–June)

Hummingbird sage

STAR-TULIP, LARGE-FLOWERED
Calochortus uniflorus
Lily family

DESCRIPTION: 2–6 inches. One showy (to 1.5 inches), mostly erect, pink flower raised barely above the ground on a short stem. Three broad, rounded petals between and below that show three narrower, pink sepals.

NOTE: Neither closed in a globe (for example, fairy lantern, p. 235) nor wide open (for example, Leichtlin's mariposa lily, p. 459) this species of *Calochortus* has petals demurely partly curled up, both revealing and concealing the reproductive parts within.

HABITAT: Damp grasslands, stream banks (to 1,800 feet); found in northwest mountains, north and central coast ranges.

WHERE AND WHEN:
Bear Valley/Walker Ridge (March–May)
Santa Lucia Range (March–May)
Point Lobos (March–May)

Ring Mountain (March–June)
Mount Tamalpais (March–June)
Salt Point (March–June)

Large-flowered star-tulip

STAR TULIP, OAKLAND   *Calochortus umbellatus*
Lily family

DESCRIPTION: 3–10 inches. Umbel-like (hence the species name) clusters of 3 to 12 open, bowl-shaped flowers (to 1 inch). Three pale pink, lavender, or white petals with small purple spots or splotches at base. California endemic. CNPS Rare and Endangered List—endangered.

NOTE: This rare, delicate, pink or white mariposa lily has to play second fiddle on Ring Mountain to its even rarer, larger, showier kin, the Tiburon mariposa lily (p. 416), which blooms a couple of months later.

HABITAT: Open, usually serpentine woodlands, grasslands (300–2,100 feet); found in north and central coast ranges.

WHERE AND WHEN:

Ring Mountain (March–April)
Red Mountain North (March–April)
Muir Woods (March–April)
Leonard Lake (March–April)
Mount Diablo (March–May)
Santa Cruz Mountains (April–June)

Oakland star-tulip

VERBENA, PURPLE SAND or
COMMON SAND VERBENA
Abronia umbellata
Four O-Clock family

DESCRIPTION: 1–3 feet. Prostrate, spreading stem with short stalks bearing umbels of eight to 27 trumpet-shaped, lavender-pink flowers. Leaves egg-shaped or diamond-shaped, not succulent.

NOTE: The non-succulent leaves of this species are an indication that it is less suited to withstanding the desiccating winds of the foredunes on the shore than its succulent relatives *A. latifolia* (p. 320) and *A. maritima* (p. 101)—it is found in the more protected areas a bit inland.

HABITAT: Dunes, coastal scrub (to 350 feet); found on coast.

WHERE AND WHEN:
Nipomo-Guadalupe Dunes (March–October)
Manchester Beach (March–October)
Torrey Pines (March–October)
Point Reyes (March–October)
Morro Bay (March–October)
MacKerricher State Park (March–October)

Purple sand verbena

WHISKERBRUSH
Leptosiphon ciliatus or *Linanthus ciliatus*
Phlox family

DESCRIPTION: 1–10 inches. Dwarf plant terminating in a head of several tiny, star-shaped, long-tubed flowers. Yellow flower tube flaring into five pink petal lobes, each with a red-purple spot or triangle at base.

NOTE: The odd, deeply lobed leaves with the narrow segments fringed with tiny hairs apparently reminded someone of an old-fashioned whiskerbrush.

HABITAT: Grasslands (to 10,000 feet); found in much of California.

WHERE AND WHEN:
Traverse Creek Botanical Area (March–April)
Santa Lucia Range (April–May)
Hite's Cove Trail (March–April)

Whiskerbrush

San Emigdio Range (April–May)
Anza-Borrego (March–April)
Meiss Meadows at Carson Pass (June–July)

BARBERRY, COAST or
WAVY-LEAF BARBERRY   *Berberis pinnata* or *Mahonia pinnata*
Barberry family

DESCRIPTION: 1–3 feet. Evergreen shrub with stems often climbing or resting on tree branches. Clusters of many bright yellow flowers (to one-fourth inch) with many sepals and petals.

NOTE: The complex flowers have nine sepals in three whorls of three and six

similar petals in two whorls of three. The new leaves are glossy and red-tinged.

HABITAT: Woodlands, rocky slopes (to 4,000 feet); found in northwest mountains, coast, coast ranges, Transverse Ranges.

WHERE AND WHEN:
San Bruno Mountain (March–May)
Channel Islands (March–May)
Bodega Head (March–May)
Santa Monica Mountains (March–May)
Stinson Beach (March–May)
Santa Lucia Range (March–May)

Coast barberry

Blazing star

BLAZING STAR   *Mentzelia laevicaulis*
Loasa family

DESCRIPTION: 1–4 feet. Stout, whitish, branching stem with several very large (to 6 inches), star-shaped flowers. Five pointed, bright yellow petals. Cluster of many long, silky yellow stamens.

NOTE: You can almost feel the heat when you find a large cluster of these plants in full, radiant bloom.

HABITAT: Sandy or rocky slopes and flats, washes (to 8,500 feet); found in much of California (except the Central Valley and the Sonoran Desert).

WHERE AND WHEN:
Carrizo Plain (March–April)
Topaz Lake (May–June)
Santa Lucia Range (May–June)
Hite's Cove Trail (June)
Trinity Alps (June–July)
San Gabriel Mountains (June–September)

BLAZING STAR, LINDLEY'S   *Mentzelia lindleyi*
Loasa family

DESCRIPTION: 0.5–2 feet. Much-branched stem bearing several stunning, five-petaled flowers (to 2 inches), each shiny yellow petal with a large, red patch at the base. Lobed, comblike leaves. California endemic.

NOTE: When these dazzling flowers form a large colony on a rocky hillside, the rock appears to have gone molten!

HABITAT: Rocky places, hillsides (to 4,000 feet); found in central and south coast ranges, San Joaquin Valley.

WHERE AND WHEN:
SR-58—east side of Temblor Range (March–April)
San Francisco Bay area (March–April)
Mount Hamilton Range (March–April)

Henry Coe St. Park (March–May)
Sunol Regional Park (March–May)
Topanga State Park (March–May)

Lindley's blazing star

BROOMRAPE, CLUSTERED   *Orobanche fasciculata*
Broomrape family

DESCRIPTION: 2–8 inches. Clusters of 5 to 20 tubular, yellow (sometimes purplish) flowers on long pedicels. Five petal lobes somewhat diamond shaped. No green leaves—a parasite.

NOTE: Despite the common name, this species of broomrape doesn't usually parasitize "brooms" (shrubs in the Pea family), but rather prefers buckwheat, sagebrush, or Aster family members.

HABITAT: Dry, sandy or gravelly flats; chaparral (to 10,000 feet); found in much of California.

WHERE AND WHEN:
Camp Nine Road (March–April)
Channel Islands (March–April)
Nipomo-Guadalupe Dunes (March–July)
Santa Monica Mountains (April–July)
Trinity Alps (May–July)
Lassen National Park (June–July)

Clustered broomrape

Butter-and-eggs

BUTTER-AND-EGGS or
JOHNNY TUCK   *Triphysaria eriantha* subsp. *eriantha*
Broomrape family (previously included in Snapdragon family)
DESCRIPTION: 2–14 inches. Spike of many long-tubular, two-lipped flowers. Narrow tube and throat white. Two upper petal lobes form purple beak; three lower lobes are swollen yellow sacs.
NOTE: These unusual, ground-hugging flowers (often with goldfields) can carpet Central Valley plains and foothill slopes with acres of golden yellow.
HABITAT: Grasslands (to 4,300 feet); found in much of California (except northeast corner, deserts, and eastern edge).
WHERE AND WHEN:
Vina Plains Preserve (March–April)
Boggs Lake (March–April)
Phoenix Park (March–April)
Jepson Prairie Preserve (March–May)
Nipomo-Guadalupe Dunes (March–May)
Santa Lucia Range (March–May)

COREOPSIS, GIANT or
GIANT SEA DAHLIA   *Leptosyne gigantea* or *Coreopsis gigantea*
Aster family
DESCRIPTION: 2–10 feet. Shrub with stout, thick, treelike trunk topped by tufts of light green, finely divided leaves and many sunny yellow flower heads (to 3 inches). Ten to 16 rays surround yellow-orange disk.
NOTE: The flowers are certainly large, but the *gigantea* undoubtedly refers to the hefty plant itself, whose treelike trunk holds the flowers high off the ground.
HABITAT: Coastal dunes, bluffs, scrub (to 200 feet); found on central and south coast.

WHERE AND WHEN:
Santa Monica Mountains
  (March–May)
Nipomo-Guadalupe Dunes
  (March–May)
Leo Carillo Beach (March–
  May)
San Luis Obispo area
  (March–May)
Channel Islands (March–
  May)
Pismo Beach (March–May)

Giant coreopsis

CREAM CUPS
Platystemon californicus
Poppy family

DESCRIPTION: 4–12 inches. One flat or shallow bowl-shaped flower (to 1.5 inches) atop hairy stem. Six yellow-tinged, creamy white petals.

NOTE: The buds are as beautiful and intriguing as the flowers—hairy, maroon, nodding cylinders. The flowers are subtly fragrant.

Cream cups

HABITAT: Grasslands, sandy soil (to 3,000 feet); found in much of California (except northeast corner).
WHERE AND WHEN:
Bear Valley (March–April)
Salt Point (March–April)
Carrizo Plain (March–May)
Red Hill Road (March–April)
Anza-Borrego (April–May)
Pinnacles (April–May)

DAHLIA, SEA   *Leptosyne maritima* or *Coreopsis maritima*
Aster family

DESCRIPTION: 1–3 feet. Several hollow stems rise well above the leaves and bear two to four terminal flower heads (to 1.5 inches) with 15–20 yellow rays surrounding a yellow disk. Leaves are fleshy and divided into needle-like segments. CNPS Rare and Endangered List—rare in California.

NOTE: Though rare in the state and highly limited in distribution, in some places (for example, Torrey Pines) these large, showy flowers decorate coastal bluffs with great patches of bright yellow.

HABITAT: Bluffs (to 75 feet); found on south coast.

WHERE AND WHEN:
Torrey Pines (March–May)
Imperial Beach (March–May)
Point Loma (March–May)
Otay Mountain (March–May)
Oceanside area (March–May)
Cabrillo National Monument
     (March–May)

Sea dahlia

DAISY, HILLSIDE or
COMMON MONOLOPIA   *Monolopia lanceolata*
Aster family

DESCRIPTION: 0.5–1.5 feet. Simple or branched stem with several bright-yellow flower heads (to 1.5 inches) with unlobed or slightly lobed rays. Narrow leaves opposite on lower stem and alternate on upper stem. Forms great masses. California endemic.

NOTE: The great fields of this bright, sunny yellow flower on the slopes of

Hillside daisy

the Temblor Range are one of central California's great floral landmarks of spring.

HABITAT: Grasslands, woodlands (to 4,000 feet); found in south coast ranges, San Joaquin Valley, southern foothills, Transverse Ranges, Peninsular Ranges, Mojave Desert.

WHERE AND WHEN:
Greenhorn Mountains (March–April)
Wind Wolves Preserve (March–May)
SR-58 (March–May)
Cuyama Valley (March–May)
Carrizo Plain (March–May)
Tehachapi Mountains (March–May)

DAISY, WALLACE'S WOOLLY

Eriophyllum wallacei or *Antheropeas wallacei*

Aster family

DESCRIPTION: 1–7 inches. Tufted plant with branching stems with tiny, rectangular or spoon-shaped, white-hairy leaves and a solitary, bright yellow flower head (to 0.5 inches). Five to 10 rays surround yellow disk.

Wallace's wooly daisy

NOTE: Although this *is* a woolly daisy, it can't hold a "hair" to its close relative, Pringle's woolly sunflower (p. 319), where you can't even see the leaves for the woolliness!

HABITAT: Sagebrush scrub, sandy flats, washes, woodlands (to 6,500 feet); found east of the Sierra, in the Transverse Ranges, Peninsular Ranges, Mojave Desert, Sonoran Desert.

WHERE AND WHEN:
Joshua Tree (March–April)
Anza-Borrego (March–April)

Mojave National Preserve (March–May)
Antelope Valley (March–May)
Alabama Hills (April–May)
San Jacinto Mountains (April–May)

LINANTHUS, GOLDEN or GOLDEN DESERT TRUMPETS
Leptosiphon aureus subsp. *aureus* or *Linanthus aureus*
Phlox family
DESCRIPTION: 2–6 inches. Threadlike, branching stems with tiny, needle-like, three- to seven-lobed leaves that appear to surround the stem. One or clusters of several funnel-shaped flowers (to 0.5 inches) with flaring, golden yellow lobes.

Golden
linanthus

NOTE: These delicate "aureus" flowers often create extensive carpets on desert floors—as if someone had poured liquid gold onto the sand.
HABITAT: Sandy flats (to 6,500 feet); found east of the Sierra, in the Transverse Ranges, Mojave Desert, Sonoran Desert.
WHERE AND WHEN:
Alabama Hills (March–April)
Anza-Borrego (March–April)
Joshua Tree (March–April)
Antelope Valley (March–April)
Mojave National Preserve (March–April)
Cuyama Valley (March–April)

LIVE FOREVER or CANYON DUDLEYA or
ROCK LETTUCE   *Dudleya cymosa*
Stonecrop family
DESCRIPTION: 4–12 inches. Cluster of two to 20 vaselike, bright yellow flowers with reddish sepals. Rosette of succulent leaves. California endemic.
NOTE: Even without the flowers, this is a stunning plant, with its large, beau-

tifully symmetrical rosette of fleshy, succulent leaves. Before the bright yellow petals open, the flowers are still striking with their scarlet or orange, teardrop sepals.

HABITAT: Cliffs, rocky outcrops, ledges (to 9,000 feet); found in coast ranges, foothills, Cascades, Sierra, Transverse Ranges.

WHERE AND WHEN:
Hite's Cove Trail (March–April)
San Bernardino Mountains (March–April)
Carrizo Plain (March–May)
Buttermilk Bend Trail (March–June)
King's Canyon/Sequoia (April–May)
Feather River Canyon (May–June)

Live forever

MALLOW, APRICOT or DESERT HOLLYHOCK *Sphaeralcea ambigua*
Mallow family

DESCRIPTION: 1–3 feet. Clusters of bowl-shaped flowers (to 2 inches) in leaf axils at intervals along stem. Five intense orange or apricot or reddish, separate or overlapping petals cradling the central column of reproductive parts. Large, crinkly, woolly leaves.

NOTE: You might want to avoid touching the stem and leaves, as they are covered with irritating hairs.

HABITAT: Desert scrub (to 8,200 feet); found east of the Sierra, in the Mojave Desert, Sonoran Desert.

WHERE AND WHEN:
Anza-Borrego (March–April)
Joshua Tree (March–April)
Death Valley (March–May)

Apricot mallow

Alabama Hills (April–May)
Haiwee Reservoir (April–May)
Topaz Lake (May–June)

MOHAVEA, LESSER or GOLDEN
DESERT SNAPDRAGON
Mohavea breviflora

Plantain family (previously included in Snapdragon family)

DESCRIPTION: 2–8 inches. Glandular plant with slender stem densely packed with alternating (almost whorled), fleshy, tonguelike leaves. Solitary yellow, two-lipped flowers nestled in leaf axils. Lower lip swollen and red-spotted.

NOTE: The species name refers to the Mojave River, where specimens were first collected, but it also tells you to look in the Mojave Desert for this little spot of sunshine.

HABITAT: Gravelly flats, washes (to 4,600 feet); found in Mojave Desert.

Lesser mohavea

WHERE AND WHEN:
Death Valley (March–April)
Mojave National Preserve
    (March–April)
Baker area (March–April)
El Paso Mountains (March–
    April)
Red Rock Canyon State Park
    (March–April)
Last Chance Range (March–May)

MONKEYFLOWER, COMMON YELLOW
Mimulus guttatus

Lopseed family (previously included in Snapdragon family)

DESCRIPTION: 0.5–3 feet. Many yellow, two-lipped flowers (to 1.5 inches) with red spots in throat. Upper leaves often fuse around the stem.

NOTE: After pollination, the petals and the stamens fall off, leaving only the swelling ovary and the calyx and the now-closed stigma at the tip of the style still on the plant.

HABITAT: Wet meadows, stream banks, seeps (to 10,000 feet); found in much of California.

WHERE AND WHEN:
Channel Islands (March–April)

Anza Borrego (March–May)
Table Mountain (March–
  May)
Carrizo Plain (March–
  September)
Modoc Plateau (May–July)
King's Canyon/Sequoia
  (June–August)

Common yellow monkeyflower

MONKEYFLOWER, WIDE-THROATED *Mimulus brevipes*
Lopseed family (previously included in Snapdragon family)
DESCRIPTION: 1–2.5 feet. Stout, unbranched, sticky-hairy stem with pairs of

opposite leaves on lower stem and narrow, clasping, pointed leaves on the upper stem. Pairs of showy, lemon yellow flowers (to 1.5 inches) on short pedicels out of leaf axils.

NOTE: These large flowers seem even larger framed by the narrow leaves of the upper stem.

HABITAT: Chaparral, burn areas (to 7,100 feet); found on south coast and coast ranges, Transverse Ranges, Peninsular Ranges.

WHERE AND WHEN:
San Gabriel Mountains
  (March–April)
Santa Rosa Plateau (March–
  April)

Wide-throated monkeyflower

Santa Ynez Mountains (March–April)
Palomar Mountain (March–April)
Figueroa Mountain (March–April)
Point Loma (March–April)

MULE EARS, EL DORADO

Wyethia reticulata or
Agnorhiza reticulata

Aster family

DESCRIPTION: 1–2 feet. Solitary flower heads (to 2 inches) atop unbranched, often reddish stems. Ten to 21 bright yellow rays around a yellow or orange disk. Triangular leaves with very distinct, often reddish veins. California endemic. CNPS Rare and Endangered List—endangered.

NOTE: The species name *reticulata,* meaning "netted," refers to the very distinct venation of the leaves.

HABITAT: Chaparral, woodlands (1,000–1,500 feet); found in foothills in El Dorado County.

WHERE AND WHEN:
Pine Hill Ecological Reserve
  (March–April)
Folsom Lake area (March–April)
Shingle Springs (March–April)

El Dorado mule ears

PEPPERGRASS, YELLOW

Lepidium flavum

Mustard family

DESCRIPTION: 4–16 inches. Usually prostrate plant forming dense mats of lemon-yellow, four-petaled flowers. Basal rosette of narrow, spoon-shaped leaves.

NOTE: In years of good rain, these spreading mats can cover large areas of the desert floor with greenish-yellow carpets.

HABITAT: Sandy, desert flats (to 4,600 feet); found east of the Sierra, in Mojave Desert, Sonoran Desert.

WHERE AND WHEN:
Alabama Hills (March–April)
Red Rock Canyon (March–April)

Yellow peppergrass

Death Valley (March–April)
Lancaster area (March–May)
San Felipe Valley (March–June)
White Mountains (April–May)

POPPY, ANNUAL or TUFTED POPPY *Eschscholzia caespitosa*
Poppy family
DESCRIPTION: 2–12 inches. Funnel-shaped or bowl-shaped flower with four separate, orange or yellow petals. Two fused sepals usually shed by blooming time. California endemic.

NOTE: These gorgeous, satiny poppies often cloak entire hillsides, sometimes growing with their larger-flowered kin, the California poppy, p. 116 (which has a distinctive platform under the flower that annual poppy doesn't have).

HABITAT: Grasslands (to 5,000 feet); found in much of California (except northeast corner, deserts, and eastern edge).

WHERE AND WHEN:
Hite's Cove Trail (March–April)
Santa Ana Mountains (March–April)

Annual poppy

Table Mountain (March–April)
Santa Lucia Range (March–April)
Red Hill Road (March–April)
Santa Gabriel Mountains (April–May)

POPPY, DESERT GOLD
Poppy family

Eschscholzia glyptosperma

DESCRIPTION: 2–14 inches. Usually several stems above basal, bluish-green, lacy leaves deeply dissected into linear segments. Solitary, four-petaled, cup-shaped, bright yellow flowers (to 2 inches) at tips of long, leafless stalk.

NOTE: The cheerful golden flowers are showcased both by their long, leafless stem and by the blue-green backdrop of the basal leaves.

HABITAT: Sandy or gravelly flats, washes (to 5,000 feet); found in Mojave Desert, Sonoran Desert.

WHERE AND WHEN:
Mojave National Preserve
    (March–April)
Salt Wells Canyon (March–
    April)
Death Valley (March–April)
Ridgecrest area (March–
    April)
Granite Mountains (March–
    April)

Desert gold poppy

Joshua Tree (March–May)

PRETTY FACE
Brodiaea family (previously included in Lily family)

Triteleia ixioides

DESCRIPTION: 0.5–1.5 feet. Large, loose umbels of four to seven golden-yellow, star-shaped flowers (to 1 inch). Six tepals with dark purple or black mid-veins. Long, grasslike leaves.

NOTE: There are several subspecies of this golden-flowered plant, some inhabiting the foothills, some the coast, and some the high mountains.

HABITAT: Dry flats and slopes, grassland, forest edges (to 10,000 feet); found in northwest mountains, coast and coast ranges, foothills, Cascades, Sierra.

WHERE AND WHEN:
Hite's Cove Trail (March–April)
Pinnacles (April–May)
Mount Shasta (May–June)
Trinity Alps (May–June)
Shirley Canyon in Tahoe (June–July)
King's Canyon/Sequoia (July)

Pretty face

PRIMROSE, BEACH *Camissonia cheiranthifolia*

Evening primrose family

DESCRIPTION: 0.5–2 feet. Prostrate or ascending stem that can form dense mats. Bright yellow flowers (to 1 inch) nestled in large, oval, fleshy, gray-green leaves. Four separate, overlapping petals. Flowers open at dawn and bloom for only one day.

NOTE: Although the stems can be more than a foot long, they sprawl across the sand, so the flowers are only slightly elevated. The bright yellow petals age pink or purple.

HABITAT: Beaches, dunes (to 300 feet); found on coast.

WHERE AND WHEN:
Monterey Peninsula (March–May)
Nipomo-Guadalupe Dunes (March–June)
Santa Monica Mountains (March–July)

Beach primrose

Salt Point (April–June)
Dunes at Arcata (April–July)
Manchester Beach (May–August)

SEDUM, DWARF CLIFF or SIERRA MOCK STONECROP
Sedella pumila or *Parvisedum pumilum*
Stonecrop family

DESCRIPTION: 2–10 inches. Ground-hugging plant with two or more sprays of tiny, five-petaled, star-shaped, yellow flowers. Succulent leaves braided into tight "lanyards."

NOTE: In rocky flats and around the edges of vernal pools, this plant can form nearly solid mats.

HABITAT: Rocky flats and outcrops, edges of vernal pools (to 4,000 feet); found in coast ranges, foothills, Central Valley.

WHERE AND WHEN:

Red Hill Road (March–April)
Wapona Falls Trail in Yosemite (March–May)
Napa area (March–May)
Table Mountain (April–May)
upper Bidwell Park (April–May)
Hell's Half-Acre (April–May)

Dwarf sedum

SENNA, DESERT
Senna armata or *Cassia armata*
Pea family

DESCRIPTION: 1–3 feet. Shrub with pinnately compound leaves with two to four leaflets. Racemes of many pinwheel-like, fragrant flowers (to 1 inch). Five golden yellow petals. Not the typical pea flower, but with typical pea pods. Twigs end in weak spines.

NOTE: The plant is leafless most of the year (greatly reducing evaporation), so the stems do most of the photosynthesizing.

HABITAT: Sandy or gravelly washes (to 3,300 feet); found in Mojave Desert, Sonoran Desert.

WHERE AND WHEN:
Anza-Borrego (March–April)
Joshua Tree (March–June)
Mojave National Preserve
    (April–May)
Yaqui Well (April–May)
Death Valley (April–May)
Red Rock Canyon State Park
    (April–June)

Desert senna

SKUNK CABBAGE, YELLOW   *Lysichiton americanus*
Arum family

DESCRIPTION: 1–2 feet. Large, cylindrical spike of tiny yellow-green flowers atop stout, fleshy stalk, which is enveloped on one side by a bright yellow

sheath (spathe). Enormous (1–5 feet), glossy, mostly erect leaves.

NOTE: The shiny yellow spathe, the gigantic leaves, and the decaying odor easily distinguish this plant.

HABITAT: Marshy areas in woods (to 4,300 feet); found on north and central coast and coast ranges.

WHERE AND WHEN:
Redwoods National Park
    (March–May)
Jughandle State Reserve
    (March–May)
Prairie Creek Redwoods
    State Park (March–May)

Yellow skunk cabbage

Russian Gulch State Park (March–May)
Patrick Point State Park (March–May)
Santa Cruz Mountains (March–June)

SUN CUP, CALIFORNIA or
MUSTARD EVENING PRIMROSE   *Camissonia californica*
Evening primrose family

DESCRIPTION: 0.5–3 feet. A few scattered, bright yellow, four-petalled flowers (to 1 inch) on short stalks. Tiny, red dots at base of petals. Very narrow, toothed leaves.

NOTE: Being a morning person will help you see these flowers in full bloom, as they usually close by early afternoon.

HABITAT: Sandy or gravelly flats, scrub, grasslands, burn areas (to 5,000 feet); found on coast and coast ranges, San Joaquin Valley, Transverse Ranges, Peninsular Ranges, Mojave Desert, Sonoran Desert.

California sun cup

WHERE AND WHEN:
Anza-Borrego (March–April)
Channel Islands (March–May)
San Gabriel Mountains (March–May)
Malibu Creek State Park (March–May)
Santa Rosa Plateau (March–June)
Santa Ynez Mountains (March–June)

SUN CUP, SOUTHERN   *Camissonia bistorta*
Evening primrose family

DESCRIPTION: 2–30 inches. Usually prostrate plant with radiating stems and narrow, slightly toothed leaves. Shallow, bowl-shaped, four-petalled, bright yellow flowers (to 1 inch) with one or two striking red spots at base of each petal.

NOTE: With the startling red dots on the bright yellow petals, you might imagine these flowers are keeping a careful "eye" on you as you approach.

HABITAT: Coastal scrub, chaparral (to 2,000 feet); found on south coast and in coast ranges, Transverse Ranges, Peninsular Ranges.
WHERE AND WHEN:
Torrey Pines (March–June)
Santa Monica Mountains
  (March–June)
Santa Rosa Plateau (March–
  June)
San Gabriel Mountains
  (March–June)
Point Loma (March–June)
Malibu Creek State Park
  (March–June)

Southern sun cup

TIDY TIPS, FREMONT'S
Layia fremontii

Aster family
DESCRIPTION: 2–12 inches. One flower head (to 1.5 inches) atop stem with three to 15 ray flowers, each with three shallow lobes, and four to 100 disk flowers. Rays yellow at base and white at tips. California endemic.
NOTE: These flowers usually form great masses, sometimes of an acre or

more—a taste of what the great Central Valley "sea" of flowers once looked like.
HABITAT: Grasslands (to 2,000 feet); found in north and central coast ranges, Central Valley, foothills.
WHERE AND WHEN:
Jepson Prairie Preserve
  (March–April)
Edgewood Preserve (March–
  April)
Vina Plains Preserve
  (March–April)
SR-36 east of Red Bluff
  (March–April)
Red Hill Road (March–April)
Ring Mountain (May–June)

Fremont's tidy tips

TWINBERRY   *Lonicera involucrata*
Honeysuckle family

DESCRIPTION: 2–10 feet. Shrub with pairs of tubular, cylindrical flowers cradled by leafy bract. Petals yellow, usually tinged with red or orange.

NOTE: This plant is dazzling in fruit—the pairs of dark black-purple, round berries are nestled in the bract, now turned purple or red.

HABITAT: Moist scrub, woodlands (to 10,800 feet); found on coast, in coast ranges, Sierra, northeast corner.

WHERE AND WHEN:

San Bruno Mountain (March–May)

Salt Point (March–May)

Nipomo-Guadalupe Dunes (March–May)

Modoc Plateau (April–June)

Santa Lucia Range (April–June)

Paige Meadows in Tahoe (July–August)

Twinberry   Twinberry

VIOLET, DOUGLAS   *Viola douglasii*
Violet family

DESCRIPTION: 2–10 inches. Usually several slender, leafless stalks with a single terminal, golden yellow flower (to 1.5 inches) at tip of each. Leaves pinnately divided into small, narrow segments.

NOTE: These large flowers are sometimes partly hidden in the grass, but their golden petals or their maroon backs will surely catch your attention, no matter what direction you approach them from.

HABITAT: Grassy, rocky areas (to 7,000 feet); found in northwest mountains, coast ranges, San Joaquin Valley, foothills, Cascades, Transverse Ranges, Peninsular Ranges.

WHERE AND WHEN:
Table Mountain (March–May)
Bartlett Springs Road (March–May)
Bear Valley (March–May)
SR-36 east of Red Bluff (March–May)
Santa Lucia Range (March–May)
Sutter Buttes (March–May)

Douglas violet

WALLFLOWER, DUNE   *Erysimum insulare*
Mustard family

DESCRIPTION: 2–24 inches. Subshrub or perennial with often-reddish stem and scattered, narrow, smooth-edged leaves. Conical or spherical raceme thick with showy, four-petaled, yellow flowers (to 1.5 inches). Long, narrow, four-sided or flattened fruit. California endemic.

NOTE: This species of wallflower is limited in distribution to coastal dunes south of San Francisco (including the Channel Islands).

HABITAT: Coastal dunes (to 1,000 feet); found on central and south coast.

WHERE AND WHEN:
Morro Bay (March–May)
Channel Islands (March–May)
Montana de Oro (March–May)

Dune wallflower

Nipomo-Guadalupe Dunes (March–June)
Point Arguello (March–June)
Point Magu (March–June)

WHISPERING BELLS, YELLOW *Emmenanthe penduliflora*
Borage family (previously included in Waterleaf family)

DESCRIPTION: 6–12 inches. Finely hairy, sticky stems with long, narrow, clasping, toothed leaves and clusters of creamy yellow, bell-shaped flowers that are erect at first, then drooping. Large, pointed, hairy sepals cradle the bells.

NOTE: These beautiful bells usually remain on the stem after they've dried, rustling in the summer breezes.

HABITAT: Scrub, chaparral, burn areas, desert flats (to 7,200 feet); found on coast and in coast ranges, San Joaquin Valley, central and southern foothills, central and southern Sierra, east of the Sierra, Transverse Ranges, Peninsular Ranges, Mojave Desert, Sonoran Desert.

WHERE AND WHEN:
Anza-Borrego (March–May)
Channel Islands (March–
    June)
White Mountains (April–
    May)
Santa Monica Mountains
    (April–May)
Santa Rosa Plateau (April–June)
Santa Cruz Mountains (April–July)

Yellow whispering bells

YELLOW CUPS *Camissonia brevipes*
Evening primrose family

DESCRIPTION: 2–30 inches. Broad, dark-green basal leaves with red veins underneath. Numerous bowl-shaped, four-petaled, bright yellow flowers (to 1.5 inches) nodding on terminal raceme and on pedicels out of leaf axils.

NOTE: These dazzling yellow flowers usually start blooming when the plant

is only a few inches tall; in years of good rain, the plant can lengthen considerably as the blooming continues.

HABITAT: Sandy or rocky flats and slopes, washes, desert scrub (to 6,000 feet); found east of the Sierra, Mojave Desert, Sonoran Desert.

WHERE AND WHEN:
Death Valley (March–April)
Mojave National Preserve
  (March–April)
Anza-Borrego (March–April)
Fish Slough (March–April)
Whipple Mountains (March–
  May)
Joshua Tree (March–May)

Yellow cups

AMSONIA or WOOLLY BLUE STAR   *Amsonia tomentosa*
Dogbane family

DESCRIPTION: 6–16 inches. Several stems with umbel-like cluster of starfish-like (although with five-petal lobes), whitish (sometimes tinged bluish or greenish), fragrant flowers (to 0.5 inches). Alternating broad diamond-shaped leaves. Milky sap.

Amsonia

NOTE: The stems and leaves are covered with matted white hairs, giving the plant a soft, pastel, almost ghostly look.

HABITAT: Sandy or gravelly flats, canyons (to 6,000 feet); found in Transverse Ranges, Mojave Desert, Sonoran Desert.

WHERE AND WHEN:
Joshua Tree (March–May)
Mojave National Preserve (March–May)
San Bernardino Mountains (March–May)
Last Chance Range (March–May)
Granite Mountains (March–May)
Old Woman Mountains (March–May)

BRODIAEA, HYACINTH or WHITE BRODIAEA   *Triteleia hyacinthina*
Brodiaea family (previously included in Lily family)
DESCRIPTION: 0.5–3 feet. One densely flowered umbel of 10–40 white flowers (to three-fourths inch) atop stiff stem. Six tepals bright white (sometimes blue-tinged) with green or black-purple mid-veins.

NOTE: This is one of the few white-flowered species of brodiaeas, but its flowers pay some homage to the other colors with their colorful mid-veins.

HABITAT: Grasslands, wet meadows, stream banks, vernal pools (to 7,200 feet); found in much of California (except northeast corner and deserts).

Hyacinth brodiaea

WHERE AND WHEN:
Phoenix Park (March–April)
San Bernardino Mountains (March–April)
Santa Lucia Range (April–May)
Boggs Lake (April–May)
Edgewood Preserve (April–June)
Trinity Alps (June–July)

BUCKBRUSH or WEDGELEAF CEANOTHUS   *Ceanothus cuneatus*
Buckbrush family
DESCRIPTION: 3–7 feet. Shrub with short, stiff branches heavy with clumps of small, creamy white or pale blue, fuzzy flowers. Sweetly fragrant.
NOTE: These shrubs, often so heavily laden with flowers that you can hardly

see the stems or leaves, are a stunning display of cream and fragrance.

HABITAT: Rocky slopes and ridges, forest edges (up to 6,000 feet); found in much of California (except northeast corner, Central Valley, and deserts).

WHERE AND WHEN:

Santa Lucia Range (March–April)

Santa Monica Mountains (March–April)

Camp Nine Road (March–May)

King's Canyon/Sequoia (April–May)

Six Rivers National Forest (April–May)

El Portal west of Yosemite (April–May)

Buckbrush

BUTTERCUP, WATERFALL

Ranunculus hystriculus or *Kumlienia hystricula*

Buttercup family

DESCRIPTION: 3–10 inches. One or two flat flowers (to three-fourths inch) atop stem usually with five or six pure white, petal-like sepals. Fruits with hooked beaks. Round or kidney-shaped, scalloped leaves. California endemic.

NOTE: There are five to 12 odd, paddlelike structures angling up and away from the sepals. You might think these are stamens, but strangely they are actually the true petals!

Waterfall buttercup

HABITAT: Stream banks, wet places among rocks (1,000–6,000 feet); found in foothills, Sierra.
WHERE AND WHEN:
Hite's Cove Trail (March–April)
Quarry Trail (March–April)
Stevens Trail (April–May)
Folsom Lake area (April–May)
Feather River Canyon (April–May)
Hetch Hetchy area in Yosemite (April–May)

CACTUS, COMMON FISHHOOK
Cactus family
DESCRIPTION: 2–12 inches. One or several cylindrical or round swollen stems covered with spines. A few creamy white or greenish-yellow flowers (to 1.5 inches across) with many petals and sepals. Red, cylindrical fruit.
NOTE: Each bump on the stem is topped by a cluster of five to 15 bristles, the central one curved at the end like a fishhook.
HABITAT: Coastal and desert scrub, washes (to 5,000 feet); found on south coast, in Peninsular Ranges, Sonoran Desert.
WHERE AND WHEN:
Torrey Pines (March–April)
Anza-Borrego (March–April)
Point Loma (March–April)
San Jacinto Mountains (March–April)
Vallecito Stage Station (March–April)
Chuckwalla Mountains (March–April)

Mammillaria dioica

Common
fishhook cactus

CHICKWEED, FIELD
Pink family
DESCRIPTION: 3–18 inches. Mat-forming, tufted or erect branching stems with several bright white flowers at tips. Five deeply notched petals, often with faint greenish veins.

Cerastium arvense

Field chickweed

NOTE: Despite its common occurrence and wide distribution, this chickweed is a delight to find, for its white petals seem to be just a notch brighter than most other white flowers.

HABITAT: Grassy fields, bluffs, seeps, shaded places (to 8,000 feet); found in northwest mountains, north and central coast and coast ranges, foothills, Sierra.

WHERE AND WHEN:
San Bruno Mountain
(March–May)
Salt Point (March–June)
Point Reyes (March–June)
Santa Lucia Range (April–May)
Vernal Falls Trail in Yosemite
(May–June)
Trinity Alps (June–July)

CHICORY, DESERT   *Rafinesquia neomexicana*
Aster family

DESCRIPTION: 6–24 inches. Showy flower heads (to 1.5 inches) with 12–18 white or creamy ray flowers only. Mostly basal leaves but also tiny, clasping stem leaves with triangular, basal lobes. Milky sap. Plant resembles white tackstem (p. 249) but without the glands on the stems.

NOTE: The flower heads have a very delicate look with their symmetrical, overlapping, straplike rays, each with five narrow teeth.

HABITAT: Sandy or gravelly flats (to 5,000 feet); found in Mojave Desert, Sonoran Desert.

WHERE AND WHEN:
Mojave National Preserve
(March–April)
Death Valley (March–April)

Desert chicory

Mission Creek Preserve (March–April)
Anza-Borrego (March–April)
El Paso Mountains (March–April)
Joshua Tree (March–May)

CHINESE HOUSES, WHITE or STICKY
CHINESE HOUSES or TINCTURE PLANT   *Collinsia tinctoria*
Plantain family (previously included in Snapdragon family)

DESCRIPTION: 0.5–2 feet. Several separated whorls of showy, two-lipped, tubular flowers (to 1 inch) on upper part of stem. Petal lobes greenish-white or yellowish with purple dots or lines.

NOTE: The leaves turn bronze or scarlet at the end of the blooming season.

HABITAT: Open woods, rocky places (2,000–8,000 feet); found in northwest mountains, north coast and coast ranges, foothills, Cascades, Sierra.

WHERE AND WHEN:
Red Hill Road (March–April)
Yosemite Falls Trail (April–June)
Bodega Head (April–July)
Traverse Creek (May–June)
Yankee Jim's Road (May–June)
Drum Powerhouse Road
    (May–June)

White Chinese houses

CUCUMBER, COAST or COAST MANROOT or
OLD-MAN-IN-THE-GROUND   *Marah oreganus*
Gourd family

DESCRIPTION: 3–20 inches. Small, somewhat starfishlike, creamy white flowers scattered on long, twisting vine. Very large, dark-green leaves with five to seven shallow, sharp-pointed lobes. Cucumberlike fruit with small or no prickles.

NOTE: The alternative common names refer to the very large, woody root that can weigh as much as 20 pounds.

HABITAT: Shrubby bluffs, canyons, forest edges (to 6,000 feet); found in northwest mountains, north and central coast and coastal ranges.

Coast cucumber

WHERE AND WHEN:
Salt Point (March–April)
Point Reyes (March–April)
Jenner-Fort Ross area
(March–April)
San Bruno Mountain
(March–May)
Santa Cruz Mountains
(March–May)
Redwood National Park
(April–May)

EVENING SNOW
Phlox family

Linanthus dichotomus

DESCRIPTION: 2–8 inches. Pinwheel-like, pure white flowers (to 1.5 inches) unfurling out of slender tube. Light pink or purple shading on back of petals. Fragrant.

Evening snow

NOTE: Suddenly at about 4:00 p.m., the blooms unfurl and the ground that appeared flowerless before is now covered with floral "snow" (see photo, p. 66, in the Alabama Hills).

HABITAT: Dry, often rocky flats (to 5,000 feet); found in much of California (except northeast corner).

WHERE AND WHEN:
Traverse Creek Botanical
Area (March–April)
Anza-Borrego (March–April)
Alabama Hills (March–
April)

Carrizo Plain (March–May)
Santa Cruz Mountains (March–May)
Tuolumne R. Canyon in Yosemite (April–June)

FIESTA FLOWER, WHITE *Pholistoma membranaceum*

Borage family (previously included in Waterleaf family)

DESCRIPTION: 0.5–3 feet. Weak, sprawling, prickly stem with arrow-shaped leaves and terminal cymes of two to 10 flat, white flowers (to 0.5 inches).

Often purple spots on petals. Green sepals show through petal lobes.

NOTE: This weak-stemmed plant often clings to other plants for support. (In the photo there is a mutual intertwining with desert mistletoe.)

HABITAT: Beaches, bluffs, desert washes, woodlands (to 4,600 feet); found in much of central and southern California (except Sierra and east of the Sierra).

WHERE AND WHEN:

Joshua Tree (March–April)
Antelope Valley (March–April)
Santa Lucia Range (March–April)
Torrey Pines (March–April)
Anza-Borrego (March–April)
Carrizo Plain (March–May)

White fiesta flower

FRITILLARY, FRAGRANT *Fritillaria liliacea*

Lily family

DESCRIPTION: 4–15 inches. One or a few bowl-shaped flowers (to 2 inches) hanging from short, down-curving pedicels. Six creamy white tepals usually with faint, yellowish-green stripes. California endemic. CNPS Rare and Endangered List—endangered.

NOTE: The common name may lead you to get down on your hands and knees to smell these beautiful blooms, but the flowers are usually odorless or only slightly sweetly fragrant.

HABITAT: Grasslands (below 750 feet); found on central coast and coast ranges, Sacramento Valley.

WHERE AND WHEN:
Point Reyes (March–April)
Coyote Ridge (March–April)
Jepson Prairie Preserve
    (March–April)
Edgewood Preserve (March–
    April)
Annadel State Park (March–
    April)
Big Sur (March–April)

Fragrant fritillary

GLOBE LILY, WHITE or FAIRY LANTERN   *Calochortus albus*
Lily family

DESCRIPTION: 1–3 feet. Several globelike flowers (to 1.5 inches), each hanging upside-down at end of pedicel arching from leaf axil. Three white pet-

als with pink nectary at base; three narrower, greenish sepals. California endemic.

NOTE: Although these globes remain mostly closed, the flower gives a hint of its treasure to insects as the pink nectaries show through the translucent petals.

HABITAT: Shady woodlands, scrubby slopes (to 5,000 feet); found in central and south coast ranges, foothills, Transverse Ranges.

WHERE AND WHEN:
Hite's Cove Trail (March–
    April)
Channel Islands (March–
    April)

White globe lily

Buttermilk Bend Trail (March–April)
Table Mountain (April–May)
Big Sur (April–May)
Santa Monica Mountains (April–May)

GRAVEL GHOST
Aster family   *Atrichoseris platyphylla*

DESCRIPTION: 0.5–5 feet. Branching, hollow stem above egg-shaped, purple-splotched, toothed, basal leaves. Terminal flower heads (to 0.5 inches) with 20–40 white, five-toothed rays only. Milky sap. Pleasant fragrance.

NOTE: The tall, slender grayish stems tend to blend in with the desert background, so it often looks like these lovely flower heads are floating free above the desert floor.

HABITAT: Sandy or gravelly flats, washes (to 4,600 feet); found in Mojave Desert, Sonoran Desert.

WHERE AND WHEN:
Death Valley (March–April)
Joshua Tree (March–April)
Mojave National Preserve (March–April)

Gravel ghost

Algodones Dunes (March–April)
Anza-Borrego (March–April)
Coachella Valley (March–April)

HELIOTROPE, ALKALI or
SALT HELIOTROPE
Heliotropium curassavicum
Borage family
DESCRIPTION: 4–24 inches. Prostrate or erect stem with scorpionlike coils crammed with bell-shaped, white flowers (to one-fourth inch) with yellowish-purple star in throat. Gray-green, tonguelike, fleshy leaves.
NOTE: In dry years, this plant may produce a couple of modest coils of flowers, but in wet years—yikes, the octopi are invading!
HABITAT: Moist or dry alkaline soils (to 6,700 feet); found in much of California.
WHERE AND WHEN:
Channel Islands (March–May)
Torrey Pines (March–May)
Anza-Borrego (March–May)
White Mountains (March–September)
Carrizo Plain (March–October)
Nipomo-Guadalupe Dunes (March–October)

Alkali
heliotrope

JOSHUA TREE
Yucca brevifolia
Agave family (previously included in Lily family)
DESCRIPTION: 3–40 feet. Tree usually well-branched with clusters of long, narrow, sharp-pointed leaves. Dense, cylindrical raceme of many waxy, cream (sometimes green-tinged), bell-shaped flowers (to 3 inches) at tip of branches. Leaves not peeling at edges.
NOTE: This plant is considered the best indicator of the Mojave Desert, not being able to survive in the hotter, drier Sonoran Desert.

Joshua tree

HABITAT: Sandy or gravelly flats and slopes (1,500–6,600 feet); found in eastern Sierra, east of the Sierra, Mojave Desert.

WHERE AND WHEN:

Ripley Desert Woodland
    (March–May)
Joshua Tree (April–May)
Tehachapi Mountains (April–
    May)
Mojave National Preserve
    (April–May)
White Mountains (April–
    May)
Death Valley (April–May)

Joshua tree

KNOTWEED, DUNE   *Polygonum paronychia*
Buckwheat family

DESCRIPTION: 1–3 feet. Prostrate or erect subshrub with small (to one-fourth inch), white or pale pink flowers tucked into clusters of stiff, narrow, pointed leaves. Five narrow, petal-like sepals, often with green midvein. Eight tiny stamens.

NOTE: The flowers sit comfortably among the clusters of leaves, a bit like royalty on a throne.

HABITAT: Dunes, coastal scrub (to 160 feet); found in north and central coast.

WHERE AND WHEN:
Monterey Peninsula (March–June)
Bodega Head (March–August)
mouth of the Russian River (March–August)
Manchester Beach (March–August)
San Bruno Mountain (May–June)
Humboldt Bay (May–August)

Dune knotweed

LAYIA, WHITE

Layia glandulosa

Aster family

DESCRIPTION: 6–12 inches. Reddish stems with sticky-hairy, narrow leaves and flower heads (to 2 inches) with three to 14 white rays surrounding yellow disk.

NOTE: Each ray has three rounded lobes; with a little imagination (okay, maybe a lot), you can see a white dove with wings furled.

HABITAT: Sandy or gravelly flats (to 7,800 feet); found on central and south coast and in coast ranges, northeast corner, San Joaquin Valley, Cascades, Sierra, east of the Sierra, Transverse Ranges, Peninsular Ranges, Mojave Desert, Sonoran Desert.

White layia

Alabama Hills (March–May)
Antelope Valley (March–May)
Carrizo Plain (March–May)
Mojave National Preserve (March–June)
Joshua Tree (March–June)
White Mountains (March–June)

LILY, GLASS   *Triteleia lilacina*
Brodiaea family (previously included in Lily family)
DESCRIPTION: 6–15 inches. Loose umbel with a few small (to 0.5 inches), white, six-tepaled flowers. Edges of tepals often somewhat rolled inward.

NOTE: Look closely at the flowers on a sunny day, and you will see the reason for the common name—the base of the tepals has tiny, glass-like bubbles that reflect the sun's glare, creating a noticeable glint or sparkle.
HABITAT: Grasslands, volcanic mesas (to 1,500 feet); found in Sacramento Valley, foothills.

Glass lily

WHERE AND WHEN:
Table Mountain (March–April)
upper Bidwell Park (March–April)
Jepson Prairie Preserve (March–April)
Vina Plains Preserve (March–April)
SR-36 east of Red Bluff (March–April)
Red Hill Road (March–April)

LINANTHUS, WHITE GOLDEN   *Leptosiphon aureus* subsp. *decorus*
                              or *Linanthus aureus* subsp. *decorus*
Phlox family
DESCRIPTION: 1–12 inches. Slender, wiry, branched stem with scattered tubular flowers (to 0.5 inches) with bright white, flaring-petal lobes. Purple throat and yellow anthers. Leaves with three to seven segments.
NOTE: It probably seems odd to call this "white, golden," but it is a white subspecies of the yellow-flowered golden linanthus (p. 212).

White golden
linanthus

HABITAT: Sandy flats (to 6,500 feet); found in south and central coast ranges, east of the Sierra, Mohave Desert, Sonoran Desert.

WHERE AND WHEN:
Alabama Hills (March–April)
Volcanic Hills (March–April)
Dos Cabezas (March–April)
Anza-Borrego (March–April)
Joshua Tree (March–April)
Carrizo Plain (March–July)

LUPINE, WHITE WHORLED *Lupinus microcarpus var. densiflorus* or *L. densiflorus* var. *densiflorus*

Pea family

DESCRIPTION: 2–3 feet. Stout, at least somewhat hairy stalk with long raceme of several separate whorls of white pea flowers. Leaves with seven to 11 broad, pointed leaflets. California endemic.

NOTE: This species of lupine has wide color variation, often with white flowers but sometimes with yellow, pink, dark rose, lavender, or blue-purple ones.

HABITAT: Dry, open flats and slopes, also roadsides—sometimes planted (to 5,200 feet); found in northwest mountains, coast and coast ranges, Sacramento Valley, foothills, Transverse Ranges.

WHERE AND WHEN:
SR-49 north of Coulterville (March–April)
Carrizo Plain (March–April)
Santa Lucia Range (March–April)

Point Reyes (March–April)
Santa Rosa Plateau (April–
    May)
Santa Cruz Mountains
    (April–July)

White whorled lupine

MANZANITA, SAN BRUNO   *Arctostaphylos imbricata*
Heath family

DESCRIPTION: 0.5–2 feet. Low mats or mounds of round, overlapping leaves and clusters of hanging, urn-shaped flowers (to one-fourth inch). Glandular, sticky, applelike fruits. California endemic. CNPS Rare and Endangered List— seriously endangered.

NOTE: The mats of this plant can extend for several feet; the species extends only as far as San Bruno Mountain and environs.

HABITAT: Coastal scrub (500– 1500 feet); found in central coast ranges.

WHERE AND WHEN:

only on *San Bruno Mountain*
    and neighboring hills
    (March–April)

San Bruno manzanita

MEADOWFOAM, DOUGLAS   *Limnanthes douglasii*
Meadowfoam family

DESCRIPTION: 4–12 inches. Several shallow bowl-shaped flowers (to 1.5 inches) with five separate white petals, often with yellow and/or rose at the base and fine purplish or rose veins. Usually forms dense mats of "foam" in wet areas.

NOTE: There are several subspecies of this meadowfoam with varying color characteristics.

HABITAT: Wet meadows, stream banks, vernal pools (to 3,200 feet); found on coast, in coast ranges, Central Valley, foothills.

WHERE AND WHEN:
Table Mountain (March–May)
Santa Lucia Range (March–May)
Phoenix Park (March–May)
Salt Point (March–May)
Jepson Prairie Preserve (March–May)
Santa Cruz Mountains (March–May)

Douglas meadowfoam

MUSTANG CLOVER   *Leptosiphon montanus* or *Linanthus montanus*
Phlox family

DESCRIPTION: 4–24 inches. Several long-tubed flowers (to 2 inches) in terminal cluster of bristly, hairy bracts. Five-petal lobes white or pink with triangular, purple spot at base. Tube yellow at throat. California endemic.

NOTE: With the bright white or soft pink-petal lobes, the intensely purple spots, and the orange anthers, this flower is quite a rainbow all by itself!

HABITAT: Grasslands, woodlands (to 6,700 feet); found in foothills.

WHERE AND WHEN:
Hite's Cove Trail (March–April)
Breckenridge Mountain (March–April)
Wards Ferry Road (March–April)

Greenhorn Range (March–April)

Traverse Creek Botanical Area (March–April)

King's Canyon/Sequoia (May–July)

Mustang clover

NEMOPHILA, FIVE-SPOT or FIVE-SPOT   *Nemophila maculata*

Borage family (previously included in Waterleaf family)

DESCRIPTION: 4–12 inches. Branching, bristly-hairy stem with solitary, five-petaled flowers (to 1.5 inches) at tips of slender pedicels from leaf axils. White flowers with purple veins and purple blotch at tip of each petal. California endemic.

Five-spot nemophila

NOTE: These gorgeous flowers just weren't satisfied with the usual nemophila monochrome—they insisted on some splashes of purple to enliven the white.

HABITAT: Grasslands, woodlands, roadbanks (to 9,000 feet); found in Central Valley, foothills, Sierra, Transverse Ranges.

WHERE AND WHEN:
Red Hill Road (March–April)
Groveland area (March–April)
San Bernardino Mountains (March–April)
Greenhorn Range (April–June)
Hodgdon Meadow in Yosemite (May–July)
King's Canyon/Sequoia (May–July)

NEMOPHILA, VARI-LEAF or
WHITE NEMOPHILA   *Nemophila heterophylla*
Borage family (previously included in Waterleaf family)

DESCRIPTION: 4–16 inches. Weak, brittle stems often form extensive, tangled masses in the shade under trees and shrubs. Shallow bowl-shaped flowers (to 0.5 inches). Five overlapping white petals.

NOTE: *Nemophila* is a wonderfully descriptive name for this genus, since many of its species are indeed lovers (*phila*, filia) of the shady grove (*nemo*).

HABITAT: Shady places in grasslands and on scrubby slopes, canyons (to 5,000 feet); found in northwest mountains, coast and coast ranges, Central Valley, foothills, Cascades, Sierra.

Vari-leaf nemophila

WHERE AND WHEN:
Hite's Cove Trail (March–April)
Santa Lucia Range (March–April)
Buttermilk Bend Trail (March–April)
Santa Cruz Mountains (March–April)
Bodega Head (March–April)
Mount Diablo (March–April)

ONION, GLASSY   *Allium hyalinum*
Onion family (previously included in Lily family)

DESCRIPTION: 0.5–1 foot. Loose umbel of six to 15 star-shaped flowers (to 0.5 inches) atop stem. Six rounded, white or pink tepals with darker midvein. Pink ovary. Two to three fingerlike leaves shorter than the stem. California endemic.

NOTE: As the common name suggests, the tepals of this onion have a glassy shine that adds sparkle and allure.

HABITAT: Grasslands (to 5,000 feet); found in central coast ranges, San Joaquin Valley, foothills.

WHERE AND WHEN:
Table Mountain (March–April)
Greenhorn Range (March–April)
Mount Diablo (March–April)
Milton Road (March–April)
Electra Road (March–April)
Merced River Canyon in Yosemite (March–May)

Glassy onion

OUR LORD'S CANDLE or
CHAPARRAL YUCCA   *Hesperoyucca whipplei* or *Yucca whipplei*
Agave family (previously included in Lily family)

DESCRIPTION: 4–12 feet. Stout flower stalk rises above basal rosette of

Our Lord's candle   Our Lord's candle

spine-tipped, swordlike leaves up to 3 feet long. Dense raceme up to 4 feet of showy, fragrant, creamy flowers (to 1.5 inches).

NOTE: These amazing plants rise well above most of their neighbors, showing off the stalk of creamy white flowers against the often blue sky. The main plant dies after fruiting, but spreads by stolons.

HABITAT: Coastal scrub, chaparral (to 5,000 feet); found in south coast ranges, southern Sierra, east of the Sierra, Transverse Ranges, Mojave Desert.

WHERE AND WHEN:
Santa Monica Mountains (March–July)
Aqua Tibia Mountains (April–May)
San Gabriel Mountains (April–June)
Santa Rosa Plateau (April–June)
Kern Plateau (April–June)
Cuyama Valley (May–June)

PINCUSHION, DESERT or
FREMONT'S PINCUSHION   *Chaenactis fremontii*
Aster family

DESCRIPTION: 4–16 inches. Mostly leafless stem rising above basal rosette of usually pinnately lobed leaves. Dome-shaped, terminal head (to 1 inch) of many white disk flowers only, the outer ones with flaring lobes.

NOTE: Although this flower head has only disk flowers, they are still very showy with their flaring, almost raylike lobes on the outer flowers.

HABITAT: Sandy or gravelly flats and slopes (to 3,500 feet); found in south coast ranges, San Joaquin Valley, east of the Sierra, Mojave Desert, Sonoran Desert.

WHERE AND WHEN:

Anza-Borrego (March–April)
Alabama Hills (March–April)
Antelope Valley (March–April)
Carrizo Plain (March–April)
Red Rock Canyon (March–April)
Joshua Tree (March–May)

Desert pincushion

POPCORN FLOWER, RUSTY   *Plagiobothrys nothofulvus*
Borage family

DESCRIPTION: 8–20 inches. Usually branching stem with small, coiled racemes of several bright white flowers (to 0.5 inches). Small flower tube flaring into five rounded, overlapping petal lobes; creamy rim around throat.

NOTE: Since the stems often blend in with their environment and so are difficult to see, a patch of these flowers dancing in the breeze may indeed remind you of a large platter of popping popcorn.

Rusty popcorn flower

HABITAT: Grasslands, woodlands (to 4,700 feet); found in much of California (except northeast corner and east of the Sierra).

WHERE AND WHEN:
Buttermilk Bend Trail (March–April)
Bodega Bay (March–April)
Santa Ana Mountains (March–April)
Table Mountain (March–May)
Carrizo Plain (March–May)
Santa Monica Mountains (March–May)

SAGE, BLACK

Salvia mellifera

Mint family

DESCRIPTION: 3–6 feet. Shrubby plant with opposite pairs of narrow, crinkly leaves and spikes of long, tubular, white or pale blue, two-lipped flow-

ers in whorls. The leaves, especially when crushed, emit a strong, pungent, minty fragrance.

NOTE: The species name means "honey-bearing," so walking through a sunny, chaparral hillside thick with these plants can be a vivid bee-and-mint experience!

HABITAT: Coastal scrub, chaparral, woodlands (to 4,000 feet); found on central and southern coast and in coast ranges, Transverse Ranges, Peninsular Ranges.

WHERE AND WHEN:
Torrey Pines (March–May)
San Francisco Bay area (March–May)
Santa Monica Mountains (March–June)
Santa Rosa Plateau (March–June)
Temblor Range (March–July)
Channel Islands (March–July)

Black sage

TACKSTEM, WHITE

Calycoseris wrightii

Aster family

DESCRIPTION: 6–15 inches. Showy flower heads (to 2 inches) with 15–25 white ray flowers only, which are usually purple-tinged underneath and have five teeth at the tip. Stems with stalked glands. Pinnately divided leaves with long, narrow segments. Milky sap.

NOTE: Although the flower heads resemble those of desert chicory (p. 231), the common name points to this plant's distinguishing characteristic—tiny, tacklike glands on the stem.

HABITAT: sandy or gravelly flats, washes (to 4,000 feet); found in Mojave Desert, Sonoran Desert.

WHERE AND WHEN:
Death Valley (March–April)
Anza-Borrego (March–April)
Joshua Tree (March–April)
Mojave National Preserve
    (March–May)
San Felipe Valley (March–May)
Ocotillo Wells (March–May)

White tackstem

THIMBLEBERRY　　　　　　　　　*Rubus parviflorus*
Rose family

DESCRIPTION: 2–7 feet. Shrub with branching, hairy stem with clusters of four to seven white, bowl-shaped flowers (to 2.5 inches) with five separate, crinkly petals. Large, slightly prickly, toothed, maplelike leaves. Red or salmon-colored, raspberrylike fruit.

NOTE: "Raspberrylike" is the magic word—these thimble-shaped, red fruits are sweet and tasty (though perhaps a bit drier than most raspberries).

HABITAT: moist forest shade (to 9,000 feet); found in much of California (except Central Valley, east of the Sierra, and deserts).

WHERE AND WHEN:
Mount Tamalpais (March–July)

Thimbleberry

Salt Point (March–July)
Palomar State Park (June–July)
Shirley Canyon in Tahoe (July–August)
King's Canyon/Sequoia (July–August)
Santa Lucia Range (July–August)

WALLFLOWER, FRANCISCAN   *Erysimum franciscanum*
Mustard family
DESCRIPTION: 0.5–2 feet. One or several stems with long racemes of four-petalled, creamy or yellow flowers. Narrow, rough-toothed leaves along

Franciscan wallflower

stem. Flattened seed pods. California endemic. CNPS Rare and Endangered List—endangered.

NOTE: The species name refers to this uncommon plant's very limited distribution—the Bay Area and some of the nearby coast and coast ranges.

HABITAT: rocky outcrops, dunes (to 1,700 feet); found on north and central coast and coast ranges.

WHERE AND WHEN:
San Bruno Mountain (March–April)
Mount Tamalpais (March–April)
Coyote Ridge (March–April)
Point Reyes (March–April)
Mount Hamilton Range (March–April)
north bank of Russian River (March–May)

YERBA MANSA   *Anemopsis californica*
Lizard's-tail family
DESCRIPTION: 0.5–2 feet. Hollow, usually leafless stem with one terminal conelike raceme of white flowers above five to eight flaring, petal-like bracts.
NOTE: The large, petal-like parts are actually bracts, as are the small, white, tonguelike parts in the cone—there are no actual petals.
HABITAT: seep springs, alkali soil (to 5,500 feet); found on central and south

coast and in coast ranges, Central Valley, east of the Sierra, Mojave Desert, Sonoran Desert.

WHERE AND WHEN:
Channel Islands (March–April)
Torrey Pines (March–April)
Alabama Hills (March–April)
Anza-Borrego (March–April)
Nipomo-Guadalupe Dunes (March–September)
White Mountains (April–July)

Yerba mansa

MISSION BELLS or CHECKER LILY
Fritillaria affinis

Lily family

DESCRIPTION: 0.5–4 feet. Several large (to 1.5 inches), nodding, bell-shaped flowers on short pedicels from leaf axils. Thick, fleshy, brown-purple tepals mottled yellow. One to four whorls of two to eight grasslike leaves.

NOTE: These striking flowers always have multicolored tepals, but it is rather difficult to tell whether they are brown-purple mottled yellow, or yellow-green mottled purple.

HABITAT: grasslands, woodlands (to 6,000 feet); found in northwest mountains, coast and coast ranges, Cascades, Sierra foothills.

WHERE AND WHEN:
San Bruno Mountain (March–April)
Mix Canyon (March–April)
Mount Tamalpais (March–April)
Santa Lucia Range (March–April)
Bodega Head (March–May)
Mount Diablo (March–May)

Mission bells

ORCHID, STREAM   *Epipactis gigantea*
Orchid family

DESCRIPTION: 1–3 feet. Stout stem with clasping, pointed leaves and three to nine multicolored flowers that arch mostly off the same side of the stem. Upper two petals pinkish, three sepals yellowish green, third petal

yellow-green with red-purple veins and mottling.

NOTE: In this orchid, the different perianth part (the third petal) is broader and more colorful than the other five parts.

HABITAT: seeps, wet meadows, stream banks (to 7,500 feet); found in much of California (except northeast corner and Central Valley).

WHERE AND WHEN:
Alabama Hills (March–May)
Santa Lucia Range (March–May)
White Mountains (March–May)
Death Valley (March–May)
along Albion River (April–May)
near Philo along Navarro River (April–May)

Stream orchid

PARSNIP, LACE   *Lomatium dasycarpum*
Carrot family

DESCRIPTION: 4–20 inches. Hairy, thick, purplish stem bearing densely flowered umbels of tiny, greenish flowers. Fernlike leaves.

NOTE: The flower heads often appear multicolored, as on some of the flowers the white hairs on the petals make the greenish flowers appear whiter.

HABITAT: grasslands, rocky (usually serpentine) outcrops (to 5,200 feet); found in coast ranges, Central Valley, foothills, Peninsular Ranges.

WHERE AND WHEN:
San Bruno Mountain (March–May)
Santa Lucia Range (March–May)
Mount Tamalpais (March–May)
Gabilan Range (March–May)
Santa Rosa Plateau (March–June)
Lake Sonoma area (March–June)

Lace parsnip

NON-NATIVE BOUQUETS

First Bouquet

Winter vetch

Winter Vetch
Vicia villosa
Pea family

DESCRIPTION: Long raceme of down-sweeping, blue-purple flowers.

EXAMPLE OF LOCATION: *Malibu Lagoon State Park.*

Robert's geranium

Robert's Geranium
Geranium robertianum
Geranium family

DESCRIPTION: Five separate pink or red-purple petals with darker rose splotches or veins.

EXAMPLE OF LOCATION: Elk area.

(First bouquet, continued)

Clasping henbit

Henbit, Clasping
Lamium amplexicaule
Mint family

DESCRIPTION: Whorls of red-purple or pink, tubular flowers with canopy upper lip; opposite pairs of scalloped leaves.

EXAMPLE OF LOCATION: Ponderosa Way.

High mallow

Mallow, High
Malva sylvestris
Mallow family

DESCRIPTION: Five pink petals with darker rose stripes. Petals notched at tip.

EXAMPLE OF LOCATION: *Santa Monica Mountains.*

Second Bouquet

Sweet Pea, Perennial
Lathyrus latifolius
Pea family

DESCRIPTION: Large, magenta or pink pea flowers along vine with flattened, winged stem. Tendrils.

EXAMPLE OF LOCATION: Feather River Canyon.

Perennial sweet pea

Spring Vetch
Vicia sativa
Pea family

DESCRIPTION: Tendriled, climbing plant with one to three rose or pink-purple pea flowers.

EXAMPLE OF LOCATION: *Santa Ana Mountains.*

Spring vetch

(Second bouquet, continued)

Scotch broom

Scotch Broom
Cytisus scoparius
Pea family

DESCRIPTION: Invasive shrub with angled stems, large, yellow pea flowers (often with red wings).

EXAMPLE OF LOCATION: Fort Bragg area.

Spanish broom

Spanish Broom
Spartium junceum
Pea family

DESCRIPTION: Invasive shrub with bright yellow, fragrant pea flowers

EXAMPLE OF LOCATION: *San Bernardino Mountains*

(Second bouquet, continued)

Moth Mullein
Verbascum blattaria
Snapdragon family

DESCRIPTION: Tall, stout stalk with long raceme of flat, yellow or white flowers; filaments covered with feathery, purple hair.

EXAMPLE OF LOCATION: Electra Road

Moth mullein

Wild Garlic or Onion Weed
Allium triquetrum
Onion family (previously included in Lily family)

DESCRIPTION: Umbel of hanging, creamy white, six-tepaled flowers with green mid-veins.

EXAMPLE OF LOCATION: Fort Bragg area

Wild garlic

APRIL

Five-spot nemophila along Red Hill Road

WHAT MARCH PROMISES in the foothills, April delivers. The explosion of spring color that began in most places in the foothills in mid-March reaches its culmination throughout April. The hills and flats become canvases of gold, blue, purple, or white, painted artistically with patches, ribbons, and dabbles of all the colors of the rainbow. The warm April sun ignites the colors and liberates the fragrances, bringing to life not only the fields and hills but the insects and birds and the human eye.

But April's gifts are not limited to the foothills: slopes and high valleys in the coast ranges and in the lower elevations of the northwest mountains are now at their absolute peak blooming; the Central Valley, though past its peak bloom, has a last spectacular downingia surprise; the Mojave Desert is still peaking or is in glorious afterglow; the coast is well on its way toward its May blooming surge; mid-mountain meadows (for example, in the Lake Tahoe Basin) are awakening from winter with buttercups and violets; and the Great Basin Desert to the east of the Sierra and Cascades is celebrating in peach and phlox. April showers may bring May flowers, but April in California up to about 6,500 feet also has its own glorious bloom.

Highlights

Northwest Mountains

Bleeding heart, candyflower, red larkspur, Tolmie's pussy ears, and **creek dogwood** in the Trinity Alps

Beaches and Bluffs Along the Coast

Western blue-eyed grass, Tolmie's pussy ears, yellow bush lupine, and **sea thrift** at Salt Point

Coast Ranges

Purple owl's-clover, tidy tips, scarlet bugler, and **thistle sage** at Shell Creek off SR-58
Desert dandelion, Parry's larkspur, common phacelia, goldfields, and **hillside daisy** at the Carrizo Plain
The rare **Mount Diablo globe lily** on Mount Diablo

Central Valley

Ithuriel's spear, blue dicks, folded downingia, and **two-horned downingia** at Phoenix Park

Folded downingia, fringed downingia, and **toothed downingia** at Jepson Prairie

Foothills

Five-spot nemophila, goldfields, and **bird's-eye gilia** at Red Hill Road
Annual poppy, purple owl's clover, Chinese houses, mustang clover, live forever, harlequin lupine, and **twining snake lily** along Hite's Cove Trail
Bleeding heart at Drum Powerhouse Road
Giant-leaf balsamroot at Pine Hill Preserve
The rare **Kern County larkspur** along the Kern River Canyon

East of the Sierra

Sandblossoms, desert dandelion, scarlet locoweed, evening snow, desert calico, and **purple mat** in the Alabama Hills
Desert peach and **long-leaf phlox** at Topaz Lake
Grape-soda lupine at the California Desert Conservation Area

Deserts

An incredible orange ocean of **California poppy** in and around Antelope Valley
Monet paintings of **Bigelow's coreopsis, spider lupine, California poppy,** and **globe gilia** on the Gorman Hills
Engleman's hedgehog cactus, beavertails, and **fishhook cactus** at Anza-Borrego
Canterbury bells at Joshua Tree

Flowers

DEER BRUSH
Buckbrush family
Ceanothus integerrimus

DESCRIPTION: 1–15 feet. Shrub with long, dense, fuzzy clusters of blue, violet, or white sweetly fragrant flowers. Oval, deciduous leaves. Flexible stems.

NOTE: This lovely shrub can form tall thickets or dense, ground-hugging mats. In either case, the neighboring air is likely to be filled with a delicious, grapelike aroma.

HABITAT: Dry slopes, ridges (to 7,000 feet); found in northwest mountains, coast ranges, foothills, Cascades, Sierra, Transverse Ranges, Peninsular Ranges.

WHERE AND WHEN:
Pine Hill Preserve (April–May)
San Jacinto Mountains (April–May)
Santa Ana Mountains (April–May)
Santa Lucia Range (April–May)
Trinity Alps (May–June)
Feather River Canyon (May–June)

Deer brush

DOWNINGIA, FOLDED
Bellflower family
Downingia ornatissima

DESCRIPTION: 3–12 inches. Small, two-lipped flowers with two narrow, pale blue or blue-purple petal lobes in the upper lip and three broader lobes of similar color in the lower lip with a large white patch. Yellow-green spots or bars and dark purple splotch toward throat. California endemic.

NOTE: The distinguishing feature of this downingia is the folding back of the two narrow, upper petal lobes.

HABITAT: Vernal pools and mud flats (to 1,000 feet); found in Central Valley, foothills.

WHERE AND WHEN:
Jepson Prairie Preserve
(April–May)
Phoenix Park (April–May)
Hell's Half Acre (April–May)
Maidu Interpretive Center
(April–May)
Arena Plains (April–May)
Mather Field (April–May)

Folded downingia

DOWNINGIA, FRINGED   *Downingia concolor*
Bellflower family

DESCRIPTION: 2–6 inches. Small, two-lipped flowers with two narrow, blue, upper petal lobes and three broader, blue and white lower lobes. Short, delicate fringes along the margins of the upper lobes; square, velvety, purple spot at the base of the lower lip. California endemic.

NOTE: These gorgeous, multicolored flowers often form dense and extensive mats along the edges of drying vernal pools.

HABITAT: Vernal pools and mud flats (to 4,600 feet); found in north and central coast ranges, Sacramento Valley, Peninsular Ranges.

Fringed downingia

WHERE AND WHEN:
Jepson Prairie Preserve (April–May)
Diablo Range (April–May)
Rohnert Park (April–May)
Santa Lucia Range (April–May)
Spring Lake (April–May)
Sonoma Valley Regional Park (April–May)

DOWNINGIA, TOOTHED   *Downingia cuspidata*
Bellflower family

DESCRIPTION: 2–6 inches. Small, two-lipped flowers with two narrow, blue petal lobes in the upper lip and three broader, blue and white lobes in the lower lip. Two yellow spots within the white patch at the base of the lower lip. California endemic.

NOTE: This species is distinguished by the lack of purple spots or splotches.

HABITAT: Vernal pools and mud flats (to 2,800 feet); found in northwest mountains, coast ranges, Central Valley, foothills, Peninsular Ranges.

WHERE AND WHEN:
Jepson Prairie Preserve (April–May)
Santa Lucia Range (April–May)
Table Mountain (April–May)
Santa Rosa Plateau (April–May)
Phoenix Park (April–May)
Boggs Lake (May–June)

Toothed downingia

DOWNINGIA, TWO-HORNED   *Downingia bicornuta*
Bellflower family

DESCRIPTION: 2–6 inches. Small, two-lipped flowers with two narrow, blue petal lobes in the upper lip and three broader blue lobes in the lower lip. Large white patch on lower lip with two yellow-green spots; purple "nipples" at throat.

NOTE: The lower stems of this species are usually decumbent, often forming great, ground-choking masses of flowers.

HABITAT: Vernal pools, mud flats (to 6,000 feet); found in north coast ranges, Central Valley, foothills, Cascades, Sierra, northeast corner.

WHERE AND WHEN:
Phoenix Park (April–May)
Arena Plains (April–May)
Mather Field (April–May)
Lake Britton area (April–
    May)
Boggs Lake (May–June)
Modoc Plateau (May–July)

Two-horned downingia

FLAX, WESTERN BLUE   *Linum lewisii*

Flax family

DESCRIPTION: 1–3 feet. Many pinwheel-like flowers (to 1.5 inches) along weak, wiry stems. Five separate, broad, blue petals with darker veins, especially at the base.

NOTE: The petals fall off shortly after blooming and dry a darker color, so you can often find the ground at the base of the plants littered with beautifully dark-blue crumples.

Western blue flax

HABITAT: Dry slopes and ridges, grassy fields to 11,000 feet); found in much of California.

WHERE AND WHEN:
Pinnacles (April–May)
San Jacinto Mountains (May–June)
east of Monitor Pass (May–June)
Modoc Plateau (May–June)
Mount Pinos (May–July)
Lake Forest in Tahoe (June–July)

INDIGO BUSH, MOJAVE   *Psorothamnus arborescens*
Pea family

DESCRIPTION: 2–4 feet. Much-branched shrub thick with pinnately compound leaves with small, nearly opposite leaflets and lupinelike racemes of many deep blue-purple pea flowers (to 0.5 inches). Red or red-purple calyx. Fruit with scattered glands.

NOTE: The deep blue-purple of the petals is even more intense in contrast with the red or red-purple calyx.

HABITAT: Canyons, washes, gravelly slopes (to 6,200 feet); found east of the Sierra, Transverse Ranges, Mojave Desert.

WHERE AND WHEN:
San Bernardino Mountains
  (April–May)
Alabama Hills (April–May)
Death Valley (April–May)
Mojave National Preserve
  (April–May)
near Big Pine (April–May)
Joshua Tree (April–May)

Mojave indigo bush

LARKSPUR, PARRY'S or
SAN BERNARDINO LARKSPUR   *Delphinium parryi*
Buttercup family

DESCRIPTION: 1–3 feet. Long raceme of three to 60 flowers (to 1.5 inches) on one-fourth to 1.5-inch ascending pedicels. Five blue sepals usually cupped slightly forward at the tips. Mostly straight nectar spur. Four small, white petals somewhat hairy. A few deeply divided leaves with narrow segments.

Parry's larkspur

NOTE: With its many large flowers on relatively short pedicels, the flowers are usually quite crowded on the stem.

HABITAT: Grasslands, chaparral, open woodlands (to 8,500 feet); found on central and southern coast and in coast ranges, Transverse Ranges, Peninsular Ranges.

WHERE AND WHEN:
Carrizo Plain (April–May)
Channel Islands (April–May)
Point Loma (April–May)
Mount Hamilton Range
   (April–June)
Gabilan Range (April–June)
Santa Monica Mountains
   (June–July)

LARKSPUR, ROYAL   *Delphinium variegatum*
Buttercup family

DESCRIPTION: 1–2 feet. Upper stem with loose racemes of 4 to 25 large (to 1.5 inches) deep-blue flowers. Nectar spur is more-or-less straight. Upper petals are whitish; the lower are blue and hairy. California endemic.

Royal larkspur

NOTE: These large, incredibly deep-blue flowers are a royal sight indeed as they bring stately beauty to spring-lush fields.

HABITAT: Grassland, forest openings (to 2,600 feet); found on coast, coast ranges, Central Valley, foothills, Cascades.

WHERE AND WHEN:
Jepson Prairie Preserve (April)
Bear Valley (April–May)
Santa Lucia Range (April–May)
Channel Islands (April–May)
Pinnacles (April–June)
Table Mountain (April–June)

LUPINE, GRAPE SODA or ADONIS LUPINE or
MOUNTAIN BUSH LUPINE
Lupinus excubitus

Pea family

DESCRIPTION: 0.5–6 feet. Subshrub or shrub with silvery-hairy stems and leaves. Palmately compound leaves with seven to 10 leaflets. Violet or lavender flowers with bright yellow patch on banner turning purple with age. Frequent fire follower.

NOTE: Finding a massive colony of these beauties is as much a treat for the nose as for the eyes.

HABITAT: Dry slopes and flats (to 10,000 feet); found in south coast ranges, southern Sierra, east of the Sierra, Transverse Ranges, Peninsular Ranges, Mojave Desert, Sonoran Desert.

WHERE AND WHEN:

California Desert Conservation Area (April–June)
Gorman Hills (April–June)
San Bernardino Mountains (April–June)
San Gabriel Mountains (April–June)
Tehachapi Mountains (April–June)
Death Valley (April–June)

Grape soda lupine

LUPINE, SEASIDE   *Lupinus littoralis*
Pea family

DESCRIPTION: 1–2 feet. Branching, usually prostrate stems with loose raceme of whorls of pea flowers. Blue wings and white or purple banner or blue

banner with large white patch. Banner shorter than wings. Silvery hairy leaves with five to nine narrow leaflets.

NOTE: This plant can form shrublike mounds, but often stretches out loosely over the sand, leaving blue and white floral "footprints" on the beach.

HABITAT: Beaches (to 300 feet); found on north and central coast.

WHERE AND WHEN:
Jenner-Fort Ross area
   (April–May)
Bodega Head (April–May)
Point Reyes (April–May)
Fort Bragg area (April–May)
Anchor Bay (April–May)
Point Arena (April–May)

Seaside lupine

PUSSY EARS, TOLMIE'S or HAIRY STAR TULIP   *Calochortus tolmiei*
Lily family

DESCRIPTION: 4–12 inches. Three pale lavender or white, wedge-shaped, purple-hairy petals with three darker purple sepals between them.

Tolmie's pussy ears

NOTE: The purple tinge comes from the sepals, the underside of the petals, and the dense hairs.

HABITAT: Grassy fields and meadows, rocky soil, woodlands (to 6,500 feet); found in northwest mountains, north and central coast and coast ranges, Sacramento Valley.

WHERE AND WHEN:
Trinity Alps (April–May)
Salt Point (April–June)
Big Basin State Park (April–June)
Point Reyes (April–June)
Fort Ross (April–June)
Six Rivers National Forest (May–June)

SAGE, THISTLE   *Salvia carduacea*
Mint family

DESCRIPTION: 0.5–3.5 feet. White-woolly, square stem with large, broad, pinnately dissected leaves with short-spiny segments. Woolly whorls of lavender, two-lipped flowers with two-lobed upper lip and fringed lower lip. Strong sage odor.

NOTE: The delicately fringed lower lip may remind you of one of those exotic aquarium fish that lure their prey with gracefully undulating "fans."

HABITAT: Sandy or gravelly flats (to 4,500 feet); found in central and southern coast ranges, San Joaquin Valley, Transverse Ranges, Peninsular Ranges, Mojave Desert, Sonoran Desert.

WHERE AND WHEN:
Red Rock Canyon (April–May)
Pinnacles (April–May)
Shell Creek Road off SR-58 (April–June)
Wind Wolves Preserve (April–June)
Carrizo Plain (April–June)
Channel Islands (April–June)

Thistle sage

Beckwith violet

VIOLET, BECKWITH or GREAT BASIN VIOLET   *Viola beckwithii*
Violet family

DESCRIPTION: 2–15 inches. Several peduncles lift flowers (to 1.5 inches) above leaves. The upper two petals are velvety purple-maroon; the lower three are the same color or are a pale violet or white. Yellow at throat with purple nectar guides.

NOTE: These delightful violets can fill an early spring field with their range of colors and sweet fragrance.

HABITAT: Sagebrush scrub (3,000–6,000 feet); found in Cascades, Sierra, northeast corner.

WHERE AND WHEN:
Martis Valley in Tahoe (April–May)
SR-36 east of Red Bluff (April–May)
Modoc Plateau (May–June)
Honey Lake area (May–June)
Lassen National Park (May–June)
Sierra Valley (May–June)

YELLOW EYES   *Lupinus flavoculatus*
Pea family

DESCRIPTION: 2–10 inches. Dense clusters of deep violet pea flowers (to 0.5 inches) practically sitting on or rising above the palmately compound leaves, which are splayed close to the ground. Bright yellow spot in center of banner. Short, round pods.

NOTE: Of the more than 70 *Lupinus* species in California, yellow eyes may have the deepest blue/violet petals of them all, especially striking in contrast with the bright yellow "eye."

HABITAT: Sandy or gravelly flats (to 7,200 feet); found east of the Sierra, Mojave Desert.

WHERE AND WHEN:
Death Valley (April–May)
Big Pine area (April–May)

Alabama Hills (April–May)
Rosamund area (April–May)
White Mountains (April–
   May)
Mojave National Preserve
   (April–May)

Yellow eyes

CACTUS, BEEHIVE or DESERT FOXTAIL CACTUS
Coryphantha vivipara or *Escobaria vivipara*

Cactus family

DESCRIPTION: 2–6 inches. One or several cylindrical beehive-like stems covered tightly with interlaced spines. Many anemone-like, pinkish or yellowish flowers (to 1 inch) with many narrow, flaring, pointed petals. Yellow anthers and a many-"fingered," creamy stigma.

NOTE: The long, white spines with the dark tips are so neatly and tightly interwoven that it looks like a painstakingly woven Indian basket.

HABITAT: Sandy or rocky flats and slopes (to 9,000 feet); found in Mojave Desert, Sonoran Desert.

WHERE AND WHEN:

Mojave National Preserve
   (April–May)
Kingston Range (April–May)
Joshua Tree (April–May)
Little San Bernardino
   Mountains (April–May)
Death Valley (April–May)
Twenty-Nine Palms (April–
   May)

Beehive cactus

CACTUS, ENGELMAN'S HEDGEHOG or
CALICO CACTUS   *Echinocereus engelmannii*
Cactus family
DESCRIPTION: 0.5–1.5 feet. Spiny, cucumberlike stems usually in cluster of up to 3 feet across. Vase-shaped, magenta flowers (to 3 inches) with many petals surrounding numerous yellow stamens and a many-fingered, green stigma.

NOTE: These magnificent flowers are "guarded" by clusters of 10–18 very sharp, straw-colored spines.

HABITAT: Dry, often rocky flats and slopes (to 7,500 feet); found east of the Sierra, Transverse Ranges, Peninsular Ranges, Mojave Desert, Sonoran Desert.

WHERE AND WHEN:
Anza-Borrego (April–May)
along Imperial Highway S2
  (April–May)
Mojave National Preserve
  (April–June)
Alabama Hills (May–June)
San Bernardino Mountains
  (May–July)
White Mountains (June)

Engelman's hedgehog cactus

CALICO, DESERT   *Loeseliastrum matthewsii*
Phlox family
DESCRIPTION: 1–6 inches. Prickly plant with narrow, pinnately lobed leaves and several scattered, two-lipped, white and pink flowers (to three-fourths inch). Lobes of upper lip pink with a red-purple arch above white base, lobes of lower lip often solid pink.
NOTE: The five petal lobes are often a bit askew with sometimes only one in the lower lip.
HABITAT: Gravelly flats, washes (to 6,000 feet); found east of the Sierra, Mojave Desert, Sonoran Desert.
WHERE AND WHEN:
Antelope Valley (April–May)

Joshua Tree (April–May)
Death Valley (April–May)
Alabama Hills (April–May)
Anza-Borrego (April–June)
Piute Mountains (April–June)

Desert calico

CHECKERMALLOW, FOOTHILL   *Sidalcea calycosa*
Mallow family

DESCRIPTION: 1–3 feet. Clusters of large (to 1 inch), bowl-shaped, delicately pink flowers, bowls sometimes deeply cupped, sometimes shallow. Upper leaves with five to 11 linear (very narrow and widely separated) segments. California endemic.

NOTE: The fingerlike leaf segments and the wet (often edges of vernal pools) habitat distinguish this species from other closely related ones.

HABITAT: Wet meadows, edges of vernal pools (to 4,000 feet); found in north coast ranges, Central Valley, foothills.

WHERE AND WHEN:
Phoenix Park (April–May)
Elk area (April–May)
Pitkin Marsh (April–May)
Dye Creek Preserve (April–May)
Mather Field (April–May)
Red Hills Road (April–May)

Foothill checkermallow

CLARKIA, ELEGANT
Evening primrose family

Clarkia unguiculata

DESCRIPTION: 1–3 feet. Tall, sparsely flowered plant with showy, four-petaled, red-purple flowers (to 1 inch). Each petal clawed with broad, fanlike tip and long, slender blade. California endemic.

NOTE: These fascinating flowers may remind you of windmills with clawed arms ready to whirl in the breeze.

HABITAT: Grassy banks, woodlands (to 5,000 feet); found in coast ranges, foothills, Transverse Ranges, Peninsular Ranges.

WHERE AND WHEN:
Carrizo Plain (April–June)
San Gabriel Mountains (April–June)
Pinnacles (April–June)
Kern River Canyon (April–June)
Yankee Jim's Road (May–June)
Santa Cruz Mountains (May–August)

Elegant clarkia

CLINTONIA, RED or BLUE BEADLILY
Lily family

Clintonia andrewsiana

DESCRIPTION: 1–2 feet. Loose umbels of 10–30 flowers atop and along slender, leafless stem. Scarlet or pink-purple six-tepaled, trumpet-shaped flowers with bright white or yellow anthers.

NOTE: This plant is certainly an illustration of intense color extremes—from scarlet flowers to shiny, bright blue berries.

HABITAT: Redwood forest shade (up to 1,300 feet); found in northwest mountains, north and central coast and coast ranges.

WHERE AND WHEN:
Redwood National Park (April–June)
Santa Cruz Mountains (April–June)
Muir Woods (April–June)
Salt Point (April–June)

Santa Lucia Range (April–June)
Kruse Rhododedron State Reserve (May)

Red clintonia

CLOVER, ANDERSON'S   *Trifolium andersonii*
Pea family

DESCRIPTION: 1–6 inches. Soft-hairy, tufted plant often forming cushions. Densely white-hairy, round heads of many pea flowers with pink-purple banners and white-tipped wings. Basal leaves with three to seven often infolded leaflets.

NOTE: These multicolored flower heads look cozy nestled in their silvery-hairy bed (of sepals and leaves).

Anderson's clover

HABITAT: Rocky places, washes, meadows (3,000–13,000 feet); found in Sierra, east of the Sierra, northeast corner.

WHERE AND WHEN:
Modoc Plateau (April–June)
Sweetwater Mountains (May–August)
White Mountains (May–August)
Bodie Hills (May–August)
Conway Summit area (May–August)

COLUMBINE, CRIMSON   *Aquilegia formosa*
Buttercup family

DESCRIPTION: 1–4 feet. Several flowers (to 1.5 inches) hanging upside-down off long, arching pedicels. Five red or orange, flaring sepals and five

red or orange tubular petals with yellow at the mouth and long nectar spurs.

NOTE: Red, upside-down, long nectar spurs—all these make this columbine the perfect flower for the hovering, long-tongued, red-seeing hummingbirds.

HABITAT: Forest openings, moist meadows, brushy slopes, seeps (to 10,000 feet); found in much of California (except Central Valley and south coast).

WHERE AND WHEN:
Traverse Creek Botanical
    Area (April–May)
San Bruno Mountain (April–
    June)
King's Canyon/Sequoia
    (May–July)

Crimson columbine

San Jacinto Mountains (June–July)
San Gabriel Mountains (June–July)
Trinity Alps (July–August)

FOUR O'CLOCK, GIANT   *Mirabilis multiflora*
Four o'clock family

DESCRIPTION: 1–3 feet. Subshrub dense with clusters of funnel-shaped magenta or rose flowers (to 2.5 inches). Petal-like sepals (no actual petals). Five partly fused bracts hold clusters of flowers together.

NOTE: This plant brings delicious sensuality to teatime (it opens at about four o'clock or early in the evening, hence the common name).

HABITAT: Sandy or rocky flats and slopes (to 8,200 feet); found in San Joaquin Valley, east of the Sierra, Transverse Ranges, Mojave Desert, Sonoran Desert.

WHERE AND WHEN:

Carrizo Plain (April–May)

Anza-Borrego (April–May)

White Mountains (April–May)

Joshua Tree (April–June)

Mojave National Preserve (April–August)

San Gabriel Mountains (June–July)

Giant four o'clock

FRINGE CUPS   *Tellima grandiflora*

Saxifrage family

DESCRIPTION: 1–3 feet. Several small, cup-shaped flowers scattered along slender, hairy stem. Five petals flare into delicate, fringed pink or green-ish-white lobes that turn pink or red with age. Broad, mostly basal, maplelike leaves.

NOTE: If you sipped out of these cups, you would get a tickle along with your drink!

HABITAT: Rocky places, canyons, damp woods (to 5,000 feet); found in northwest mountains, north and central coast and coast ranges, foothills, Cascades, Sierra.

WHERE AND WHEN:

Fort Ross (April–June)

Santa Cruz Mountains (April–June)

Feather River canyon (April–June)

Santa Lucia Range (April–June)

Mount Tamalpais (May–July)

Trinity Alps (June–August)

Fringe cups

FRITILLARY, SCARLET   *Fritillaria recurva*
Lily family

DESCRIPTION: 1–3 feet. Several bell-shaped flowers (to 2 inches) with six yellow-mottled, red or orange-red tepals that curve back at the tips. One to five whorls of grasslike leaves and a few single, alternating leaves on upper stem.

Scarlet fritillary

NOTE: Scarlet fritillary is one of the few California fritillaries that is brilliant scarlet (with a little yellowish tinge inside).

HABITAT: Woodland, scrub (2,000–6,000 feet); found in northwest mountains, north coast ranges, foothills, Cascades, Sierra.

WHERE AND WHEN:
Lake Sonoma area (April–May)
Hell's Half-Acre (April–May)
Mount Sanhedrin (May–June)
SR-36 west from Red Bluff (May–June)
Yuba River Canyon (May–June)
Trinity Alps (May–June)

GILIA, GREAT BASIN or NEVADA GILIA   *Gilia brecciarum*
Phlox family

DESCRIPTION: 3–12 inches. Branching stem above basal rosette of pinnately lobed and toothed leaves. Clusters of multicolored, tubular flowers (to one-fourth inch). Flower tubes yellow with purple splotches. Flaring, pink petal lobes white at base. Blue or turquoise anthers.

NOTE: This rainbow-flowered gilia is similar to showy gilia (p. 280), but the flowers are much smaller and the calyx has distinctive black, stalked glands.

HABITAT: Sandy flats (to 7,500 feet); found in south coast ranges, northeast corner, eastern Sierra, east of the Sierra, Transverse Ranges, Mojave Desert

WHERE AND WHEN:
Alabama Hills (April–May)
San Gabriel Mountains (April–May)
Sawmill Pass Trail (April–May)
Carrizo Plain (April–May)

White Mountains (April–
May)
Piute Mountains (April–
May)

Great Basin gilia

GILIA, SHOWY   *Gilia cana*

Phlox family

DESCRIPTION: 4–12 inches. Much-branched stem usually with many multi-colored, tubular flowers (to three-fourths inch). Flower tube dark purple with yellow band and flaring petal lobes pink with splotches of white. Basal rosette of pinnately lobed, cobwebby leaves. California endemic.

NOTE: To complete the rainbow theme, the anthers are usually blue-purple or turquoise.

HABITAT: Sandy or gravelly flats, washes (2,500–10,000 feet); found in eastern Sierra, east of the Sierra, Transverse Ranges, Mojave Desert.

WHERE AND WHEN:

Alabama Hills (April–May)
San Bernardino Mountains
   (April–May)
Red Rock Canyon State Park
   (April–May)
Death Valley (April–May)
White Mountains (April–
May)
Mosquito Pass trail (May–
July)

Showy gilia

GILIA, YARROW-LEAF or MANY-LEAF GILIA *Gilia millefoliata*
Phlox family
DESCRIPTION: 3–12 inches. Terminal clusters of two to six small, multicolored, tubular flowers. Yellow flower tube with dark purple splotches flar-

ing out into rounded, pink lobes. Narrow, erect sepals partly conceal the flower tube. Pinnately lobed leaves. California endemic. CNPS Rare and Endangered List—endangered.
NOTE: The entire plant is glandular-hairy and strongly (rather unpleasantly) scented.
HABITAT: Dunes (to 30 feet); found in north and central coast.
WHERE AND WHEN:
Mattole Beach (April–June)
Humboldt Bay (April–June)
Bodega Bay (April–June)
Point Reyes (April–June)
Bodega Head (April–June)
MacKerricher State Park (April–June)

Yarrow-leaf gilia

HOP SAGE *Grayia spinosa*
Goosefoot family
DESCRIPTION: 2–4 feet. Shrub with stiff branches becoming spinelike, needlelike leaves, and spiky clusters of petal-less, inconspicuous flowers. Colorful creamy or rosy bracts.
NOTE: Only the female flowers have the colorful bracts, forming saclike structures surrounding the seeds.
HABITAT: Sandy or gravelly flats, sagebrush scrub (1,600–9,000 feet); found in south coast ranges, Sierra, east of the Sierra, northeast corner, Mojave Desert, Sonoran Desert.
WHERE AND WHEN:
Mojave National Preserve (April–June)
White Mountains (April–June)
Alabama Hills (April–June)
Carrizo Plain (April–June)
Lava Beds National Monument (April–June)
Antelope Valley (April–June)

Hop sage

LARKSPUR, KERN COUNTY   *Delphinium purpusii*
Buttercup family

DESCRIPTION: 1–4 feet. Stout stem with short, bristly hairs. Broad, dark-green, shallowly palmately lobed leaves, mostly on lower half of stem. Large flowers with narrow, somewhat drooping, pink and white sepals. California endemic. CNPS Rare and Endangered List—limited distribution.

NOTE: This is the only species of *Delphinium* native to North America with consistently rose-pink flowers (sepals).

HABITAT: Moist places on cliffs, rock walls, talus (to 4,500 feet); found in southern Sierra, Mojave Desert.

WHERE AND WHEN:

Kern River Canyon (April–May)

Long Canyon Reservoir Natural Area (April–May)

Piute Mountains (April–May)

Inspiration Point Botanical Area (April–May)

Kern County larkspur

LUPINE, CHICK

Lupinus microcarpus var. *microcarpus* or
L. subvexus var. *subvexus*

Pea family

DESCRIPTION: 8–24 inches. Several distinct whorls of many pea flowers on upper part of stem. Amazing variability in color—pink, rose, purple, yellow, white, or lavender. Stem and leaves usually hairy. Five to 11 leaflets.

NOTE: The long, shaggy hairs adorn not only the leaves but also the calyx of the flowers, providing a soft "bed" for the colorful, showy petals.

HABITAT: Grassy fields; roadsides and other disturbed places (to 5,200 feet); found in much of California.

WHERE AND WHEN:
Jenner-Fort Ross area
  (April–May)
Channel Islands (April–May)
Edgewood Preserve (April–
  May)
San Bernardino Mountains
  (April–May)
Bodega Head (April–May)
Tehachapi Mountains (April–
  May)

Chick lupine

MALLOW, BUSH or
CHAPARRAL MALLOW

Malacothamnus fasciculatus

Mallow family

DESCRIPTION: 3–15 feet. Shrub with thin, flexible branches with a few broad, densely hairy leaves with three to five lobes. Clusters of bowl-shaped, pink or lavender flowers (to 1.5 inches) from the leaf axils with five graceful, fragile-looking petals. Frequent fire follower.

NOTE: The delicate flowers have an even more delicate fragrance.

HABITAT: Chaparral, scrub, disturbed places (to 2,000 feet); found on coast and coast ranges, Transverse Ranges, Peninsular Ranges, Mojave Desert.

WHERE AND WHEN:
Santa Monica Mountains (April–September)
Point Loma (April–August)
Santa Rosa Plateau (April–September)
San Gabriel Mountains (April–September)

Santa Ynez River area
(April–September)
Malibu Creek State Park
(April–September)

Bush mallow

MARIPOSA LILY, KENNEDY or
DESERT MARIPOSA LILY
Lily family

Calochortus kennedyi

DESCRIPTION: 4–8 inches (to 2 feet). Short plant if out in the open, taller if supported by other plants. Umbel-like raceme of one to six large (to 2.5 inches), bowl-shaped, bright orange (sometimes red or purplish) flowers.
NOTE: Whether the typical orange or more red or purple, the color of this lily is as dazzling as it is unusual for the genus.

HABITAT: Rocky flats and slopes, desert scrub (2,000–7,200 feet); found east of the Sierra, Transverse Ranges, Mojave Desert.

WHERE AND WHEN:
Haiwee Reservoir (April–May)
Randsburg area (April–May)
Death Valley (April–May)
Mount Pinos (April–May)
Mojave National Preserve (April–June)
White Mountains (April–June)

Kennedy mariposa lily

MARIPOSA LILY, STRIPED or
ALKALI MARIPOSA LILY
Calochortus striatus

Lily family

DESCRIPTION: 1–12 inches. Umbel-like raceme of one to five bowl-shaped flowers (to 1.5 inches). Pink petals with dark red-purple lines. CNPS Rare and Endangered List—endangered.

NOTE: Although this beautiful, striped mariposa lily is rare, you can find many of the plants on Edwards Air Force Base (and in Ash Meadows, just east of Death Valley just over the Nevada border).

HABITAT: Alkaline flats, moist desert scrub (2,500–4,500 feet); found in Transverse Ranges, Mojave Desert.

WHERE AND WHEN:
Lake Isabella (April–May)
Edwards Air Force Base
  (April–May)
Tejon Ranch (April–May)
Red Rock Canyon (April–
  May)
San Gabriel Mountains
  (April–June)
San Bernardino Mountains
  (April–June)

Striped mariposa lily

MARIPOSA LILY, WEAK-STEM or
WINDING MARIPOSA LILY
Calochortus flexuosus

Lily family

DESCRIPTION: 4–8 inches. Usually sprawling stem with one to six bowl-shaped, pink or lilac or white flowers with various types of banding and red-purple arches at base. One to two basal, grasslike leaves withering early.

NOTE: The stem is indeed "flexuosus," usually snaking along the ground or relying on support from neighboring shrubs.

HABITAT: Gravelly or rocky flats, sagebrush scrub (2,000–5,600 feet); found in Mojave Desert, Sonoran Desert.

WHERE AND WHEN:
Death Valley (April–May)
Bakersfield area (April–May)

Whipple Mountains (April–
May)
Clark Mountains in Mojave
National Preserve (April–
May)
Chuckwalla Mountains
(April–May)

Weak-stem mariposa lily

MILKVETCH, FRECKLED or PAPER LOCOWEED

Astragalus lentiginosus

Pea family

DESCRIPTION: 4–16 inches. Erect or sprawling stems with silvery green, pinnately compound leaves with nine to 19 leaflets. Raceme of red-purple pea flowers extended well above the leaves. Banner with white stripes.

NOTE: As is often the case with locoweeds, the seed-pods are distinguishing, in this case papery, strongly inflated, and speckled with a distinct mid-groove and with a pointed beak.

HABITAT: Sandy or gravelly flats and slopes (to 11,800 feet); found in central and south coast ranges, San Joaquin Valley, southern foothills, Sierra, east of the Sierra, northeast corner, Mojave Desert, Sonoran Desert.

WHERE AND WHEN:

Anza-Borrego (April–May)
Carrizo Plain (April–May)

Freckled milkvetch

Alabama Hills (April–May)
Tehachapi Mountains (April–May)
Lava Beds National Monument (April–June)
White Mountains (April–July)

Freckled milkvetch

MILKWEED, PURPLE
Asclepias cordifolia

Dogbane family (previously included in Milkweed family)

DESCRIPTION: 1–2.5 feet. Stout, branching stems with umbels of many flowers on long pedicels. Deep red-purple, reflexed, winglike petals beyond which project white or pale purple horns, which resemble teeth or corn kernels.

Purple milkweed

NOTE: Odd in shape and unusual in color, they are definitely worth a close look.

HABITAT: Forest openings, rocky slopes, lava flows (to 6,500 feet); found in northwest mountains, north coast ranges, foothills, Cascades, Sierra, northeast corner, Mojave Desert.

WHERE AND WHEN:
Pine Hill (April–May)
Yuba River canyon (April–May)
Greenhorn Range (April–May)
Tehachapi Mountains (April–June)
Warner Mountains (May–July)
Trinity Alps (June–July)

MONKEYFLOWER, PANSY   *Mimulus angustatus*
Lopseed family (previously included in Snapdragon family)

DESCRIPTION: 2–4 inches. One two-lipped flower (to 1 inch) at the tip of the very short stem. All of the five equal-petal lobes are pink or magenta with a large, dark purple spot. Flower throat yellow with small, red-purple spots. California endemic.

NOTE: The flower is so large and long-tubed for its dwarf plant that it almost seems the flower was mistakenly stuck on the stem.

HABITAT: Wet depressions (to 4,000 feet); found in north coast ranges, San Joaquin Valley, foothills.

WHERE AND WHEN:
Table Mountain (April–May)
Cohasset Ridge (April–May)
Traverse Creek Botanical
    Area (April–May)
Clear Lake area (April–May)
Hell's Half Acre (April–May)
Grass Valley area (April–
    May)

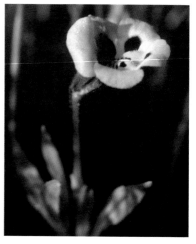

Pansy monkeyflower

MONKEYFLOWER, SCARLET   *Mimulus cardinalis*
Lopseed family (previously included in Snapdragon family)

DESCRIPTION: 1–3 feet. Several two-lipped, scarlet flowers (up to 2 inches). All five petal lobes are swept back.

NOTE: There are many monkeyflowers that are various shades of red-

Scarlet monkeyflower

purple or pink, but this is the only species in California that is consistently solid scarlet—and satiny scarlet at that!

HABITAT: Stream banks, seeps (to 8,000 feet); found in much of California (except northeast corner).

WHERE AND WHEN:

Anza-Borrego (April–May)
Channel Islands (April–May)
White Mountains (April–June)
Yankee Jim's Road (April–June)
Santa Monica Mountains (May–October)
Mount Whitney Trail (June–July)

ONION, FRINGED or DESERT ONION *Allium fimbriatum*
Onion family (previously included in Lily family)

DESCRIPTION: 2–12 inches. Ground-covering plant with densely flowered umbel of six to 75 flowers practically on ground. Flowers deep purple to

Fringed onion

pale rose (or white) with darker mid-veins. One leaf, round in cross section, usually curled up close to the ground.

NOTE: You can often find great patches of desert sand carpeted with these deep purple onions.

HABITAT: Dry, sandy flats and slopes (to 10,000 feet); found in coast ranges, southern foothills, east of the Sierra, Transverse Ranges, Peninsular Ranges, Mojave Desert, Sonoran Desert.

WHERE AND WHEN:

California Desert Conservation Area (April–June)
Jacumba area (April–May)

Greenhorn Range (April–June)
Channel Islands (April–June)
San Emigdio Mountains (April–June)
Red Rock Canyon (April–June)

ONION, ROSY or COAST ONION · *Allium dichlamydeum*

Onion family (previously included in Lily family)

DESCRIPTION: 4–12 inches. Stout stem with a tight umbel of five to 30 deep rose-purple flowers. Tepals erect in inner and outer circles, inner tepals sometimes finely toothed. California endemic.

NOTE: This lovely and unusual onion (with its erect, rosy tepals) forms rosy clumps that stand out even from quite a distance.

HABITAT: Dry, sandy or clay soil on sea cliffs (150–500 feet); found on north and central coast and coast ranges.

WHERE AND WHEN:

Dillon Beach (April–June)
Santa Lucia Range (April–June)
San Bruno Mountain (April–June)
Edgewood Preserve (April–June)
Point Reyes (April–June)
Salt Point (May–July)

Rosy onion

ORCHID, CALYPSO or FAIRY SLIPPER · *Calypso bulbosa*

Orchid family

DESCRIPTION: 3–10 inches. Single, showy flower (to 1.5 inches) hangs from tip of leafless stem. Three narrow sepals and two similar petals are solid pink. Lower middle petal slipperlike, white mottled with orange, brown, and/or yellow. One broad, oval, basal leaf.

NOTE: In calypso orchid, the one different petal is dramatically different in shape, size, and color.

HABITAT: Woodlands (to 6,000 feet); found in northwest mountains, north and central coast and coast ranges.

WHERE AND WHEN:

Geyser Peak (April–July)

Mount Tamalpais (April–
July)
South Kelsey Historical Trail
(April–July)
Trinity Alps (May–June)
Redwood National Park
(May–July)
Lamphere-Christensen
Dunes (May–July)

Calypso orchid

PAINTBRUSH, DESERT   *Castilleja angustifolia* or *C. chromosa*
Broomrape family (previously included in Snapdragon family)
DESCRIPTION: 0.5–1.5 feet. White-hairy plant with three- to five-lobed
green leaves and bright scarlet, three- to five-lobed bracts. Actual flowers
are mostly hidden, yellow-green tubes.
NOTE: The scarlet color of the bract tips is in dramatic contrast with the
chocolate brown bases—you won't confuse this paintbrush with any other.
HABITAT: Dry flats, washes, sagebrush scrub (3,000–9,800 feet); found in

Desert paintbrush

eastern Sierra, east of the Sierra, northeast corner, Transverse Ranges, Mojave Desert.

WHERE AND WHEN:
Alabama Hills (April–May)
Sawmill Pass Trail (April–May)
Warner Mountains (April–July)
Death Valley (April–May)
San Bernardino Mountains (April–May)
White Mountains (April–July)

PEA, SILKY BEACH   *Lathyrus littoralis*
Pea family

DESCRIPTION: 0.5–2 feet. Trailing or ascending stem terminating in cluster of bi-colored, pea flowers. Banner is pink-purple and wings are white. Tendrils. California endemic.

NOTE: This plant has chosen the ocean beachcombing life—you won't find it out of the sand or far from the water, or more than a few yards above sea level.

HABITAT: Beaches, dunes (to 20 feet); found in north and central coast.

WHERE AND WHEN:
Humboldt Bay (April–May)
Point Reyes (April–May)
Stinson Beach (April–May)
Bodega Bay (April–May)
Monterey Peninsula (April–May)
Lamphere-Christensen Dunes (April–June)

Silky beach pea

PEACH, DESERT   *Prunus andersonii*
Rose family

DESCRIPTION: 2–6 feet. Shrub with spine-tipped branches and clusters of pink or rose flowers (to 0.5 inches). Five widely separate petals. Small, pulpy, peachlike fruits.

NOTE: Like the cherry trees in Washington, D.C., desert peach (a fellow Rose family member) ushers in spring (in the deserts and east of the Sierra) with delightful, soft color and delicious, subtle fragrance.

HABITAT: Dry, shrubby slopes; rocky places; canyons; open woods (3,000–

Desert peach

8,500 feet); found in eastern Sierra, east of Sierra, northeast corner, Mojave Desert.

WHERE AND WHEN:
Topaz Lake (April–May)
Death Valley (April–May)
west of Walker (April–May)
Walker Pass (April–May)
Mono Basin (April–May)
Honey Lake area (May–June)

PENSTEMON, GRINNELL'S   *Penstemon grinnellii*
Plantain family (previously included in Snapdragon family)
DESCRIPTION: 0.5–3 feet. Stout stem with opposite pairs of thick, toothed, often infolded leaves. Glandular inflorescence of many two-lipped, tubular, pink or lavender flowers on branching pedicels. Flowers distinctly swollen with long-protruding, golden-hairy staminode. California endemic.

Grinnell's penstemon

NOTE: These cute, "chubby" flowers are strongly and deliciously fragrant.

HABITAT: Chaparral, woodlands (1,500–9,000 feet); found in south coast ranges, southern Sierra, Transverse Ranges, Peninsular Ranges.

WHERE AND WHEN:
Wind Wolves Preserve
(April–June)
Kern River Canyon (April–July)
Mount Pinos (April–July)
Santa Ynez Mountains
(April–July)
Cuyama Valley (April–July)
Santa Lucia Mountains
(April–July)

PENSTEMON, SCENTED or
PALMER'S PENSTEMON   *Penstemon palmeri*
Plantain family (previously included in Snapdragon family)

DESCRIPTION: 1–6 feet. Stout stem thick with inflated, two-lipped, pale pink flowers (to 1.5 inches). Dark red-purple stripes on lower petal lobes. Protruding yellow-bearded staminode. Opposite pairs of clasping, triangular, toothed leaves with upper leaves joined to surround stem. Fragrant.

NOTE: These dazzling flowers are as deliciously fragrant as they are stunningly beautiful, attracting swams of bees and herds of flower lovers.

HABITAT: Sandy or gravelly flats, washes, canyons, desert scrub (3,500–7,500 feet); found in Peninsular Ranges, Mojave Desert.

WHERE AND WHEN:
San Jacinto Mountains (April–June)
Providence Mountains in Mojave National Preserve (April–June)
Kingston Range (April–June)
Clark Mountains (April–June)
Death Valley (May–June)

Scented penstemon

PHLOX, SHOWY   *Phlox speciosa*
Phlox family

DESCRIPTION: 0.5–2 feet. Several pinwheel-like flowers (to 1.5 inches) on opposite pairs of slender pedicels from leaf axils. Five heart-shaped pink petals white at the base.

NOTE: *Phlox* means "flame" for the bright-colored flowers of many species, although in showy phlox, the fires simmer subdued and subtle.

HABITAT: Shady places (to 8,000 feet); found in northwest mountains, north coast and coast ranges, foothills, Cascades, Sierra.

WHERE AND WHEN:
Independence Trail (April–May)
Lake Sonoma area (April–May)
King's Canyon/Sequoia (April–June)
Mount Shasta (April–June)
Trinity Alps (May–June)
Butterfly Valley (May–June)

Showy phlox

SAGE, TALL PURPLE or SAN LUIS PURPLE SAGE *Salvia leucophylla*
Mint family
DESCRIPTION: 3–5 feet. Shrub with gray appearance due to short, woolly, grayish hairs on stem, leaves, and calyx. Square stem. Tonguelike, felty leaves with toothed edges. Many widely separated whorls of long, tubular, rose-lavender flowers. Grows in large masses on hillsides. California endemic.

NOTE: As with most *Salvia* species, this plant is extremely attractive to bees, so watch out where you put your nose.

HABITAT: Chaparral, scrub (to 2,500 feet); found on south coast and coast ranges, Transverse Ranges.

WHERE AND WHEN:
Malibu Creek State Park
    (April–June)
Santa Monica Mountains
    (April–July)
San Gabriel Mountains
    (April–July)
Cuyama Valley (April–July)
Carrizo Plain (April–July)
Tejon Ranch (April–July)

Tall purple sage

SCARLET BUGLER   *Penstemon centranthifolius*
Plantain family (previously included in Snapdragon family)

DESCRIPTION: 1–4 feet. Cluster of stems (sometimes woody at base) with thick, clasping leaves. Opposite pairs of bracts on stem, out of which arching pedicels bear long, slender, tubular, bright red flowers.

NOTE: The tubular flowers barely open at the tip—just enough for hummingbird access.

HABITAT: Chaparral, woodlands (to 6,000 feet); found in coast ranges, foothills, Central Valley, Transverse Ranges, Peninsular Ranges.

WHERE AND WHEN:
Eaton Canyon (April–May)
Wind Wolves Preserve
    (April–May)
Malibu Creek State Park
    (April–May)
Joshua Tree (April–May)
Santa Monica Mountains
    (April–June)
Shell Creek Road off SR-58
    (April–June)

Scarlet bugler

SEA THRIFT or SEA PINK   *Armeria maritima*
Leadwort family

DESCRIPTION: 4–20 inches. Round, terminal umbel of small pink, star-shaped flowers, usually with darker rose streaks on petals. Petals are papery and may last on plant well after they've faded to brown or beige. California endemic.

NOTE: With their densely flowered spheres atop such slender stems, these plants often dance in the sea breezes.

HABITAT: Coastal bluffs, grasslands (to 650 feet); found on coast.

WHERE AND WHEN:
Monterey Peninsula (April–June)
Point Reyes (April–June)
Salt Point (April–June)
Bodega Head (April–June)
San Bruno Mountain (April–July)
Torrey Pines (May–June)

Sea thrift

SNAKE LILY, TWINING   *Dichelostemma volubile*
Brodiaea family (previously included in Lily family)
DESCRIPTION: 2–5 feet. Umbel of 10–30 pink flowers at end of long, twining, reddish stem. Six tepals only partly flare out of short, stubby tube. California endemic.

Twining snake lily

NOTE: The stem is so weak that it will twine around anything in the vicinity to help it hold the flowers up—even around itself.

HABITAT: Woodland, scrub (to 2,500 feet); found in north coast ranges, foothills.

WHERE AND WHEN:

Red Hill Road (April–May)

Buttermilk Bend Trail (April–May)

Hite's Cove trail (April–May)

Merced River Canyon(April–May)

Pine Hill (April–May)

Greenhorn Range (April–June)

STAR-FLOWER, PACIFIC   *Trientalis latifolia*

Myrsine family (previously included in Primrose family)

DESCRIPTION: 2–12 inches. Whorl of three to eight broad leaves at tip of slender stem. A few star-shaped flowers each at tip of slender pedicel from leaf axil. Five to seven separate, pointed, pink or white petals.

NOTE: These lovely, six-pointed (sometimes five- or seven-pointed) flowers light up their often-dark forest habitat like twinkling stars in a night sky.

HABITAT: Woodlands (to 4,500 feet); found in northwest mountains, coast, coast ranges, foothills, Cascades, Sierra.

WHERE AND WHEN:

Santa Lucia Range (April–June)

Salt Point (April–June)

Redwoods National Park (April–July)

Trinity Alps (May–June)

Butterfly Valley (May–June)

Kruse Rhododendron State Reserve (May–June)

Pacific star-flower

THISTLE, COBWEB
Cirsium occidentale

Aster family

DESCRIPTION: 2–4 feet. Branching stem with one or several flower heads (to 3 inches across), each with scores of pink, red-purple, or white, threadlike disk flowers. Flower head rather short and broad with spiny bracts that are

cobwebby at the base. California endemic.

NOTE: There are several varieties of this species, varying a bit in color and cobwebbiness, among other things.

HABITAT: Grasslands, forest openings (to 11,500 feet); found in much of California (except San Joaquin Valley and east of the Sierra).

WHERE AND WHEN:
Hite's Cove Trail (April–May)
Camp Nine Road (April–May)
Kern River Canyon (April–May)
Drum Powerhouse Road (April–May)
Torrey Pines (April–May)
San Gabriel Mountains (April–July)

Cobweb thistle

WILLOWHERB, WATSON'S
Epilobium ciliatum subsp. *watsonii*

Evening primrose family

DESCRIPTION: 0.5–3 feet. Robust plant with long, leafy raceme with many small, four-petaled flowers. Deeply bilobed petals are pink or rose-purple. Tonguelike, slightly toothed leaves.

NOTE: The most interesting and noticeable aspect of this plant is the long, ribbed, reddish inferior ovary (not a value judgment!) dwarfing the tiny flowers.

HABITAT: Stream banks, seeps, disturbed places (to 1,200 feet); found on north and central coast.

WHERE AND WHEN:
Jenner-Fort Ross area (April–May)
Santa Lucia Range (April–May)
MacKerricher State Park (April–May)
north of Point Arena (May–July)

Sea Ranch (May–July)
San Bruno Mountains (May–
July)

Watson's willowherb

AGOSERIS, ANNUAL   *Agoseris heterophylla*

Aster family

DESCRIPTION: 2–16 inches. Solitary flower head atop slender stem with five-to-many slender ray flowers (no disk flowers). Narrow, white-hairy leaves smooth-edged or with a few fine teeth.

NOTE: The underside of the rays and/or the outside of the phyllaries are often tinged or striped reddish or purplish.

Annual agoseris

HABITAT: Dry, open, often rocky flats (to 7,500 feet); found in much of California (except eastern edges).

WHERE AND WHEN:
Traverse Creek Botanical Area (April–May)
Anza-Borrego (April–May)
Santa Ana Mountains (April–May)
Yosemite Valley (April–June)
Santa Lucia Range (April–June)
Trinity Alps (May–June)

BALSAMROOT, GIANT-LEAF or DELTOID BALSAMROOT   *Balsamorhiza deltoidea*

Aster family
DESCRIPTION: 0.5–3 feet. One or several large flower heads (to 3 inches) with 13–21 bright yellow rays surrounding a brownish-orange disk. Huge, triangular, shiny leaves (to 2 feet) with heart-shaped base.

NOTE: These very large leaves look smooth, but if you touch them, you will discover that they are covered with short, stiff hairs.

HABITAT: Grasslands, forest openings (to 7,000 feet); found in northwest mountains, coast ranges, foothills, Sierra, Transverse Ranges.

WHERE AND WHEN:
Pine Hill Preserve (April–May)
Mount Pinos (May–June)
Six Rivers National Forest (May–June)
Yosemite Valley (May–June)
Mount Sanhedrin (June–July)
San Gabriel Mountains (June–July)

Giant-leaf balsamroot

BALSAMROOT, HOOKER'S   *Balsamorhiza hookeri*

Aster family
DESCRIPTION: 4–12 inches. Several leafless stems with one flower head (to 3 inches) at tips with 10–21 bright yellow rays. Cluster of long, basal, deeply pinnately divided leaves with further lobed or divided segments.

Hooker's balsamroot

NOTE: The leaves (with their pinnate leaflets) distinguish this species from its close relative arrow-leaf balsamroot (p. 376) with whom Hooker's balsamroot sometimes hybridizes (with resulting intermediate leaves).
HABITAT: Dry, grassy slopes and flats; open woods (2,500–7,000 feet); found in Cascades, Sierra, east of Sierra, northeast corner.
WHERE AND WHEN:
Martis Valley in Tahoe (April–May)
Warner Mountains (April–May)
Markleeville area (April–May)
Honey Lake area (April–May)
Modoc Plateau (May–June)
Gazelle Mountain (June–July)

BLACKBRUSH
Coleogyne ramosissima
Rose family
DESCRIPTION: 1–6 feet. Spiny shrub thick with clusters of tiny, white-hairy leaves and scattered lemon-yellow flowers (to 0.5 inches). Four leathery, petal-like sepals and cluster of reproductive parts.
NOTE: The flowers of this shrub have the many reproductive parts typical of the Rose family, but they don't have the typical five petals—they have only four, and these aren't even actual petals.
HABITAT: Desert scrub, woodlands (2,000–5,200 feet); found east of the Sierra, in Transverse Ranges, Mojave Desert, Sonoran Desert.
WHERE AND WHEN:
Death Valley (April–June)
San Bernardino Mountains (April–June)
Rand Mountains (April–June)

Blackbrush

Anza-Borrego (April–June)
Red Rock Canyon (April–June)
Mojave National Preserve (April–July)

BLAZING STAR, VENUS
Loasa family

Mentzelia nitens

DESCRIPTION: 4–12 inches. Whitish stems rising above basal rosette of deeply pinnately lobed, gray-green leaves. A few showy, glossy yellow

flowers (to 1.5 inches), each solitary at tip of short pedicel.

NOTE: Although this species doesn't have the enormous radiating-sun flowers of *M. laevicaulis* (p. 206) or the shiny, silvery-cream flowers of *M. involucrata* (p. 125), it nonetheless dazzles with its satiny yellow petals (sometimes adorned with an orange spot).

HABITAT: Sandy flats and slopes, washes (1,500–7,000 feet); found east of the Sierra; Mojave Desert.

WHERE AND WHEN:
volcanic mesa above Bishop
(April–May)

Venus blazing star

Death Valley (April–May)
Alabama Hills (April–May)
El Paso Mountains (April–May)
Antelope Valley (April–May)
White Mountains (April–June)

BUCKWHEAT, CUSHION   *Eriogonum cespitosum*
Buckwheat family

DESCRIPTION: 1–4 inches. Leafless stems rise above compact mat or cushion of small, gray-felty leaves. Spherical flower heads of tiny, yellow flowers (sepals), which can be red early or late.

NOTE: Though small and close to the ground, these flower heads are dazzling, for the bright yellow of the "fresh" flowers contrasts dramatically with the deep red or orange of the buds and often of the aging blooms.

HABITAT: Sandy or gravelly flats and slopes (5,000–8,600 feet); found in northeast corner, east of the Sierra.

WHERE AND WHEN:

White Mountains (April–June)
Sweetwater Mountains (April–June)
Portola area (May–July)
Warner Mountains (May–July)
Benton area (May–July)
Ravendale area (May–July)

Cushion buckwheat

BUTTERCUP, WATER PLANTAIN   *Ranunculus alismifolius*
Buttercup family

DESCRIPTION: 2–20 inches. Sprawling or erect stem with many shiny, bright yellow flowers (to 1 inch). Five to 22 overlapping petals. Narrow, fleshy, unlobed leaves.

NOTE: One of the first bloomers in mid-elevation meadows just melted off from winter snows, this buttercup often forms extensive masses, bringing spring sunshine where not long before lay the cloak of winter.

Water plantain buttercup

HABITAT: Wet meadows, stream banks (to 12,000 feet); found in northwest mountains, north coast ranges, Cascades, Sierra, east of the Sierra, northeast corner, Transverse Ranges, Peninsular Ranges.

WHERE AND WHEN:
Martis Valley in Tahoe
    (April–May)
Modoc Plateau (April–May)
Lassen National Park (May–
    June)
San Bernardino Mountains
    (May–June)
San Jacinto Mountains
    (May–June)
Sweetwater Mountains
    (May–July)

COREOPSIS, BIGELOW or
BIGELOW'S TICKSEED   *Leptosyne bigelovii* or *Coreopsis bigelovii*
Aster family

DESCRIPTION: 4–24 inches. One stem or many with mostly basal, pinnately divided leaves. Solitary flower head at tip of nearly leafless stem with five to 10 bright yellow rays and 20–50 disk flowers. California endemic.

NOTE: In some grassland areas (for example, in the Gorman hills and along SR-58), these sunny flowers create masses that can be seen from miles away.

HABITAT: Grasslands, open woodlands, deserts (to 5,000 feet); found in south coast ranges, foothills, Transverse Ranges, Mojave Desert, Sonoran Desert.

WHERE AND WHEN:
Gorman Hills (April–May)
Death Valley (April–May)

Santa Monica Mountains
  (April–May)
SR-58 (April–May)
Joshua Tree (April–May)
Walker Pass (April–June)

Bigelow coreopsis

DAISY, PANAMINT or
LARGE-FLOWERED SUNRAY
Aster family
Enceliopsis covillei

DESCRIPTION: 1–1.5 feet. Several leafless stems rising above cluster of large, basal, silvery-gray leaves. Gigantic (up to 5.5 inches across) bright yellow flower heads with 20–35 rays surrounding dome-shaped disk. Green, pointed phyllaries in three series. CNPS Rare and Endangered List— endangered.

NOTE: The raised disk of this giant "sunflower" can itself be two to three inches across—larger than many daisylike flower heads with disk and rays combined!

HABITAT: Rocky flats and slopes, canyons (1,500–4,000 feet); found in Mojave Desert.

Panamint daisy

Wildrose Canyon in Death Valley (April–June)
Panamint Range in Death Valley (April–June)
Jail Canyon in Death Valley (April–June)
Surprise Canyon in Death Valley (April–June)

DANDELION, SEASIDE   *Agoseris apargioides*
Aster family

DESCRIPTION: 4–18 inches. Decumbent or erect, leafless stem with one large, yellow flower head at tip. Many overlapping, square-tipped, toothed ray flowers; no disk. Basal rosette of narrow, pinnately lobed or toothed, dark-green shiny leaves.

NOTE: This is quite similar to the invasive lawn dandelion, but it is a native that brings bright, sunny color to wild seaside gardens (with the smaller goldfields in the photo).

HABITAT: Dunes, grasslands, bluffs (to 1,600 feet); found on coast and coast ranges.

WHERE AND WHEN:
Salt Point (April–June)
Point Reyes (April–June)
Channel Islands (April–June)
Dillon Beach (April–June)
Monterey Peninsula (April–June)
Santa Cruz Mountains (April–August)

Seaside dandelion

DESERT PLUME or PRINCE'S PLUME   *Stanleya pinnata*
Mustard family

DESCRIPTION: 2–5 feet. Subshrub with woody stems and deeply pinnately lobed leaves. Stems terminate in bottlebrush-like raceme (to over a foot long) crowded with lemon-yellow, four-petaled flowers (to three-fourths inch), hairy at the base.

NOTE: As with most mustards, the fruits (in this case cylindrical pods) rival the flowers for showiness.

HABITAT: Sandy or gravelly flats and slopes, washes, canyons (to 6,100 feet); found on south coast and in coast ranges, east of the Sierra, northeast corner, Transverse Ranges, Peninsular Ranges, Mojave Desert.

WHERE AND WHEN:
Death Valley (April–May)
Alabama Hills (April–July)
Joshua Tree (April–July)
Susanville area (May–July)
White Mountains (May–
   September)
Carrizo Plain (May–December)

Desert plume

FAIRY LANTERN, GOLDEN or
GOLDEN GLOBE LILY
Calochortus amabilis

Lily family

DESCRIPTION: 0.5–2 feet. Two or several golden-yellow, globe-shaped flowers (to 1 inch) hang upside-down from short pedicels arching out of leaf axils. Three yellow petals form globe; three yellow sepals flare out horizontally above globe. California endemic.

NOTE: The thick, green, winged seedpods nodding from the arching pedicels are even larger and almost as striking as the nodding flowers!

HABITAT: Woodlands; shady, brushy hillsides (to 3,200 feet); found on north and central coast and in coast ranges.

WHERE AND WHEN:
Bear Valley (April–May)
Boggs Lake (April–May)

Golden fairy lantern

Mix Canyon Road (April–May)
SR-36 west of Red Bluff (April–May)
Pope Valley area (April–June)
Lake Sonoma area (April–June)

FLANNELBUSH or SLIPPERY ELM
Fremontodendron californicum subsp. *californicum*
Mallow family (previously included in Cacao family)

DESCRIPTION: 4–15 feet. Shrub or small tree with broad, thick, downy, three-lobed leaves and somewhat waxy, lemon-yellow flowers (to 2 inches). No true petals but petal-like sepals. Peeling bark.

NOTE: The bark peels from a gelatinous stem, hence the alternate common name. The downy hairs on the leaves can cause skin irritation.

HABITAT: Chaparral, washes, oak woodlands (to 6,500 feet); found in much of California (except northeast corner and deserts).

WHERE AND WHEN:
Kern River Canyon (April–July)
Santa Cruz Mountains (April–July)
Mount Pinos (April–July)
San Bernardino Mountains (April–July)
Santa Ynez Mountains (April–July)
Clear Lake area (April–July)

Flannelbush

GLOBE LILY, MOUNT DIABLO or
MOUNT DIABLO FAIRY LANTERN   *Calochortus pulchellus*
Lily family

DESCRIPTION: 4–12 inches. One or several large (to 1.5 inches), light yellow, globe-shaped flowers nod on short pedicels. Conspicuous nectary swelling on the exterior of the petals. California endemic. CNPS Rare and Endangered List—endangered.

NOTE: The plants and flowers of this species closely resemble those of golden fairy lantern (p. 308), but are a bit larger on a shorter plant and are usually a paler yellow or greenish-yellow.

HABITAT: Shade around trees or shrubs on brushy slopes (300–2500 feet); found in central coast ranges—only on Mount Diablo and vicinity.

WHERE AND WHEN:
Mount Diablo (April–June)
*Carquinez Straits Regional
    Park* (April–June)
Briones Regional Park
    (April–June)

Mount Diablo globe lily

GOLD NUGGETS *Calochortus luteus*

Lily family

DESCRIPTION: 0.5–2 feet. One or several erect, bowl-shaped flowers atop a slender, leafless stem. Three golden yellow, wedge-shaped petals, each with a central, reddish-brown spot above the nectary and reddish, vertical lines or speckles. California endemic.

NOTE: In gold nuggets, unlike in several of the other yellow species of *Calochortus*, the gold can shine forth unimpeded by hair and largely undistracted by other colors.

HABITAT: Grasslands, woodlands (to 3,000 feet); found in northwest mountains, coast and coast ranges, Central Valley, foothills.

WHERE AND WHEN:
Jepson Prairie Preserve (April–
    May)
Pine Hill Reserve (April–May)
Santa Lucia Range (April–May)
Table Mountain (April–May)
Monterey Peninsula (April–May)
Greenhorn Range (April–June)

Gold nuggets

Rayless goldenhead

GOLDENHEAD, RAYLESS   *Acamptopappus sphaerocephalus*
Aster family

DESCRIPTION: 1–3 feet. Much-branched, rounded subshrub with narrow leaves sometimes in bundles, and many flower heads (single or in clusters) with 13–27 pale yellow disk flowers only.

NOTE: Although the flower heads are rayless, this is a very showy plant, as the discoid flower heads can almost completely cover the stems and leaves, neatly blanketing the rounded outline of the plant.

HABITAT: Rocky or gravelly flats and slopes, woodlands (to 7,200 feet); found east of the Sierra, Transverse Ranges, Peninsular Ranges, Mojave Desert, Sonoran Desert.

WHERE AND WHEN:
Alabama Hills (April–May)
Joshua Tree (April–May)
Anza-Borrego (April–May)
Antelope Valley (April–May)
Lone Pine area (April–June)
Mojave National Preserve (April–June)

GOLDEN STARS   *Bloomeria crocea*
Brodiaea family (previously included in Lily family)

DESCRIPTION: 0.5–1.5 feet. Naked stem with large, open umbel of 30–50 starlike, six-tepaled, straw-yellow flowers. Tepals with brown-purple central stripe. Usually just one grasslike leaf that often withers early.

NOTE: Closely resembling its more northern relative pretty face (p. 218), the tepals of this species are separate all the way to the base instead of being fused into a tube at the base.

HABITAT: Woodlands, grasslands, chaparral (to 5,500 feet); found on south coast and in coast ranges, southern foothills, Transverse Ranges, Peninsular Ranges.

WHERE AND WHEN:

Tehachapi Mountains (April–July)

San Emigdio Mountains (April–July)

Channel Islands (April–July)

Greenhorn Mountains (April–July)

Santa Rosa Plateau (April–July)

Temblor Range (April–July)

Golden stars

LAYIA, GOLDEN   *Layia glandulosa* subsp. *lutea*

Aster family

DESCRIPTION: 4–12 inches. Slender, glandular stems with scattered narrow, comblike basal and lower stem leaves and smooth-edged upper leaves.

Three to 14 yellow or cream ray flowers surrounding a yellow disk, each ray three-toothed.

NOTE: This plant with the lovely creamy-yellow ray flowers is a subspecies of the more frequent and widespread white-flowered *L. glandulosa* (p. 239).

HABITAT: Sandy flats (to 8,000 feet); found in south coast ranges.

WHERE AND WHEN:

Shell Creek off SR-58 (April–May)

Tehachapi Mountains (April–May)

Golden layia

LOTUS, BICOLORED or
WITCHES' TEETH   *Hosackia gracilis* or *Lotus formosissimus*

Pea family

DESCRIPTION: 0.5–2 feet. Sprawling or ascending stems terminating in an umbel of three to nine pea flowers. Banner yellow with dark veins; wings pink-purple fading white. Small, pinnately compound leaves with three to seven leaflets in opposite pairs.

Bicolored lotus

NOTE: At first glance, you might think you were looking at a patch of two separate flowers—one yellow and one pink or white.

HABITAT: Seashores, wet meadows, ditches (to 2,100 feet); found on coast and coast ranges.

WHERE AND WHEN:

Kruse Rhododendron State Park (April–July)

Santa Lucia Range (April–July)

Mount Tamalpais (April–July)

Santa Cruz Mountains (April–July)

Monterey Peninsula (April–July)

Salt Point (May–June)

LUPINE, YELLOW BUSH   *Lupinus arboreus*

Pea family

DESCRIPTION: 3–5 feet. Shrub dense with racemes of pea flowers usually yellow (occasionally lilac or purple). Palmately compound leaves with five to 12 narrow, pointed leaflets often fringed with short, silvery hairs.

NOTE: Usually growing on windswept beaches (probably native to the central California coast and planted elsewhere to stabilize dunes), this shrub often forms smoothly "pruned" mounds. In many places, it has become an aggressive invader.

HABITAT: Dunes, bluffs (below 300 feet); found on coast.

WHERE AND WHEN:

Salt Point (April–June)

Carmel (May–June)

Big Sur (May–June)

Point Reyes (May–June)

Manchester Beach (May–
August)
Humboldt Bay (May–
August)

Yellow bush lupine

MADIA, COMMON
Aster family

Madia elegans

DESCRIPTION: 0.5–3 feet. Simple or branching glandular stems with several flat flower heads. Five to 21 deeply lobed, fan-shaped, lemon-yellow ray flowers, often with purple blotches at base. Twenty-five to 50 yellow or maroon disk flowers.

NOTE: The heavy, pungent aroma clinging to your hands after you touch the leaves may not be as pleasing as the flowers!

HABITAT: Grasslands, openings in woods (to 11,000 feet); found in much of California (except deserts).

WHERE AND WHEN:
Hite's Cove Trail (April–May)
King's Canyon/Sequoia
(April–May)
Trinity Alps (April–June)
Yosemite Valley (April–June)
Carrizo Plain (May–June)
Santa Monica Mountains
(June–August)

Common madia

MARIGOLD, DESERT
Aster family

Baileya multiradiata

DESCRIPTION: 8–20 inches. Mostly leafless stems rising above basal, pinnately divided leaves, each stem bearing terminal bright-yellow flower head (to 2 inches). Fifty to 60 overlapping rays, each with three conspicuous lobes. Stems and leaves covered with matted white hairs.

Desert marigold

NOTE: Talk about intense golden suns—each flower head consists of scores of overlapping rays but still finds room for a central golden disk as well.

HABITAT: Sandy flats, washes (2,000–5,200 feet); found in Mojave Desert.

WHERE AND WHEN:
Joshua Tree (April–June)
Death Valley (April–July)
Anza-Borrego (April–July)
eastern San Bernardino
  Mountains (April–July)
Coachella Valley (April–July)
Mojave National Preserve
  (April–July, October)

MONKEYFLOWER, YELLOW-AND-WHITE
Lopseed family (previously included in Snapdragon family)

Mimulus bicolor

DESCRIPTION: 4–12 inches. Several two-lipped, tubular flowers along stem on short pedicels from leaf axils. Two petal lobes of upper lip are white; three lobes of lower lip are yellow with red spots. California endemic.

Yellow-and-white monkeyflower

NOTE: The bicolored flowers are unusual for a *Mimulus*—the solid-colored common yellow monkeyflower (also in the photo) is more typical.
HABITAT: Moist, grassy area (to 6,000 feet); found in northwest mountains, foothills, Cascades, Sierra.
WHERE AND WHEN:
Traverse Creek Botanical Area (April–May)
Shower Lake area (April–May)
Wawona Meadow in Yosemite (April–May)
near Potato Patch Campground (April–May)
King's Canyon/Sequoia (April–June)
upper Bidwell Park (May–July)

POND LILY, YELLOW *Nuphar lutea or N. polysepala*
Water lily family
DESCRIPTION: 2–6 feet. Globe-shaped, bright yellow flowers (to 2 inches) floating or a foot or so above the water surface. Eight or more leathery, petal-like sepals surround smaller petals and reproductive parts.
NOTE: The enormous leaves often clog the surface of small ponds, sometimes completely hiding the water.
HABITAT: Ponds, slow streams (to 7,500 feet); found in northwest mountains, north and central coast and coast ranges, Cascades, Sierra, northeast corner.
WHERE AND WHEN:
Nipomo-Guadalupe Dunes (April–June)
Jenner-Fort Ross area (April–July)
Modoc Plateau (May–June)
Grass Lake at Luther Pass (July)
Crane Flat in Yosemite (July)
Trinity Alps (July–August)

Yellow pond lily

PUSSY EARS, YELLOW or
YELLOW STAR TULIP
Calochortus monophyllus

Lily family

DESCRIPTION: 3–8 inches. One or several bowl-shaped flowers with bright yellow petals, dense with yellow hairs. Usually small, red spots toward base. A single, grasslike leaf that usually far outreaches the flowers.

Yellow pussy ears

NOTE: This is certainly among the brightest and the hairiest (along with Tolmie's pussy ears, p. 269) of all the many *Calochortus* species in California.

HABITAT: Woodlands (1,200–4,000 feet); found in foothills.

WHERE AND WHEN:
Pine Hill Preserve (April–May)
Hell's Half-Acre (April–May)
Traverse Creek Botanical Area (April–May)
Table Mountain (April–May)
Yuba River canyon (April–June)
Drum Powerhouse Road (April–June)

SCALE BUD
Anisocoma acaulis

Aster family

DESCRIPTION: 2–8 inches. Leafless stalks with terminal, showy flower head (to 1 inch) of lemon-yellow, straplike rays only, each with five tiny teeth. Basal rosette of pinnately toothed or divided leaves. Milky sap.

Scale bud

NOTE: The phyllaries under the flower head are almost as striking as the flower heads themselves—with their maroon stripes and often maroon dots and/or reddish tips.

HABITAT: Sandy flats, washes (2,000–7,900 feet); found in south coast ranges, San Joaquin Valley, eastern Sierra, east of the Sierra, northeast corner, Transverse Ranges, Peninsular Ranges, Mojave Desert, Sonoran Desert.

WHERE AND WHEN:
Carrizo Plain (April–May)
Doyle area (April–May)
Bishop Creek (April–May)
Joshua Tree (April–May)
Mojave National Preserve (April–June)
Horseshoe Meadow Road (June)

SEDUM, PACIFIC   *Sedum spathulifolium*
Stonecrop family

DESCRIPTION: 2–12 inches. Branched inflorescence of five to 50 lemon-yellow, star-shaped flowers (to 0.5 inches) on stem coming from center of leaves. Pale green, succulent, rounded, overlapping leaves.

NOTE: Whereas the leaves of most sedums are longer than broad, and form basal rosettes of leaves radiating from the center, these leaves are short and rounded and delicately overlapping.

HABITAT: Shady, often rocky places (to 7,500 feet); found in northwest mountains, coast and coast ranges, foothills, Cascades, Sierra, Transverse Ranges.

Pacific sedum

Independence Trail (April–May)
Mount Tamalpais (April–May)
El Paso Canyon (April–May)
Six Rivers National Forest (April–May)
Santa Lucia Range (April–May)
Tenaya Canyon in Yosemite (June–July)

SILVERWEED, PACIFIC

Argentina egedii **subsp.** *egedii* **or**
Potentilla anserina **subsp.** *pacifica*

Rose family

DESCRIPTION: 1–6 inches. Tufted plant from runners with single bright yellow, five-petaled flower (to 1 inch) atop slender pedicel. Cluster of 20–25

stamens. Dark green, crinkly, pinnately compound feathery leaves with three to 15 toothed leaflets per side.

NOTE: The "footsteps" of this plant always seem to be heading toward the ocean.

HABITAT: Bluffs, dunes, coastal marshes, stream banks (to 500 feet); found on coast, Transverse Ranges.

WHERE AND WHEN:
Channel Islands (April–May)
Salt Point (April–June)
Muir Beach (April–June)
Bodega Head (April–June)
San Bernardino Mountains
(April–June)
San Bruno Mountains
(April–June)

Pacific silverweed

SUNFLOWER, PRINGLE'S WOOLLY

Eriophyllum pringlei

Aster family

DESCRIPTION: 1–3 inches. Tufted plant with wedge-shaped, three-lobed leaves usually hidden under dense, cobwebby, white-woolly hairs. Yellow flower heads (to 0.5 inches) of 10–25 disk flowers (no rays) resting on leaves.

NOTE: Of all the hairy desert plants (presumably to help reduce evaporation), this woolly sunflower probably out-woollies all the rest.

HABITAT: Sandy flats, desert scrub, sagebrush scrub, woodlands (to 7,300 feet); found in south coast ranges, Transverse Ranges, eastern Sierra, east of the Sierra, Mojave Desert, Sonoran Desert.

WHERE AND WHEN:
Alabama Hills (April–May)
Sawmill Pass Trail (April–May)
Carrizo Plain (April–May)
Anza-Borrego (April–May)
San Bernardino Mountains (April–June)
White Mountains (April–June)

Pringle's woolly sunflower

VERBENA, YELLOW SAND or
COASTAL SAND VERBENA
Abronia latifolia

Four o'clock family

DESCRIPTION: 1–6 feet. Trailing stem forming large mats across the sand. Many tight, ball-shaped umbels of bright yellow, shallow bowl-shaped flowers at tips of peduncles coming out of the leaf axils.

NOTE: The stems and fleshy leaves are sticky, so you'll usually find grains of sand stuck fast.

HABITAT: Dunes, scrub (to 350 feet); found on coast.

Yellow sand verbena

WHERE AND WHEN:
Channel Islands (April–May)
Monterey Peninsula (April–July)
Point Reyes (April–August)
Manchester Beach (April–August)
mouth of Santa Maria River (April–August)
Humboldt Bay (May–August)

VIOLET, FAN or SHELTON VIOLET   *Viola sheltonii*
Violet family
DESCRIPTION: 2–9 inches. Clusters of several stems, each with terminal flower (to 1 inch) with bright yellow petals, the upper two with brown-purple tinge on the back. Palmately compound, blue-green leaves with narrow, lobed segments.

NOTE: "Fan violet" is a perfect name for this species, for its palmately compound leaves with the many narrow segments do resemble soft-green fans.
HABITAT: Woodlands (2,500–8,000 feet); found in northwest mountains, coast ranges, foothills, Sierra, northeast corner, Transverse Ranges.
WHERE AND WHEN:
Drum Powerhouse Road
  (April–May)
Greenhorn Range (April–
  May)
Diablo Range (April–May)
Warner Mountains (May–
  June)
Yosemite Valley (May–June)
Trinity Alps (June–July)

Fan violet

APACHE PLUME   *Fallugia paradoxa*
Rose family
DESCRIPTION: 1–6 feet. Much-branched shrub with gray, peeling stems and clusters of deeply lobed, needlelike leaves. One to three flowers (to 2 inches) at tips of long stems with five crinkly, bright white petals and many reproductive parts.

Apache plume

NOTE: As lovely as the flowers are, this plant is showiest when it goes to fruit, for the many styles are reddish, sinuous, and feathery.

HABITAT: Rocky slopes, woodlands (3,000–7,200 feet); found in Mojave Desert, Sonoran Desert.

WHERE AND WHEN:
Death Valley (April–June)
Anza-Borrego (April–June)
Clark Mountains in Mojave National Preserve (April–June)
Granite Mountains in Mojave National Preserve (April–June)
Kingston Range in Mojave National Preserve (April–June)

BITTERROOT   *Lewisia rediviva*
Miner's lettuce family (previously included in Purslane family)

DESCRIPTION: 1–4 inches. Several very showy, bowl-shaped flowers (to 3 inches). Ten to 19 white, pink, or rose petals cradling six to eight creamy, wormlike stigmas and 30–50 stamens with pink anthers.

NOTE: Although the species name *rediviva* (meaning "brought back to life") refers to a quality of the plant, you may feel "revived" just looking at these amazing blossoms!

HABITAT: Rocky or sandy soil, sagebrush scrub, open woodlands (to 10,000 feet); found in northwest mountains, coast ranges, foothills, Sierra, east of the Sierra, northeast corner, Transverse Ranges, Peninsular Ranges, Mojave Desert.

WHERE AND WHEN:
Bear Valley (April–May)
Red Hill Road (April–May)
Santa Lucia Range (April–May)

Santa Monica Mountains
(April–June)
Mount Pinos (May–July)
Warner Mountains (June–
July)

Bitterroot

BUCKWHEAT, CALIFORNIA   *Eriogonum fasciculatum*
Buckwheat family
DESCRIPTION: 0.5–6.5 feet. Branched shrub two to 10 feet in diameter, thick with clusters of small, leathery leaves and densely flowered umbels of white (pinkish tinged) flowers.

NOTE: The red anthers and the subtle, reddish markings at the throat give the otherwise white flowers a bit of colorful garnish, which intensifies when the flowers dry (pink then burnt orange).
HABITAT: Sandy or gravelly flats and slopes, washes, canyons (to 7,500 feet); found in much of central and southern California (except San Joaquin Valley).
WHERE AND WHEN:
Alabama Hills (April–May)
Mojave National Preserve (April–June)

California buckwheat

White Mountains (April–June)
Carrizo Plain (April–October)
San Gabriel Mountains (April–October)
Santa Monica Mountains (April–October)

DOGWOOD, CREEK or AMERICAN DOGWOOD   *Cornus sericea*
Dogwood family

DESCRIPTION: 3–12 feet. Shrub with large, round-topped clusters of creamy white, four-petaled flowers (to 0.5 inches). Red stems and opposite pairs of broad, veined, dark-green leaves.

NOTE: Although the flowers are smaller and not as showy as those of the familiar dogwood tree (p. 396), this species is striking for contrasts—white

flowers, dark-green leaves, and red or red-purple stems.

HABITAT: Moist thickets, stream banks, seeps (to 9,200 feet); found in much of California (except northeast corner and deserts).

WHERE AND WHEN:
Big Sur (April–May)
Trinity Alps (April–June)
San Jacinto Mountains
   (May–June)
Yosemite Valley (May–June)
Lassen National Park (June–
   July)
San Bernardino Mountains
   (July–August)

Creek dogwood

EVENING PRIMROSE, TUFTED   *Oenothera caespitosa*
Evening primrose family

DESCRIPTION: 1–8 inches. Several large, showy, white flowers (to 4 inches) close to the ground. Four heart-shaped, crinkly petals. Fragrant. Large, tonguelike leaves.

NOTE: Since this is a night-bloomer, in the early morning or late afternoon, you will often find a few flowers in glorious white bloom while several others, which bloomed a day or so earlier, are in delicious pink wilting.

HABITAT: Desert scrub, woodlands (to 10,000 feet); found in eastern Sierra, east of the Sierra, northeast corner, Mojave Desert, Sonoran Desert.

WHERE AND WHEN:
Antelope Valley (April–May)
Topaz Lake (May)

Tufted evening
primrose

Death Valley (May–June)
Modoc Plateau (May–June)
White Mountains (May–June)
Bishop Creek (June)

KECKIELLA, WHITE-FLOWERED or
BUSH BEARDTONGUE   *Keckiella breviflora*
Plantain family (previously included in Snapdragon family)
DESCRIPTION: 0.5–6 feet. Shrub with opposite pairs of two-lipped flowers.

Petal lobes creamy white, usually with purple or pink lines.

NOTE: The pairing of the flowers is endearingly like a matched pair of tropical lovebirds sitting on a branch.

HABITAT: Dry, rocky places; shrubby slopes (to 8,900 feet); found in coast ranges, Central Valley, foothills, Sierra, Transverse Ranges.

WHERE AND WHEN:
Buck Meadows area (April–
    May)
Kern River Canyon (May–June)
San Gabriel Mountains (May–
    June)
Geyser Peak (May–June)
upper Bidwell Park (May–July)
Santa Lucia Range (May–July)

White-flowered keckiella

Labrador tea

LABRADOR TEA

Ledum glandulosum or
Rhododendron neoglandulosum

Heath family

DESCRIPTION: 1–4 feet. Evergreen shrub thick with round clusters of shallow bowl-shaped, white or creamy, half-inch flowers. Eight to 10 long-protruding stamens. Rosettes of shiny, sticky, yellow-green, tonguelike leaves.

NOTE: If you rub a leaf, you will be enveloped in a strong medicinal smell.

HABITAT: Boggy meadows, edges of ponds and lakes (4,000–12,000 feet); found in northwest mountains, coast and coast ranges, Cascades, Sierra, east of the Sierra.

WHERE AND WHEN:

Salt Point (April–June)
Santa Lucia Range (May–June)
Trinity Alps (June–August)
King's Canyon/Sequoia (July–August)
Lassen National Park (July–August)
Mosquito Flat trail (July–August)

LOVAGE, CELERY-LEAF or
CELERY-LEAF LICORICEROOT

Ligusticum apiifolium

Carrot family

DESCRIPTION: 1–5 feet. Stout stem with terminal umbel of many umbellets of tiny, white flowers. Threadlike bracts just under primary umbel often project above flowers.

NOTE: Many members of the Carrot family have finely, pinnately divided,

Celery-leaf lovage

almost fernlike leaves, but celery-leaf lovage, with its lacy, much divided leaves *and* its threadlike bracts, looks especially delicate and airy.

HABITAT: Meadows, bluffs, woodlands (to 6,000 feet); found on north and central coast and in coast ranges.

WHERE AND WHEN:
Jenner-Fort Ross area
(April–May)
San Bruno Mountains
(April–June)
Santa Cruz Mountains
(April–June)
Sea Ranch (May–June)
Salt Point (May–June)
Mount Sanhedrin (May–June)

MOUNTAIN MISERY or BEAR CLOVER   *Chamaebatia foliolosa*
Rose family

DESCRIPTION: 0.5–2 feet. Evergreen shrub with many white, five-petaled flowers sitting atop the finely divided, fernlike, rough, glandular leaves. Plants often form dense knee-high or ankle-high thickets. California endemic.

Mountain misery

NOTE: The glandular, resinous leaves are strongly, not-so-pleasantly scented and sticky, leaving a stain when touched ... maybe not exactly misery, but not a delight, either.

HABITAT: Forests edges and clearings (1,800–7,000 feet); found in foothills, Cascades, Sierra, east of the Sierra.

WHERE AND WHEN:
Drum Powerhouse Road
(April–May)
Greenhorn Range (April–May)
King's Canyon/Sequoia
(April–May)

Burney area (April–May)
Crowley Lake area (April–May)
Foresta area in Yosemite (May–June)

NAVARRETIA, NEEDLE
Navarretia intertexta
Phlox family

DESCRIPTION: 2–8 inches. Dwarf plant (often forming mats) with spiny heads of small, tubular flowers. Flower tube and five flaring, rounded petal lobes are pure white or slightly blue. Hairy leaves with narrow, pinnate, needlelike leaf segments.

NOTE: These spiny-looking plants with the lovely white flowers often provide palettes in drying vernal pools for the blue painting of the downingias.

HABITAT: Wet meadows, vernal pools (to 7,000 feet); found in northwest mountains, coast ranges, Central Valley, foothills, Cascades, Sierra, northeast corner, Transverse Ranges.

WHERE AND WHEN:
Bogg's Lake (April–May)
Greenhorn Range (April–May)
San Gabriel Mountains (April–May)
Modoc Plateau (May–June)
Santa Lucia Range (May–June)
Martis Valley in Tahoe (June)

Needle navarretia

NOLINA, PARRY'S
Nolina parryi
Ruscus family (previously included in Lily family)

DESCRIPTION: 3–7 feet. Thick, woody, unbranched or branched stem with basal rosette of 60–200 very narrow, swordlike leaves. Long flowering stalk with hundreds of small (to one-fourth inch), creamy flowers. Six tepals in two whorls. California endemic.

NOTE: This conspicuous desert plant resembles our Lord's candle (p. 246) from a distance, but close inspection shows quite different flowers—much smaller and persisting as dry, papery remains.

HABITAT: Dry slopes and ridges (to 6,000 feet); found in southern Sierra, Transverse Ranges, Peninsular Ranges, Mojave Desert, Sonoran Desert.

WHERE AND WHEN:
Joshua Tree (April–June)
Kingston Mountains (April–June)
Kern Plateau (April–June)
San Bernardino Mountains (April–June)
Palomar Mountain (April–June)
Little San Bernardino Mountains (April–June)

Parry's nolina

POPPY, MATILIJA   *Romneya coulteri*
Poppy family

DESCRIPTION: 3–8 feet. Shrub with gray-green, three- to five-lobed leaves and numerous crepe-papery, six-petaled, fragrant, white flowers (to 6 inches across). Large dome of yellow reproductive parts in center. California endemic. CNPS Rare and Endangered List—endangered.

NOTE: This striking flower is the largest of any plant native to California. How could any self-respecting pollinator possibly miss this bloom!

Matilija poppy

HABITAT: Dry washes, canyons (to 4,000 feet); found on south coast and coast ranges, Transverse Ranges, Peninsular Ranges.

WHERE AND WHEN:

Eaton Canyon Nature Center (April–May)
Cozy Dell Trail (April–May)
Torrey Pines (May–July)
Santa Ana Mountains (May–July)
Santa Monica Mountains (May–July)
San Gabriel Mountains (May–July)

ROCK NETTLE, DESERT or STING BUSH   *Eucnide urens*
Loasa family

DESCRIPTION: 1–1.5 feet. Subshrub with prickly white hairs and broad, stiff-toothed leaves. Clusters of translucent, creamy white or pale yellow, tubular flowers (to 2 inches) with five flaring petals.

NOTE: Be careful not to touch this bristly-hairy plant—it is not named "rock nettle" and "sting bush" for nothing.

HABITAT: rocky slopes, washes, cliffs (to 4,600 feet); found in Mojave Desert, Sonoran Desert.

WHERE AND WHEN:

Death Valley (April–May)
Whipple Mountains (April–May)
Anza-Borrego (April–May)
Red Rock Canyon (April–May)
El Paso Mountains (April–May)
Mojave National Preserve (April–May)

Desert rock nettle

SAGE, PITCHER or WOODBALM   *Lepechinia calycina*
Mint family

DESCRIPTION: 3–6 feet. Shrub with opposite pairs of rough, toothed leaves above which rise racemes of many pendant, broad-tubular, two-lipped, white or pale lavender flowers (to 1.5 inches). Broad lower lip hangs down below tube. Swollen, veined, rough-haired calyx. California endemic.

NOTE: Although the leaves aren't altogether pleasantly scented, you could

Pitcher sage

easily imagine some delicious, creamy or lavender liquid pouring out of these lovely pitchers.

HABITAT: Chaparral, scrub, rocky slopes (to 3,000 feet); found in coast ranges, north and central foothills, Transverse Ranges.

WHERE AND WHEN:
Lake Sonoma area (April–June)
San Bruno Mountain (April–June)
Santa Ynez Mountains (April–June)
Pinnacles (May–June)
Mount Diablo (May–June)
Ukiah area (May–June)

SOLOMON'S SEAL, STAR-FLOWERED FALSE
Maianthemum stellatum or *Smilacina stellata*
Ruscus family (previously included in Lily family)

DESCRIPTION: 1–3 feet. Loose raceme of five to 20 small, creamy white,

Star-flowered false Solomon's seal

star-shaped flowers on short pedicels. Six widely separated, pointed tepals. Berries first greenish-yellow, then purple or black.

NOTE: The raceme stem usually gently zigzags between the flowers, mirroring the plant stem's zigzagging between the alternating leaves.

HABITAT: Stream banks, moist forest openings, moist meadows (to 8,000 feet); found in much of California (except northeast corner and deserts).

WHERE AND WHEN:
Boggs Lake (April–May)
Santa Lucia Range (April–May)

Trinity Alps (June–July)
San Jacinto Mountains (June–July)
Lassen National Park (June–July)
San Bernardino Mountains (July)

YUCCA, MOJAVE or SPANISH DAGGER *Yucca schidigera*
Agave family (previously included in Lily family)

DESCRIPTION: 3–15 feet. Shrub or small tree with rosette of long, stiff, swordlike leaves and dense clusters of hanging, creamy white flowers (to 2 inches). Leaves have distinctive, peeling fibers on edges. Fruits are thick, cylindrical, hanging pods.

NOTE: The leaves are as dangerous as the name implies!

HABITAT: Desert scrub (to 8,200 feet); found on south coast and in coast ranges, Transverse Ranges, Peninsular Ranges, Mojave Desert, Sonoran Desert.

WHERE AND WHEN:
Anza-Borrego (April–May)
Joshua Tree (April–May)
Mojave National Preserve
   (April–May)
Torrey Pines (April–May)
Channel Islands (April–May)
San Jacinto River (April–
   May)

Mojave yucca

CHOLLA, SILVER *Cylindropuntia echinocarpa* or *Opuntia echinocarpa*
Cactus family

DESCRIPTION: 2–5 feet. Much-branched, treelike plant with cylindrical, jointed stems with silver-gray spines in clusters of 3 to 20. Bowl-shaped, yellow-green flowers with many petals.

NOTE: This species overlaps in distribution with buckhorn cholla (p. 415), which closely resembles it (except, usually, in flower color) and sometimes hybridizes with it.

Silver cholla

HABITAT: Desert flats and slopes, washes (to 4,600 feet); found east of the Sierra, Mojave Desert, Sonoran Desert.

WHERE AND WHEN:
Death Valley (April–May)
Joshua Tree (April–May)
White Mountains (April–May)
Anza-Borrego (April–May)
Mojave National Preserve (May–June)
Benton area (June)

Silver cholla

PARSLEY, DESERT   *Lomatium mohavense*
Carrot family

DESCRIPTION: 4–16 inches. Thick stem rising above basal, fernlike, pinnately compound leaves with terminal umbel of long, arching spokes, each with spherical umbel of tiny (to one-eighth inch), black-purple to maroon (sometimes yellow) flowers.

NOTE: You expect white, yellow, pink, or even greenish Queen Anne's lace-like flowers in Carrot family members, so these black-purple flowers are a stunning surprise.

HABITAT: sandy flats, desert scrub, woodlands (3,000–6,500 feet); found in south coast ranges, east of the Sierra, Transverse Ranges, Mojave Desert.

WHERE AND WHEN:

Carrizo Plain (April–May)
White Mountains (April–May)
Alabama Hills (April–May)
San Gabriel Mountains (April–May)
Anza-Borrego (April–May)
Antelope Valley (April–May)

Desert parsley

NON-NATIVE BOUQUETS

First Bouquet

Sea fig

Sea Fig
Carpobrotus chilensis
Fig-marigold family

DESCRIPTION: Fleshy, three-sided leaves form extensive mats; magenta or purple flowers with many fringelike petals.

EXAMPLE OF LOCATION: Salt Point.

Tamarisk

Tamarisk or Salt Cedar
Tamarix ramosissima
Tamarisk family

DESCRIPTION: Shrub or small tree with spikes of small, pink flowers.

EXAMPLE OF LOCATION: *Alabama Hills.*

(First bouquet, continued)

ice Plant, Slender-Leaved or False Ice Plant
Conicosia pugioniformis
Fig-marigold family

DESCRIPTION: Narrow, fleshy, three-sided leaves; many very narrow, threadlike yellow petals.

EXAMPLE OF LOCATION: *Nipomo-Guadalupe Dunes*

Slender-leaved ice plant

Second Bouquet

Flax, Wild or Pale Flax
Linum bienne
Flax family

DESCRIPTION: Threadlike stem with one pinwheel-like, white or pale blue flower at tip.

EXAMPLE OF LOCATION: Salt Point

Wild flax

(Second bouquet, continued)

Poison hemlock

Stinging nettle

Poison Hemlock
Conium maculatum
Carrot family

DESCRIPTION: Stout stem with many umbels of tiny, white flowers; lacy leaves; very toxic plant; purple splotches on stems.

EXAMPLE OF LOCATION: *Stinson Beach.*

Stinging Nettle
Urtica dioica
Nettle family

DESCRIPTION: Stout stem with plumes of tiny, greenish flowers; stinging hairs on upper surface of leaves.

EXAMPLE OF LOCATION: Sea Ranch

MAY

Speckled clarkia along Kern River Canyon

WITH THE COMING of May, the Central Valley bloom is mostly over; but the coast, the coast ranges, and the foothills are continuing to peak, complementing the carryover of the spectacular April bloom with a new wave of gorgeous flowering. In the foothills and in the coast ranges, this is the month for the rich blue or blue-purple brodiaeas and the startling pink or red-purple clarkias (many of which are endemic to California) bidding their farewells to spring. May is also the month for stunning thickets of azaleas and rhododendrons on brushy slopes and in forests along the coast. Now, too, the Great Basin desert east of the Sierra and Cascades, especially on the Modoc Plateau, is coming into full spring flower, and finally even the high country (at least its lower altitudes up to about 7,000 feet) is awakening from the winter snow to its first flowers, some of which create dazzling masses of brilliant color.

Highlights

Beaches and Bluffs Along the Coast

Windflower, Columbia lily, calypso orchid, false lily-of-the-valley, and **red clintonia** in Redwoods National and State Parks
Rosy butter-and-eggs, rosy onion, dwarf brodiaea, coast dudleya, and **sea thrift** at Salt Point
Rhododendron and **azalea** at Kruse Rhododendron State Park

Coast Ranges

Long-rayed hyacinth, ruby chalice clarkia, and the rare **Tiburon mariposa lily** on Ring Mountain
Pitcher plant and **mountain dogwood** at Butterfly Valley
Two-horned downingia at Boggs Lake
The rare **Mount Diablo globe lily** on Mount Diablo
Spotted downingia, splendid mariposa lily, and **Vasey's prickly pear** on the Santa Rosa Plateau
Fairy fan and **Douglas spineflower** at Pinnacles

Foothills

Elegant clarkia, bilobed clarkia, and **Williamson's clarkia** along Yankee Jim's Road
Speckled clarkia, elegant clarkia, wine-cup clarkia, and **gunsight clarkia** in the Kern River Canyon
Bleeding hearts and **white Chinese houses** along Drum Powerhouse Road
Bridge's brodiaea and the rare **Pine Hill flannelbush** at Pine Hill Preserve

Sierra

Camas lily and **alpine shooting star** at Sagehen Creek
Miles of **bush monkeyflower** in Feather River Canyon

Transverse Ranges

Large-flowered phacelia, golden yarrow, climbing penstemon, bush monkeyflower, and **our Lord's candle** in the San Gabriel and San Bernardino Mountains
Bush mallow, tall purple sage, and **scarlet monkeyflower** in the Santa Monica Mountains

Northeast Corner

Sand lily, big-headed clover, Beckwith violet, showy penstemon, and **Hooker's balsamroot** on the Modoc Plateau
Heart-leaf arnica in the Warner Mountains

East of the Sierra

Bigelow's monkeyflower in the Benton area
Apricot mallow and **tufted evening primrose** at Topaz Lake
Fringed onion, desert calico, purple sage, and **grape soda lupine** at the California Desert Conservation Area
Anderson's larkspur and **flat-stemmed onion** at Monitor Pass

Deserts

Apache plume, desert willow, and **banana yucca** at Anza-Borrego
Desert gold at Death Valley

Flowers

BRODIAEA, BRIDGE'S   *Triteleia bridgesii* or *Brodiaea bridgesii*
Brodiaea family (previously included in Lily family)
DESCRIPTION: 1–2 feet. Loose umbel of up to 20 blue-purple, violet, or lilac funnel-shaped flowers with six wide-spreading tepals. White at base of tepals. Blue anthers.
NOTE: Of the several rather similar species of *Brodiaea* and *Triteleia*, this one is distinguished by the loose umbel, the white at the base of the tepals, and the blue anthers.
HABITAT: Forest edges, rocky places (to 3,000 feet); found in northwest mountains, north coast ranges, foothills.

WHERE AND WHEN:
Pine Hill Ecological Preserve
(May–June)
SR-36 east of Red Bluff
(May–June)
upper Bidwell Park (May–
June)
west of Ukiah (May–June)
Plaskett Meadow (May–
June)
Jedediah Smith State Park
(May–June)

Bridge's brodiaea

BRODIAEA, ELEGANT or HARVEST BRODIAEA   *Brodiaea elegans*
Brodiaea family (previously included in Lily family)
DESCRIPTION: 4–16 inches. Loose umbel of up to 10 blue-purple or violet funnel-shaped flowers at tip of stem. Six flaring tepals with darker purple mid-vein and tips curved back. Three narrow, erect, white staminodes standing away from the erect stamens close to the tepals.

NOTE: The positioning of the staminodes helps differenti-ate this species from many of the other species with similar flowers.

HABITAT: Grasslands, open woods (to 7,000 feet); found in northwest mountains, north and central coast ranges, foothills, Sierra, Transverse Ranges.

WHERE AND WHEN:
Hite's Cove Trail (May)
Ring Mountain (May–June)
Diablo Range (May–June)
Table Mountain (May–July)
King's Canyon/Sequoia
(May–July)
Trinity Alps (June–July)

Elegant broadiaea

Dwarf brodiaea

BRODIAEA, DWARF   *Brodiaea terrestris*
Brodiaea family (previously included in Lily family)
DESCRIPTION: 2–10 inches. Loose umbel of purple, funnel-shaped flowers on short pedicels. Six flaring tepals with tips curved back. Three broad, erect, waxy, white or pink staminodes close to the stamens and enclosing them.
NOTE: The flowers usually appear to be scattered directly on the grass.
HABITAT: Grasslands (to 5,000 feet); found in northwest mountains, coast, coast ranges, Central Valley, foothills, Transverse Ranges, Peninsular Ranges.
WHERE AND WHEN:
Aqua Tibia Mountains (May–June)
Phoenix Park (May–June)
Diablo Range (May–June)
Salt Point (May–July)
Santa Lucia Range (May–July)
Trinity Alps (June–July)

BRODIAEA, PURDY'S   *Brodiaea purdyi*
Brodiaea family (previously included in Lily family)
DESCRIPTION: 0.5–1 foot. Loose umbel of only a few spreading, blue-violet flowers. Six narrow tepals with dark purple mid-veins. Conspicuous, white staminodes at center of flower.
NOTE: This species of *Brodiaea* is distinguished from others by its very loose umbel of only a few flowers; the very narrow, widely separated tepals with the dark purple stripe; the white, fleshy, erect staminodes; and its often-serpentine habitat.
HABITAT: Woodlands, often serpentine (to 2,000 feet); found in Sacramento Valley, northern foothills, northern Sierra.
WHERE AND WHEN:
Drum Powerhouse Road (May–June)

Purdy's brodiaea

Traverse Creek Botanical Area (May–June)
Phoenix Park (May–June)
Hell's Half-Acre (May–June)
Lake Britton area (May–June)
Quincy area (May–July)

CAMAS LILY   *Camassia quamash*
Agave family (previously included in Lily family)
DESCRIPTION: 1–2 feet. Open raceme of many star-shaped flowers (to 1.5
inches) on short, ascending pedicels. Six narrow, pointed, deep-blue tepals
with one slightly longer than the rest.
NOTE: In early spring, some wet meadows can become "lakes" of camas lilies, dazzling the eye with acres of nearly solid floral blue.

Camas lily

HABITAT: Wet meadows, stream banks (2,000–8,000 feet); found in northwest mountains, north coast ranges, Cascades, Sierra, northeast corner.

WHERE AND WHEN:
Sagehen Meadows in Tahoe (May)
Lassen National Park (May–June)
Butterfly Valley (May–June)
Trinity Alps (May–June)
Warner Mountains (May–June)
Mount Sanhedrin (May–June)

DOWNINGIA, SPOTTED or HOOVER'S DOWNINGIA *Downingia bella*
Bellflower family

DESCRIPTION: 0.5–1.5 feet. Sprawling or erect stem with narrow leaves and many showy, two-lipped flowers (to three-fourths inch). Petal lobes deep blue, lower lip with two yellow spots on squarish white patch. Three rich purple spots at throat. California endemic.

NOTE: Occasionally you will find exquisite pink variations in startling contrast to their deep blue neighbors.

HABITAT: Vernal pools, wet meadows, lake margins (to 5,300 feet); found in Central Valley, south coast ranges, Transverse Ranges.

WHERE AND WHEN:
Santa Rosa Plateau (May–June)
Boggs Lake (May–June)
Phoenix Park (May–June)
Jepson Prairie (May–June)
near Merced in the San Joaquin Valley (May–June)

Spotted downingia

LARKSPUR, ANDERSON'S   *Delphinium andersonii*
Buttercup family

DESCRIPTION: 0.5–2 feet. Loose raceme of many flowers on upper half of reddish stem. Dark blue sepals with long, ascending spur with down-curving tip. The two tiny upper petals are white, the two lower petals are blue and bilobed.

NOTE: All larkspurs are striking; Anderson's has the added touch of the contrast of the deep blue flowers with the reddish stems.

HABITAT: Sagebrush scrub, talus (4,000–7,500 feet); found in northern Sierra, east of the Sierra, northeast corner.

WHERE AND WHEN:
east of Monitor Pass (May–June)
near Honey Lake (May–June)
Martis Valley in Tahoe (May–June)
Conway Summit (May–June)
Warner Mountains (May–June)
Lava Beds National Monument (May–June)

Anderson's larkspur

PENSTEMON, DESERT or MOJAVE BEARDTONGUE

Penstemon incertus

Plantain family (previously included in Snapdragon family)

DESCRIPTION: 1.5–3 feet. Shrub thick with narrow, often in-rolled leaves and deep blue, tubular, two-lipped flowers (to 1.5 inches) on opposite pairs of long pedicels. Flowers purple-tinged on outside, whitish on inside.

NOTE: All penstemons have four stamens and one staminode (i.e., an infertile stamen with no anther). In this species, the staminode is densely "bearded."

Desert penstemon

HABITAT: Sandy flats, washes, canyons, sagebrush scrub (3,300–5,600 feet); found in southern Sierra, Transverse Ranges, Mojave Desert.

WHERE AND WHEN:
Alabama Hills (May–June)
Walker Pass (May–June)
Horseshoe Meadow Road (May–June)
Onyx area (May–June)
Antelope Valley area (May–June)
Tehachapi Mountains (May–June)

PENSTEMON, SHOWY or
ROYAL PENSTEMON   *Penstemon speciosus*
Plantain family (previously included in Snapdragon family)

DESCRIPTION: 0.5–2 feet. Densely flowered racemes of rich blue, tubular, two-lipped, somewhat potbellied flowers (to 2 inches) red-purple at throat.

NOTE: Most of the flowers come off the same side of the stem, giving the plant a bit of an unbalanced look.

HABITAT: Sandy or gravelly flats and slopes, forest openings, rocky ridges (to 10,500 feet); found in northwest mountains, Cascades, Sierra, northeast corner, east of the Sierra, Transverse Ranges, Mojave Desert.

WHERE AND WHEN:
Modoc Plateau (May–June)
Monitor Pass (June)
Fallen Leaf Lake in Tahoe
    (June–July)
Lassen National Park (June–
    July)
Piute Mountains (June–July)
Lakes Basin (July)

Showy penstemon

PHACELIA, BOLANDER'S   *Phacelia bolanderi*
Borage family (previously included in Waterleaf family)

DESCRIPTION: 1–2 feet. Loose coils of shallow bowl-shaped, papery, pale blue or purple flowers (to three-fourths inch) along erect or decumbent, glandular-hairy stem. Broad, crinkly, dark green, toothed, distinctly veined leaves.

NOTE: Count yourself lucky to see these lovely flowers in bloom, for they fall off shortly after opening.

HABITAT: Bluffs, canyons, brushy slopes, disturbed places (to 4,600 feet); found in northwest mountains, north coast and coast ranges.

WHERE AND WHEN:
Fort Bragg area (May–June)
Standish-Hickey State Park
(May–June)
Stewart's Point (May–July)
east of Gualala (May–July)
Jenner-Fort Ross area (May–
July)
Greenwood Road east of Elk
(May–July)

Bolander's phacelia

PHACELIA, LINEAR-LEAF or
THREADLEAF PHACELIA
Phacelia linearis

Borage family (previously included in Waterleaf family)

DESCRIPTION: 3–24 inches. Small clusters of delicate, violet, bowl-shaped flowers with white or pale blue throat. Very narrow leaves.

NOTE: Most phacelias have caterpillar-like coils of flowers; this species is usually much simpler, with few-flowered clusters.

HABITAT: Sandy or gravelly flats, sagebrush scrub (3,000–6,500 feet); found in Cascades, Sierra, east of the Sierra, northeast corner.

WHERE AND WHEN:
Modoc Plateau (May–June)
Lassen National Park (May–
June)
Lava Beds National
Monument (May–June)
Weed area (May–June)
Warner Mountains (May–
June)
Beckwourth Pass (May–
June)

Linear-leaf phacelia

Purple sage

SAGE, PURPLE　　　　　　　　　　　　　　*Salvia dorrii*
Mint family

DESCRIPTION: 1–2.5 feet. Shrub with many violet, two-lipped flowers whorled around upper stems. Hairy, red-purple calyx. Blue-green, ovate or spoon-shaped leaves. Fragrant.

NOTE: These shrubs can cover wide areas, usually in sagebrushy terrains, announcing their presence "loudly" with the striking flowers and the clouds of minty fragrance.

HABITAT: Dry, gravelly or rocky places (3,000–13,000 feet); found in Cascades, Sierra, east of the Sierra, northeast corner, Tranverse Ranges, Mojave Desert.

WHERE AND WHEN:
Alabama Hills (May–June)
Mojave National Preserve (May–June)
Sawmill Pass Trail (May–June)
Antelope Valley (May–June)
White Mountains (May–July)
San Gabriel Mountains (May–July)

SQUAW CARPET or MAHALA MAT　　　　*Ceanothus prostratus*
Buckbrush family

DESCRIPTION: 2–8 inches. Wide-spreading, ground-hugging shrub with many clusters of small, pale blue flowers with five clawed petals. Stiff, toothed, hollylike leaves. Red-purple fruits.

NOTE: Sometimes a patch of these plants almost looks like liquid flowing

Squaw carpet

over the ground—the mats of leaves contour the ground, revealing as much as concealing the terrain.

HABITAT: Forest openings; dry, open slopes (3,000–7,800 feet); found in northwest mountains, north coast ranges, Cascades, Sierra, northeast corner.

WHERE AND WHEN:
Pole Creek in Tahoe (May–June)
Mount Shasta (May–June)
Boggs Lake (May–June)
Lakes Basin (May–June)
Trinity Alps (May–June)
Modoc Plateau (May–July)

STAR LAVENDER or CAT'S BREECHES   *Hydrophyllum capitatum*
Borage family (previously included in Waterleaf family)
DESCRIPTION: 1–6 inches. Globe-shaped clusters of lavender or pale blue star-shaped flowers close to the ground, mostly hidden under arching, deeply lobed leaves. Long-protruding reproductive parts.
NOTE: In bud, the clusters of fuzzy white balls look a bit like some bird's clutch of eggs.
HABITAT: Sagebrush flats, moist slopes (3,000–7,000 feet); found in Cascades, Sierra, east of the Sierra, northeast corner.
WHERE AND WHEN:
Kyburz Flat (May–June)
Warner Mountains (May–June)
Martis Valley in Tahoe (May–June)
Markleeville area (May–June)
Modoc Plateau (May–June)
Winnemucca Lake trail at Carson Pass (June–July)

Star lavender

AZALEA, WESTERN *Rhododendron occidentale*
Heath family

DESCRIPTION: 2–14 feet. Shrub with many-flowered clusters of large (to 3 inches), showy, fragrant flowers. Five pink or white petal lobes with pink veins, upper lobe with large yellow patch.

NOTE: Azalea thickets look a bit like a sea of pink and yellow starfish.

HABITAT: Forests, stream banks, shrubby slopes (to 7,500 feet); found in northwest mountains, coast, coast ranges, foothills, Cascades, Sierra, Peninsular Ranges.

WHERE AND WHEN:
Kruse Rhododendron State Park (May–June)

Western azalea

Gabilan Range (May–June)
Feather River Canyon (May–June)
Santa Rosa Plateau (May–June)
Smith River (May–June)
King's Canyon/Sequoia (June–July)

CANCHALAGUA   *Zeltnera venusta* or *Centaurium venustum*
Gentian family
DESCRIPTION: 0.5–1 foot. Several delicate, red-purple, five-petaled flowers
(to 0.5 inches). Short stamens with corkscrew, yellow anthers, and slender,
long-protruding pistil with yellow stigma. California endemic.
NOTE: This is certainly an unusual representative of the Gentian family—
five flaring petals above an inconspicuous and mostly concealed flower
tube and a long-protruding pistil.
HABITAT: Grasslands, forest openings (to 9,000 feet); found in central and
south coast and coast ranges, Central Valley, foothills, Cascades, Sierra,
Transverse Ranges, Peninsular Ranges.
WHERE AND WHEN:
Traverse Creek Botanical Area (May–June)
Torrey Pines (May–June)
San Jacinto Mountains (May–July)
Santa Rosa Plateau (May–August)
Yosemite Valley (June)
Santa Monica Mountains (June–July)

Canchalagua

CLARKIA, BILOBED   *Clarkia biloba*
Evening primrose family
DESCRIPTION: 1–3 feet. Many four-petaled, magenta, pink, or lavender
flowers (to 1 inch) clustered toward the tip of the slender, unbranched
stem. Each petal widest at tip and narrowing at base, two-lobed at tip with

red spots toward base. California endemic.

NOTE: Look for these late-spring bloomers forming masses on hillsides along foothills roads bidding "farewell to spring."

HABITAT: Grassy banks, roadsides (to 4,000 feet); found on central coast and coast ranges, foothills.

WHERE AND WHEN:
Yankee Jim's Road (May–June)
Traverse Creek (May–June)
Ponderosa Way (May–June)
Hetch Hetchy in Yosemite (May–June)
Mount Diablo (May–June)
Los Osos area (May–June)

Bilobed clarkia

CLARKIA, GUNSIGHT
Clarkia xantiana

Evening primrose family

DESCRIPTION: 0.5–3 feet. Wiry stem with a few linear leaves and several mostly flat, four-petaled pink or red-purple flowers (to 1.5 inches), each

Gunsight clarkia

petal deeply notched at tip with spinelike tooth in center of notch. Some or all the petals with red-purple spot or diamond on white patch. California endemic.

NOTE: You can understand the reason for the unusual common name, as the spine in the center of the petal notch points straight and true.

HABITAT: Grasslands, woodlands (to 6,600 feet); found in southern foothills, southern Sierra, Transverse Ranges.

WHERE AND WHEN:
Kern River Canyon (May–June)
Greenhorn Mountains (May–June)
Tehachapi Mountains (May–June)

Ruby chalice
clarkia

CLARKIA, RUBY CHALICE   *Clarkia rubicunda*
Evening primrose family

DESCRIPTION: 1–3 feet. Often branching, slender stem with several showy, four-petaled flowers (to 2 inches). Rounded petals pink with dark red patch at base. Very narrow, sessile leaves. California endemic.

NOTE: The dark-red patch at the base of the petals creates a glowing, red "eye" at the center of the flower.

HABITAT: Grasslands, woodlands, scrub (to 1,600 feet); found on central coast and coast ranges.

WHERE AND WHEN:
Santa Lucia Range (May–June)
San Bruno Mountain (May–June)
San Francisco Bay area (May–June)
Angel Island (May–June)
Ring Mountain (May–July)
Edgewood Preserve (May–July)

CLARKIA, SPECKLED
Clarkia cylindrica

Evening primrose family

DESCRIPTION: 0.5–2 feet. Wiry stem with linear leaves and several slightly cupped, four-petaled, pink or lavender flowers with small, bright red-purple spot at base. Petals usually with pink flecks. Buds nodding. California endemic.

NOTE: In late spring, masses of these lovely flowers can tint entire hillsides pink.

HABITAT: Grasslands, woodlands, chaparral (to 4,000 feet); found in south coast ranges, central and southern foothills, Transverse Ranges.

WHERE AND WHEN:

Kern River Canyon (May–June)

Santa Monica Mountains (May–June)

Figueroa Mountain (May–June)

SR-58 (May–June)

Temblor Range (May–June)

San Gabriel Mountains (May–July)

Speckled clarkia

CLARKIA, WILLIAMSON'S
Clarkia williamsonii

Evening primrose family

DESCRIPTION: 1–3 feet. Clusters of open, bowl-shaped, four-petaled, multicolored flowers at leaf nodes along stem. Petals lavender or pink with white center and dark, red-purple spot at tip. California endemic.

NOTE: Wow, if this is how the flowers say "farewell" to spring (as the clarkias collectively do), maybe it is not so bad to see spring pass! The combination of colors is both softly appealing and dazzling.

HABITAT: Grassy banks, woodlands (to 5,000 feet); found in foothills.

WHERE AND WHEN:

Yankee Jim's Road (May–June)

Hell's Half-Acre (May–June)

Yosemite Valley (May–June)

Red Hill Road (May–June)

Williamson's clarkia

Hetch Hetchy area in Yosemite (May–June)
Coarsegold area (May–June)

CLARKIA, WINE-CUP   *Clarkia purpurea* subsp. *quadrivulnera*
Evening primrose family

DESCRIPTION: 1.5–2 feet. Wiry stem with several nearly flat or shallowly cupped, four-petaled flowers (to three-fourths inch) on long, inferior

ovary out of leaf axil. Petals lavender or purple or dark wine-red.

NOTE: In some flowers the petals are lighter-colored with a rose spot near the middle or at the tip, but often the petals are a solid wine-red purple.

HABITAT: Grasslands, scrub (to 2,000 feet); found in much of California (except northeast corner and deserts).

WHERE AND WHEN:
Santa Rosa Plateau (May–June)
Ponderosa Way (May–June)
Pinnacles (May–June)
Hell's Half-Acre (May–June)
Kern River Canyon (May–June)
Ukiah area (May–June)

Wine-cup clarkia

CLOVER, BIG-HEADED   *Trifolium macrocephalum*
Pea family

DESCRIPTION: 4–12 inches. Large, round, densely flowered head of pink or bicolored pea flowers. Short wings are pink or rose and banner is pink or white. Palmately compound leaves with five to nine wedge-shaped, toothed leaflets.

NOTE: An individual plant is impressive with its large head of flowers; an entire field of these beauties (which often happens) is dazzling.

HABITAT: Sagebrush scrub, ridges (2000–5,500 feet); found in northwest mountains, foothills, Cascades, Sierra, east of the Sierra, northeast corner.

WHERE AND WHEN:
Modoc Plateau (May–June)

SR-36 east of Red Bluff
   (May–June)
Mount Shasta (May–June)
Sierra Valley (May–June)
Warner Mountains (May–
   June)
Lassen National Park (May–
   June)

Big-headed clover

DOGBANE, SPREADING or INDIAN HEMP
Apocynum androsaemifolium

Dogbane family

DESCRIPTION: 0.5–1.5 feet. Low, much-branched plant with clusters of bell-shaped, white (with pink tinges) flowers (to one-fourth inch). Tonguelike dark-green leaves.

NOTE: The alternative common name refers to the tough, sinewy stems, which can be used to weave rope.

HABITAT: Rocky places, forest clearings, chaparral scrub (to 9,500 feet); found in much of California (except Central Valley and deserts).

WHERE AND WHEN:

Bishop Creek (May–July)

Lassen National Park (May–July)

San Jacinto Mountains (May–July)

Onion Valley (June–July)

San Bernardino Mountains (June–July)

Warner Mountains (June–August)

Spreading
dogbane

DUDLEYA, POWDERY or
CHALK LIVEFOREVER
Dudleya pulverulenta
Stonecrop family

DESCRIPTION: 1–2 feet. Several branching stems rise above a large, basal rosette of fleshy, tonguelike, pointed leaves. Stems with smaller, alternating

leaves and many cylindrical, dark red flowers. Sepals, stems, leaves, and underside of flowers covered with dense, white, mealy powder or chalky wax.

NOTE: The flowers are oddly and strikingly reminiscent of red-and-white-striped barber poles.

HABITAT: Dry, rocky places (to 5,000 feet); found in central and south coast ranges, Transverse Ranges, Mojave Desert, Sonoran Desert.

WHERE AND WHEN:
Mojave National Preserve (May–July)
Laguna Coast Wilderness Park (May–July)
Santa Monica Mountains (May–July)
Torrey Pines (May–July)
Anza-Borrego (May–July)
Santa Rosa Plateau (May–July)

Powdery dudleya

FAIRY FAN or BREWER'S CLARKIA
Clarkia breweri
Evening primrose family

DESCRIPTION: 2–8 inches. Low plant with linear leaves and a few shallowly cupped, pink or lavender flowers (to 1.5 inches). Four petals each with three lobes, the center lobe much narrower and longer than the outer two. Long-protruding reproductive parts. California endemic. CNPS Rare and Endangered List—limited distribution.

NOTE: This uncommon beauty has an uncommonly spicy fragrance as well.

HABITAT: Woodlands, chaparral (to 3,000 feet); found in central and south coast ranges.

WHERE AND WHEN:
Pinnacles (May–June)
Mount Hamilton Range (May–June)
Henry Coe State Park (May–June)

Fairy fan

FIRECRACKER FLOWER

Dichelostemma ida-maia

Brodiaea family (previously included in Lily family)

DESCRIPTION: 1–3 feet. Loose umbel of 6 to 20 long-tubular, nodding flowers (up to 1.5 inches) at tip of tall, weak stem. Flower tube bright red with curled white or greenish tips.

NOTE: The shape and color of these odd and striking flowers may indeed remind you of a Fourth of July celebration!

HABITAT: Coastal grassland, forest edges (to 6,600 feet); found in northwest mountains, north coast and coast ranges.

WHERE AND WHEN:

Jenner–Fort-Ross area
    (May–July)
Shasta Lake (May–July)
SR-36 west of Red Bluff
    (May–July)
Six Rivers National Forest
    (May–July)
Coastal Trail near Requa
    (May–July)
Trinity Alps (May–July)

Firecracker flower

Sierra gooseberry

GOOSEBERRY, SIERRA   *Ribes roezlii*
Gooseberry family
DESCRIPTION: 1–3 feet. Shrub with spines at nodes. Clusters of one to three tubular flowers with red-purple, reflexed sepals and less conspicuous, small white petals. California endemic.
NOTE: The globular, red, spiny fruits are a bit intimidating (they look like land mines), but are tasty if you can de-spine them.
HABITAT: Woodlands (to 9,200 feet); found in northwest mountains, coast ranges, Cascades, Sierra, Transverse Ranges, Peninsular Ranges, northeast corner.

WHERE AND WHEN:
King's Canyon/Sequoia
  (May–June)
Santa Lucia Range
  (May–June)
Yosemite Valley (May–
  June)
San Jacinto Mountains
  (June–July)
Trinity Alps (May–July)
Lakes Basin (June)

Sierra gooseberry

HONEYSUCKLE, HAIRY or PINK HONEYSUCKLE *Lonicera hispidula*

Honeysuckle family

DESCRIPTION: 6–20 feet. Climbing, woody vine with reddish stems bearing pairs of broad, dark-green leaves, the upper pairs fused around the stem. Spikes of flowers out of upper leaf axils. Two-lipped, pink, trumpet-shaped flowers with long-protruding stamens. Bright red berries.

NOTE: As you might expect with a honeysuckle, these flowers are as deliciously fragrant as they are gracefully beautiful.

HABITAT: Woodlands, canyons, stream banks (to 2,500 feet); found in northwest mountains, coast and coast ranges, foothills, Transverse Ranges.

WHERE AND WHEN:

Redwood National Park
(May–June)
San Lucia Range (May–June)
Yuba River Canyon (May–June)
Santa Monica Mountains
(May–June)
Mount Tamalpais (May–June)
Salt Point (May–July)

Hairy honeysuckle

INDIGO BUSH, NEVADA *Psorothamnus polydenius*

Pea family

DESCRIPTION: 1–5 feet. Much-branched shrub covered with fine, white hairs and dense with spikelike racemes of small, pink-purple pea flowers (to one-fourth inch). Noticeable red-purple glands on twigs.

NOTE: Distinguishing this indigo bush from the more "typical" and common *P. arborescens* (p. 266) are the red-purple spots (glands) on the stems and the non-indigo color of the flowers.

HABITAT: Sandy flats and slopes (3,000–7,400 feet); found east of the Sierra, Mojave Desert, Sonoran Desert.

WHERE AND WHEN:

Joshua Tree (May–June)
Death Valley (May–June)
Little San Bernardino Mountains (May–June)
Mono Lake Basin (May–June)

Coyote Mountain (May–
June)
White Mountains (May–
September)

Nevada indigo bush

LUPINE, GRAY'S or SIERRA LUPINE   *Lupinus grayi*
Pea family

DESCRIPTION: 0.5–1 foot. Loose raceme of purple pea flowers. Banner with distinct yellow patch. Palmately compound leaves with 5 to 11, white-hairy leaflets. California endemic.

NOTE: This lupine can be distinguished by its flowers, which are more red-purple than the usual blue-purple or blue, and by the yellow, rather than the more usual white, patch on the banner.

HABITAT: Forest openings (2000–8,000 feet); found in foothills, Sierra.

WHERE AND WHEN:
Meeks Bay in Tahoe (May–June)
SR-36 west of Red Bluff (May–June)

Gray's lupine

Kern Plateau (May–June)
Greenhorn Range (May–June)
Quincy area (May–June)
Yosemite Valley (May–July)

MARIPOSA LILY, SPLENDID or
LILAC MARIPOSA LILY   *Calochortus splendens*
Lily family

DESCRIPTION: 0.5–2 feet. Branching stems with long, basal, grasslike leaves that wither early. Bowl-shaped, pink or lilac flowers (to 1.5 inches). Base of petals with white or yellow hairs and only occasionally a red-purple blotch.

NOTE: Even without the colorful blotches or chevrons characteristic of so many California species of mari-posa lily, this flower is truly "splen-dens" with its lovely, soft pastel color.

HABITAT: Grasslands, brushy slopes, chaparral (to 9,200 feet); found in central and south coast ranges, Transverse Ranges, Peninsular Ranges.

WHERE AND WHEN:
Santa Rosa Plateau (May–June)
Santa Lucia Mountains (May–July)
Santa Monica Mountains (May–July)
Diablo Range (May–July)
Cuyama Valley (May–July)
Palomar Mountain (May–July)

Splendid mariposa lily

MILKVETCH, PURSH'S or
WOOLLYPOD MILKVETCH   *Astragalus purshii*
Pea family

DESCRIPTION: 2–6 inches. Low plant with loose racemes of 2 to 10 intensely red-purple (sometimes pink or white) pea flowers. Banner with large white patch.

NOTE: The seedpods are as eye-catching as the flowers—they are densely white-woolly, cotton "pellets" that might lead you to believe that some rabbit left its calling card!

HABITAT: Sagebrush scrub; dry, rocky flats; fellfields (to 11,000 feet); found in northwest mountains, coast ranges, Cascades, Sierra, east of the Sierra, northeast corner, Transverse Ranges, Mojave Desert mountains.

Pursh's
milkvetch

WHERE AND WHEN:
Martis Valley in Tahoe (May–June)
Mount Pinos (May–June)
Piute Mountains (May–June)
Anthony Peak (May–June)
Red Lake Peak at Carson Pass (June)
Dana Plateau in Yosemite (July–August)

MILKVETCH, SHAGGY   *Astragalus malacus*
Pea family
DESCRIPTION: 4–16 inches. Branching stem with dense racemes of 9 to 35 pea flowers. Pink, white, or violet flowers with recurved banner. Pinnately compound leaves with 3 to 10 opposite pairs of small leaflets and one terminal leaflet.

NOTE: As the common name suggests, the stems, leaves, sepals, and seedpods are covered with dense, shaggy, white hair.

HABITAT: Sagebrush scrub (3,400–7,700 feet); found east of the Sierra, northeast corner, Mojave Desert.

WHERE AND WHEN:
Topaz Lake (May–June)
Benton area (May–June)
Modoc Plateau (May–June)
Warner Mountains (May–June)
Conway Summit (May–June)
Mojave National Preserve (May–June)

Shaggy milkvetch

MILKWEED, SHOWY
Asclepias speciosa
Dogbane family (previously included in Milkweed family)

DESCRIPTION: 2–6 feet. Stout stem thick with opposite pairs of broad, felty leaves. Large clusters of oddly shaped flowers with five pink, tonguelike, reflexed petals and five white or pink horns.

NOTE: These intricately flowered plants are also fascinating in bud and fruit—fuzzy grapes to rough, beaked pods.

HABITAT: Dry flats, sagebrush scrub, disturbed places (to 6,000 feet); found in much of California.

WHERE AND WHEN:
Mount Tamalpais (May–June)
Mount Sanhedrin (May–June)
Lake Sonoma area (May–July)
Yosemite Valley (May–July)
White Mountains (July–August)
Trinity Alps (July–August)

Showy milkweed

MOUNTAIN PRIDE
Penstemon newberryi
Plantain family (previously included in Snapdragon family)

DESCRIPTION: 0.5–1 foot. Subshrub with many tubular, two-lipped, cherry-red flowers (to 1.5 inches). Woolly-haired anthers and bearded throat. Opposite pairs of broad, leathery, toothed leaves.

NOTE: Early bloomers, these bright red flowers bring cascades of cheery and cherry spring to rocky slopes and cliffs.

HABITAT: Rocky slopes, outcrops, talus, cliffs (2,000–11,500 feet); found in northwest mountains, north coast ranges, Cascades, Sierra.

WHERE AND WHEN:
SR-36 west of Red Bluff (May–June)
Greenhorn Range (May–June)
Piute Mountains (May–June)
Trinity Alps (June–July)
Lassen National Park (June–July)
Tioga Pass Road in Yosemite (July)

Mountain pride

ONION, CRINKLED
Allium crispum or
A. peninsulare subsp. *crispum*

Onion family (previously included in Lily family)

DESCRIPTION: 5–10 inches. Loose umbel of 10–40 rose-purple flowers with the inner three tepals narrower than the outer three, and wrinkled. Two to three long, grasslike leaves that often wither early. California endemic.

NOTE: Maybe this is a good way to think of ourselves as we age and wrinkle—crinkled and crisp!

HABITAT: Grasslands, woodlands, chaparral (to 2,500 feet); found in central and south coast ranges.

WHERE AND WHEN:
Pinnacles (May–June)
Wind Wolves Preserve (May–June)
Figueroa Mountain area (May–June)
Mount Hamilton Range (May–June)
Cuyama Valley (May–June)
Santa Lucia Mountains (May–June)

Crinkled onion

ONION, FLAT-STEMMED   *Allium platycaule*
Onion family (previously included in Lily family)

DESCRIPTION: 1–6 inches. Densely flowered, spherical umbel of 20–90 pink, star-shaped flowers at the tip of a short, leafless stem. Six narrow tepals with a darker mid-rib. Stem and two grasslike leaves are flattened.

NOTE: With its dense, ball-like umbel of pink flowers and the unusually narrow tepals, this onion puts on quite a "star-studded" show.

HABITAT: Sandy or gravelly flats and slopes (4,000–8,000 feet); found in Cascades, Sierra, northeast corner.

WHERE AND WHEN:

east of Monitor Pass (May–June)

Warner Mountains (May–June)

south fork Feather River (May–June)

Lassen National Park (June–July)

Lakes Basin (June–July)

Donner Pass (June–July)

Flat-stemmed onion

ONION, LEMMON'S   *Allium lemmonii*
Onion family (previously included in Lily family)

DESCRIPTION: 0.5–1 foot. Crowded terminal umbel of 10–40 rose, pink, or white flowers with six pointed tepals of solid color. Two papery bracts under umbel.

NOTE: Many onions grow in very dry places, many others in very wet places. Lemmon's onion is less extreme, preferring moist, drying meadows.

HABITAT: Drying, grassy meadows (3,500–6,000 feet); found in Cascades, Sierra, east of the Sierra, northeast corner.

WHERE AND WHEN:

west of Monitor Pass (May–June)

Martis Valley in Tahoe (May–June)

Modoc Plateau (May–June)

Adobe Flat (May–June)

Sierra Valley (May–June)

Gray's Valley (May–June)

Lemmon's onion

ONION, SIERRA   *Allium campanulatum*

Onion family (previously included in Lily family)

DESCRIPTION: 0.5–1 foot. Rather loose umbel (long pedicels) of 15–40 pink or rose-purple, six-tepaled, star-shaped flowers.

NOTE: Of the several dry-environment onions in California, this one is dis-

tinguished by the rose-colored crescent at the base of each tepal above the nectar gland.

HABITAT: Dry flats and slopes (2,000–8,900 feet); found in much of mid-elevation California (except northeast corner and deserts).

WHERE AND WHEN:

Haiwee Reservoir (May–June)

Drum Powerhouse Road (May–June)

San Jacinto Mountains (June–July)

Santa Lucia Range (June–July)

Trinity Alps (June–August)

Castle Peak (July–August)

Sierra onion

Mendocino
coast
paintbrush

PAINTBRUSH, MENDOCINO COAST   *Castilleja mendocinensis*
Broomrape family (previously included in Snapdragon family)

DESCRIPTION: 1.5–2 feet. Much-branched, shaggy white-hairy stems thick with scarlet or red-orange "flowers" (bracts). Bracts widely wedge-shaped with very wide central lobe. California endemic. CNPS Rare and Endangered List—limited distribution.

NOTE: Of all the bright red or orange paintbrush species in California, this species might have the most intensely colored, incandescent bracts.

HABITAT: Coastal scrub (to 350 feet); found on north coast—only in Mendocino and Humboldt counties.

WHERE AND WHEN:

Manchester Beach (May–July)

Jughandle State Reserve (May–July)

north of Fort Bragg (May–July)

Mendocino area (May–July)

Patrick's Point State Park (May–July)

Elk area (May–July)

PENSTEMON, ROSY or
PANAMINT BEARDTONGUE   *Penstemon floridus*
Plantain family (previously included in Snapdragon family)

DESCRIPTION: 1–4 feet. Stout stem with many rosy-pink, two-lipped flowers in opposite pairs or whorled. Long, swollen flower tube and small flaring lobes. Opposite pairs of sawtoothed leaves.

NOTE: The swollen, potbellied flower tube makes the flower look like an eccentric, pink puffer fish.

HABITAT: Gravelly flats, washes, canyons, sagebrush scrub (3,000–8,000 feet); found in eastern Sierra, east of the Sierra, Mojave Desert.

WHERE AND WHEN:

Benton area (May–June)

Big Pine Creek (May–July)

Inyo Mountains (May–July)
White Mountains (May–July)
Death Valley (May–July)
Conway Summit (May–July)

Rosy penstemon

PITCHER PLANT, CALIFORNIA or
DARLINGTONIA   *Darlingtonia californica*
Pitcher plant family
DESCRIPTION: 0.5–2 feet. Upraised, cobralike, tubular leaves with mustache-like, yellow-green or purple appendages. Single flower nods off a separate, taller stem. Five yellow-green sepals with purple veins and five red-purple, veined petals. CNPS Rare and Endangered List—limited distribution.
NOTE: Unfortunate insects end up trapped inside the curled part of the leaf and become plant food!

California
pitcher plant

HABITAT: Bogs, seeps (to 6,000 feet); found in northwest mountains, foothills, Cascades, Sierra, northeast corner.

WHERE AND WHEN:
Butterfly Valley (May–August)
Trinity Alps (July–August)
Bear Basin Butte Botanical Area
    (July–August)
Stony Creek Bog (July–August)
Mount Shasta (July–August)
Warner Mountains (July–August)

California pitcher plant

RED RIBBONS   *Clarkia concinna*
Evening primrose family

DESCRIPTION: 2–12 inches. Several flowers in leaf axils along stem. Four bright pink petals, usually darker at the base and with a white, vertical streak. Each petal with three nearly equal, clawed lobes. California endemic.

NOTE: With its deeply lobed petals, the flower may remind you of a pink snowflake.

HABITAT: Coastal scrub, woodlands (to 5,000 feet); found in northwest mountains, north and central coast and coast ranges, Sierra.

WHERE AND WHEN:
Jenner area (May–June)
Six Rivers National Forest
    (May–June)
Feather River Canyon (May–June)
Stevens Creek Canyon in
    (May–June)

Red ribbons

Mount Diablo (May–July)
Mount Tamalpais (June–July)

RHATANY, WHITE

Krameria bicolor

Rhatany family

DESCRIPTION: 1–2 feet. Gray-green (matted, white hairs), parasitic shrub with spreading branches whose tips are spiny. Four or five deep red-purple, reflexed, petal-like sepals. Three tiny, upright, red-purple "flag" petals.

White rhatany

NOTE: The true petals are much less conspicuous than the petal-like sepals—the three "flag" petals are tiny; the other two petals are hard to even find, having been modified into fleshy scales that flank the ovary.

HABITAT: Dry, sandy or rocky places (to 4,500 feet); found in Mojave Desert, Sonoran Desert.

WHERE AND WHEN:
Joshua Tree (May–June)
Granite Mountains (May–June)
Anza-Borrego (May–June)
San Felipe Valley (May–June)
Algodones Dunes (May–June)
Chuckwalla Mountains (May–June)

RHODODENDRON, PACIFIC or CALIFORNIA ROSE-BAY

Rhododendron macrophyllum

Heath family

DESCRIPTION: 5–10 feet. Shrub thick with clusters (to 6 inches across) of many pink or red-purple flowers (to 1.5 inches). Five petals, often with dark red splotches or spots. Long, scarlet filaments.

NOTE: The northern coast and northern coast ranges are blessed with this spectacular rhododendron and its close kin, western azalea (p. 350), which often grow together.

HABITAT: Woodlands (to 3,600 feet); found in northwest mountains, north and central coast and coast ranges, Sierra.

WHERE AND WHEN:
Kruse Rhododendron State
Park (May–June)
Santa Cruz Mountains
(May–June)
Mount Tamalpais (May–
June)
Santa Lucia Range (May–
June)
Del Norte Redwoods (May–
June)
along Smith River (May–
June)

Pacific rhododendron

ROSE, NOOTKA   *Rosa nutkana*
Rose family

DESCRIPTION: 1–6 feet. Prickly shrub that often forms thickets. Two thorns
at leaf axils. One to four shallow, bowl-shaped flowers (to 2 inches) at ends
of branching stem. Five sepa-
rate pink or rose petals, often
white at base, around a dense
cluster of yellow anthers.

NOTE: With its delicate pink
or rose heart-shaped petals
and its delicious, sweet fragrance, this rose lulls you
into forgetting its sharp
thorns.

HABITAT: Moist, shrubby flats;
woodlands (to 2,300 feet);
found in northwest moun-
tains, coast.

WHERE AND WHEN:
Jenner-Fort Ross area (May–
June)
Sea Ranch (May–June)

Nootka rose

Kruse Rhododendron State Park (May–June)
Russian Gulch State Park (May–June)
Salt Point (May–June)
Trinity Alps (June–July)

SHOOTING STAR, ALPINE — *Dodecatheon alpinum*
Primrose family

DESCRIPTION: 0.5–2 feet. Flowers, from 1 to clusters of 10, hang upside-down from arching pedicels. Flowers are turned inside-out with black-purple "nose" holding reproductive part sticking out from four reflexed petals. Short, basal, tonguelike leaves.

NOTE: After pollination, these flowers move to an erect position, letting pollinators and wildflower lovers alike know their fulfilled state.

HABITAT: Wet meadows, stream banks (6,000–12,000 feet); found in northwest mountains, north coast ranges, Cascades, Sierra, northeast corner, Transverse Ranges, Peninsular Ranges.

WHERE AND WHEN:
Sagehen Creek meadow (May–June)
Paige Meadows in Tahoe (May–July)
Lakes Basin (June)
San Jacinto Mountains (June–July)
Lassen National Park (June–August)
Tuolumne Meadows in Yosemite (July–August)

Alpine shooting star

SPINEFLOWER, DOUGLAS — *Chorizanthe douglasii*
Buckwheat family

DESCRIPTION: 0.5–1.5 feet. Slender stem with umbels of many tiny (to one-fourth inch) flowers with six bright pink or white, petal-like sepals. Pink, spiny bracts under flowers that appear as triangles from above. Whorl of needlelike stem leaves. California endemic. CNPS Rare and Endangered List—limited distribution.

NOTE: These unusual and uncommon plants create gorgeous, vibrant pink, spiny "mini-forests" in sandy openings.

HABITAT: Woodlands (to 5,000 feet); found in south coast ranges.

WHERE AND WHEN:
Pinnacles (May–June)
Point Lobos State Reserve (May–June)
Fort Ord (May–June)
Big Sur (May–June)
Carrizo Plain (May–June)
Santa Lucia Mountains (May–June)

Douglas spineflower

THISTLE, MOJAVE · *Cirsium mohavense*
Aster family

DESCRIPTION: 2–5 feet. Stout stem branching above with many large, spiny leaves and clusters of roundish, pink (sometimes white) flower heads. Phyllaries are sharp spines sticking out at all angles. Plant covered with dense, white hairs.

NOTE: Every day in the desert with this plant is the Fourth of July, as the flower fireworks explode all around you.

HABITAT: Damp places around springs, canyons, washes (1,300–9,200 feet); found in foothills, Cascades, Sierra, Transverse Ranges, Mojave Desert.

Mojave thistle

WHERE AND WHEN:
Alabama Hills (May–June)
San Bernardino Mountains (May–June)
White Mountains (May–July)
Tehachapi Mountains (May–June)
Antelope Valley (May–July)
Joshua Tree (May–June)

WILLOW, DESERT
Bignonia family

Chilopsis linearis

DESCRIPTION: 6–20 feet. Willowlike shrub or tree with long, narrow, deciduous leaves and clusters of long tubular, inflated, two-lipped, pink flowers (to 2 inches). Yellow ridges and purple lines in throat and on lower lip.

NOTE: These large, sweetly fragrant flowers look quite a bit like pink "monkeys" (i.e., monkeyflowers) playing in a tree (although they aren't even in the monkeyflower's family).

HABITAT: Sandy washes (to 5,000 feet); found in Transverse Ranges, Peninsular Ranges, Mojave Desert, Sonoran Desert.

WHERE AND WHEN:
Mount San Jacinto (May–July)
Manzanita Indian Reservation (May–July)
Anza-Borrego (May–September)
Chuckwalla Mountains (May–September)
Mojave National Preserve (May–September)
Joshua Tree (May–September)

Desert willow

ARNICA, HEART-LEAF
Aster family

Arnica cordifolia

DESCRIPTION: 0.5–2 feet. One terminal flower head (to 1.5 inches) and two to four other flower heads at tips of opposite pedicels originating in leaf axils. Six to 15 bright yellow, pointed rays. Two to four opposite pairs of heart-shaped leaves.

Heart-leaf arnica

NOTE: The plants are heliotropic, so the flower faces can all be staring at or away from you, depending on where you are in relationship to the sun.

HABITAT: Openings in woods, meadows (3,500–10,000 feet); found in northwest mountains, north and central coast ranges, Cascades, Sierra, northeast corner.

WHERE AND WHEN:
Warner Mountains (May–June)
Mount Sanhedrin (May–June)
Shirley Canyon in Tahoe (June–July)
Lassen National Park (June–July)
Trinity Alps (June–August)
Gaylor Lakes in Yosemite (July–August)

BALSAMROOT, ARROW-LEAF   *Balsamorhiza sagittata*
Aster family

DESCRIPTION: 0.5–2 feet. Many flower heads (to 2 inches) of broad, over-lapping, bright yellow rays surrounding a raised yellow-orange disk. Large, basal, arrow-shaped leaves on arching petioles.

NOTE: Very much like mule ears (p. 385), with which it grows, but with non-woolly, arrow-shaped, arching (i.e., non-erect) leaves.

HABITAT: Dry, open slopes; sagebrush scrub, forest openings (4,000–8,300 feet); found in Cascades, Sierra, east of the Sierra, northeast corner.

WHERE AND WHEN:
King's Canyon/Sequoia (May–June)
Modoc Plateau (May–June)

Walker Pass (May–June)
Shirley Canyon in Tahoe (June–
    July)
Yosemite Valley (June–July)
Warner Mountains (June–July)

Arrowleaf balsamroot

BEE PLANT, YELLOW   *Cleome lutea*
Cleome family (previously included in Caper family)
DESCRIPTION: 1–3 feet. Terminal cluster of many lemon-yellow, four-petaled flowers. Palmately compound leaves with three to seven narrow, fingerlike leaflets. Hanging, bananalike seedpods.

NOTE: Although it often grows
weedily along roadsides and in
other disturbed places, this
plant is quite attractive with its
symmetrically distributed hanging fruits.

HABITAT: Dry, sandy flats, desert
scrub, roadsides (3,600–7,900
feet); found east of the Sierra,
Mojave Desert.

WHERE AND WHEN:
along U.S. 395 near Bishop
    (May–June)
Coachella Valley (May–June)
White Mountains (May–June)
Joshua Tree (May–June)
Mojave National Preserve
    (May–June)
west of Bishop (May–June)

Yellow bee plant

Bitterbrush

BITTERBRUSH or ANTELOPE BUSH   *Purshia tridentata*
Rose family

DESCRIPTION: 1–8 feet. Shrub heavy with pale yellow or creamy, five-petaled flowers with cluster of many reproductive parts. Three-lobed, mitten-like leaves.

NOTE: The flowers have a gentle, cinnamonlike aroma that can fill the air on hot, sun-baked days.

HABITAT: Sagebrush scrub, forest clearings (2,800–11,200 feet); found in northwest mountains, north coast ranges, Cascades, Sierra, east of the Sierra, northeast corner, Transverse Ranges, Peninsular Ranges, Mojave Desert.

WHERE AND WHEN:
Modoc Plateau (May–June)
Kern Plateau (May–June)
San Gabriel Mountains (May–June)
Jacumba area (May–June)
Topaz Lake (May–June)
Meiss Meadows at Carson Pass (June)

CRYPTANTHA, GOLDEN or
BASIN YELLOW CAT'S EYE   *Cryptantha confertiflora*
Borage family

DESCRIPTION: 0.5–1.5 feet. Coarse, bristly stem with tonguelike, hairy leaves and dense clusters of yellow, pinwheel-like flowers (to 0.5 inches). Five rounded petal lobes; yellow-toothed rim around throat.

NOTE: The fruits in cryptanthas are often interesting and distinctive—in golden cryptantha they are four smooth, sleek, triangular nutlets.

HABITAT: Dry, rocky places (4,000–9,000 feet); found in Sierra, east of the

Sierra, Transverse Ranges, Mojave Desert.

WHERE AND WHEN:
Death Valley (May–June)
Convict Lake (May–June)
Fish Slough (May–June)
White Mountains (May–July)
San Bernardino Mountains
    (May–July)
King's Canyon/Sequoia
    (May–July)

Golden cryptantha

DAISY, RAYLESS or RAYLESS SHAGGY FLEABANE
Erigeron aphanactis

Aster family

DESCRIPTION: 3–10 inches. Solitary, flat-topped button head of yellow disk flowers only. Narrow leaves covered with bristly, white hair.

NOTE: This daisy is without the usual showy rays, having only the yellow disk—subtle but still quite striking, especially in contrast with the gray-green leaves.

HABITAT: Sagebrush scrub (4,300–8,500 feet); found east of the Sierra, northeast corner, Transverse Ranges, Mojave Desert.

WHERE AND WHEN:
Topaz Lake (May–June)

Rayless daisy

San Bernardino Mountains (May–June)
Frog Lake at Carson Pass (June–July)
White Mountains (June–July)
Modoc Plateau (June–July)
Sweetwater Mountains (June–July)

DUDLEYA, COAST or BLUFF LETTUCE *Dudleya farinosa*
Stonecrop family
DESCRIPTION: 4–16 inches. Large, basal rosette of thick, succulent, gray-green leaves that often turn red at or after blooming time. Clusters of three to 11 pale yellow, star-shaped flowers.

NOTE: Even without the flowers, this is a fascinating and striking plant with its gorgeous rosettes of voluptuously succulent leaves clinging to the often otherwise-barren rocks.
HABITAT: Rocky outcrops along the coast (to 500 feet); found on north and central coast.
WHERE AND WHEN:
Monterey Peninsula (May–July)
Salt Point (May–August)
Bodega Head (May–August)
Jughandle State Reserve (May–September)
Santa Lucia Range (June–July)
San Bruno Mountain (July–August)

Coast dudleya

DUDLEYA, LANCELEAF *Dudleya lanceolata*
Stonecrop family
DESCRIPTION: 1–1.5 feet. Succulent stem rising from one side of the basal rosette of narrow, pointed, succulent leaves. Lateral branches with two to 20 urn-shaped, waxy, yellow or orange or reddish, star-shaped flowers (to one-fourth inch) with tiny, reddish, pointed sepals.
NOTE: Everything about this species is sharp—from the lancelike leaves to the pointed star flowers.

HABITAT: Dunes, rocky flats and cliffs (to 4,000 feet); found on south coast and in coast ranges, Transverse Ranges, Peninsular Ranges, Mojave Desert.

WHERE AND WHEN:
Pinnacles (May–July)
Montana del Oro (May–July)
Santa Monica Mountains
  (May–July)
Santa Rosa Plateau (May–
  July)
Nipomo-Guadalupe Dunes
  (May–July)
Temblor Range (May–July)

Lanceleaf dudleya

EVENING PRIMROSE, HOOKER'S   *Oenothera elata* subsp. *hookeri*
Evening primrose family

DESCRIPTION: 1–7 feet. Stout, usually reddish stem with many long, narrow leaves and a spike of showy, shallow bowl-shaped, four-petaled, creamy yellow flowers (to 3 inches) aging reddish. Sticky stigma with four narrow lobes. Very fragrant.

NOTE: This species has two subspecies, one of which is widespread and the other only occurring in low-elevation coastal bluffs.

HABITAT: Moist areas in grasslands, ditches (to 9,200 feet); found in much of California.

WHERE AND WHEN:
Cuyama Valley (May–August)
Nipomo-Guadalupe Dunes (May–
  October)
Santa Rosa Plateau (June–
  September)
Santa Monica Mountains (June–
  August)
Tioga Pass Road (July–September)
Tahoe Basin (July–September)

Hooker's evening primrose

FALSE LUPINE, CALIFORNIA *Thermopsis macrophylla*
Pea family

DESCRIPTION: 1–3 feet. Densely flowered raceme of yellow pea flowers (to three-fourths inch). Pinnately compound leaves with three oval leaflets. CNPS Rare and Endangered List—rare.

NOTE: This sure looks like a yellow-flowered lupine, until you look at the leaves—they have only three leaflets rather than the many palmate leaflets characteristic of all lupines.

HABITAT: Grasslands, brushy slopes, woodlands, disturbed places (to 6,900 feet); found in northwest mountains, coast ranges, foothills, Cascades, northeast corner, Transverse Ranges, Peninsular Ranges.

WHERE AND WHEN:
Mount Tamalpais (May–June)
Santa Lucia Range (May–June)
Jenner area (May–June)
Modoc Plateau (May–June)
Ring Mountain (May–June)
Trinity Alps (June–July)

California false lupine

FLANNELBUSH, PINE HILL or PINE HILL FREMONTIA
Fremontodendron decumbens or *F. californicum* subsp. *decumbens*
Mallow family (previously included in Cacao family)

DESCRIPTION: 2–3 feet. Shrub thick with open, orange or coppery flowers (to 2.5 inches) and broad, hairy, usually three-lobed leaves. Three sepal-like bracts under each flower. Five petal-like sepals (no true petals). California endemic. CNPS Rare and Endangered List—limited distribution.

NOTE: Although this species is relatively common, this subspecies, with the short and wide growth form (*decumbens*), is rare, occurring only in the Pine Hill area and vicinity.

HABITAT: Rocky, serpentine flats and ridges (at about 3,000 feet); found in foothills—only at Pine Hill and neighboring areas.

Pine Hill flannelbush

JOHNNY-NIP   *Castilleja ambigua*
Broomrape family (previously included in Snapdragon family)
DESCRIPTION: 4–12 inches. Densely flowered spike of three to nine lobed, greenish bracts with creamy white or yellow tips. Yellowish or purplish

flowers nestled in the bracts with purple-haired beak. Un-lobed or lobed leaves often reddish.

NOTE: The odd, multicolored spike of flowers might re-mind you of purple afros shyly peering out of a creamy white tree!

HABITAT: Bluffs, grasslands, marshes (to 500 feet); found on north and central coast and coast ranges.

WHERE AND WHEN:
Humboldt Bay (May–June)
Salt Point (May–July)
Sea Ranch (May–July)
Pitkin Marsh (May–July)
Manchester Beach (May–
July)
Monterey Bay (May–August)

Johnny-nip

LILY, COLUMBIA
Lily family
Lilium columbianum

DESCRIPTION: 1–3 feet. One or several very showy flowers (to 2 inches) nodding at end of long, arched pedicels. Six orange, yellow, or red tepals with darker spots curved back at tips. Stamens all parallel or barely spreading. Two to nine whorls of leaves.

NOTE: Some lilies are deliciously fragrant; this one makes up for not stimulating the nose by dazzling the eyes.

HABITAT: Woodlands, scrub (to 4,300 feet); found in northwest mountains, north coast and coast ranges.

WHERE AND WHEN:
Kruse Rhododendron State
　　Reserve (May–June)
Redwood National Park
　　(May–July)
Patrick's Point State Park
　　(May–July)
Crescent City area (May–
　　July)
Salt Point (May–July)
Prairie Creek State Park
　　(June–July)

Columbia lily

LILY, LEOPARD
Lily family
Lilium pardalinum

DESCRIPTION: 3–8 feet. As many as 35 large (to 4 inches) flowers, each nodding off a long, ascending pedicel. Six tepals orange at the tip and yellow with red spots toward the base. Tepals strongly recurved. California endemic.

NOTE: There are graceful curves everywhere on this robust plant—arching pedicels, curved-back tepals, and gentle whorls of leaves.

HABITAT: Stream banks, coastal bluffs (to 6,600 feet); found in much of California (except northeast corner, desert, and eastern edge).

WHERE AND WHEN:
Traverse Creek Botanical Area (May–June)
Cuyamaca Mountains (May–June)
Santa Lucia Range (May–June)

Feather River Canyon (May–June)

Lakes Basin (June–July)

Redwood National Park (June–July)

Leopard lily

MULE EARS, WOOLLY   *Wyethia mollis*

Aster family

DESCRIPTION: 1–3 feet. Several showy flower heads (to 3.5 inches) with 10–20 widely separate rays around a raised disk with many yellow-orange

disk flowers. Broad, usually erect, white-woolly leaves.

NOTE: These sunny flowers often occur in large masses on dry (especially volcanic) hillsides—with their long roots, they can tap into the water-table deep below the porous soil.

HABITAT: Dry, open hillsides; forest openings (4,500–10,600 feet); found in northwest mountains, Cascades, Sierra, east of Sierra, northeast corner.

WHERE AND WHEN:

Modoc Plateau (May–June)

Shirley Canyon in Tahoe (June–July)

Woolly mule ears   Butterfly Valley (June–August)

Lassen National Park (June–August)
Lakes Basin (July–August)
Wright's Lake (July–August)

PRICKLY PEAR, MOJAVE or
BROWN-SPINED PRICKLY PEAR   *Opuntia phaeacantha*
Cactus family

DESCRIPTION: 1–4 feet. Broad, flattened pods at right angles. Clusters of one to four straw-colored spines, red-brown near base. Many bowl-shaped flowers (to 3 inches) with many yellow-orange petals, red at base. California endemic.

NOTE: The flowers are open for only a day or two, starting yellow and becoming more orange or peach.

HABITAT: Dry flats and slopes (to 7,300 feet); found in south coast ranges, Transverse Ranges, Peninsular Ranges, Mojave Desert, Sonoran Desert.

WHERE AND WHEN:
San Bernardino Mountains (May–June)
Mojave National Preserve (May–June)
San Felipe Valley (May–June)
Anza-Borrego (May–June)
California Polytechnic State University (May–July)
Cuyama Valley (May–July)

Mojave
prickly pear

PRICKLY PEAR, VASEY'S or
APRICOT PRICKLY PEAR   *Opuntia vaseyi* or *O. littoralis* var. *vaseyi*
Cactus family

DESCRIPTION: 1–3 feet. Sprawling, spreading shrub with flattened stem segments (pads). One to six spines only on upper two-thirds of each pad—areoles on lower third are spineless. Bright yellow or orange petals with darker orange or red at base. Scores of stamens with soft yellow anthers

surrounding pink style with greenish stigma.

NOTE: This is a natural hybrid between *O. littoralis* and *O. phaeacantha*, and so technically is spelled *Opuntia xvaseyi* (the "x" indicating a hybrid).

HABITAT: Chaparral, disturbed places (to 1,700 feet); found on south coast and coast ranges.

WHERE AND WHEN:
Santa Rosa Plateau (May–June)
Carrizo Plain (May–June)
Crystal Cove State Park (May–June)

Vasey's prickly pear

SUNFLOWER, WOOLLY   *Eriophyllum lanatum*
Aster family

DESCRIPTION: 0.5–1 foot. Subshrub. One or a few broad, bright yellow flower heads with 10–20 rays surrounding a slightly raised disk.

NOTE: The white-woolly covering on the stems and foliage of these hardy plants helps them adapt to dry conditions all the way from the foothills to high above timberline.

HABITAT: Dry slopes and flats, alpine ridges (to 11,500 feet); found in much of California (except deserts).

WHERE AND WHEN:
Drum Powerhouse Road (May–June)

Woolly
sunflower

Santa Lucia Range (May–June)
San Bernardino Mountains (May–June)
Modoc Plateau (May–June)
Trinity Alps (June–July)
Mount Dana in Yosemite (July–August)

TANSY, DUNE or CAMPHOR TANSY   *Tanacetum camphoratum*
Aster family

DESCRIPTION: 4–10 inches. Branched, hairy stem sometimes forming mounds with flat-topped clusters of 3 to 15 buttonlike, yellow flower heads with disk flowers only.

Pinnately compound, fern-like leaves with many small, pinnately lobed segments.

NOTE: If these are the buttons, imagine the coat!

HABITAT: Dunes (to 100 feet); found on north and central coast.

WHERE AND WHEN:
San Bruno Mountain (May–
    July)
Salt Point (May–August)
Humboldt Bay (May–
    August)
Rodeo Lagoon (May–
    August)
Bodega Head (May–August)
Manchester Beach (June–
    August)

Dune tansy

VIOLET, PINEWOODS or MOUNTAIN VIOLET   *Viola purpurea*
Violet family

DESCRIPTION: 1–5 inches. Several peduncles each tipped with a bright yellow flower (to 1 inch) with purple veins mostly on lower middle-petal lobe. Broad, dark-green deeply veined leaves with smooth or slightly toothed edges.

NOTE: The bright yellow petal lobes with the purple veins and the brown-purple on the backs create a stunning contrast with the lush green leaves.

HABITAT: Forest openings, sagebrush scrub (to 11,000 feet); found in much of California (except Central Valley).

San Bruno Mountain (May–June)
Piute Mountains (May–June)
Warner Mountains (May–June)
Yosemite Valley (May–July)
Santa Lucia Range (May–July)
King's Canyon/Sequoia (June–July)

Pinewoods violet

YELLOW-EYED GRASS, CALIFORNIA or CALIFORNIA GOLDEN-EYED GRASS   *Sisyrinchium californicum*

Iris family

DESCRIPTION: 0.5–2 feet. One or a few star-shaped, golden yellow, six-tepaled flowers near tip of flattened stem. Flat, dark green, grasslike leaves.

NOTE: Its grasslike leaves blend in perfectly with the blades of real grass it often grows with, so the yellow starlike flowers seem a bit disconnected, like yellow starfish floating freely on a sea of green.

HABITAT: Moist grassland (to 2,000 feet); found in northwest mountains, north and central coast and coast ranges.

WHERE AND WHEN:
Kruse Rhododendron State Park (May–June)
Monterey Peninsula (May–June)
Sea Ranch (May–June)
Santa Lucia Range (May–June)
San Bruno Mountain (May–June)
Trinity Alps (June)

California yellow-eyed grass

Alumroot

ALUMROOT   *Heuchera micrantha*
Saxifrage family

DESCRIPTION: 1–3 feet. Delicate, branching stem with many tiny (to one-fourth inch), drooping, white or pink flowers. Reddish sepals. Broad, maplelike, lobed, toothed, mostly basal leaves on petioles.

NOTE: The tiny, drooping flowers on the slender, candelabra-like branches tremble in the breeze like delicate, miniature wind chimes.

HABITAT: Moist, rocky banks, cliffs (to 8,200 feet); found in northwest mountains, north and central coast and coast ranges, foothills, Cascades, Sierra.

WHERE AND WHEN:
Feather River Canyon (May–June)
Santa Lucia Range (May–June)
Salt Point (May–June)
Yosemite Valley (May–July)
Trinity Alps (June–July)
Pole Creek in Tahoe (July–August)

BISTORT or DIRTY SOCKS   *Bistorta bistortoides* or
                                      Polygonum bistortoides
Buckwheat family

DESCRIPTION: 0.5–2 feet. Thumblike cluster of tiny white or pinkish flowers at tip of leafless stem. Crinkly, crepe-papery sepals (no petals). Mostly basal, long, narrow leaves.

NOTE: The name "dirty socks" is a tipoff to the pungent aroma that fills the air over any field of these buckwheats!

HABITAT: Wet meadows, stream-banks (5,000–10,500 feet); found in much of California.

WHERE AND WHEN:
Sagehen Creek meadows
(May–June)
Greenhorn Range (May–June)
Piute Mountains (May–June)
Pitkin Marsh (June–July)
San Jacinto Mountains (June–July)
Trinity Alps (June–August)

Bistort

BLEPHARIPAPPUS or ROUGH EYELASH   *Blepharipappus scaber*
Aster family

DESCRIPTION: 4–12 inches. Branching stem with several flower heads (to three-fourths inch) with two to eight white, three-lobed rays and a few

white disk flowers. Many small, narrow, alternating leaves.

NOTE: The white, three-lobed rays (which look a bit like some swept-wing fighter jet) are unusual, but maybe even more interesting are the delicate, purple, hairy anthers.

HABITAT: Dry flats and slopes, sagebrush scrub (3,000–6,000 feet); found in northwest mountains, Cascades, Sierra, northeast corner.

WHERE AND WHEN:
northwest of Monitor Pass
(May)
Lake Britton (May–July)
Blepharipappus   Modoc Plateau (May–July)

Susanville area (May–July)
Eagle Lake area (May–July)
Lava Beds National Monument (May–July)

BUCKEYE, CALIFORNIA   *Aesculus californica*
Soapberry family (previously included in Buckeye family)
DESCRIPTION: 0–20 feet. Large shrub or tree with dense, cylindrical clusters of white or pink flowers. Four or five separated, clawed petals and long-protruding reproductive parts. California endemic.

NOTE: Although these shrubs or trees offer us beautiful, showy flower displays, all parts of the plant are toxic—so don't even think about eating the pearlike fruits.

HABITAT: Edges of woods, canyons, dry slopes (to 5,000 feet); found in northwest mountains, coast, Central Valley, coast ranges, foothills, Cascades, Mojave Desert

WHERE AND WHEN:
Feather River Canyon May–
    June)
Kern River Canyon (May–June)
Monterey Peninsula (May–June)
Yankee Jim's Road (May–June)
Trinity Alps (June)
King's Canyon/Sequoia (June)

California buckeye

BUCKWHEAT, NUDE   *Eriogonum nudum*
Buckwheat family
DESCRIPTION: 0.5–3 feet. Tall, leafless, slender, branching stems with round heads of tiny, crepe-papery, white or pink-tinged flowers (to one-fourth inch). Basal, tonguelike, dark-green leaves.
NOTE: The leaves are well suited for this plant's hot, dry habitat—basal (out of the wind) and covered with a mat of gray hairs.
HABITAT: Dry flats, rocky places (to 12,500 feet); found in much of California (except northeast corner).
WHERE AND WHEN:
Drum Powerhouse Road (May–June)
Lassen National Park (June–July)

Yosemite Valley (June–July)
San Jacinto Mountains
    (June–July)
Carrizo Plain (June–
    December)
Trinity Alps (July–August)

Nude buckwheat

BUTTERCUP, AQUATIC or
WATER BUTTERCUP   *Ranunculus aquatilis*
Buttercup family
DESCRIPTION: 1–5 feet. Branching stem, mostly underwater, with several small, white flowers on short pedicels. Five widely separate, rounded pet-als yellow at base.

NOTE: Masses of the stringy-looking leaves often clog the surface of ponds and streams or spread out fingerlike in the current just under the surface. You can sometimes even find the flowers bloom-ing underwater!

HABITAT: Ponds, lakes, slow-moving streams (to 10,000 feet); found in much of Cali-fornia (except deserts).

WHERE AND WHEN:
Martis Valley in Tahoe
    (May–June)
Santa Rosa Plateau (May–
    June)

Aquatic buttercup

Santa Lucia Range (May–June)
Santa Cruz Mountains (May–July)
Bodega Bay Marsh (May–July)
Lassen National Park (June–August)

CHAMAESARACHA, DWARF
Chamaesaracha nana
Nightshade family

DESCRIPTION: 2–10 inches. Since the plant stem crawls along the ground, the flowers (to three-fourths inch) lie prostrate on their bed of broad, dark-green leaves. Five petals united into white saucer, yellow-green at the throat.

NOTE: The saucerlike flowers are reminiscent of those of the shrubby and toxic nightshades (*Solanum* genus), but these are flat on the ground and much more be-nevolent.

HABITAT: Sagebrush scrub, sandy flats, forest clearings (5,000–9,000 feet); found in northwest mountains, Cascades, Sierra, northeast corner, east of the Sierra.

WHERE AND WHEN:
SR-44 east of Lassen (May–June)
Modoc Plateau (May–June)
Glass Mountain area (May–June)
Conway Summit (May–July)
Mount Eddy (May–July)
Lakes Basin (July)

Dwarf chamaesaracha

CHOKE CHERRY, WESTERN
Prunus virginiana
Rose family

DESCRIPTION: 3–12 inches. Shrub or small tree heavy with elongated, neatly cylindrical clusters of five-petaled, white flowers. Many reproductive parts. Oval, finely toothed, pointed leaves. Dark red or black berries.

NOTE: As the common name indicates, it is not a good idea to eat the berries!

HABITAT: Rocky slopes, canyons, woodlands (to 8,200 feet); found in much of California (except deserts).

WHERE AND WHEN:
San Bruno Mountain (May–June)
Feather River Canyon (May–June)

Trinity Alps (May–June)
Santa Lucia Range (May–
June)
Yosemite Valley (May–June)
Diablo Range (May–June)

Western choke cherry

COLLOMIA, GRAND or MOUNTAIN COLLOMIA *Collomia grandiflora*
Phlox family
DESCRIPTION: 8–30 inches. Terminal head of long-tubular flowers (to 1 inch) with five flaring petal lobes that are creamy white, yellowish, salmon, apricot, or pale orange. Blue pollen.
NOTE: With its many large, trumpetlike flowers and their unusual and variable color, this "flora" is grand indeed!
HABTIAT: Dry flats and slopes, grasslands, sagebrush scrub, forest openings

(to 8,000 feet); found in much of California (except northeast corner and deserts).

WHERE AND WHEN:
Yosemite Valley (May–June)
Santa Cruz Mountains
(May–July)
Palomar Mount State Park
(May–July)
Santa Lucia Range (June–
July)
Barker Pass in Tahoe (June–
July)
Lassen National Park (July–
August)

Grand collomia

Mountain dogwood

DOGWOOD, MOUNTAIN or PACIFIC DOGWOOD   *Cornus nuttallii*
Dogwood family

DESCRIPTION: 5–75 feet. Tree with green twigs becoming dark red to almost black. Broad leaves with distinct veins. Large, bright white "flowers" with four to seven petal-like bracts.

NOTE: The large, showy, glistening white "flowers" are not actually flowers at all—the petal-like structures are bracts, while the true flowers at the center of the bracts are tiny and greenish-white.

HABITAT: Forests (to 6,500 feet); found in much of California (except northeast corner and deserts).

WHERE AND WHEN:
Butterfly Valley (May–June)
Santa Lucia Range (June–July)
west of Carson Pass (June–July)
San Jacinto Mountains (June–July)
King's Canyon/Sequoia (June–July)
San Bernardino Mountains (June–July)

DRAPERIA   *Draperia systyla*
Borage family (previously included in Waterleaf family)

DESCRIPTION: 4–16 inches. Decumbent or erect stem with terminal cyme of many narrow, white or pale lavender, tubular flowers. Stems and cyme covered with long, soft hairs. California endemic.

NOTE: With its upraised, tubular flowers projecting out of the cyme in all

directions, this plant looks like it is joyfully "trumpeting" some wonderful tidings to all who will listen.

HABITAT: Open woods, rocky places (2,400–8,000 feet); found in northwest mountains, foothills, Cascades, Sierra.

WHERE AND WHEN:
Drum Powerhouse Road (May–June)
upper Bidwell Park (May–June)
Yosemite Valley (May–June)
King's Canyon/Sequoia (May–June)
Shasta Lake (May–June)
Trinity Alps (June–July)

Draperia

FALSE LILY-OF-THE-VALLEY
Maianthemum dilatatum

Ruscus family (previously included in Lily family)

DESCRIPTION: 6–15 inches. Spike of tiny, white, faintly scented, four-petaled flowers (not shown in photo) rises above large, shiny, dark-green, deeply parallel-veined, heart-shaped leaves. Mottled beige or greenish berries turn red.

NOTE: The multicolored berries (photo) are a spectacular show in themselves!

HABITAT: Forest shade (to 1,600 feet); found in northwest mountains, north and central coast and coast ranges.

WHERE AND WHEN:
Redwood National Park (May–June)
Lamphere-Christensen Dunes (May–June)
Sea Ranch (May–June)
San Bruno Mountain (May–June)
Point Reyes (May–June)
Big Basin Redwoods State Park (May–June)

False lily-of-the-valley

HESPEROCHIRON, CALIFORNIA   *Hesperochiron californicus*
Borage family (previously included in Waterleaf family)
DESCRIPTION: 1–4 inches. Ground-hugging plant with several bowl-shaped or funnel-shaped flowers (to 1 inch) lying among basal rosette of shiny, tonguelike leaves. Five (sometimes six) petal lobes bright white or pink.
NOTE: In early spring, grassy meadows at mid-elevation are often lit up by large clusters of these showy, white and/or pink flowers.
HABITAT: Damp meadows (4,000–9,000 feet); found in northwest mountains, Cascades, Sierra, east of the Sierra, northeast corner, Transverse Ranges.
WHERE AND WHEN:
Kyburz Flat (May–June)
Pohono Trail in Yosemite
    (May–June)
Modoc Plateau (May–June)
San Bernardino Mountains
    (June–July)
Meiss Meadows Trail at
    Carson Pass (June–July)
Hope Valley in Tahoe (June–
    July)

California hesperochiron

HYACINTH, LONG-RAYED or
LONG-RAYED BRODIAEA   *Triteleia peduncularis*
Brodiaea family (previously included in Lily family)
DESCRIPTION: 0.5–3 feet. Tall, stout stem terminating in large, open umbel of many six-tepaled, white (flushed violet) flowers (to 1 inch). The rays in the umbel can be up to 6.5 inches. California endemic.
NOTE: Along with the very long rays, the most striking aspect of this plant is the lovely violet tinge to the underside of the tepals.
HABITAT: Wet grasslands, stream banks (to 2,600 feet); found in northwest mountains, north and central coast ranges.
WHERE AND WHEN:
Ring Mountain (May–June)
Tiburon area (May–June)
Santa Lucia Range (May–June)
Point Reyes (May–July)
Pitkin Marsh (May–July)
Mount Tamalpais (May–July)

Long-rayed hyacinth

IRIS, HARTWEG'S *Iris hartwegii*
Iris family

DESCRIPTION: 1–2 feet. One or up to three showy flowers (to 3 inches). Broad, spreading sepals and narrower, erect petals usually cream or pale yellow with darker veins, but sometimes bluish or purple. California endemic.

Hartweg's iris

NOTE: Since many irises vary in color, often the most reliable way to distinguish them is the position of the ovary—in Hartweg's iris it is directly under the blossom.

HABITAT: Forest openings (2,000–7,500 feet); found in foothills, Cascades, Sierra, Transverse Ranges.

WHERE AND WHEN:
Drum Powerhouse Road (May–June)
Yankee Jim's Road (May–June)
King's Canyon/Sequoia (May–June)
Butterfly Valley (May–June)
Greenhorn Range (May–June)
Feather River Canyon (May–June)

Nuttall's
linanthus

LINANTHUS, NUTTALL'S *Leptosiphon nuttallii*
Phlox family

DESCRIPTION: 4–8 inches. Many stems form low, shrublike plant. Several pinwheel-like, white, half-inch flowers at tips of long pedicels. Yellow flower tube with five narrow, widely separated, flaring petal lobes.

NOTE: This plant usually forms densely flowered mats or shrublike mounds where the flowers all but conceal the leaves and stems.

HABITAT: Dry flats, sagebrush scrub, forest openings (1,600–10,000 feet); found in northwest mountains, north coast ranges, Cascades, east of the Sierra, northeast corner, Transverse Ranges.

WHERE AND WHEN:
Santa Ana Mountains (May–June)
San Bernardino Mountains (May–June)
Bishop Creek (June–July)
Modoc Plateau (July–August)
Trinity Alps (July–August)
Freel Peak (July–August)

MALLOW, MAPLE-LEAF *Sidalcea malachroides*
Mallow family

DESCRIPTION: 2–5 feet. Branching, bristly hairy stem with dense, spikes of flowers (to 1 inch). Five separate petals notched at tips. Large, dark-green maplelike leaves. CNPS Rare and Endangered List—limited distribution.

NOTE: When you think "mallow," you probably think "pink," so these unusual bright white flowers are more than a bit of a surprise.

HABITAT: Woodlands (to 2,500 feet); found on north and central coast and in coast ranges.

WHERE AND WHEN:
Salt Point (May–June)

Santa Lucia Range (May–June)
near Santa Cruz (May–June)
north of Gualala River (May–June)
Monterey Peninsula (May–June)
east of Gualala (May–June)

Maple-leaf mallow

MARIPOSA LILY, BUTTERFLY   *Calochortus venustus*
Lily family

DESCRIPTION: 4–24 inches. Umbel-like inflorescence of up to six bell-shaped flowers (to 2 inches). Petals white, pink, or lavender with more-or-

less rectangular or square, red markings in a line from the petal base to the tip.

NOTE: Although the petal color can vary greatly, the red markings are quite consistent, the one at mid-petal with a yellow border, the one at the tip without it.

HABITAT: Grasslands, woodlands (to 9,000 feet); found in central coast ranges, foothills, Transverse Ranges.

WHERE AND WHEN:

Santa Monica Mountains (May–July)
California Spring area (May–July)
San Gabriel Mountains (May–July)

Butterfly mariposa lily

Santa Lucia Mountains (May–July)
Temblor Range (May–July)
Grass Valley area (May–July)

MARIPOSA LILY, SUPERB — *Calochortus superbus*
Lily family

DESCRIPTION: 1.5–2 feet. A single or up to three showy, bowl-shaped flowers (to 2 inches) at tip of stem. Three rounded, white (sometimes yellow, lavender, or purple) petals with reddish-haired, inverted V-shaped gland near base and yellow-bordered, red-purple spot above.

NOTE: The markings in this species are truly *superbus*!

HABITAT: Grasslands, open woods (to 5,600 feet); found in northwest mountains, coast and coast ranges, foothills, Transverse Ranges, Peninsular Ranges.

WHERE AND WHEN:
Traverse Creek Botanical
    Area (May–June)
Greenhorn Range (May–
    June)
Pine Hill (May–June)
Electra Road (May–June)
San Bernardino Mountains
    (May–June)
Big Meadow in Yosemite
    (June–July)

Superb mariposa lily

MARSH MARIGOLD or ELKSLIP MARSHMARIGOLD — *Caltha leptosepala*
Buttercup family

DESCRIPTION: 0.5–1 foot. Several bright white, shallow, bowl-shaped flowers (to 1.5 inches) with 5 to 11 petal-like sepals and dense cluster of yellow reproductive parts. Fleshy, dark green, kidney-shaped leaves.

NOTE: These plants spread by runners, so they usually form dense masses in boggy areas.

HABITAT: Marshes, wet meadows, stream banks, pond edges (4,500–10,000 feet); found in northwest mountains, Cascades, Sierra, northeast corner.

WHERE AND WHEN:
Sagehen Creek in Tahoe (May–June)

Marsh marigold

Echo Summit in Tahoe (May–June)
Glacier Point area in Yosemite (May–June)
Modoc Plateau (May–June)
Lassen National Park (May–July)
Trinity Alps (June–July)

MOCK ORANGE   *Philadelphus lewisii*
Hydrangea family

DESCRIPTION: 3–10 feet. Shrub with clusters of four-petaled, clean white flowers (to 1.5 inches). Many reproductive parts. Stamens with yellow pollen. Opposite pairs of broad, dark-green leaves.

NOTE: With its large, four-petaled flowers, its broad, dark-green leaves, and its reddish stems, this lovely shrub may remind you a bit of dogwood.

HABITAT: Forest openings and edges, canyons (to 6,000 feet); found in northwest mountains, north coast ranges, foothills, Cascades, Sierra, Transverse Ranges.

Mock orange

Pine Hill Ecological Preserve (May–June)
Feather River Canyon (May–June)
Drum Powerhouse Road (May–June)
Trinity Alps (May–June)
San Gabriel Mountains (May–June)
Yosemite Valley (May–June)

ONION, PITTED
Allium lacunosum

Onion family (previously included in Lily family)

DESCRIPTION: 4–15 inches. Slender stem with a terminal, densely flowered umbel of five to 45 small, white or pale pink flowers. Darker mid-veins. Two grasslike leaves. California endemic.

NOTE: The dark red or green mid-veins are a striking contrast with the white (or pale pink) tepals. "Pitted" refers to the bulb coat.

HABITAT: Dry hillsides, serpentine outcrops (to 3,500 feet); found in central and south coast ranges, foothills, east of the Sierra, Transverse Ranges, Mojave Desert.

Pitted onion

WHERE AND WHEN:
Ring Mountain (May–June)
Santa Rosa Plateau (May–June)
Channel Islands (May–June)
Santa Ana Mountains (May–June)
Santa Lucia Range (May–June)
Edgewood Preserve (May–June)

PHLOX, SPREADING
Phlox diffusa

Phlox family

DESCRIPTION: 4–12 inches. Low, spreading, woody plant covered with many pinwheel-like flowers. Five broad, overlapping petal lobes, usually white early and pink or purple after pollination.

NOTE: This is one of the first flowers to bloom across its wide elevational range.

HABITAT: Dry, rocky slopes and flats, ridges (to 13,300 feet); found in much of California (except deserts).

WHERE AND WHEN:
Shirley Canyon in Tahoe (May–June)

Spreading phlox

Mount Pinos (May–June)
King's Canyon/Sequoia (May–July)
Trinity Alps (May–July)
Lassen National Park (June–August)
Mount Dana in Yosemite (July)

SALAL   *Gaultheria shallon*

Heath family

DESCRIPTION: 0.5–5 feet. Shrub, though you will often find it only a foot or so tall. Many white or pink-tinged, urn-shaped flowers hang from glandular, red or pink pedicels. Broad, dark green, leathery, evergreen leaves.

NOTE: The juicy dark-purple berries were an important food source for the coastal Indians.

HABITAT: Forest edges and openings (to 2,600 feet); found in northwest mountains, coast, coast ranges.

WHERE AND WHEN:

Santa Ynez Mountains (May–June)

Santa Lucia Range (May–July)

Salt Point (May–July)

Big Basin State Park (May–July)

Kruse Rhododendron State Park (May–July)

San Bruno Mountain (May–July)

Salal

SAND LILY   *Leucocrinum montanum*
Agave family (previously included in Lily family)
DESCRIPTION: 1–4 inches. Stemless. Several showy (to 1.5 inches), star-shaped flowers atop rosette of narrow leaves. Six bright white tepals united into long, narrow flower tube.

NOTE: In some places on the Modoc Plateau in a good year, you can see thousands of these showy tufts scattered on sandy flats among the sagebrush and junipers.

HABITAT: Moist, sandy flats; sagebrush scrub (3,300–5,000 feet); found in Cascades, northeast corner.

WHERE AND WHEN:
SR-44 east of Lassen (May–June)
Glass Mountain (May–June)
U.S. 199 west of Alturas (May–June)
Said Valley Reservoir area (May–June)
Lava Beds National Monument (May–June)
Ravendale area (May–June)

Sand lily

SANDPAPER PLANT   *Petalonyx thurberi*
Loasa family
DESCRIPTION: 1–3 feet. Subshrub with clasping, heart-shaped leaves and dense terminal clusters of tiny (to one-fourth inch), creamy, star-shaped, fragrant flowers. Long-protruding reproductive parts.

NOTE: Touch the leaves and stems—they are covered with tiny, bristly hairs that create a sandpaper-like texture.

HABITAT: Sandy or gravelly flats, dunes, washes, desert scrub (to 4,000 feet); found in Mojave Desert, Sonoran Desert.

WHERE AND WHEN:
Anza-Borrego (May–July)
Joshua Tree (May–July)
along Imperial Highway S2 (May–July)
Rand Mountains (May–July)
Mojave National Preserve (May–July, September–November)
Death Valley (May–July, September–November)

Sandpaper
plant

SANDWORT, NUTTALL'S or BRITTLE SANDWORT
Minuartia nuttallii

Pink family

DESCRIPTION: 1–8 inches. Mat-forming plant with short, needlelike leaves and star-shaped, white flowers (to 0.5 inches). Glandular-sticky stems and leaves.

NOTE: There is a delightful symmetry about these delicate, white stars— five radiating petals, 10 radiating, threadlike stamens, and five pointed sepals showing between the petals.

HABITAT: Sandy, gravelly, or rocky flats and slopes (2,100–12,500 feet); found in northwest mountains, north coast ranges, Cascades, Sierra, northeast corner, east of the Sierra.

WHERE AND WHEN:

Lassen National Park (May–August)
Mount Sanhedrin (June–July)
Trinity Alps (July–August)
Freel Peak (July–August)
Saddlebag Lake in Yosemite (July–August)
White Mountains (July–August)

Nuttall's
sandwort

Sego lily

SEGO LILY or BRUNEAU MARIPOSA LILY   *Calochortus bruneaunis*
Lily family

DESCRIPTION: 8–16 inches. Umbel-like inflorescence of one to four showy, bowl-shaped flowers (to 2 inches). Three white, rounded petals with point at tip and maroon chevrons over yellow, hairy spot at base. Central greenish stripe on tepals. Grasslike leaves.

NOTE: This is a sagebrush scrub plant of the Great Basin, coming into northern California only along the eastern edges of the Sierra/Cascades and east to the Nevada border.

HABITAT: Sagebrush scrub (5,000–9,900 feet); found in northeast corner, eastern Sierra, east of the Sierra.

WHERE AND WHEN:
Topaz Lake (May–June)
Onion Valley (May–June)
Modoc Plateau (May–June)
Lakes Basin (May–June)
White Mountains (May–June)
Inyo Mountains (May–June)

SILVERTOP, BEACH   *Glehnia littoralis*
Carrot family

DESCRIPTION: 1–6 inches. Prostrate, often densely hairy plant with umbels of tiny, white flowers. Broad, pinnately compound, leathery leaves with toothed leaflets. Deep taproot. Balls of winged fruits.

NOTE: The deep taproot not only stabilizes the individual plant in the shifting sands but "holds" the species to sea level—it is one of the very few northern California species with an elevational range of only a few feet.

HABITAT: Beaches (at about sea level); found on north coast.

WHERE AND WHEN:
Salt Point (May–June)
Lamphere-Christensen Dunes (May–June)

Beach silvertop

Dillon Beach (May–June)
Redwood National Park (May–June)
Point Arena (May–June)
Fort Bragg area (May–June)

SOAP PLANT
Chlorogalum pomeridianum

Agave family (previously included in Lily family)

DESCRIPTION: 1–3 feet. Thick, branching stem rising above basal rosette of long, wavy-edged leaves. Long racemes of many scattered, starfishlike, six-tepaled, white flowers. Very narrow, widely separated, tepals with green or purple mid-vein. Night bloomer.

NOTE: It is amazing how quickly these flowers can open in late afternoon or early evening—almost while you watch.

HABITAT: Grasslands, openings in woods (to 5,000 feet); found in much of California (except northeast corner, deserts, and eastern edge).

WHERE AND WHEN:
Ring Mountain (May–June)
Edgewood Preserve (May–June)
Laguna Coast Wilderness Park (May–June)
Santa Rosa Plateau (May–June)
Hite's Cove trail (May–June)
Santa Monica Mountains (May–June)

Soap plant

Steer's head

STEER'S HEAD
Dicentra uniflora
Poppy family

DESCRIPTION: 1–3 inches. Solitary, white flower nodding off long, slender, often prostrate stem. Flowers resembling sun-bleached steer skull—the inner two petals form the "snout," the outer two petals the "horns."

NOTE: You would think such a strange and distinctive flower would be easy to spot, but it can blend in with its rocky habitat, so it can be difficult to find.

HABITAT: Gravelly or rocky flats (5,400–12,000 feet); found in northwest mountains, north coast ranges, Cascades, Sierra.

WHERE AND WHEN:
Goose Meadows in Tahoe (May)
Lakes Basin (May–June)
Six Rivers National Forest (May–June)
Mount Shasta (May–June)
Lassen National Park (May–June)
Castle Peak (June)

SWERTIA, WHITE-MARGINED or
WHITE-STEM ELKWEED
Swertia albicaulis
Gentian family

DESCRIPTION: 1–2 feet. Dense cluster of many four-petaled, waxy, white or greenish or pale blue flowers (to 0.5 inches) along slender plant stem. Opposite pairs of long, narrow leaves.

NOTE: As the common name indicates, the leaves have distinct narrow, white margins.

HABITAT: Dry hillsides, open woods (500–6,200 feet); found in northwest mountains, north coast ranges, foothills, Cascades, Sierra, northeast corner.

WHERE AND WHEN:
Pine Hill (May–June)

Sierra Valley (May–June)
McCourtney Road outside
  Grass Valley (May–June)
Modoc Plateau (May–June)
Washington area (June–July)
Weed area (June–July)

White-margined swertia

THISTLE, PEREGRINE
Cirsium cymosum

Aster family

DESCRIPTION: 1–3 feet. Cobwebby stem and leaves. One or a few mushroomlike flower heads above broad involucres crowded with pointed

phyllaries. Dull white, erect, tubular disk flowers. Long, narrow, clasping, spiny leaves.

NOTE: Perhaps grabbing a spiny leaf of this thistle would be a bit like being grabbed by the talons of the falcon—ouch!

HABITAT: Sagebrush scrub, open woods, grassy meadows (to 5,000 feet); found in northwest mountains, coast ranges, Cascades, Sierra, northeast corner.

WHERE AND WHEN:
Modoc Plateau (May–June)
Weed area (May–June)
Diablo Range (May–June)
Warner Mountains (May–
June)

Peregrine thistle

Tehachapi Mountains (May–June)
Boggs Lake (May–June)

THISTLE, STEMLESS or ELK THISTLE or
DRUMMOND'S THISTLE or DWARF THISTLE   *Cirsium scariosum*
Aster family

DESCRIPTION: 1–6 inches. Usually stemless plant with one or several creamy white or brownish flower heads (to 2 inches across) nestled atop rosette of prickly, pinnately divided leaves.

NOTE: Although some of these plants do have stems, the more typical version is stemless with flower head(s) directly atop the spiny, leafy bed.

HABITAT: Moist meadows, sagebrush scrub (to 11,000 feet); found in northwest mountains, Cascades, Sierra, east of the Sierra, south coast ranges, Transverse Ranges, Peninsular Ranges.

WHERE AND WHEN:

White Mountains (May–August)
Santa Rosa Plateau (May–August)
Kirkwood west of Carson Pass (June–July)
Lassen National Park (July–August)
east of Carson Pass (July–August)
San Jacinto Mountains (July–August)

Stemless
thistle

VIOLET, MACLOSKEY'S or SMALL WHITE VIOLET   *Viola macloskeyi*
Violet family

DESCRIPTION: 1–5 inches. Single (to 0.5 inches) bright white flower at tip of peduncle. Middle petal lobe of lower lip with purple nectar guides. Round or kidney-shaped leaves.

NOTE: You will usually see thick patches of these flowers, for the plants spread by rhizomes.

HABITAT: Wet meadows, seeps (3,300–11,200 feet); found in much of California (except deserts).

WHERE AND WHEN:
Butterfly Valley (May–June)
Warner Mountains (June–
    July)
King's Canyon/Sequoia
    (June–July)
San Jacinto Mountains
    (June–July)
Lassen National Park (June–
    July)
Castle Peak in Tahoe (July)

Macloskey's violet

WINDFLOWER, COLUMBIA   *Anemone deltoidea*
Buttercup family

DESCRIPTION: 4–12 inches. One flat, pure white flower atop stender stem. Five rounded, petal-like sepals surrounding cluster of many stamens and

pistils. Usually one compound leaf surrounding stem part-way up with three whorled, toothed leaflets.

NOTE: With its pure white color it almost seems as if the flower is a magical and fragile embodiment of the wind itself.

HABITAT: Woodlands, redwood forest (to 6,600 feet); found in northwest mountains, north coast and coast ranges.

WHERE AND WHEN:
Redwoods National Park
    (May–June)
*Big Basin Redwoods State
    Park* (May–June)

Columbia windflower

Prairie Creek Redwoods State Park (May–June)
Trinity Alps (June–July)
Russian Peak Wilderness (June–July)
Salmon Mountains (June–July)

YERBA SANTA, CALIFORNIA *Eriodictyon californicum*
Borage family (previously included in Waterleaf family)
DESCRIPTION: 3–10 feet. Sticky, evergreen shrub with densely flowered clusters of narrow, tubular, white, pinkish, or bluish flowers (to 1 inch). Five petal lobes flare out of broad tube.
NOTE: Apparently bees and butterflies understand the meaning of the common name ("holy herb"), for you will usually find swarms of them "worshipping" the flowers.
HABITAT: Open woods, dry slopes, roadsides (to 5,500 feet); found in northwest mountains, north and central coast ranges, Central Valley, foothills, Cascades, Sierra, Transverse Ranges.
WHERE AND WHEN:
Trinity Alps (May–June)
Kern Canyon Road (May–June)
Hite's Cove Trail (May–June)
Big Basin Redwoods State Park (May–June)
Santa Lucia Range (June–July)
Bear Basin Butte (June–July)

California
yerba santa

YUCCA, BANANA or SPANISH BAYONET *Yucca baccata*
Agave family (previously included in Lily family)
DESCRIPTION: 1–3 feet. Shrub with one or a few flowering stalks surrounded by basal rosettes of stiff, swordlike, sharp-pointed, blue-green leaves whose margins shred. Clusters of hanging, bell-shaped, cream-colored (often with purple tinges) flowers (to 3 inches).

Banana yucca

NOTE: This plant has no true above-ground stem. As the common name indicates, the fruits are banana-like.

HABITAT: Desert woodlands (2,600–4,300 feet); found in Mojave Desert.

WHERE AND WHEN:
Kingston Range in Mojave National Preserve (May–June)
Mount San Jacinto (May–June)
Granite Mountains in Mojave National Preserve (May–June)
Providence Mountains in Mojave National Preserve (May–June)
New York Mountains in Mojave National Preserve (May–June)
Clark Mountains in Mojave National Preserve (May–June)

BUCKHORN CHOLLA

Cylindropuntia acanthocarpa or *Opuntia acanthocarpa*

Cactus family

DESCRIPTION: 3–6 feet. Many-branched, treelike plant with narrow, cylindrical, jointed stems. Six to 25 straw-colored or silvery spines per cluster. Bowl-shaped, yellow-orange to bronze-red flowers (to 3 inches) with many petals.

NOTE: The spines are covered with a straw-colored sheath which comes off easily, revealing the usually darker spines beneath.

Buckhorn cholla

HABITAT: Desert scrub, woodlands (to 4,500 feet); found in Transverse Ranges, Mojave Desert, Sonoran Desert.

WHERE AND WHEN:

Mojave National Preserve (May–June)

Joshua Tree (May–June)

San Gabriel Mountains (May–June)

Algodones Dunes (May–June)

Granite Mountains in Mojave National Preserve (May–June)

Inyokern area (May–June)

FRITILLARY, PURPLE or
SPOTTED MOUNTAIN BELLS   *Fritillaria atropurpurea*
Lily family

DESCRIPTION: 4–24 inches. A few star-shaped flowers (to three-fourths inch) nod from along the stem. Six narrow, pointed tepals purplish-brown with greenish-yellow or white mottling, often yellow-edged.

NOTE: Many of the fritillaries have large, dramatically showy flowers; the purple fritillary has smaller flowers but is no less strikingly multicolored.

Purple fritillary

HABITAT: Sagebrush scrub, grassy fields, forest clearings (6,000–10,500 feet); found in northwest mountains, foothills, Cascades, Sierra, east of the Sierra, northeast corner, Transverse Ranges, Mojave Desert, Sonoran Desert.

WHERE AND WHEN:

SR-44 east of Lassen (May–June)

White Mountains (June–July)

Martis Valley in Tahoe (June–July)

San Bernardino Mountains (June–July)

Trinity Alps (June–July)

Warner Mountains (June–July)

MARIPOSA LILY, TIBURON   *Calochortus tiburonensis*
Lily family

DESCRIPTION: 4–24 inches. Usually branching stem bearing two to seven spectacular, erect, bowl-shaped, yellow-green flecked flowers with purple-brown streaks or lining. Petals fringed with yellowish hairs. Three sepals

Tiburon mariposa lily

project thornlike between the petals. California endemic. CNPS Rare and Endangered List—seriously endangered.

NOTE: Despite its large and dazzling flowers, this rare mariposa lily is sometimes difficult to spot, even when it is right in front of you, as its flowers find camouflage in their dry, rocky habitat.

HABITAT: Rocky areas in serpentine grassland (150–500 feet); found in central coastal ranges.

WHERE AND WHEN:

only on *Ring Mountain* (May–June)

PEONY, WESTERN or BROWN'S PEONY   *Paeonia brownii*
Peony family

DESCRIPTION: 0.5–1.5 feet. Branching stem with five to 12 bowl-shaped flowers (up to 2 inches) hanging upside-down. Many rounded, brownish-

Western peony

maroon petals with yellow edges. Large, deeply lobed, waxy blue-green leaves.

NOTE: It is amazing to see this plant in fruit—the ovaries swell and swell into "sausages" up to 2 inches long whose weight can pull the flower almost to the ground.

HABITAT: Forest openings, sagebrush scrub (3,000–8,600 feet); found in northwest mountains, north and central coast ranges, Cascades, Sierra, foothills, Peninsular Ranges.

WHERE AND WHEN:
Sagehen Creek (May)
Butterfly Valley (May)

Palomar Mountain (May–June)
Lassen National Park (May–June)
Trinity Alps (June)
Lakes Basin (June)

YOUTH-ON-AGE or PIG-A-BACK PLANT   *Tolmiea diplomenziesii*
Saxifrage family
DESCRIPTION: 1–3 feet. Long, flowering stem rising well above basal, heart-shaped leaves. Tubular flowers with four brown-purple, threadlike, sinuous petals.

NOTE: The common name refers to this plant's unusual backup, asexual, method of reproduction—a short stem grows out of a bud at the base of a mature leaf, falls to the ground with the withering leaf, and sprouts.
HABITAT: Wet places in forests (to 6,000 feet); found in northwest mountains, north and central coast and coast ranges.
WHERE AND WHEN:
Santa Cruz Mountains (May–June)
Russian Gulch State Park (May–July)
Plaskett Meadows (May–July)
Van Damme State Park (May–July)
Salt Point (May–July)
Marble Mountains (May–July)

Youth-on-age

NON-NATIVE BOUQUET

Crimson clover

Crimson Clover
Trifolium incarnatum
Pea family

DESCRIPTION: Cylindrical spike of scarlet pea flowers.

EXAMPLE OF LOCATION: Jenner-Fort Ross area.

Foxglove

Foxglove
Digitalis purpurea
Plantain family (previously included in Snapdragon family)

DESCRIPTION: Spike of large, tubular, two-lipped, purple or white, spotted flowers.

EXAMPLE OF LOCATION: Salt Point.

JUNE

Elegant clarkia and linanthus in the Kern River Canyon

IF YOU SEEK wildflowers, with the coming of June, you will shift your attention to mid-mountain elevations. Although there will still be some blooming along the coast, in the coast ranges, and in the foothills, the flowers will largely have left the Central Valley with the arrival of the searing summer heat. For you and the flowers, the band of greatest blooming will now be between about a mile and a mile and a half above sea level—mid-mountain meadows and slopes and the high Great Basin desert along the eastern edges of the state. In the far north, the bloom will be peaking at somewhat lower elevations.

At the lower edges of this blooming band, in places like Yosemite Valley, the Smith River corridor, Sagehen Meadows north of Tahoe, the Modoc Plateau, and Benton east of Yosemite, summer will be well under way. If you are missing spring, don't despair; just go higher, to places like Winnemucca Lake south of Tahoe, Monitor Pass east of the Sierra, the Warner Mountains, the Trinity Alps, or the San Bernardino Mountains. And if you don't mind a little lingering snow, you can experience the graceful **fawn lily** along the Loch Leven Trail west of Tahoe and in Lassen National Park and the dazzling, blue-tinged, white **Drummond's anemone** near Squaw Valley, north of Lake Tahoe. If you're even more adventurous, you can bloom with the spectacular **daggerpod** high in the rocks up Red Lake Peak at Carson Pass.

June is both a culmination and a transition—full summer in the lower mountains and spring up above.

Highlights

The Northwest Mountains

Merten's coralroot, giant trillium, calypso orchid, red ribbons, few-flowered bleeding heart, phantom orchid, and **leopard lily** in the Trinity Alps and along the Smith River

The Coast

Blue blossom, seaside daisy, sea thrift, coast sun cup, yellow bush lupine, Johnny-nip, and **rosy onion** at Salt Point
Coast buckwheat at the Dunes of Arcata

The Cascades

Fawn lily at Mount Lassen

The Foothills

Elegant clarkia in the Kern River Canyon

The Sierra

Western blue flag and **daggerpod** at Carson Pass
Elegant brodiaea and **canchalagua** in Yosemite Valley
Bladderwort, swamp onion, and **tofieldia** in Osgood Swamp in the Tahoe Basin
Fawn lily on the Loch Leven trail
Drummond's anemone in the Pole Creek area in the Tahoe Basin
Sugar stick along the Vikingsholm trail in the Tahoe Basin
Bog asphodel at Butterfly Valley

The Northeast Corner

Bach's downingia, Beckwith violet, Hooker's balsamroot, and **tansy-leaf evening primrose** on the Modoc Plateau
Bitterroot and **heart-leaf arnica** in the Warner Mountains

East of the Sierra

Prickly poppy, rayless daisy, sego lily, apricot mallow, white-flowered keckiella, and **blazing star** at Topaz Lake
Mojave prickly pear and **silver cholla** in the Benton area

Flowers

DOWNINGIA, BACH'S or BACH'S CALICOFLOWER   *Downingia bacigalupii*
Bellflower family

DESCRIPTION: 2–12 inches. Two-lipped flowers with two narrow, hornlike, blue-violet petal lobes in the upper lip and three blue lobes with a white patch in the lower lip. Two large, yellow-orange spots within the white patch.

NOTE: The easiest way to distinguish this downingia from others is by the narrow, tubular, periscope-like anther tube rising above the corolla.

HABITAT: Vernal pools, grassy meadows (to 7,500 feet); found in Cascades, Sierra, northeast corner.

WHERE AND WHEN:
Sagehen Creek meadow (June)
Warner Mountains (June–July)
Modoc Plateau (June–July)
Madeline area (June–July)

Bach's
downingia

Sierra Valley (June–July)
Lake Almanor area (June–July)

HEAVENLY BLUE or GIANT WOOLLY STAR   *Eriastrum densifolium*
Phlox family
DESCRIPTION: 0.5–2 feet. Often-spreading subshrub with dense clusters of light blue, funnel-shaped flowers (to 0.5 inches). Petal lobes flaring star-like. Needlelike leaves and spiky bracts under the flowers.
NOTE: These plants often form wide, dense displays—pieces of beautiful blue sky come to rest on the desert floor, often among sagebrush.
HABITAT: Sandy, gravelly flats and slopes, dunes, dry river beds (to 9,500 feet); found in much of central and southern California.
WHERE AND WHEN:
Anza-Borrego (June–July)
San Jacinto Mountains (June–July)
Horseshoe Meadows Road (June–August)
Santa Lucia Range (June–August)
Sawmill Pass Trail (June–August)
Monterey Peninsula (June–August)

Heavenly blue

IRIS, WILD or BLUE FLAG or
ROCKY MOUNTAIN IRIS
Iris missouriensis

Iris family

DESCRIPTION: 1–2 feet. One to four large (to 2.5 inches), showy, blue or blue-purple flowers at the tip of the stem. Three tonguelike, arching sepals with yellow-white veins; three erect petals without veins.

NOTE: The other erect structures are the pistils that spring up after receiving pollen.

HABITAT: Moist, grassy meadows, creek banks (3,000–11,000 feet); found in coast ranges, Sierra, east of the Sierra, northeast corner, Transverse Ranges, Peninsular Ranges.

WHERE AND WHEN:

Winnemucca Lake Trail (June–July)

Mount Pinos (June–July)

Bridgeport area just north of Yosemite (June–July)

Monitor Pass area (June–July)

King's Canyon/Sequoia (June–July)

east of Cedarville (June–July)

Wild iris

LUPINE, BROAD-LEAF
Lupinus polyphyllus

Pea family

DESCRIPTION: 1–5 feet. Stout stem with long (to 18 inches) raceme packed with whorls of blue pea flowers. Often with white or yellow patch on the banner that turns rosy with age. Palmately compound leaves with five to 17 broad leaflets.

NOTE: This plant often occurs in great masses—you can almost see the cloud of fragrance hovering above the flowers.

HABITAT: Wet meadows, stream banks (to 9,800 feet); found in much of California (except Central Valley, south coast, and deserts).

WHERE AND WHEN:

Lake Forest in Tahoe (June–July)

Piute Mountains (June–August)

Greenhorn Range (June–August)

Mount Shasta (June–August)

Lakes Basin (July)
King's Canyon/Sequoia (July–August)

Broad-leaf lupine

MONKSHOOD *Aconitum columbianum*
Buttercup family
DESCRIPTION: 1–6 feet. Stout stem bearing numerous, oddly shaped, deep blue-purple flowers on short pedicels. Upper sepal forms head; lower sepals form wings that cradle the large cluster of reproductive parts. Two very small, inconspicuous petals inside the sepals.

NOTE: In profile, the upper sepal looks much more like a duck's head than a monk's hood!

HABITAT: Stream banks, wet meadows, moist forest openings (4,000–8,700 feet); found in northwest mountains, Cascades, Sierra, east of the Sierra, northeast corner.

WHERE AND WHEN:
Paige Meadows in Tahoe (June–July)

Monkshood

Modoc Plateau (June–July)
Greenhorn Range (June–July)
Lassen National Park (July–August)
Yolla Bolly-Middle Eel Wilderness (July–August)
Saddlebag Lake in Yosemite (August–September)

PENSTEMON, WOODLAND or
WOODLAND BEARDTONGUE *Nothochelone nemorosa*
Plantain family (previously included in Snapdragon family)
DESCRIPTION: 1–3 feet. Slender, often-leaning stem bearing loose, few-flowered clusters of pink-purple, tubular flowers. Opposite, toothed leaves.

NOTE: Although not a true penstemon, these flowers share with penstemons their interesting characteristic of one infertile (antherless) stamen—called a staminode.

HABITAT: Rocky places in forests (3,200–4,600 feet); found in northwest mountains, Cascades.

WHERE AND WHEN:
Mount Shasta (June–July)
Green Pass (June–July)
Bear Basin Butte Botanical
　　Area (June–July)
Marble Mountain
　　Wilderness (June–July)

Woodland penstemon

PHACELIA, DWARF *Phacelia humilis*
Borage family (previously included in Waterleaf family)
DESCRIPTION: 2–8 inches. Coiling racemes of small, violet or blue-purple, bowl-shaped flowers. Long-protruding, white stamens. Broad, deeply veined leaves. Often forms extensive carpets.

NOTE: With its hairy stems and leaves and its many protruding, threadlike stamens, you might think this plant would have been named something like "fuzzy blue bowl."

HABITAT: Sandy or gravelly flats, forest openings (2,600–9,400 feet); found in Sierra, east of the Sierra, northeast corner.

Dwarf phacelia

WHERE AND WHEN:
Sagehen Creek (June)
Sweetwater Mountains (June–July)
Warner Mountains (June–July)
Owens Peak (June–July)
Monitor Pass (June–July)
Mount Dana in Yosemite (July–August)

POLEMONIUM, GREAT or GREAT JACOB'S LADDER or WESTERN POLEMONIUM
Polemonium occidentale

Phlox family

DESCRIPTION: 2–3 feet. Slightly sticky stem with long raceme of many shallow, bowl-shaped, blue or blue-purple flowers (to 1 inch). White throats with dark purple lines. Pinnately compound leaves with 9 to 27 leaflets.

Great polemonium

NOTE: The alternate name for plants in the *Polemonium* genus is "Jacob's ladder," in reference to the pinnately compound leaves with the ladder-rung leaflets.

HABITAT: Wet meadows, stream banks (3,000–11,000 feet); found in northwest mountains, Sierra, east of the Sierra, northeast corner, Transverse Ranges.

WHERE AND WHEN:

Paige Meadows in Tahoe (June–July)
Sweetwater Mountains (June–July)
Warner Mountains (June–July)
Bishop Creek (June–July)
San Bernardino Mountains (June–July)
Tioga Pass in Yosemite (July)

PORTERELLA   *Porterella carnosula*
Bellflower family

DESCRIPTION: 1–12 inches. Loose racemes of many multicolored, two-lipped flowers (to three-fourths inch). Lower lip (three lobes) with white patch at its base with two bright yellow spots and blue-purple at the tip.

NOTE: Porterella is closely related to the downingias and, like them, forms extensive mats in drying vernal pools, but in the high mountains.

HABITAT: Vernal pools; wet, grassy meadows (5,000–10,000 feet); found in Cascades, Sierra, east of Sierra, northeast corner.

WHERE AND WHEN:

Pole Creek in Tahoe (June–July)
Lassen National Park (June–July)
Warner Mountains (June–July)
Clover Meadow south of Yosemite (June–July)
Modoc Plateau (June–July)
Kern Plateau (June–July)

Porterella

SELF HEAL
Prunella vulgaris
Mint family

DESCRIPTION: 4–20 inches. Square stem ending in thick, somewhat pine-cone-like spike of two-lipped purple flowers emerging from greenish or purple, scalelike bracts. Upper two petal lobes form canopy; lower three form broad, ragged bib and two wings.

NOTE: The former scientific name of the Mint family was *Labiatae,* mean-

ing "lip," in reference to the larger, landing-pad, middle petal lobe of the lower lip.

HABITAT: Moist meadows, forest openings (to 7,500 feet); found in much of California (except northeast corner, Central Valley, and deserts).

WHERE AND WHEN:
Salt Point (June)
Trinity Alps (June–July)
Monterey Peninsula (June–July)
Lassen National Park (June–July)
Palomar Mount State Park (July–August)
Osgood Swamp in Tahoe (July–August)

Self heal

STICKSEED, VELVETY
Hackelia velutina
Borage family

DESCRIPTION: 1–3 feet. Many blue, pinwheel-like flowers (up to 1 inch) on branched raceme. Broad petal lobes with raised white rim around the

throat. Long, tonguelike leaves with soft white hairs. California endemic.

NOTE: The fruits are round or oval nutlets covered with prickly barbs that attach the fruit to fur, legs, shoes, socks, and anything else that they touch.

HABITAT: Dry flats and slopes, forest openings (to 10,000 feet); found in foothills, Cascades, Sierra.

WHERE AND WHEN:
Paige Meadows in Tahoe (June–July)

Velvety stickseed

Greenhorn Mountains (June–July)
Crane Flat in Yosemite (June–July)
King's Canyon/Sequoia (June–August)
Kirkwood west of Carson Pass (July)
Grass Lake at Luther Pass (July)

BLEEDING HEART, FEW-FLOWERED or
SHORT-HORNED STEER'S HEAD   *Dicentra pauciflora*
Poppy family

DESCRIPTION: 1–10 inches. Dwarf plant with one to three nodding, pale pink, lavender, or brownish, flattened, more-or-less heart-shaped flowers. Deeply divided, fernlike leaves. California endemic.

NOTE: At first you might think you've come across a steer's head (see p. 410) with a fat face and short horns, then you realize that it is a pale, squarish bleeding heart on a very short plant.

HABITAT: Rocky places, forest openings (4,000–10,000 feet); found in northwest mountains, northern and southern Sierra.

WHERE AND WHEN:
Mount Eddy (June–July)
Trinity Alps (June–July)
King's Canyon/Sequoia (June–July)

Few-flowered bleeding heart

CINQUEFOIL, PURPLE or
MARSH CINQUEFOIL   *Comarum palustre* or *Potentilla palustris*
Rose family

DESCRIPTION: 0.5–3 feet. A few star-shaped flowers (to 1.5 inches). Five separate, pointed, wine-red petals surrounding red sphere of many reproductive parts. Five red-purple sepals extend well beyond petals.

NOTE: Wine and water—some people don't think the two ever mix. But here they do—wine-red petaled flowers on plants that grow in bogs and marshes.

HABITAT: Bogs, marshes (to 8,000 feet); found in north coast, Sacramento Valley, Cascades, Sierra, northeast corner.

WHERE AND WHEN:
Coastal Trail near Requa (June–July)

Warner Mountains (June–
   July)
Osgood Swamp in Tahoe
   (July–August)
Grass Lake at Luther Pass
   (July–August)
Mount Shasta (July–August)
Lassen National Park (July–
   August)

Purple cinquefoil

CLARKIA, TONGUE or FOREST CLARKIA   *Clarkia rhomboidea*
Evening primrose family
DESCRIPTION: 1–3 feet. A few rose-purple flowers (to 1 inch) scattered loosely on short pedicel (above which is inferior ovary). Four diamond-

shaped, clawed, widely separated petals. Buds nod, flowers
ascend. Narrow, ovate leaves
with pair of stipules.

NOTE: The lovely rose-purple of
the petals is enhanced by white
splotches at the base with delicate red-purple spots.

HABITAT: Woodlands; dry, rocky
slopes (to 8,000 feet); found in
much of California (except deserts).

WHERE AND WHEN:
Modoc Plateau (June–July)
Santa Lucia Range (June–July)
Trinity Alps (June–July)
Diablo Range (June–July)
Mount Tamalpais (June–July)
Palomar Mount State Park
   (June–July)

Tongue clarkia

CORALROOT, MERTEN'S or WESTERN CORALROOT
Corallorhiza mertensiana

Orchid family

DESCRIPTION: 0.5–2 feet. Many small flowers along reddish stem. Five narrow, reddish petals and sepals; lower (middle) petal is white or red with red lines or splotches and spur underneath. No green leaves—saprophyte.

NOTE: There are two other species of coralroot in California: one with red spots on the lower petal and the other with yellow and red stripes. Merten's coralroot has less-defined red coloration.

HABITAT: Forest shade (to 7,200 feet); found in northwest mountains, north coast, Cascades.

WHERE AND WHEN:

Klamath Mountains along Klamath River (June–July)

Trinity Alps (June–August)

Fort Ross area (June–July)

Bear Basin Butte Natural Area (June–July)

Six Rivers National Forest (June–July)

Jughandle Creek (June–July)

Merten's coralroot

COYOTE MINT or SERPENTINE MONARDELLA
Monardella villosa

Mint family

DESCRIPTION: 1–1.5 feet. Slender stem with terminal, round flower head densely packed with scores of small, two-lipped, pink or purple (sometimes white) flowers. The plant is gently covered with soft white hairs.

NOTE: As with many mints, these flowers attract bees in great buzzing multitudes!

HABITAT: Woodlands, rocky places (to 6,000 feet); found on north and central coast and in coast ranges, foothills.

WHERE AND WHEN:

Ring Mountain (June–July)

Salt Point (June–July)

Monterey Peninsula (June–July)

Coyote mint

Jenner area (June–July)
Mount Tamalpais (June–July)
Santa Lucia Range (June–July)

DAGGERPOD ***Phoenicaulis cheiranthoides***

Mustard family

DESCRIPTION: 2–8 inches. Loose raceme of four-petaled flowers (to 0.5 inches) on long, upcurving stems. Separate, pink or red-purple, rounded petals. Basal rosette of broad, gray-hairy leaves and a few stem leaves.

Daggerpod

NOTE: An early bloomer at mid-elevations; its dagger-pods (long, knifelike seed-pods) will be fully ripe when most neighboring flowers are just coming into bloom.

HABITAT: Rocky outcrops, ridges (3,800–10,700 feet); found in northwest mountains, north coast ranges, Cascades, Sierra, east of the Sierra, northeast corner.

WHERE AND WHEN:
Warner Mountains (June)
Pole Creek in Tahoe (June–July)

Trinity Alps (June–July)
Red Lake Peak at Carson Pass (June–July)
Mount Shasta (June–July)
Bishop Creek (June–July)

DAISY, WANDERING   *Erigeron peregrinus*
Aster family

DESCRIPTION: 0.5–2.5 feet. Slender stem with one or a few flower heads (to 1 inch) with 30–100 crowded, narrow, pink or lavender or white rays (usually upcurving) around a yellow-orange disk. Glandular-sticky phyllaries. Mostly basal, long narrow leaves.

NOTE: The wanderings of these delightful daisies take them all the way from the American West to eastern Asia.

HABITAT: Wet meadows, forest openings, talus slopes (4,200–11,100 feet); found in northwest mountains, Cascades, Sierra, east of the Sierra, northeast corner.

WHERE AND WHEN:
Paige Meadows in Tahoe
    (June–July)
Lassen National Park (June–
    July)
Tenaya Canyon in Yosemite
    (June–July)
Warner Mountains (July)
Lakes Basin (July–August)
Trinity Alps (July–August)

Wandering daisy

GILIA, SCARLET   *Ipomopsis aggregata*
Phlox family

DESCRIPTION: 1–3 feet. Usually dense clusters of many trumpetlike, scarlet flowers, mostly nodding off one side of sticky plant stem. Often mottled yellow or white in throat.

NOTE: Whereas its trumpet-flowered, close relative, pink gilia (p. 482) might play soft, romantic, mood music, the flowers of this richer-colored gilia would probably wail red-hot jazz!

HABITAT: Brushy slopes, often with sagebrush, forest openings (3,500–

10,800 feet); found in north-west mountains, Cascades, Sierra, northeast corner.

WHERE AND WHEN:
Barker Pass in Tahoe (June–July)
Modoc Plateau (June–July)
Kern Plateau (June–July)
Pohono Trail in Yosemite (July–August)
Trinity Alps (July–August)
Lakes Basin (July)

Scarlet gilia

LEWISIA, QUILL-LEAF or LEE'S LEWISIA   *Lewisia leana*
Miner's lettuce family (previously included in Purslane family)

DESCRIPTION: 0.5–1 foot. Candelabra-like plant with slender, much-branched stems and scattered pink, six- to eight-petaled, star-shaped flow-

ers (to 0.5 inches). Basal rosette of fleshy, mostly erect, narrow leaves.

NOTE: Despite their small size, the pink flowers are quite striking, especially as there are no stem leaves (except for much-reduced bracts) to compete for attention.

HABITAT: Rocky places, forest openings (4,000–10,500 feet); found in northwest mountains, north coast ranges.

WHERE AND WHEN:
Kangaroo Lake (June–August)

Quill-leaf lewisia

Marble Mountains (June–August)
Mount Eddy (June–August)
Salmon Mountains (June–August)
Trinity Alps (June–August)
Cedar Basin Research Natural Area (June–August)

MALLOW, BOG
Sidalcea oregana
Mallow family

DESCRIPTION: 0.5–3 feet. Dense or loose spikelike cluster of flowers (to 1 inch) along the upper stem. Five separate, pink or rose petals with veins. Large, broad, deeply palmately lobed leaves, more deeply lobed higher on stem.

NOTE: The delicate pink or rose flowers resemble those of the other mallows, but occur in dense, cylindrical spikes instead of loose clusters.

HABITAT: Wet meadows, marshes (to 9,800 feet); found in northwest mountains, Cascades, Sierra, east of the Sierra, northeast corner, Peninsular Ranges.

WHERE AND WHEN:
Trinity Alps (June–July)
Greenhorn Mountains (June–July)
Modoc Plateau (June–July)
San Jacinto Mountains (June–August)
Mount Shasta (July)
Pole Creek in Tahoe (July)

Bog mallow

MILKWEED, NARROW-LEAF or
MEXICAN WHORLED MILKWEED
Asclepias fasciculatus
Dogbane family (previously included in Milkweed family)

DESCRIPTION: 1–3 feet. Umbel-like clusters of gray-pink or rose flowers with reflexed, tonguelike petals above which are five white or pinkish, erect, cuplike "horns." Whorls of three to five very narrow, often infolded leaves.

NOTE: The seedpods are like erect green beans.

HABITAT: Dry flats and slopes (to 7,000 feet); found in much of California.

WHERE AND WHEN:
Santa Monica Mountains
(June–July)
Hetch Hetchy in Yosemite
(June–July)
White Mountains (June–July)
Trinity Alps (June–July)
Alabama Hills (June–July)
Santa Cruz Mountains
(June–August)

Narrow-leaf milkweed

MONKEYFLOWER, TORREY'S   *Mimulus torreyi*
Lopseed family (previously included in Snapdragon family)
DESCRIPTION: 2–8 inches. Ground-hugging plant with several two-lipped, pink or magenta flowers (to 0.5 inches). Two golden-yellow stripes with

dark rose margins in throat. Flower tube longer than corolla is wide. California endemic.

NOTE: These small but striking flowers often create extensive magenta carpets on otherwise bare, dry ground.

HABITAT: Forest openings, sandy or gravelly flats (to 8,000 feet); found in Cascades, foothills, Sierra.

WHERE AND WHEN:
upper Bidwell Park (June–July)
Traverse Creek (June–July)
Hope Valley east of Carson Pass (June–July)

Torrey's monkeyflower

Lassen National Park (June–July)
Hetch Hetchy area in Yosemite (June–July)
French Meadows Reservoir area (June–July)

OLD MAN'S WHISKERS or PRAIRIE SMOKE　　*Geum triflorum*
Rose family

DESCRIPTION: 6–20 inches. One or several flowers, each hanging from tip of arching pedicel. Five pink sepals cradle five smaller pink or cream petals to form puckered kiss.

NOTE: As interesting as are the hanging-kiss flowers, the fruits are amazing—spiraling wonderlands of sinuous, red threads adorned with silver hairs.

HABITAT: Sagebrush scrub; grassy meadows; forest openings (4,000–11,000 feet); found in northwest mountains, Cascades, Sierra, east of the Sierra, northeast corner.

WHERE AND WHEN:
Pole Creek in Tahoe (June–July)
Lakes Basin (June–July)
Modoc Plateau (June–July)
Marble Mountains (June–July)
Mount Shasta (June–July)
Meiss Meadows at Carson Pass (July)

Old man's whiskers

Old man's whiskers

ONION, SWAMP   *Allium validum*
Onion family (previously included in Lily family)
DESCRIPTION: 1–3 feet. One large, terminal umbel of 15–40 rose-purple, six-tepaled, fragrant flowers. Tepals mostly erect rather than spreading. Long-protruding reproductive parts. Three to six flattened, grasslike leaves much shorter than stem.

NOTE: The onion fragrance of these flowers is so strong it can create pungent clouds of odor that hover over the plants.

HABITAT: Wet meadows, seeps (4,000–10,000 feet); found in northwest mountains, north coast ranges, Cascades, Sierra, northeast corner.

WHERE AND WHEN:
Sagehen Creek meadow (June–July)
Warner Mountains (June–July)
King's Canyon/Sequoia (June–July)
Mount Eddy (June–July)
Onion Valley (June–July)
Trinity Alps (July–August)

Swamp onion

PAINTBRUSH, APPLEGATE'S or
WAVY-LEAF PAINTBRUSH   *Castilleja applegatei*
Broomrape family (previously included in Figwort family)
DESCRIPTION: 0.5–2.5 feet. Glandular-hairy stem and leaves. Unlobed or three-lobed, mittenlike, wavy-edged leaves. Bracts usually three-lobed and red, orange, or yellow. Yellow-green, tubular flowers protrude beyond bracts.
NOTE: This paintbrush provides quite a range of colors, sometimes even on the same plant.
HABITAT: Dry slopes, forest openings, sagebrush scrub (to 11,000 feet); found in much of California (except Central Valley).
WHERE AND WHEN:
Kern Plateau (June–July)
Mount Pinos (June–July)
Trinity Alps (June–July)
Barker Pass in Tahoe (June–July)
Modoc Plateau (June–July)
Lakes Basin (July)

Applegate's paintbrush

PENSTEMON, BRIDGE'S or
SCARLET PENSTEMON
Penstemon rostriflorus

Plantain family (previously included in Snapdragon family)

DESCRIPTION: 1–3.5 feet. Long, tubular, two-lipped flowers. Bright red flowers with gaping, reflexed, lower lip. Opposite pairs of narrow leaves. Plant often shrubby at base.

NOTE: Unlike the similar narrow-tubed, red-flowered scarlet bugler (p. 296), this species, with its slightly open "mouth," appears to have a lot to say!

HABITAT: Sagebrush scrub, woodlands, talus slopes (5,000–10,700 feet); found in central and southern Sierra, east of the Sierra, Transverse Ranges, Peninsular Ranges, Mojave Desert.

WHERE AND WHEN:
along Vernal Falls trail in Yosemite (June–July)
San Gabriel Mountains (June–August)
San Jacinto Mountains (June–August)

Bridge's penstemon

Granite Mountains (June–August)
San Bernardino Mountains (June–August)
east of Monitor Pass (July)

PUSSYPAWS   *Calyptridium umbellatum*
Miner's lettuce family (previously included in Purslane family)

DESCRIPTION: 2–10 inches. Round clusters of tiny, crepe-papery, pink or white flowers at tips of long, reddish stems. Basal rosette of spoon-shaped leaves, between which radiate flower stems.

NOTE: This plant is a temperature indicator—the flower stems lie flat when the ground is cold and angle sharply upward when it heats up.

HABITAT: Dry, sandy or rocky flats and slopes, forest openings (2,500–14,000 feet); found in northwest mountains, north coast ranges, foothills, Cascades, Sierra, east of the Sierra, northeast corner.

WHERE AND WHEN:
Lakes Basin (June)
King's Canyon/Sequoia (June–July)
San Bernardino Mountains (June–July)
Lassen National Park (June–September)
Castle Peak (July)
Mount Dana in Yosemite (July–August)

Pussypaws

ROSE, WOOD'S   *Rosa woodsii*
Rose family

DESCRIPTION: 3–6 feet. Shrub with prickles and many, mostly flat, five-petaled, rose or pink, very fragrant flowers. Dark-red torpedolike buds and deep-red rose hips (fruits).

NOTE: You will often find these plants growing in dense, thorny thickets, so inhaling the sweet aroma may come with a price!

Wood's rose

HABITAT: Creekbanks, seeps (3,500–11,500 feet); found in Cascades, Sierra, east of the Sierra, northeast corner, Transverse Ranges, Mojave Desert, Sonoran Desert.

WHERE AND WHEN:
Pole Creek in Tahoe (June–July)
Mount Tallac in Tahoe (July–August)
Honey Lake area (June–July)
San Gabriel Mountains (July–August)
Dana Plateau in Yosemite (July–August)
San Bernardino Mountains (July–August)

SALMONBERRY   *Rubus spectabilis*
Rose family

DESCRIPTION: 3–9 feet. Shrub with deep pink-purple, five-petaled flowers (to 1.5 inches) and large, toothed, deeply veined leaves.

Salmonberry

NOTE: The red, yellow, or orange raspberry-like berries are quite tasty—to four-leggeds and two-leggeds alike!

HABITAT: Moist places in forests, stream banks (to 4,600 feet); found in northwest mountains, north and central coast and coast ranges.

WHERE AND WHEN:
along Navarro River (June–July)
Lamphere-Christensen Dunes (June–July)
Van Damme State Park (June–July)
Prairie Creek Redwoods State Park (June–July)
Fort Bragg area (June–July)
Salt Point (June–July)

SNOWPLANT   *Sarcodes sanguinea*
Heath family

DESCRIPTION: 4–12 inches. Christmas-tree spike dense with bright red, urn-shaped flowers. No green leaves—saprophyte with small, red scales. Early bloomer right after the snow melts.

Snowplant

NOTE: The Latin name means "fleshy blood-red," which describes well the impression this strange, clammy, sticky, leafless plant conveys!

HABITAT: Forest shade (4,000–8,000 feet); found in northwest mountains, north coast ranges, Cascades, Sierra, Transverse Ranges, Peninsular Ranges.

WHERE AND WHEN:
King's Canyon/Sequoia
    (June–July)
Trinity Alps (June–July)
Pole Creek in Tahoe (June–
    July)
Lassen National Park (June–
    July)
San Jacinto Mountains
    (June–July)
San Gabriel Mountains
    (June–July)

TWINFLOWER   *Linnaea borealis* var. *longiflora*
Twinflower family (previously included in Honeysuckle family)

DESCRIPTION: 2–8 inches. Pairs of slender, fringed, trumpet-shaped, pink-tinged flowers (to three-fourths inch) hanging gracefully from short pedicels in Y-shape at top of slender plant stem. Opposite pairs of basal, shiny, leathery leaves.

NOTE: The plant spreads by long runners from which sprout numerous stems, often creating a "mini-forest" of these adorable flowers.

HABITAT: Moist places in forest duff (to 8,000 feet); found in northwest mountains, Cascades, northeast corner.

WHERE AND WHEN:
Warner Mountains (June–August)
Cedar Basin Research Natural Area (June–August)
Mount Shasta (June–August)
Six Rivers National Forest (June–August)
Trinity Alps (June–August)
along Smith River near Gasquet (June–August)

Twinflower

BLADDERWORT   *Utricularia macrorhiza* or *Utricularia vulgaris*
Bladderwort family

DESCRIPTION: 2–12 inches. Aquatic plant. Five to 20 yellow, two-lipped flowers along the above-water portion of the stem. Floating leaves finely dissected into threadlike segments bearing bladders that trap and digest insects.

NOTE: When tiny, aquatic insects trigger the hairs on the bladder pods, the poor unsuspecting visitors become permanent guests.

HABITAT: Ponds (to 9,000 feet); found in northwest mountains, north and central coast and coast ranges, Cascades, Sierra, east of the Sierra, northeast corner, Transverse Ranges, Mojave Desert.

WHERE AND WHEN:
Modoc Plateau (June–July)
Osgood Swamp in Tahoe (June–August)
Butterfly Valley (July–August)
Sea Ranch (July–August)

Bladderwort

Fish Slough (July–August)
Santa Ana Mountains (July–August)

BOG ASPHODEL, CALIFORNIA   *Narthecium californicum*
Bog asphodel family (previously included in Lily family)
DESCRIPTION: 0.5–2 feet. Stem thick with overlapping, six-tepaled, starlike, yellow flowers on short pedicels. Red anthers. Narrow, mostly erect, basal leaves. California endemic.

California bog asphodel

NOTE: Since the plants are often connected by a rhizome, you will frequently find bog asphodel "forests" in wet meadows, bogs, and fens.
HABITAT: Wet meadows, stream banks, fens (to 8,000 feet); found in northwest mountains, north coast ranges, Cascades, north and central Sierra.
WHERE AND WHEN:
Butterfly Valley (June–August)
Trinity Alps (June–August)
Red Mountain North (June–August)

Lakes Basin (July–August)
Osgood Swamp in Tahoe (July–August)
Stony Creek Bog (July–August)

DRABA, LEMMON'S or GRANITE DRABA   *Draba lemmonii*

Mustard family

DESCRIPTION: 1–5 inches. Mat-forming plant with clusters of 3 to 30 lemon-yellow, four-petaled flowers (to 0.5 inches). Tiny, oval leaves. Oddly twisted seedpods. California endemic.

NOTE: Although the flowers are lemony yellow in color, this is not the source of the name (Lemmon with two M's).

HABITAT: Talus slopes, rock crevices, rocky flats (8,500–14,000 feet); found in Sierra.

WHERE AND WHEN:

Mount Dana in Yosemite (July–August)
Freel Peak (July–August)
Mount Conness in Yosemite (July–August)
King's Canyon/Sequoia (July–August)
Donahue Pass in Yosemite (July–August)
John Muir Wilderness (July–August)

Lemmon's
draba

EVENING PRIMROSE, TANSY-LEAF   *Camissonia tanacetifolia*

Evening primrose family

DESCRIPTION: To 2 inches. Stemless. Cup-shaped, bright yellow flowers (to 2 inches) atop long ovaries. Flowers wither red. Four separate petals and reflexed, pointed sepals. Flowers open in the morning and wilt later the same day.

NOTE: The flowers hug the ground, as there is no plant stem, though the spreading leaves are on petioles.

HABITAT: Moist flats and slopes, open fields (2,300–8,500 feet); found in foothills, Cascades, Sierra, east of Sierra, northeast corner.

Tansy-leaf
evening
primrose

WHERE AND WHEN:
Hope Valley east of Carson Pass (June–July)
Modoc Plateau (June–July)
Lake Almanor (June–July)
Sierra Valley (June–July)
Lassen National Park (June–July)
Lava Beds National Monument (June–July)

GLACIER LILY or YELLOW FAWN LILY   *Erythronium grandiflorum*
Lily family

DESCRIPTION: 0.5–1 foot. One or two spreading flowers (to 2 inches) nod from tip of mostly leafless stem. Bright yellow tepals swept back at tips

exposing pistil and linear yellow, cream, or red anthers. Pair of long, tongue-like, shiny green, mostly basal leaves.

NOTE: Blooming shortly after the snow leaves, these beautiful blossoms can fill a meadow or slope with a "glacier" of yellow cheer.

HABITAT: Meadows, slopes (to 6,000 feet); found in northwest mountains, north coast ranges.

WHERE AND WHEN:
Trinity Alps (June–July)

Glacier lily

Bear Basin Butte Natural Area (June–July)
Anthony Peak (June–July)
Yolla-Bolly-Middle Eel Wilderness (June–July)
Black Rock Mountains (June–July)
Marble Mountains (June–July)

Spineless
horsebrush

HORSEBRUSH, SPINELESS   *Tetradymia canescens*
Aster family
DESCRIPTION: 0.5–3 feet. Shrub with brushy, more-or-less flat-topped clusters of yellow flower heads. Disk flowers only. Narrow, fingerlike, gray-felty leaves.
NOTE: The gray-felty phyllaries form long, swollen-looking "vases" holding the yellow bouquets.
HABITAT: Sagebrush scrub, woodlands (to 10,000 feet); found east of the Sierra, northeast corner, Transverse Ranges, Mojave Desert.
WHERE AND WHEN:
Kingsbury Grade east of Tahoe (June–July)
Kern Plateau (June–July)
White Mountains (June–July)
Modoc Plateau (June–July)
Piute Mountains (June–July)
San Gabriel Mountains (July–August)

PRICKLY PEAR, GRIZZLY BEAR   *Opuntia polyacantha* var.
                                        erinacea or *O. erinacea*
Cactus family
DESCRIPTION: 1–2 feet. Very large (to 3 inches), bowl-shaped flowers with many translucent lemon-yellow petals that turn reddish with age, or red petals. Cluster of yellow stamens and green, globular stigma. Large round leaves (pads) with long sharp spines.
NOTE: The many thin yellow petals, especially when backlit, seem to warm the ground with a golden glow; the red petals light a fire.

HABITAT: Desert, scrub (2,500–9,200 feet); found in Sierra, east of the Sierra, Transverse Ranges, Peninsular Ranges, Mojave Desert.

WHERE AND WHEN:
near Benton (June)
Joshua Tree (June)
San Bernardino Mountains
   (June)
Sweetwater Mountains
   (June–July)
San Jacinto Mountains
   (June–July)
Kern Plateau (June–July)

Grizzly bear prickly pear

SNEEZEWEED, BIGELOW'S   *Helenium bigelovii*
Aster family

DESCRIPTION: 1–4 feet. Large, terminal flower heads with raised, dome-

shaped disk and many yellow rays. Alternating, tongue-like, clasping stem leaves and similar but petioled basal leaves.

NOTE: These plants often form large masses, bringing hundreds or thousands of bright suns to wet places in meadows.

HABITAT: Wet meadows, marshes, bogs (to 10,000 feet); found in northwest mountains, coast ranges, foothills, Cascades, Sierra, Transverse Ranges, Peninsular Ranges.

WHERE AND WHEN:
Yosemite Valley (June–July)

Bigelow's sneezeweed   *Mount Pinos* (June–July)

Fallen Leaf Lake in Tahoe (June–July)
San Bernardino Mountains (June–August)
Bishop Creek (July–August)
Trinity Alps (July–August)

STENOTUS, SHORT-STEMMED or
STEMLESS MOCK GOLDENWEED   *Stenotus acaulis*
Aster family

DESCRIPTION: 2–6 inches. Ground-hugging plant with rather diamond-shaped leaves and flower heads of six to 15 bright yellow rays surrounding a raised yellow-orange disk.

NOTE: The showy flower heads up to 1.5 inches across seem disproportionately large for the short stems.

HABITAT: Rocky flats (to 10,500 feet); found in foothills, Cascades, Sierra, east of the Sierra, northeast corner, Mojave Desert.

WHERE AND WHEN:
Freel Peak (June–July)
White Mountains (June–July)
Mount Tallac in Tahoe (June–July)
Sweetwater Mountains (June–July)
Sonora Pass (June–July)
Warner Mountains (June–July)

Short-stemmed
stenotus

ANEMONE, DRUMMOND'S   *Anemone drummondii*
Buttercup family

DESCRIPTION: 4–10 inches. Usually one bowl-shaped flower to 1.5 inches at tip of stem. Five to eight white petal-like sepals with bluish tinge, especially on the underside. Fernlike leaves.

NOTE: These flowers bloom early as the snow is melting off, and from a distance, these blooms may appear to be just more patches of snow, perhaps with a bit of bluish shadow.

HABITAT: Rocky slopes, forest edges (to 10,000 feet); found in northwest mountains, foothills, Cascades, Sierra.

WHERE AND WHEN:
Pole Creek (June–July)
Mount Eddy (June–July)
Sonora Pass (June–July)
Lassen National Park (June–August)
Tioga Pass in Yosemite (July–August)
Trinity Alps (July–August)

Drummond's anemone

BEARGRASS   *Xerophyllum tenax*
Trillium family (previously included in Lily family)

DESCRIPTION: 1–5 feet. Dense clusters of hundreds of creamy white flowers (to one-fourth inch) along upper parts of stem, usually culminating in

swollen-looking, conical inflorescence. Tough, wiry, basal grasslike leaves.

NOTE: The plants may take several years to produce flowers, after which they die, though the dried leaves may persist for some time.

HABITAT: Dry, open slopes; forest openings (to 6,000 feet); found in northwest mountains, central coast, north and central coast ranges, Cascades, northern Sierra.

WHERE AND WHEN:
Butterfly Valley (June–July)
Trinity Alps (June–July)
Van Damme State Park (June–July)

Beargrass

Mount Tamalpais (June–July)
Russian Gulch State Park (June–July)
Monterey Peninsula (June–July)

BUCKBEAN   *Menyanthes trifoliata*
Buckbean family

DESCRIPTION: 6–15 inches. Raceme of several star-shaped flowers on leaf-less scape. Bright white petals fringed with white hairs. Compound leaves with three broad leaflets.

NOTE: Many flower stems sprout from a rhizome, so these plants usually form huge masses, often nearly choking bogs and lake edges.

HABITAT: Lake and pond edges, bogs, very wet meadows (up to 10,500 feet); found on north and central coast, foothills, Cascades, Sierra, northeast corner.

WHERE AND WHEN:
Point Reyes (June)
MacKerricher State Park
    (June)
Grass Lake at Luther Pass
    (June–July)
Warner Mountains (June–
    July)
Lake Almanor (June–July)
Lassen National Park (June–July)

Buckbean

BUCKWHEAT, COAST   *Eriogonum latifolium*
Buckwheat family

DESCRIPTION: 1–3 feet. Stout, much-branched stem with many large, spherical heads of small, cream-to-red, papery flowers at tips of spreading rays. Ovate or oblong, wavy-margined, white-hairy leaves basal and on lower part of stem.

NOTE: Many of the heads have both cream and pink or red flowers, giving the impression that something is ripening.

HABITAT: Coastal bluffs, scrub, dunes (to 500 feet); found on north and central coast.

WHERE AND WHEN:
Dunes of Arcata (June–September)

Point Reyes (June–
    September)
Salt Point (June–September)
Stinson Beach (June–
    September)
Bodega Bay (June–
    September)
MacKerricher State Park
    (June–September)

Coast buckwheat

CRYPTANTHA, LOW or
ROUNDSPIKE CRYPTANTHA

Cryptantha humilis

Borage family

DESCRIPTION: 2–12 inches. Low plant with several stems bearing spherical or cylindrical cluster of many pinwheel-like white flowers (to 0.5 inches). Small, raised rim around throat.

NOTE: Although this plant may be "low" and *humilis* (humble), its large, ball-like or cylindrical clusters of flowers put on quite a floral show, especially when they adorn some rocky ridge above the timberline.

Low cryptantha

HABITAT: Sandy, gravelly, or rocky flats and slopes; ridges (6,000–11,400 feet); found in Sierra, east of the Sierra, northeast corner.

WHERE AND WHEN:
Sweetwater Mountains (June–July)
Warner Mountains (June–July)
White Mountains (June–July)
Red Lake Peak at Carson Pass (June–August)
Mount Warren in Yosemite (July–August)
Desolation Wilderness in Tahoe (July–August)

DEATH CAMAS   *Zigadenus venenosus*
Trillium family (previously included in Lily family)

DESCRIPTION: 0.5–2 feet. Stout stem with usually conical inflorescence along top several inches. Six white tepals with greenish-yellow gland at base. Six radiating stamens with white or yellowish anthers.

NOTE: This is an extremely poisonous plant—all parts contain toxic alkaloids.

HABITAT: Wet meadows, rocky hillsides (to 9,200 feet); found in much of California (except Central Valley).

WHERE AND WHEN:
Shirley Canyon in Tahoe
(June–July)
Santa Lucia Range (June–July)
Trinity Alps (June–July)
Tehachapi Mountains (June–July)
El Capitan Meadows in
Yosemite (June–July)
Carson Pass (July–August)

Death camas

DOGWOOD, CANADIAN or BUNCHBERRY   *Cornus canadensis*
Dogwood family

DESCRIPTION: 4–8 inches. Bright white "flowers" (to three-fourths inch) with four petal-like bracts nestled atop whorls of four to seven broad, dark-green deeply veined leaves. The actual sepals and petals are tiny, forming an inconspicuous cluster at the center of the bracts.

NOTE: The plants spread by rhizomes, so you will often find them in large gatherings on the forest floor.

HABITAT: Moist places in forests, bogs (to 3,600 feet); found in northwest mountains, north coast ranges.

WHERE AND WHEN:
Trinity Alps (June–July)
Fort Bragg area (June–July)

Canadian dogwood

DUCK POTATO or ARROWHEAD *Sagittaria cuneata*
Water plantain family

DESCRIPTION: 1–4 feet. Long, leafless stem, mostly underwater, usually bearing whorls of female flowers below water and whorls of up to three male flowers above. Three separate round petals and many reproductive parts. Broad, floating arrow-shaped leaves.

NOTE: The floating arrow-shaped leaves look like speedboats revving up for a race!

HABITAT: Ponds, slow-moving streams (to 7,500 feet); found in northwest mountains, coast ranges, Cascades, Sierra, east of the Sierra, northeast corner, Transverse Ranges.

Duck potato

WHERE AND WHEN:
Boggs Lake (June–July)
Bishop area (June–July)
Modoc Plateau (June–July)
San Bernardino Mountains (June–July)
Lassen National Park (July–August)
Osgood Swamp in Tahoe (September)

FAWN LILY, PLAIN-LEAF   *Erythronium purpurascens*
Lily family

DESCRIPTION: 4–10 inches. One to several showy, star-shaped flowers (to 2 inches) nod off arching pedicels. Six strongly recurved, white tepals yellow at base. Long-protruding stamens with creamy yellow anthers. Broad, nearly basal leaves wavy on edges. California endemic.

NOTE: The white petals age pink-purple, so you will often see purple flowers and white flowers on the same plant.

HABITAT: Forest openings, rocky places (4,000–8,000 feet); found in northwest mountains, Cascades, Sierra, northeast corner.

WHERE AND WHEN:
Loch Leven Lakes (June)
Illouette Creek in Yosemite (June)
Warner Mountains (June–July)
Trinity Alps (June–July)
Lassen National Park (June–July)
Butterfly Valley (June–July)

Fawn lily

INDIAN PIPE
Monotropa uniflora

Heath family

DESCRIPTION: 2–10 inches. Single, white, nodding flower at tip of white, fleshy stem. Nearly transparent, white, scalelike leaves. Saprophyte. CNPS Rare and Endangered List—endangered in California.

Indian pipe

NOTE: Coming across a miniature "forest" of these ghostly plants in a dark woods is an eerie experience.

HABITAT: Forests (to 500 feet); found in northwest mountains, north coast.

WHERE AND WHEN:
Redwood National Park (June–July)
Requa area (June–July)
Prairie Creek Redwoods State Park (June–July)
along Smith River (June–July)
Jedediah Smith Redwoods State Park (June–July)

LEWISIA, THREE-LEAF
Lewisia triphylla

Miner's lettuce family (previously included in Purslane family)

DESCRIPTION: 1–4 inches. Slender, branching stem with half-inch flowers, either single or in clusters of up to 10. Five to nine narrow, white or pink petals, usually with pink mid-veins. Two green sepals.

NOTE: This is a wonderful flower for hands-and-knees inspection—glistening petals with pink veins, tiny reddish anthers on delicate stalks, and succulent, tentacle-like leaves.

Three-leaf lewisia

HABITAT: Moist meadows, forest openings (5,000–11,200 feet); found in northwest mountains, north coast ranges, Cascades, Sierra, northeast corner.

WHERE AND WHEN:
Paige Meadows in Tahoe (June–July)
Lassen National Park (June–July)
Mount Shasta (June–August)
Trinity Alps (July)
Warner Mountains (July–August)
Tioga Crest in Yosemite (July–August)

LOCOWEED, WHITNEY'S or BALLOONPOD MILKVETCH
Astragalus whitneyi

Pea family

DESCRIPTION: 2–10 inches. Prostrate stems bearing several loose racemes of 5 to 16 pea flowers. White, cream, pink, or purple flowers. Five to 21 narrow leaflets per leaf.

NOTE: The seedpods are the most conspicuous feature—swollen, papery, red-mottled, gold sausages!

HABITAT: Sandy, gravelly, or rocky flats and slopes (2,500–12,000 feet); found in northwest mountains, north coast ranges, Sierra, east of the Sierra, northeast corner, Transverse Ranges.

WHERE AND WHEN:
Modoc Plateau (June–July)
Barker Peak in Tahoe (June–July)
Mount Pinos (June–July)
Trinity Alps (July)
White Mountains (July–August)
Warner Mountains (July–August)

Whitney's locoweed

MANZANITA, GREENLEAF   *Arctostaphylos patula*
Heath family

DESCRIPTION: 3–6 feet. Evergreen shrub thick with stiff, oval leaves mostly tipped up on edge. Hanging clusters of white or pink, urn-shaped flowers.

Little applelike edible fruits.

NOTE: Shake the ants out and eat these delicious flowers.

HABITAT: Forest openings, scrub (2,000–11,000 feet); found in northwest mountains, coast ranges, Cascades, Sierra, Transverse Ranges, Peninsular Ranges.

WHERE AND WHEN:
Lassen National Park (June)
Trinity Alps (June)
Lakes Basin (June)
San Jacinto Mountains
    (June–July)
San Bernardino Mountains
    (June–July)
San Gabriel Mountains
    (June–July)

Greenleaf manzanita

MARIPOSA LILY, LEICHTLIN'S   *Calochortus leichtlinii*
Lily family

DESCRIPTION: 0.5–2 feet. Umbel-like raceme of one to five bowl-shaped flowers (to 1.5 inches). Three broad, rounded, white petals with black or

dark-purple chevrons at the base above the nectar glands. Yellow hairs in throat.

NOTE: Although this mariposa lily has dark-colored chevrons and yellow hairs, the main impression it gives is bright, clean, exuberant white.

HABITAT: Gravelly flats and slopes, forest openings (4,000–11,000 feet); found in Sierra, northeast corner.

WHERE AND WHEN:
east of Monitor Pass (June–

Leichtlin's mariposa lily   July)

Meiss Meadow trail at Carson Pass (June–July)
Greenhorn Range (June–July)
Castle Peak (July)
Modoc Plateau (July–August)
Mount Dana in Yosemite (July–August)

Dwarf onion

ONION, DWARF or RED SIERRA ONION   *Allium obtusum*
Onion family (previously included in Lily family)

DESCRIPTION: 1–3 inches. Dense umbel of 6 to 10 white flowers (sometimes tinged pink) at tip of short stem. Six tepals with purplish mid-veins. California endemic.

NOTE: This plant is very easy to overlook, for its flowers are practically on the ground, and they blend with their rocky environment.

HABITAT: Rocky flats and ridges (to 12,000 feet); found in foothills, Cascades, Sierra.

WHERE AND WHEN:
Lake Aloha in Tahoe (June–July)
Lakes Basin (June–July)
Kirkwood west of Carson Pass (July–August)
Wright's Lake west of Tahoe (July–August)
Red Lake Peak at Carson Pass (July–August)
Gaylor Lakes in Yosemite (July–August)

ORCHID, PHANTOM   *Cephalanthera austiniae* or
Eburophyton austiniae
Orchid family

DESCRIPTION: 0.5–2 feet. Stout white stem with numerous white flowers in leaf axils. Small, yellow patch on lower lip. No green leaves—just reduced white bracts. Saprophyte.

NOTE: To come across one of these bright white "lights" in the dark of a coniferous forest is exhilarating and a bit spooky.

HABITAT: Forest (to 7,000 feet); found in northwest mountains, coast ranges, Cascades, Sierra, Transverse Ranges, Peninsular Ranges.

WHERE AND WHEN:
Trinity Alps (June–July)
Mount Shasta (June–July)
Smith River area (June–July)
Mount Lassen (June–July)
Mount Sanhedrin (June–July)
Santa Lucia Range (June–July)

Phantom orchid

ORCHID, SIERRA REIN

Platanthera dilatata var. *leucostachys* or *P. leucostachys*

Orchid family

DESCRIPTION: 0.5–2.5 feet. Dense spike of bright white flowers. Five simi-

lar, narrow, pointed petals; sixth lower petal ends in long, curving spur. Grasslike leaves.

NOTE: Because it grows in such wet areas, you might think that the name was "rain orchid," but instead it's "rein orchid" in reference to the long spur.

HABITAT: Wet meadows, stream banks, seeps (to 11,000 feet); found in much of California (except Central Valley and deserts).

WHERE AND WHEN:
Paige Meadows in Tahoe (June–July)
San Jacinto Mountains (June–July)

Sierra rein orchid

King's Canyon/Sequoia (June–July)
Modoc Plateau (June–July)
San Gabriel Mountains (July–August)
Butterfly Valley (July–August)

PASQUEFLOWER or MOUSE-ON-A-STICK   *Anemone occidentalis*
Buttercup family

DESCRIPTION: 0.5–2 feet. Thick, densely white-hairy stem with one terminal, bowl-shaped flower (to 3 inches). Five to eight bright white, petal-like
sepals cradling large cluster of yellow stamens and greenish pistils.

NOTE: What a character—downy stems poking through the snow, bright
white, showy flowers, and comi-
cal, mop-head "mouse-on-a-
stick" fruits!

HABITAT: Meadows, rocky slopes
(to 10,000 feet); found in northwest mountains, foothills, Cascades, Sierra, northeast corner.

WHERE AND WHEN:
near Upper Merced Pass Lake in
    Yosemite (June–July)
Mount Tallac in Tahoe (June–
    July)
Warner Mountains (July–
    August)
Lassen National Park (July–
    August)
Trinity Alps (July–August)
Mount Shasta (July–
    September)

Pasqueflower

Pasqueflower

Pennyroyal

PENNYROYAL or
MOUNTAIN MONARDELLA   *Monardella odoratissima*
Mint family

DESCRIPTION: 0.5–2 feet. Square stem with one round, flat-topped flower head (to 1 inch) densely packed with numerous small, two-lipped white, lavender, purple, or pink flowers. Five narrow, widely separated petal lobes.

NOTE: This is one of the most fragrant of all California plants, the leaves have a powerful, pleasant mint aroma that is liberated in "clouds" when they are crushed.

HABITAT: Sagebrush scrub, dry flats, forest openings (3,000–11,400 feet); found in northwest mountains, north coast ranges, Cascades, Sierra, northeast corner, Transverse Ranges.

WHERE AND WHEN:
San Bernardino Mountains (June–July)
Monitor Pass (June–July)
Greenhorn Range (June–July)
Lassen National Park (July)
Warner Mountains (July)
Tioga Pass in Yosemite (July)

PHACELIA, VARI-LEAF   *Phacelia heterophylla*
Borage family (previously included in Waterleaf family)

DESCRIPTION: 1–4 feet. Stout, hairy stem with many densely flowered coils of dirty-white, bowl-shaped flowers (to 0.5 inches). Many oval, unlobed, hairy leaves toward top of stem and larger leaves, usually with lateral lobes toward bottom.

NOTE: It looks a bit like this stout plant is swarming with coiling, green and white caterpillars.

HABITAT: Dry, sandy or gravelly flats; sagebrush scrub (to 9,000 feet); found in north coast ranges, northwest mountains, Cascades, Sierra, east of the Sierra, northeast corner.

WHERE AND WHEN:
Lakes Basin (June–July)
Modoc Plateau (June–July)
Mount Tallac in Tahoe (June–July)
Feather River Canyon (June–July)
Yosemite Valley (June–July)
Six Rivers National Forest (June–July)

Vari-leaf phacelia

QUEEN'S CUP or BRIDE'S BONNET · *Clintonia uniflora*
Lily family

DESCRIPTION: 2–6 inches. Single, showy, six-tepaled, white flower (to 1.5 inches) at tip of slender stem. Two to three large, dark green, tongue-like leaves.

NOTE: The large, shiny leaves will probably catch your attention first, but the bright white flowers are quite striking, especially on the dark forest floor.

HABITAT: Forest (3,500–6,000 feet); found in northwest mountains, north coast ranges, foothills, Cascades, Sierra.

Queen's cup

WHERE AND WHEN:
Siskiyou Mountains (June–July)
Calaveras Big Trees State Park (June–July)
Trinity Alps (June–July)
Yosemite National Park (June–July)
King's Canyon/Sequoia (June–July)
Bear Basin Butte Natural Area (June–July)

SUGARSTICK or CANDYSTICK *Allotropa virgata*
Heath family
DESCRIPTION: 0.5–2 feet. Fleshy, sticky stem with numerous small, urn-shaped white flowers with red stamens and five petals. Stems have red and

white stripes. No green leaves—saprophyte.
NOTE: It is always a surprise to come across this pepper-mint-striped "candy cane" (without the curved handle) in an otherwise-dark forest.
HABITAT: Forests (to 10,000 feet); found in northwest mountains, north coast ranges, Cascades, Sierra.
WHERE AND WHEN:
Vikingsholm in Tahoe (June)
Russian Peak Wilderness (June)
Greenhorn Mountains (June–July)
Mount Shasta (June–August)
Trinity Alps (July–August)
Lassen National Park (July–August)

Sugarstick

TOBACCO BRUSH *Ceanothus velutinus*
Buckthorn family
DESCRIPTION: 3–6 feet. Evergreen shrub heavy with large clusters of small, creamy white flowers (to one-fourth inch) with five clawed petals. Rather lilac-like fragrance. Broad, shiny, evergreen leaves with strong aroma.
NOTE: The shiny leaves have a highly flammable oil that encourages fires—competing plants are killed, while the tobacco brush quickly resprouts from root crowns.
HABITAT: Dry, open slopes; forest clearings (to 10,000 feet); found in north-

west mountains, north coast
ranges, Cascades, Sierra, east
of the Sierra, northeast corner.

WHERE AND WHEN:
5 Lakes Basin in Tahoe
  (June–July)
Trinity Alps (June–July)
Mount Tallac in Tahoe
  (June–July)
Warner Mountains (June–
  July)
Lassen National Park (June–
  July)
Mount Shasta (June–August)

Tobacco brush

TOFIELDIA or WESTERN FALSE ASPHODEL
Triantha occidentalis or *Tofieldia occidentalis*
Toad lily family (previously included in Lily family)

DESCRIPTION: 8–30 inches. Dense, spherical head of small, white or greenish, six-tepaled flowers atop long, leafless stem. Mostly basal, long, grasslike leaves.

NOTE: This plant resembles
death camas (p. 454) with its
clusters of six-tepaled white
flowers, but the raceme of tofieldia is much smaller, the
plant is not poisonous, and it
is much less common in California, occurring mostly in
bogs.

HABITAT: Wet meadows, bogs,
lake edges (to 10,000 feet);
found in northwest moun-
tains, Cascades, Sierra.

WHERE AND WHEN:
Osgood Swamp in Tahoe
  (June–July)
Tenaya Canyon in Yosemite
  (June–July)

Tofieldia

Lakes Basin (July)
Trinity Alps (July–August)
Butterfly Valley (July–August)
Lassen National Park (July–August)

FRITILLARY, DAVIDSON'S or
PINE WOODS MISSION BELLS
Fritillaria pinetorum
Lily family

DESCRIPTION: 4–16 inches. Several, showy, multicolored, star-shaped flowers (to 2 inches) on short pedicels off upper stem. Six tepals united into a shallow bowl with six points. Tepals mottled purple or yellow-green. Red anthers.

NOTE: Although the mottled flowers are well camouflaged for their scrubby environment, a close look reveals a stunning bloom—a large, brown-purple, speckled, yellowish-green starfish!

HABITAT: Dry, gravelly flats and slopes (6,000–10,500 feet); found in central and southern Sierra, Transverse Ranges.

Davidson's fritillary

WHERE AND WHEN:
June Lake (June–July)
Tehachapi Mountains (June–July)
Mount Dana trail in Yosemite (June–July)
Piute Mountains (June–July)
San Bernardino Mountains (June–July)
Gaylor Lakes in Yosemite (June–August)

JULY

Mule ears and lupine in the Tahoe Basin

WITH THE SEARING July heat in the deserts and the Central Valley, the flowers there are only a memory, but in mid-to-high elevations in the mountains across the state, the summer blooming has reached its peak, and the mountains are vibrant with lush gardens of color and fragrance.

This is the month to see the shoulder-high rainbow gardens that the coast ranges, the northwest mountains, and the great spine of the Cascades and Sierra are famous for—those wet meadow and seep gardens where scores of species of robust, rambunctious plants clamor with their bright flowers for your attention and delight. Some of these gardens (for example, along the Winnemucca Lake trail at Carson Pass) are renowned, but many are only locally known, if known at all.

And July also brings the bloom to the very high mountains, to the alpine fellfields above timberline, where the plants huddle down out of the wind, pulling their "furry coats" tight around them. Up here above human habitation, you are in a very different world of crisp, clear, thin air, endless blue skies, distant views, and unique flowers specially adapted to this special environment. Most of these plants will require special effort and energy from you, too, for to reach them you'll have to hike several miles at high altitudes, exposed to the same conditions the plants endure. Mount Lassen, the shoulder of Mount Shasta, Mount Eddy west of Shasta, Freel

Peak in Tahoe, Mount Dana and Mount Conness in Yosemite, White Mountain in the range of that name, Mount Wilson, Mount Baldy, and San Jacinto Peak in the Transverse and Peninsular Ranges, and, of course, Mount Whitney—from mid-July (in some cases earlier) through August and sometimes September, these, and other, towering peaks offer dazzling blooms along with their sky-piercing majesty.

Be sure to find the stunning, rare hybrid **alpine pink columbine** high in the granite of Yosemite, and celebrate the "merging" of the land and the sky with the sky-blue **sky pilot** atop California's highest spot—Mount Whitney. Although finding this gorgeous plant at the juncture of sky and earth may seem like the culminating floral experience of the year, if you can come back to earth from this lofty spot and return to mid-mountain elevations, there are still some floral gifts to come—some of California's most striking flowers are yet to bloom in August.

Highlights

Northwest Mountains

Phantom orchid, leopard lily, and **fire-cracker flower** in the Trinity Alps
Mount Eddy lupine, swamp onion, pitcher plant, leopard lily, stream orchid, bear grass, and **few-flowered bleeding heart** on Mount Eddy
Nuttall's larkspur, Tolmie's pussyears, pitcher plant, Lee's lewisia, and **Scott Mountain phacelia** at Kangaroo Lake Botanical Area
Redwood keckiella along the Smith River

Coast

Coast buckwheat, ladies tresses, and **yellow sand verbena** at the Dunes of Arcata
Leopard lily and **windflower** in Redwoods National and State Parks
Coast dudleya at Salt Point

Cascades

Washington lily and **scarlet gilia** at Mount Shasta

Sierra

Bog asphodel and **pitcher plant** at Butterfly Valley
Bluebells, glaucous larkspur, bull elephant's-head, Lewis monkey-flower, great red paintbrush, arrowleaf senecio, corn lily, and **deer's tongue** on the Winnemucca Lake Trail at Carson Pass
Rosy sedum, Sierra primrose, red heather, and **white heather** above Winnemucca Lake at Carson Pass

Swamp onion at Onion Valley
Sky pilot and alpine pink columbine in Yosemite
Mule ears throughout the Tahoe Basin

Flowers

BLUEBELLS, MOUNTAIN or LUNGWORT   *Mertensia ciliata*
Borage family
DESCRIPTION: 2–3 feet. Clusters of bell-shaped flowers nod off drooping
stems. Flower tube constricted at base. Flowers pink in bud, then blue,
sometimes with pink tinges in bloom.
NOTE: With all the clusters of drooping, bell-like flowers, you might expect
to hear sweet music—the blues, no doubt.
HABITAT: Wet meadows, stream banks (5,000–10,000 feet); found in Sierra,
east of the Sierra, northeast corner.
WHERE AND WHEN:
Echo Summit in Tahoe (July–August)
Meiss Meadows Trail at Carson Pass (July–August)
Tenaya Canyon in Yosemite (July–August)
White Mountains (July–August)
Lakes Basin (July–August)
Modoc Plateau (July–August)

Mountain
bluebells

BLUE-EYED GRASS, IDAHO   *Sisyrinchium idahoense*
Iris family
DESCRIPTION: 4–16 inches. One or a few star-shaped flowers at tip of flattened stem. Six blue or blue-purple tepals with darker purple veins. Flowers with bright yellow "eye" in throat.

NOTE: These delightful flowers may be "blue eyes," but it is the bright yellow centers that may catch most of the attention.

HABITAT: Moist, grassy meadows; stream banks (to 10,000 feet); found in northwest mountains, foothills, Cascades, Sierra, east of the Sierra, northeast corner, south coast ranges, Transverse Ranges, Peninsular Ranges.

WHERE AND WHEN:
San Jacinto Mountains (July–August)
San Bernardino Mountains (July–August)
Osgood Swamp in Tahoe (July–August)
Lassen National Park (July–August)
Tioga Pass area in Yosemite (July–August)
Mount Pinos (July–August)

Idaho blue-eyed grass

GENTIAN, SIERRA   *Gentianopsis holopetala*

Gentian family

DESCRIPTION: 2–16 inches. Solitary, long-tubular flower at tip of each mostly leafless peduncle. Flowers funnel-shaped with dark blue or blue-purple tube and four flaring petal lobes. Mostly basal, spoon-shaped leaves.

NOTE: Some of the species originally in the genus *Gentiana* were split off into *Gentianella* (small gentian) and *Gentianopsis* (gentianlike).

HABITAT: Moist meadows (6,000–11,000 feet); found in Sierra, east of the Sierra.

WHERE AND WHEN:
Tuolumne Meadows in Yosemite
   (July–August)
King's Canyon/Sequoia (July–
   August)
Butterfly Valley (July–August)
Mono Basin (July–August)
White Mountains (July–August)
Kern Plateau (July–August)

Sierra gentian

HAREBELL, CALIFORNIA

Asyneuma prenanthoides or
Campanula prenanthoides

Bluebell family

DESCRIPTION: 0.5–2 feet. Slender stem with scattered, ovate, slightly toothed, sessile or short-petioled leaves and scattered, bell-shaped blue flowers. Long style well exserted from corolla.

NOTE: With the narrow, spreading calyx lobes, the equally narrow, spreading petal lobes, and the very long, slender, snoutlike style, this flower is all "arms and legs"—angular and a bit gangly, but nonetheless delicate and graceful.

HABITAT: Openings in woods (to 6,500 feet); found on north and central coast and coast ranges, foothills, Cascades, north and central Sierra.

California harebell

WHERE AND WHEN:

Trinity Alps (June–August)
Stony Creek (July–August)
Lake Sonoma area (July–August)
along Smith River (July–August)
Van Damme State Park (July–
    August)
Red Mountain North (July–
    August)

LARKSPUR, GLAUCOUS

Delphinium glaucum

Buttercup family

DESCRIPTION: 3–6 feet. Robust plant with stout stem and long raceme of many dark-blue flowers (to 2 inches) with long nectar spur. Four tiny petals inside large, showy sepals. Many large, maplelike leaves with sharp lobes (smaller leaves with narrow segments toward the top of plant).

NOTE: The "glaucous" and *glaucum* parts of the name refer to the white, powdery covering on the lower stem.

HABITAT: Wet meadows, stream banks, seeps (5,000–10,000 feet); found in northwest mountains, Sierra, east of the Sierra, northeast corner, Transverse Ranges.

WHERE AND WHEN:

Paige Meadows in Tahoe (July)
Trinity Alps (July–August)

San Gabriel Mountains (July–August)
Warner Mountains (July–August)
Mount Dana in Yosemite (July–August)
San Bernardino Mountains (July–August)

Glaucous larkspur

NAMA, ROTHROCK'S   *Nama rothrockii*
Borage family (previously included in Waterleaf family)
DESCRIPTION: 0.5–1 foot. Silky-hairy plant with terminal spherical clusters of many purple or pinkish, bowl-shaped flowers (to 0.5 inches) with white throats. Narrow, pinnately lobed or toothed leaves.

Rothrock's
nama

NOTE: Now this is a hairy plant—long, non-sticky white hairs and shorter, glandular-sticky hairs cover leaf, stem, and calyx. If you touch the sticky ones, a heavy fragrance will cling to your fingers.

HABITAT: Sandy flats, meadows, rocky places (7,000–10,000 feet); found in Sierra, east of the Sierra, Transverse Ranges.

WHERE AND WHEN:
Onion Valley (July–August)
Lee Vining Canyon (July–August)
Horseshoe Meadow Road (July–August)
Glass Mountain area (July–August)
San Bernardino Mountains (July–August)
Kern Plateau (July–August)

PENSTEMON, ALPINE or DAVIDSON'S PENSTEMON *Penstemon davidsonii*

Plantain family (previously included in Figwort family)

DESCRIPTION: 1–6 inches. Dwarf subshrub with one or a few large (to 1.5 inches long), tubular, blue-purple or red-purple flowers. Sometimes hybridizes with mountain pride (*P. newberryi*, p. 364) to produce rose-pink flowers.

NOTE: This plant often forms large mats on high-elevation rocky flats and slopes, providing a dazzling display of color and form.

HABITAT: Rocky ridges and outcrops, alpine fellfields (9,000–12,000 feet); found in northwest mountains, Cascades, Sierra, east of the Sierra, northeast corner.

Alpine penstemon

WHERE AND WHEN:
Warner Mountains (July–August)
Mount Dana in Yosemite (July–August)
Freel Peak (July–August)
Mount Shasta (July–August)
Sweetwater Mountains (July–August)
Mount Eddy (July–August)

POLEMONIUM, SHOWY or
SHOWY JACOB'S LADDER   *Polemonium pulcherrimum*
Phlox family

DESCRIPTION: 2–12 inches. Usually decumbent stems forming mounds. Clusters of bell-shaped flowers with five blue-purple petal lobes and yellow throat. Nine to 21 small leaflets per leaf.

NOTE: It is easy to see the reason for the name "Jacob's Ladder," as it seems that a mini-you could climb right up the ladder-rung leaflets to the heavenly flower!

HABITAT: Talus, rocky slopes, ridges (6,000–12,000 feet); found in northwest mountains, north coast ranges, Cascades, Sierra, east of the Sierra, northeast corner.

WHERE AND WHEN:
Frog Lake at Carson Pass (July–August)
Trinity Alps (July–August)
Lassen National Park (July–August)
Mount Shasta (July–August)
Mount Dana in Yosemite (July–August)
Warner Mountains (July–August)

Showy polemonium

Sky pilot

SKY PILOT
Polemonium eximium

Phlox family

DESCRIPTION: 4–12 inches. Densely flowered, spherical clusters of blue flowers. Five rounded petal lobes form pinwheel or shallow bowl. Mostly basal, pinnately compound leaves with many opposite pairs of tiny leaflets. California endemic.

NOTE: This is a strictly alpine plant, occurring only at or near the summits of the highest peaks in Yosemite and south.

HABITAT: Rocky outcrops, talus, ridges and summits (10,000–14,200 feet); found in central and southern Sierra.

WHERE AND WHEN:

Mount Dana in Yosemite (July–August)
King's Canyon/Sequoia (July–August)
Mount Lyell in Yosemite (July–August)
Mount Whitney (July–August)
Mount Conness in Yosemite (July–August)
Matterhorn Peak in Yosemite (July–August)

VERONICA, CUSICK'S or CUSICK'S SPEEDWELL *Veronica cusickii*

Plantain family (previously included in Snapdragon family)

DESCRIPTION: 2–8 inches. Raceme of many deep blue, two-lipped flowers on short pedicels. One large petal lobe in the upper lip, three narrower lobes in the lower lip. CNPS Rare and Endangered List—limited distribution.

NOTE: Veronicas are unusual in having four petal lobes but not the same number of stamens—only two.

HABITAT: Wet, rocky places; wet meadows; seeps (8,000–9,000 feet); found

in Cascades, northern and central Sierra.

WHERE AND WHEN:
Kirkwood Meadows west of
  Carson Pass (July–
  August)
Mount Fillmore (July–
  August)
Granite Chief in Tahoe
  (July–August)
Tuolumne Peak in Yosemite
  (July–August)
Desolation Wilderness in
  Tahoe (July–August)
above Winnemucca Lake
  (July–August)

Cusick's veronica

BUCKWHEAT, LOBB'S   *Eriogonum lobbii*
Buckwheat family
DESCRIPTION: 1–6 inches. Ground-hugging plant with densely flowered umbels of tiny flowers at ends of long, prostrate, leafless stems. Flowers are cream or pink with darker midveins turning rosy with age.
NOTE: What beautiful symmetry in the leaf rosette and the "moat" of flower umbels ringing it!

HABITAT: Rocky or gravelly flats and slopes (to 11,500 feet); found in northwest mountains, north coast ranges, foothills, Cascades, Sierra, east of Sierra, northeast corner.

WHERE AND WHEN:
Shirley Canyon in Tahoe
  (July)
Desolation Wilderness in
  Tahoe (July–August)
Freel Peak (July–August)
Lakes Basin (July–August)
Dana Plateau in Yosemite
  (July–August)
Lobb's buckwheat   Trinity Alps (July–August)

Alpine pink
columbine

COLUMBINE, ALPINE PINK

Aquilegia pubescens or
Aquilegia formosa hybrid

Buttercup family

DESCRIPTION: 1–2 feet. Very similar to alpine columbine (p. 503), except that the sepals and nectar tubes are usually pink instead of white, the flowers are rarely erect but are of an angle somewhere between upright and upside-down, and the terminal leaf lobes are broader.

NOTE: Since hybrids are infertile, this gorgeous flower becomes even more of a treasured discovery since it won't reproduce—some bee will have to hybridize the two source plants all over again.

HABITAT: Rocky slopes; around boulders (9,000–10,500 feet); found in central Sierra.

WHERE AND WHEN:

Morgan Pass in Yosemite (July–August)

Tioga Crest in Yosemite (July–August)

DAISY, DWARF ALPINE or PYGMY FLEABANE   *Erigeron pygmaeus*

Aster family

DESCRIPTION: 1–3 inches. Solitary flower heads (to 1 inch) at tip of mostly leafless stem. 15–35 pink, purple, or lavender rays surrounding a raised yellow disk. Basal cluster of glandular, linear leaves.

NOTE: The plant is definitely dwarf (the flower head is practically on the ground), but the flower head is anything but dwarf and looks even bigger being on such a short stem.

HABITAT: Rocky flats and ridges, summits (10,000–12,000 feet); found in Sierra, east of Sierra.

WHERE AND WHEN:

Freel Peak (July–August)

Dwarf alpine daisy

Mosquito Flat trail (July–August)
Mount Dana in Yosemite (July–August)
Sweetwater Mountains (July–August)
Bodie Hills (July–August)
King's Canyon/Sequoia (July–August)

ELEPHANT'S-HEAD, BULL   *Pedicularis groenlandica*
Broomrape family (previously included in Snapdragon family)
DESCRIPTION: 1–3 feet. Spike of many pink or red-purple (occasionally pure white), two-lipped, elephant-head flowers (to 0.5 inches).
NOTE: Sometimes little elephant's-head (*P. attolens*) grows with the bulls

Bull elephant's-head

and is pollinated by the same bees, but differences in the location of the reproductive parts help the bees keep the pollens separate.
HABITAT: Wet meadows, stream banks, bogs (5,000–11,200 feet); found in northwest mountains, Cascades, Sierra, northeast corner.
WHERE AND WHEN:
Paige Meadows in Tahoe (July)
Lassen National Park (July)
Lakes Basin (July)
Modoc Plateau (July–August)
King's Canyon/Sequoia (July–August)
Castle Peak (July–August)

FIREWEED   *Chamerion angustifolium* or *Epilobium angustifolium*

Evening primrose family

DESCRIPTION: 2–9 feet. Stout stem with many four-petaled flowers in long, terminal spike. Four separate, clawed, rose or magenta petals with four narrower, darker rose sepals between.

NOTE: Late in the blooming, the leaves turn scarlet or bronze, creating a bit of late summer or fall color.

HABITAT: Moist meadows; stream banks; forest openings; disturbed places (up to 10,500); found in northwest mountains, north coast and coast ranges, Cascades, Sierra, east of the Sierra, Transverse Ranges, Mojave Desert.

WHERE AND WHEN:

Shirley Canyon in Tahoe
    (July–August)
King's Canyon/Sequoia (July–
    August)
San Bernardino Mountains
    (July–August)
Salt Point (August)
Trinity Alps (August–
    September)
along Klamath River
    (August–September)

Fireweed

FIREWEED, ALPINE or
DWARF FIREWEED   *Chamerion latifolium* or *Epilobium latifolium*

Evening primrose family

DESCRIPTION: 4–20 inches. A few four-petaled flowers (to 1.5 inches) usually nodding from the leaf axils along the decumbent stem. Narrow, red-purple sepals between broader, lighter purple or pink petals.

NOTE: An arctic/alpine species infrequent in California. The flowers resemble those of common fireweed (above), but usually they form extensive, nearly ground-hugging masses on rocky, otherwise nearly bare slopes.

HABITAT: Rocky slopes, glacial outwashes, stream banks (7,600–11,400 feet); found in northwest mountains, northern and central Sierra.

WHERE AND WHEN:

above Winnemucca Lake at Carson Pass (July)

Alpine fireweed

Marble Mountains (July–August)
Mount Conness in Yosemite (July–August)
Siskiyou Mountains (July–August)
Saddlebag Lake area (July–August)
Sonora Pass (July–August)

FUCHSIA, CALIFORNIA *Epilobium canum*
Evening primrose family
DESCRIPTION: 0.5–2 feet. Subshrub with many long-tubular, scarlet flowers from the leaf axils on the upper stems. Four notched petals.
NOTE: Although fuchsia begins blooming in July in the southern mountains, it is such a spectacular member of the northern autumn flora beginning to bloom in August, I include it under August as well.
HABITAT: Cliffs, talus, rock crevices (to 10,000 feet); found in much of California (except northeast corner and eastern edge).

California
fuchsia

WHERE AND WHEN:
Torrey Pines (July)
Santa Monica Mountains (July–October)
San Gabriel Mountains (July–October)
Santa Lucia Range (July–October)
Lassen National Park (August)
Santa Rosa Plateau (August–October)

GILIA, PINK   *Ipomopsis tenuituba*
Phlox family

DESCRIPTION: 1–3 feet. Often-dense clusters of trumpetlike pink or white flowers (to 1.5 inches) coming mostly off one side of stem. Pinnately divided leaves with very narrow segments.

NOTE: This flower is very similar to the scarlet gilia (see p. 434), but it has much paler pink or white flowers, and is now considered a separate species.

HABITAT: Gravelly or rocky flats and slopes (7,900–10,000 feet); found in Sierra, east of the Sierra, northeast corner.

WHERE AND WHEN:
Red Lake Peak at Carson
    Pass (July–August)
Modoc Plateau (July–
    August)
Castle Peak (July–August)
Sweetwater Mountains
    (July–August)
Sonora Pass (July–August)
Bishop Creek (July–August)

Pink gilia

HEATHER, PINK MOUNTAIN   *Phyllodoce empetriformis*
Heath family

DESCRIPTION: 0.5–2 feet. Shrub with dense clusters of pink or rose-purple, dangling or erect, cup-shaped flowers (to 0.5 inches). Needlelike leaves.

NOTE: It's almost shocking to come across a mass of these sometimes almost fluorescent flowers lighting up a meadow or open slope.

HABITAT: Moist, open slopes; rocky places (4,800–8,700 feet); found in

northwest mountains, Cascades.

WHERE AND WHEN:
Mount Shasta (July–August)
Cedar Basin Research
    Natural Area (July–
    August)
Lake Anna area in Trinity
    Alps (July–August)
Mount Eddy (July–August)
Grizzly Lake area in Trinity
    Alps (July–August)
Marble Mountains (July–
    August)

Pink mountain heather

HEATHER, RED
Heath family

Phyllodoce breweri

DESCRIPTION: 0.5–1 foot. Shrub with terminal clusters of pink or rose, cup-shaped flowers with 10 long-protruding stamens. Many alternating, needlelike leaves. California endemic.

NOTE: This lovely, spreading shrub often brings its rose-colored blossoms to rocky places in the high mountains, not infrequently growing with its fellow heath, white heather (p. 506).

Red heather

HABITAT: Moist, rocky places; forest clearings (6,000–12,000 feet); found in Cascades, Sierra, Transverse Ranges.

WHERE AND WHEN:
King's Canyon/Sequoia (July–August)
Lassen National Park (July–August)
Dana Plateau in Yosemite (July–August)
Kirkwood west of Carson Pass (July–August)
above Winnemucca Lake at Carson Pass (July–August)
Mount Shasta (July–August)

KECKIELLA, REDWOOD or RED BEARDTONGUE
Keckiella corymbosa or *Penstemon corymbosus*
Plantain family (previously included in Snapdragon family)

DESCRIPTION: 1–2 feet. Shrub with many opposite pairs of small, leathery, dark-green leaves, usually slightly toothed. Clusters of long-tubular, two-lipped, red or pink flowers. Upper lip narrow hoodlike, lower lip three spreading, reflexed petal lobes.

NOTE: Resembling a penstemon, but, as with most *Keckiella* species, the lower lip is reflexed, considerably opening up the throat.

HABITAT: Forest, rocky slopes, riverbanks (to 5,000 feet); found in northwest mountains, coast and coast ranges.

WHERE AND WHEN:
along Trinity River (July–August)
Salt Point (July–August)
along Klamath River (July–August)
Santa Lucia Range (July–August)
Henry Coe State Park (July–August)

Redwood keckiella

LAUREL, SWAMP or BOG LAUREL
Kalmia polifolia or *Kalmia microphylla*
Heath family

DESCRIPTION: 2–8 inches. Low, evergreen shrub. Two to six saucer-shaped, rose-purple or pink flowers.

Swamp laurel

NOTE: The anthers are held in pockets on the corolla, creating "spring-loaded" filaments. When a bee "trips" the wire, the anthers fly up, shaking pollen all over the surprised (but probably delighted) visitor.

HABITAT: Wet meadows; bogs; rock crevices (3,200–12,000 feet); found in northwest mountains, Cascades, Sierra, northeast corner.

WHERE AND WHEN:

King's Canyon/Sequoia (July–August)
Trinity Alps (July–August)
Gaylor Lakes in Yosemite (July–August)
Warner Mountains (July–August)
Mount Shasta (July–August)
Winnemucca Lake at Carson Pass (July–August)

MONKEYFLOWER, LEWIS   *Mimulus lewisii*

Lopseed family (previously included in Snapdragon family)

DESCRIPTION: 1–3 feet. Two-lipped, pink flowers (to 2 inches) at tip of ped-icels. Two hairy yellow ridges on center petal lobe of lower lip. Several opposite pairs of broad, toothed, sessile leaves.

NOTE: With the large flowers, you can easily see the beige, hinged stigma that closes permanently only if touched with pollen from the same species but a different plant.

HABITAT: Stream banks, seeps (4,000–10,000 feet); found in northwest mountains, foothills, Cascades, Sierra, northeast corner.

WHERE AND WHEN:

Paige Meadows in Tahoe (July)
Lakes Basin (July)
King's Canyon/Sequoia (July–August)

Lewis monkeyflower

Lassen National Park (July–August)
Sentinel Meadows in Yosemite (July–August)
Trinity Alps (July–August)

PAINTBRUSH, ALPINE   *Castilleja nana*
Broomrape family (previously included in Snapdragon family)

DESCRIPTION: 1–6 inches. Dwarf plant. Clustered stems with inflorescence often more than half their length. Bracts three- to five-lobed, red-purple, yellowish, grayish, or brownish-red at tips. California endemic.

NOTE: A close look will reveal some fascinating color variations and even some intense hues.

HABITAT: Rocky flat and ridges, alpine fellfields (6,400–12,000 feet); found in Sierra, east of the Sierra.

WHERE AND WHEN:
Tioga Crest in Yosemite (July–August)
Kirkwood west of Carson Pass (July–August)
Winnemucca Lake Trail at Carson Pass (July–August)

Alpine paintbrush

Sweetwater Mountains (July–August)
Mount Tallac in Tahoe (July–August)
Wright's Lake west of Tahoe (July–August)

PAINTBRUSH, GREAT RED   *Castilleja miniata*
Broomrape family (previously included in Snapdragon family)
DESCRIPTION: 1–3 feet. Long raceme of bright red, three-lobed bracts.
Long-protruding, greenish flower beaks. Alternating, narrow, pointed
leaves.
NOTE: This robust plant with the bright, showy bracts often forms lush
clusters in wet meadows with broad-leaf lupine (p. 424), creating a star-

tling red-blue rainbow gar-
den.
HABITAT: Wet meadows (to
11,500 feet); found in much
of California (except Central
Valley, foothills, and des-
erts).
WHERE AND WHEN:
Lakes Basin (July–August)
San Jacinto Mountains (July–
  August)
Modoc Plateau (July–
  August)
Trinity Alps (July–
  September)
King's Canyon/Sequoia (July–
  September)
Kirkwood west of Carson

Great red paintbrush   Pass (July–September)

PAINTBRUSH, HAIRY   *Castilleja pilosa*
Broomrape family (previously included in Snapdragon family)
DESCRIPTION: 3–12 inches. Short inflorescence with rounded, pink or red-
purple, or yellowish bracts with thin white margins. Hairy leaves three-
lobed or unlobed.
NOTE: Less common than many of its fellow paintbrushes and with unusually colored bracts—pinkish with white margin (though they can also be
yellowish)—hairy paintbrush is a startling addition to a grassy meadow or
alpine fellfield.
HABITAT: Sagebrush scrub, grassy meadows, fellfields (5,000–10,000 feet);
found in Sierra, east of the Sierra, northeast corner, Transverse Ranges.

Hairy paintbrush

WHERE AND WHEN:
Sagehen Creek meadow (July–August)
Desolation Wilderness in Tahoe (July–August)
Dana Plateau in Yosemite (July–August)
San Bernardino Mountains (July–August)
Modoc Plateau (July–August)
Mosquito Flat trail (July–August)

PAINTBRUSH, LEMMON'S   *Castilleja lemmonii*
Broomrape family (previously included in Snapdragon family)
DESCRIPTION: 4–12 inches. Short inflorescence with pointed, three- to five-lobed, magenta or pink-purple bracts. Narrow, unlobed or three-lobed leaves. Glandular-hairy stems and leaves. California endemic.
NOTE: Although a few paintbrushes are gray, yellow, white, or orange, most are some shade of red—from scarlet, to red-purple, to pink. Lemmon's is "normal" in that respect, but its shade of red is distinctive—magenta or pink-purple.
HABITAT: Moist, grassy meadows (7,000–11,500 feet); found in Cascades, Sierra.
WHERE AND WHEN:
Tuolumne Meadows in Yosemite (July–August)
Desolation Wilderness in Tahoe (July–August)
Donner Summit area in Tahoe (July–August)
Mosquito Flat trail (July–August)
Lassen National Park (July–August)
Sonora Pass (July–August)

Lemmon's paintbrush

PRIMROSE, SIERRA   *Primula suffrutescens*
Primrose family

DESCRIPTION: 0.5–1 foot. Subshrub with branching racemes of many five-petaled, pinwheel-like, rose or pink flowers. Petals are notched or lobed and are yellow at the base. Basal rosette of spoon-shaped, fleshy, toothed leaves. California endemic.

NOTE: These wonderful, warm flowers form extensive rose-colored gardens in rocky areas of the high mountains.

Sierra primrose

HABITAT: Around rocks, crevices, cliffs (6,500–13,000 feet); found in north-west mountains, Sierra, east of the Sierra.
WHERE AND WHEN:
King's Canyon/Sequoia (July–August)
above Winnemucca Lake (July–August)
Lakes Basin (July)
Mount Hoffman in Yosemite (July–August)
Pole Creek in Tahoe (July)
Trinity Alps (July–August)

ROCK FRINGE   *Epilobium obcordatum*
Evening primrose family
DESCRIPTION: 1–6 inches. Several four-petaled, red-purple or rose flowers (to 2 inches) along upper stem. Petals heart-shaped with darker rose veins. Small, roundish, toothed leaves.
NOTE: These gorgeous flowers usually form extensive mats of rose around rocks shortly after the snow melts.
HABITAT: Around rocks, talus (6,500–13,000 feet); found in northwest mountains, Cascades, Sierra, northeast corner.
WHERE AND WHEN:
Pole Creek in Tahoe (July–August)
Trinity Alps (July–August)
Gaylor Lakes in Yosemite (July–August)
King's Canyon/Sequoia (July–August)
Lakes Basin (July–August)
Lassen National Park (July–August)

Rock fringe

Rosy sedum

SEDUM, ROSY or LEDGE STONECROP

Rhodiola integrifolia subsp. *integrifolia* or *Sedum roseum*

Stonecrop family

DESCRIPTION: 4–10 inches. Usually shrublike with clusters of up to 50 wine-red flowers. Flower tube with four petal lobes (sometimes five) that don't fully open.

NOTE: Succulence is a very effective strategy for surviving very dry areas, for the leaves, camel-like, can store moisture through extended dry periods.

HABITAT: Wet places on rocky flats and slopes, ridges, summits, talus (6,500–12,500 feet); found in northwest mountains, Sierra, east of the Sierra, northeast corner.

WHERE AND WHEN:

Castle Peak (July–August)

Desolation Wilderness in Tahoe (July–August)

above Winnemucca Lake at Carson Pass (July–August)

Warner Mountains (July–August)

Mount Dana in Yosemite (July–August)

White Mountains (July–August)

SORREL, MOUNTAIN   *Oxyria digyna*

Buckwheat family

DESCRIPTION: 2–10 inches. Densely flowered spike of tiny, crepe-papery flowers. Sepals (no true petals) reddish or yellowish-green turning to reddish fruits. Broad, fleshy, kidney-shaped, basal leaves.

NOTE: The leaves are tartly tasty and energizing. Of course, if you try a leaf, be absolutely certain it is a mountain sorrel plant and only nibble a little—to spare yourself and the plant.

HABITAT: Rock crevices, cliffs, talus (to 13,000 feet); found in northwest mountains, foothills, Cascades, Sierra, east of the Sierra, northeast corner, Transverse Ranges, Peninsular Ranges.

WHERE AND WHEN:
San Jacinto Mountains (July–August)
Mount Tallac in Tahoe (July–August)
Trinity Alps (July–August)
Mount Dana in Yosemite (July–August)
Mount Shasta (July–September)
Lassen National Park (July–September)

Mountain sorrel

SPIRAEA, DOUGLAS   *Spiraea douglasii*
Rose family

DESCRIPTION: 2–6 feet. Shrub with many shoots and branches, and alternating oval leaves. Elongated clusters of many tiny, five-petaled, pink flowers fuzzy with masses of reproductive parts.

NOTE: This species has flowers similar to the mountain spiraea's (p. 493), but they are in long, narrow racemes instead of round ones. Very fragrant.

HABITAT: Moist meadows, forest openings (to 6,700 feet); found in northwest mountains, north coast, Cascades, northern Sierra, northeast corner.

WHERE AND WHEN:
Lakes Basin (July–August)
Mount Shasta (July–August)
Lassen Peak (July–August)
Cedar Basin Research Natural Area (July–August)
Trinity Alps (July–August)
Dunes of Arcata (July–August)

Douglas spiraea

Mountain spiraea

SPIRAEA, MOUNTAIN or ROSE MEADOWSWEET
Spiraea splendens var. *splendens* or *S. densiflora*

Rose family

DESCRIPTION: 1–3 feet. Shrub with many flat-topped clusters (to 3 inches) of small, five-petaled, rose-colored, shallow bowl-shaped flowers. Dark-green toothed, oval leaves. California endemic.

NOTE: The flowers of all the members of the Rose family have clusters of many reproductive parts, but in spiraea the parts are so many and so thick that they almost conceal the small petals, creating a fragrant mass of rosy fuzz.

HABITAT: Open woods, scrubby slopes (2,000–11,100 feet); found in northwest mountains, Cascades, Sierra, northeast corner.

WHERE AND WHEN:

Castle Peak (July–August)
Lakes Basin (July–August)
Trinity Alps (July–August)
Warner Mountains (July–August)
Tioga Crest in Yosemite (July–August)
Desolation Wilderness in Tahoe (July–August)

THISTLE, ANDERSON'S   *Cirsium andersonii*

Aster family

DESCRIPTION: 1–3 feet. Branching stem with one or a few cylindrical flower heads. Brushy heads with scores of red-purple, tubular disk flowers above spiny involucres.

NOTE: With its long, tubular, red flowers, this is a perfect hummingbird plant, and so a great place for hummingbird lovers to hang out at dusk!

HABITAT: Dry flats, forest openings (4,000–10,500 feet); found in northwest mountains, foothills, Cascades, Sierra, northeast corner.

WHERE AND WHEN:
Glacier Point Road in Yosemite (July–August)
Warner Mountains (July–August)
Greenhorn Range (July–August)
Lassen National Park (July–August)
Barker Pass in Tahoe (July–August)
Piute Mountains (July–August)

Anderson's thistle

WINTERGREEN, BOG

Pyrola asarifolia

Heath family

DESCRIPTION: 0.5–1.5 feet. Several small, cup-shaped flowers nod off an elongated raceme. Five pink and white petal lobes with a projecting, bent style. Round, dark-green, leathery, basal leaves.

NOTE: The oddly bent style is characteristic of several of the species of the *Pyrola* genus and of some other close relatives in the Heath family.

HABITAT: Moist forests, stream banks, seeps (to 10,000 feet); found in northwest mountains, north coast and coast ranges, Cascades, Sierra, northeast corner, Transverse Ranges.

WHERE AND WHEN:
Osgood Swamp in Tahoe (July)
San Bernardino Mountains (July–August)
Mount Shasta (July–August)
San Gabriel Mountains (July–August)
Mirror Lake in Yosemite (July–August)
Warner Mountains (July–August)

Bog wintergreen

Alpine gold

ALPINE GOLD
Hulsea algida

Aster family

DESCRIPTION: 4–16 inches. Solitary flower head (to 2 inches) at tip of glandular-sticky stem. Golden yellow rays surround a raised orange disk. Narrow, crinkled, glandular-sticky, irregularly toothed leaves.

NOTE: To see this plant you will have to climb to rocky ridges and summits of the highest Sierra peaks. Be sure to gently rub the leaves or stem, and a wonderful, sweet fragrance—truly alpine gold—will linger on your hands.

HABITAT: Rocky or gravelly flats and ridges, summits (9,500–14,000 feet); found in Sierra, east of the Sierra.

WHERE AND WHEN:

Mount Dana in Yosemite (July–August)
Sweetwater Mountains (July–August)
Freel Peak (July–August)
White Mountains (July–August)
Mount Tallac in Tahoe (July–August)
Bodie Hills (July–August)

ARNICA, SEEP-SPRING
Arnica longifolia

Aster family

DESCRIPTION: 1–2 feet. Branching stems with 3 to 20 broad flower heads of 8 to 13 yellow, pointed rays surrounding yellow or orange disk. Five to seven opposite pairs of long, narrow leaves.

NOTE: The stems of this species are often clustered, forming large masses of the bright yellow flower heads.

HABITAT: Wet meadows, stream banks, open forests (5,000–11,000 feet); found in northwest mountains, north coast ranges, Cascades, Sierra, east of the Sierra, northeast corner.

WHERE AND WHEN:

Mount Tallac in Tahoe (July–August)
Modoc Plateau (July–August)

Seep-spring
arnica

McGee Creek (July–August)
Sweetwater Mountains (July–August)
Lassen National Park (July–August)
Snow Mountain (July–August)

BUTTERCUP, ALPINE   *Ranunculus eschscholtzii*
Buttercup family
DESCRIPTION: 1–6 inches. Dwarf plant with large (to 1.5 inches), shallow, bowl-shaped flower at tip of stem. Five shiny yellow petals. Several broad leaves with three to five pointed lobes.
NOTE: It is always a surprise to find clumps of these large, glistening flowers in the rocks on some alpine ridge or summit.
HABITAT: Rocky slopes, ledges, ridges, summits (5,500–13,300 feet); found in northwest mountains, Cascades, Sierra, east of the Sierra, northeast corner, Transverse Ranges, Peninsular Ranges.
WHERE AND WHEN:
above Winnemucca Lake at Carson Pass (July–August)
Trinity Alps (July–August)
Mount Dana in Yosemite (July–August)

Alpine buttercup

San Bernardino Mountains (July–August)
Bodie Hills (July–August)
Warner Mountains (July–August)

Fan-leaf
cinquefoil

CINQUEFOIL, FAN-LEAF   *Potentilla flabellifolia*
Rose family
DESCRIPTION: 4–12 inches. Several bright yellow flowers in branching raceme. Five separate petals notched at tip and cluster of many reproductive parts. Dark-green fan-shaped leaves with three broad, wedge-shaped, toothed leaflets.
NOTE: *Potentilla* presumably refers to the plant's medicinal qualities—but it could just as easily be describing the dazzling, intense color of the flowers.
HABITAT: Moist meadows, stream banks (5,800–12,000 feet); found in northwest mountains, Cascades, Sierra, northeast corner.
WHERE AND WHEN:
Winnemucca Lake trail at Carson Pass (July–August)
Trinity Alps (July–August)
Dana Plateau in Yosemite (July–August)
Mount Shasta (July–August)
Lakes Basin (July–August)
Warner Mountains (July–August)

DANDELION, ORANGE MOUNTAIN   *Agoseris aurantiaca*
Aster family
DESCRIPTION: 0.5–2 feet. Solitary flower head at tip of stem. Burnt-orange (sometimes red) square-tipped rays. No disk. Basal, lancelike leaves.
NOTE: The rays cover quite a color range, from burnt orange or brick red in bloom, to dark purple or pink when dry.

HABITAT: Grassy meadows, stream banks, openings in woods (5,500–11,500 feet); found in northwest mountains, north coast ranges, Cascades, Sierra, east of the Sierra, northeast corner.

WHERE AND WHEN:
Pole Creek in Tahoe (July–August)
Trinity Alps (July–August)
Glen Aulin in Yosemite (July–August)
Modoc Plateau (July–August)
Lassen National Park (July–August)
Bishop Creek (July–August)

Orange mountain dandelion

HAWKWEED, SHAGGY · *Hieracium horridum*
Aster family

DESCRIPTION: 4–15 inches. Branching stem with numerous small flower heads, each with six to 15 bright yellow ray flowers (no disk). Stems, phyllaries, and tonguelike leaves covered with long, fine, white hairs.

NOTE: If you are allergic to hairs, this amazingly shaggy plant might be "horridum"; otherwise it is delightfully astonishing.

HABITAT: Rocky slopes and ledges, crevices (5,000–11,000 feet); found in

Shaggy hawkweed

northwest mountains, Cascades, Sierra, east of the Sierra, northeast corner, Peninsular Ranges.

WHERE AND WHEN:
San Jacinto Mountains (July)
Mono Pass in Yosemite (July–August)
White Mountains (July–August)
Greenhorn Mountains (July–August)
Mount Tallac in Tahoe (July–August)
Lassen National Park (July–August)

LILY, SIERRA TIGER or ALPINE LILY   *Lilium parvum*
Lily family
DESCRIPTION: 2–6 feet. Showy, bell-shaped, bright orange or dark red, maroon-spotted flowers (to 2 inches). Six flaring tepals recurved at tips. Usually 2 to 10 flowers, but as many as 40. California endemic.

NOTE: Unlike most lilies in California, the flowers of tiger lily are usually erect (not nodding) on the stem (though the buds nod), and the tepals curve only at the tips, not all the way back.
HABITAT: Wet meadows, along creeks (4,000–8,000 feet); found in Sierra.
WHERE AND WHEN:
Castle Peak (July–August)
Tenaya Canyon in Yosemite
   (July–August)
Osgood Swamp in Tahoe
   (July–August)
Carson Pass (July–August)
Greenhorn Mountains (July–
   August)
Mosquito Flat trail (July–
   August)

Sierra tiger lily

LUPINE, MOUNT EDDY   *Lupinus croceus*
Pea family
DESCRIPTION: 1–2 feet. Broad racemes up to a foot long of bright yellow or yellow-orange pea flowers. Palmately compound leaves with five to eight broad leaflets. California endemic.
NOTE: There are a few yellow-flowered lupines, but in this species, the

flowers usually have an orange tinge somewhere on the petals.

HABITAT: Rocky, dry places; forest openings (3,000–9,000 feet); found in northwest mountains, Cascades.

WHERE AND WHEN:
Mount Eddy (July–August)
Scott Mountain (July–August)
Trinity Alps (July–August)
Cedar Basin Research Natural Area
(July–August)
Kangaroo Lake Botanical Area
(July–August)

Mount Eddy lupine

SENECIO, ARROWLEAF   *Senecio triangularis*
Aster family

DESCRIPTION: 2–4 feet. Robust plant with dark green, arrow-shaped toothed leaves. Many clusters of 10–30 small flower heads with only a few scattered yellow rays surrounding a yellow disk.

NOTE: Most *Senecio* species have a rather scraggly look because the rays are irregularly spaced and differently angled.

HABITAT: Wet meadows, stream banks (4,000–11,000 feet); found in northwest mountains, foothills, Cascades, Sierra, east of the Sierra, northeast corner, Transverse Ranges, Peninsular Ranges.

WHERE AND WHEN:
San Bernardino Mountains
(July–August)
Modoc Plateau (July–August)

Arrowleaf senecio

San Gabriel Mountains (July–August)
San Jacinto Mountains (July–August)
Paige Meadows in Tahoe (July–August)
Trinity Alps (August)

STONECROP, LANCE-LEAF   *Sedum lanceolatum*
Stonecrop family
DESCRIPTION: 2–8 inches. As many as 25 star-shaped flowers (to 0.5 inches) in cluster at tip of fleshy stem. Five bright-yellow petal lobes, often with reddish mid-ribs. Narrow, pointed, succulent stem leaves.

NOTE: These juicy-leaved plants with the blazing yellow star flowers are the perfect example of floral BYOB—they definitely bring their own moisture!

HABITAT: Rocky flats and slopes, outcrops, ridges, talus (6,000–12,000 feet); found in northwest mountains, foothills, Cascades, Sierra.

WHERE AND WHEN:
Red Lake Peak at Carson
    Pass (July–August)
Mount Eddy (July–August)
Dana Plateau in Yosemite
    (July–August)
Desolation Wilderness in
    Tahoe (July–August)
Ebbetts Pass (July–August)
Mosquito Flat trail (July–
    August)

Lance-leaf stonecrop

SULPHUR FLOWER   *Eriogonum umbellatum*
Buckwheat family
DESCRIPTION: 4–12 inches. An umbel of several slender rays at the tip of a leafless stem, each ray ending in a spherical umbellet of tiny, lemon-yellow flowers that often turn red with age. Crepe-papery petal-like sepals (no petals).
NOTE: Distinguishing this species from many other yellow-flowered buckwheats is the whorl of narrow, upcurving, leaflike bracts just below the primary umbel.
HABITAT: Dry, open, often rocky flats and slopes (to 12,100 feet); found in much of California (except Central Valley).

Sulphur flower

WHERE AND WHEN:
Mount Tallac in Tahoe (July–August)
Santa Lucia Range (July–August)
Lassen National Park (July–August)
Trinity Alps (July–August)
rims of Yosemite Valley (July–August)
San Gabriel Mountains (July–August)

BUCKWHEAT, ONION-HEAD or INYO BUCKWHEAT
Buckwheat family   *Eriogonum latens*

DESCRIPTION: 4–20 inches. Leafless stem rising above mat of round, leathery, basal leaves. Terminal, spherical heads (to 2 inches) of tiny, creamy, papery flowers. Six petal-like sepals, no true petals.

NOTE: Many buckwheats have more-or-less round heads of flowers, but this head is unusually large and showy.

HABITAT: Granitic sand (6,500–11,000 feet); found in central and southern Sierra, east of the Sierra, Mojave Desert.

WHERE AND WHEN:
White Mountains (July–August)
Taboose Pass (July–August)
Death Valley (July–August)
Big Pine Creek (July–August)

Onion-head buckwheat

Convict Lake (July–August)
Olancha Peak (July–August)

COLUMBINE, ALPINE *Aquilegia pubescens*
Buttercup family
DESCRIPTION: 6–20 inches. Bright white, spurred flowers (to 2 inches) at ends of branching stems. Five petals are long tubes ending in nectar spurs; five sepals flare out between the petals. Many long-protruding stamens. California endemic.

NOTE: These flowers are delicately beautiful and stunning in size and color. They sometimes hybridize with *Aquilegia formosa* (p. 277).
HABITAT: Rocky flats, ridges (9,000–12,000 feet); found in Sierra.
WHERE AND WHEN:
Dana Plateau in Yosemite area (July–August)
Bishop Creek (July–August)
Mono Pass in Yosemite (July–August)
Mosquito Flat trail (July–August)
King's Canyon/Sequoia (July–August)
Donahue Pass in Yosemite (July–August)

Alpine columbine

CORN LILY or FALSE HELLEBORE *Veratrum californicum*
Trillium family (previously included in Lily family)
DESCRIPTION: 3–6 feet. Stout stem with elongated raceme of many white flowers (to 1 inch). Six pointed tepals with green glands at the base. Large, broad, deeply veined, dark-green cornlike leaves.
NOTE: This poisonous plant forms great masses in wet areas—a jungle toxic to humans, animals, and even some insects.
HABITAT: Wet meadows, stream banks, seeps (to 11,000 feet); found in much of California (except south coast and deserts).
WHERE AND WHEN:
Castle Peak (July–August)
Trinity Alps (July–August)

Crane Flat in Yosemite (July–
  August)
Palomar Mount State Park (July–
  August)
Greenhorn Range (July–August)
San Jacinto Mountains (July–
  August)

Corn lily

Corn lily

DAISY, COULTER'S or
LARGE MOUNTAIN FLEABANE *Erigeron coulteri*
Aster family

DESCRIPTION: 1–3 feet. Usually one flower head (but sometimes as many as four) atop slender stem. Flower head crowded with 45–150 narrow, white rays surrounding yellow disk. Oblong, basal leaves on petioles and smaller, clasping stem leaves.

NOTE: This species is characterized by scores of very narrow, pure white rays.

Coulter's daisy

HABITAT: Wet meadows, creekbanks, forest openings (6,000–11,000 feet); found in Sierra, northeast corner, Transverse Ranges, Peninsular Ranges.

WHERE AND WHEN:
Pole Creek in Tahoe (July–August)
Warner Mountains (July–August)
Tuolumne Meadows in Yosemite (July–August)
Lakes Basin (July–August)
San Bernardino Mountains (July–August)
San Jacinto Mountains (July–August)

DEER'S TONGUE or MONUMENT PLANT   *Swertia radiata*
Gentian family

DESCRIPTION: 3–6 feet. Towering, stout stem, dense with scores and scores of flat, four-petaled flowers (to 1.5 inches). Greenish-white petals with purple spots and pink nectar glands.

NOTE: It is not surprising that it takes two years for this robust plant to produce the flowers—the first year is just for the leaves.

HABITAT: Grassy slopes, open woods (6,800–10,000 feet); found in northwest mountains, north coast ranges, Sierra, northeast corner.

WHERE AND WHEN:
Winnemucca Lake trail at Carson Pass (July)
Warner Mountains (July–August)
Crane Flat in Yosemite (July–August)
Kirkwood west of Carson Pass (July–August)
Six Rivers National Forest (July–August)
Mount Sanhedrin (July–August)

Deer's tongue

Fringed grass-
of-Parnassus

GRASS-OF-PARNASSUS, FRINGED   *Parnassia fimbriata*
Grass-of-Parnassus family

DESCRIPTION: 1–2 feet. Flat, five-petaled, white flowers (to 1 inch) at tips of mostly leafless stems. Petals with white fringes between them and yellow-green glands at base. Round, basal, scalloped leaves.

NOTE: Despite its "conservative" white color, this flower apparently lives on the fringes.

HABITAT: Wet meadows, rocky seeps (6,500–9,000 feet); found in north-west mountains, Cascades, northern Sierra, northeast corner.

WHERE AND WHEN:
Pole Creek in Tahoe (July)
Warner Mountains (July–August)
Trinity Alps (July–August)
Lassen National Park (July–August)
Kangaroo Lake (July–August)
Marble Mountains (July–August)

HEATHER, WHITE   *Cassiope mertensiana*
Heath family

DESCRIPTION: 6–12 inches. Matted, creeping shrub with many half-inch, nodding, upside-down, bell-shaped flowers. Petal lobes white with tiny, narrow red sepals on top.

NOTE: You will usually find this plant forming dense canopies of flowers over the branches and leaves, looking like a sea of white bobbing bells being held and jangled by little red fingers.

HABITAT: Moist, rocky places (5,900–12,000 feet); found in northwest mountains, Cascades, Sierra, northeast corner.

WHERE AND WHEN:
Mount Tallac in Tahoe (July–August)

White heather

Trinity Alps (July–August)
above Winnemucca Lake at Carson Pass (July–August)
Warner Mountains (July–August)
Cathedral Peak in Yosemite (July–August)
Lakes Basin (July–August)

LADIES TRESSES, WHITE *Spiranthes romanzoffiana*
Orchid family

DESCRIPTION: 4–20 inches. Spiraling spike of many tubular, white or cream, half-inch flowers. Middle petal of lower lip is constricted below tip. Long, parallel-veined, basal leaves.

White ladies tresses

NOTE: Since the short stems are often hidden by surrounding grass, these twisted, white "braids" often appear to emerge directly from the wet ground.

HABITAT: Wet meadows, marshes, bogs, seeps (to 10,000 feet); found in northwest mountains, north and central coast ranges, foothills, Cascades, Sierra, northeast corner, Transverse Ranges, Peninsular Ranges.

WHERE AND WHEN:
Tenaya Canyon in Yosemite (July)
Trinity Alps (July–August)
Osgood Swamp in Tahoe (July–August)
San Jacinto Mountains (July–August)
Santa Lucia Range (July–August)
San Bernardino Mountains (July–August)

LILY, WASHINGTON   *Lilium washingtonianum*
Lily family

DESCRIPTION: 2–8 feet. Up to 26 very large (to 3 inches), trumpet-shaped flowers at tips of long pedicels. Six white, tonguelike tepals curving at the tips, often with purple dots. One to nine whorls of broad, pointed leaves.

NOTE: The subspecies *purpurescens*, found in California only in the Cascades and the northwest corner, has more recurved, purple-tinged tepals that age pink.

HABITAT: Forest openings; dry, bushy slopes (4,000–7,400 feet); found in northwest mountains, foothills, Cascades, Sierra, northeast corner.

Washington lily

WHERE AND WHEN:
Modoc Plateau (July–
    August)
Trinity Alps (July–August)
Mount Tallac in Tahoe (July–
    August)
Smith River (July–August)
Chinquapin in Yosemite
    (July–August)
Mount Shasta (July–August)

LOUSEWORT, COILED BEAK   *Pedicularis contorta*
Broomrape family (previously included in Snapdragon family)

DESCRIPTION: 4–16 inches. Loose spike of many creamy white or pale yellow two-lipped flowers. Upper two petal lobes form stout, downcurving beak; lower three lobes are spreading "ears." CNPS Rare and Endangered List—limited distribution in California.

NOTE: The common name and species name are perfect descriptions, as the curving beak and slightly askew flowers definitely give a twisted impression.

HABITAT: Stream banks, meadows, bogs, forest openings (5,000–8,000 feet); found in northwest mountains.

WHERE AND WHEN:
Trinity Alps (July–August)
Salmon Mountains (July–August)
Russian Peak Wilderness (July–August)
Klamath Range (July–August)
Marble Mountains (July–August)

Coiled beak lousewort

PARTRIDGE FOOT   *Luetkea pectinata*
Rose family

DESCRIPTION: 4–12 inches. Evergreen, mat-forming subshrub thick with cylindrical clusters of tiny (to one-fourth inch), white flowers and small, deeply divided leaves. Many reproductive parts.

NOTE: The deeply divided leaves presumably reminded someone of a partridge's foot!

HABITAT: Moist places around rocks, often near snow (5,900–9,200 feet); found in northwest mountains, Cascades.

Partridge foot

WHERE AND WHEN:
Mount Shasta (July–August)
Cedar Basin Research Natural Area (July–August)
Trinity Alps (July–August)
Heart Lake (July–August)
Marble Mountain Wilderness (July–August)
Siskiyou Mountains (July–August)

PENSTEMON, HOT-ROCK   *Penstemon deustus*
Plantain family (previously included in Snapdragon family)
DESCRIPTION: 0.5–1.5 feet. Many narrow-tubed, two-lipped flowers on short pedicels. Petal lobes white with purple markings; upper two lobes small and inconspicuous. Glandular inflorescence. Pairs of opposite leaves.

NOTE: The two petal lobes of the upper lip look like they got burned by that hot rock!

HABITAT: Rocky places (2,000–10,000 feet); found in northwest mountains, north coast ranges, Cascades, Sierra, east of the Sierra, northeast corner.

WHERE AND WHEN:
Warner Mountains (July–
    August)
Trinity Alps (July–August)
Echo Summit in Tahoe
    (July–August)
Mount Shasta (July–August)
Mount Lassen (July–August)
Bear Basin Butte (July–
    August)

Hot-rock penstemon

PHACELIA, SCOTT MOUNTAIN   *Phacelia dalesiana*
Borage family (previously included in Waterleaf family)
DESCRIPTION: 2–6 inches. Ground-hugging, glandular-hairy plant with basal rosette of elliptic leaves. Several shallowly bowl-shaped white flowers with purple markings in throat. Black anthers. California endemic. CNPS Rare and Endangered List—limited distribution.
NOTE: This rare plant occurs only on ultramafic soils (i.e., serpentine and peridotite) that are high in magnesium and iron.

Meadows, forest openings (5,000–6,500 feet); found in northwest mountains.
WHERE AND WHEN:
Kangaroo Lake Botanical
 Area (July–August)
Scott Mountain (July–
 August)
Mount Eddy (July–August)
Trinity Alps (July–August)

Scott Mountain phacelia

PHLOX, CUSHION or CONDENSED PHLOX   *Phlox condensata*
Phlox family

DESCRIPTION: 2–12 inches. Dense, rounded cushion, woody at the base, covered with white or pink, pinwheel-like, half-inch flowers. Yellow flower tube flaring into five rounded petal lobes.

NOTE: Cushion plants are wonderfully adapted to alpine environments—the leaves are so dense that the wind and cold can't penetrate.

HABITAT: Rocky flats, ridges (6,000–13,000 feet); found in Sierra, east of the Sierra, northeast corner, Transverse Ranges.

Cushion phlox

WHERE AND WHEN:
Modoc Plateau (July)
Mount Dana in Yosemite (July–August)
White Mountains (July–August)
Freel Peak (July–August)
Sweetwater Mountains (July–August)
San Bernardino Mountains (July–August)

PINEDROPS
Pterospora andromedea
Heath family

DESCRIPTION: 1–3 feet. Thick, fleshy, clammy, red or orangish stem with many small, urn-shaped flowers nodding on short, arching pedicels along extended raceme. White or creamy yellow corolla with tiny, fingerlike, red sepals. No green leaves—saprophyte.

NOTE: Pinedrops join snowplants (p. 443) as common forest saprophytes with tall, flowering stalks (even taller in pinedrops).

HABITAT: Forest shade (to 8,500 feet); found in northwest mountains, north coast ranges, Cascades, Sierra, northeast corner, Transverse Ranges, Peninsular Ranges.

Pinedrops

WHERE AND WHEN:
Yosemite Valley (July)
San Gabriel Mountains (July)
San Jacinto Mountains (July–August)
Trinity Alps (July–August)
Echo Summit in Tahoe (July–August)
Lassen National Park (July–August)

RANGER'S BUTTONS or SWAMP WHITEHEADS
Sphenosciadium capitellatum
Carrot family

DESCRIPTION: 2–5 feet. Stout stem with several large, loose umbels of small, white or pinkish spheres, each sphere a tight umbel of many tiny flowers.

NOTE: Of the many tall Carrot family members with umbels of white flow-

Ranger's
buttons

ers, this species is unique with its buttonlike (buttons for a pea jacket, perhaps) flower heads.

HABITAT: Wet meadows, stream banks (3,000–10,400 feet); found in north
coast ranges, Cascades, Sierra, east of Sierra, northeast corner, south coast,
Transverse Ranges, Peninsular Ranges.

WHERE AND WHEN:
King's Canyon/Sequoia (July–August)
Lakes Basin (July–August)
Rafferty Creek trail in Yosemite (July–August)
Warner Mountains (July–August)
San Jacinto Mountains (July–August)
San Bernardino Mountains (July–August)

SAXIFRAGE, TOLMIE'S   *Saxifraga tolmiei*
Saxifrage family

DESCRIPTION: 1–6 inches. Matted plant with slender, trailing, branching,
leafless stem with several small flowers with five separate petals. Tiny,
basal, round, shiny, fleshy leaves.

NOTE: The name *saxifrage*, meaning "stone breaker," seems very appropriate for this species—it usually grows around rocks on high mountain
ridges and fellfields.

HABITAT: Rocky ridges, fellfields (8,500–11,800 feet); found in northwest
mountains, north coast ranges, Cascades, Sierra, northeast corner.

WHERE AND WHEN:
Freel Peak (July–August)
Trinity Alps (July–August)

Pole Creek in Tahoe (July–
  August)
Lassen National Park (July–
  August)
Morgan Pass (July–August)
Warner Mountains (July–
  August)

Tolmie's saxifrage

SUNDEW, ROUND-LEAF   *Drosera rotundifolia*
Sundew family

DESCRIPTION: 2–12 inches. A few tiny, five-petaled, white flowers (not in bloom in photo) along slender, leafless stem. Basal rosette of round leaves covered with red-stalked, sticky hairs.

NOTE: This bog plant is deadly to insects, snaring them with the sticky hairs for slow digestion. Sometimes you will even find dragonflies stuck to the leaves of several plants.

HABITAT: Bogs (to 8,000 feet); found in northwest mountains, north coast and coast ranges, Cascades, Sierra.

WHERE AND WHEN:

Grass Lake at Luther Pass (July)

Round-leaf
sundew

Big Lagoon County Park (July)
Osgood Swamp in Tahoe (July)
Crane Flat in Yosemite (July)
Butterfly Valley (July)
Lassen National Park (July–August)

WINTERGREEN, WHITE-VEINED · *Pyrola picta*
Heath family

DESCRIPTION: 4–8 inches. Several cup-shaped, white (sometimes pink-tinged) flowers (up to 0.5 inches) hang upside-down from short, arching

pedicels spread loosely along stem. Broad, basal, dark-green leathery leaves with white veins.

NOTE: The width of the white veins indicates the recent amount of sunlight the plant has received—with a lot of sun, the chlorophyll is replenished and the veins shrink.

HABITAT: Forest shade (to 10,000 feet); found in much of California (except Central Valley and deserts).

WHERE AND WHEN:
King's Canyon/Sequoia (July–August)
Trinity Alps (July–August)
San Jacinto Mountains (July–August)
Santa Lucia Range (July–August)
Butterfly Valley (July–August)
Warner Mountains (July–August)

White-veined wintergreen

YAMPAH, PARISH'S · *Perideridia parishii*
Carrot family

DESCRIPTION: 0.5–2 feet. One or a few flat-topped, lacy umbels of tiny white flowers. Only a few leaves with only a few narrow, needlelike segments. Plants often form large masses on hillsides and flats. California endemic.

NOTE: Though it's generally not easy to distinguish among species of the numerous Queen Anne's lace–type genera in northern California, yampah (*Perideridia*) is distinguishable from other genera by its needlelike leaf segments.

HABITAT: Meadows, dry slopes, forest openings (3,500–11,200 feet); found

Parish's yampah

in northwest mountains, Cascades, Sierra, east of Sierra, Transverse Ranges, Peninsular Ranges.

WHERE AND WHEN:
Lakes Basin (July)
Castle Peak (July–August)
Bishop Creek (July–August)
Trinity Alps (July–August)
Yosemite Valley (July–August)
San Jacinto Mountains (July–August)

CLOVER, BOWL · *Trifolium cyathiferum*
Pea family

DESCRIPTION: 4–12 inches. Slender, branching stem with bowl-like terminal heads of many tiny pea flowers. Greenish-white or yellowish-brown flowers with greenish, membraneous bracts.

NOTE: You might not recognize this as a pea, unless you look carefully at one of the tiny individual flowers and see the typical banner, wings, and keel.

Bowl clover

HABITAT: Seeps, ditches, moist forest openings (to 8,000 feet); found in northwest mountains, north coast and coast ranges, Central Valley, foothills, Cascades, Sierra, east of the Sierra, northeast corner, south coast ranges.

WHERE AND WHEN:
Hope Valley east of Carson Pass (July)
along Tuolumne River in Yosemite (July)
Mount Pinos (July–August)
Lassen National Park (July–August)
Barker Pass in Tahoe (July–August)
Warner Mountains (July–August)

WINTERGREEN, ONE-SIDED   *Orthilia secunda* or *Pyrola secunda*
Heath family

DESCRIPTION: 4–8 inches. Round, shiny, green, often leathery stem leaves near base of plant. Slender, bending stem with numerous greenish, urn-shaped flowers hanging from one side.

NOTE: It certainly looks like all the flowers are of one mind—all taking the same side!

HABITAT: Forests (3,000–10,500 feet); found in northwest mountains, north coast ranges, Cascades, Sierra, northeast corner, Transverse Ranges, Peninsular Ranges.

WHERE AND WHEN:
Warner Mountains (July–August)
San Jacinto Mountains (July–August)
Castle Peak (July–August)
Lassen National Park (July–August)
Trinity Alps (July–August)
San Bernardino Mountains (July–August)

One-sided wintergreen

AUGUST

Red paintbrush at 11,000 feet just east of Yosemite

AUGUST IS A TIME of continuance and transition for the California flowers. In the beginning of the month, most of the high-country blooming that peaked in July is still in fine form, but toward the end of the month it is definitely winding down toward fall and winter. However, nature gives us a special gift as abundant recompense for the passing of another year's wildflower season—a few spectacular species that wait almost to the end to come into their glory.

These late-summer bloomers are dazzling indeed—deep, rich blue **gentians** and **asters**, blazing scarlet **fuchsia**, soft rose or pink **eupatorium**, white **corydalis** and **alpine gentian**, greenish **twayblade**, and yellow **goldenrod**. These are not usually the lush rainbow gardens of July, but rather intense patches of bright colors and intriguing forms.

Although some of these bloom in the mountains of the southern part of the state, most of the August bloomers are especially prevalent in the northern mountains—the Cascades, the Warners, the Trinity Alps, the Marbles, Salmons, and Siskyous, and the northern and central Sierra. **California fuchsia**, with its intensely scarlet, tubular flowers, is one of the few members of the August northern flora that also is prevalent in the south (for example, in the Santa Monica Mountains and the San Gabriel Mountains), where it starts blooming in July, so it is included in the July section, but because it is such a spectacular and frequent component of the August-blooming northern flora, it is included again here in the August section.

Highlights

Northwest Mountains

Explorer's gentian, hiker's gentian, and **alpine gentian** in the Trinity Alps

Sierra

Explorer's gentian, hiker's gentian, alpine gentian, and **great red paintbrush** in Yosemite

Sierra corydalis, western eupatorium, great red paintbrush, monkshood, swamp onion, glaucous larkspur, and **California fuchsia** in the Tahoe Basin

Northeast Corner

Eupatorium in the Warner Mountains

Flowers

GENTIAN, EXPLORER'S   *Gentiana calycosa*
Gentian family
DESCRIPTION: 0.5–2 feet. One broad, vaselike flower (to 2 inches) at tip of stem, sometimes several more in leaf axils of upper stem. Five deep-blue petal lobes with green spots and fringes between them.
NOTE: The deep, deep blue of this flower is like a crystal autumn sky come to earth.

Explorer's
gentian

HABITAT: Wet, rocky places (4,000–10,500 feet); found in northwest mountains, Cascades, Sierra, northeast corner.

WHERE AND WHEN:
Mount Tallac in Tahoe (August–September)
Mount Eddy (August–September)
Kirkwood at Carson Pass (August–September)
Warner Mountains (August–September)
Tenaya Creek in Yosemite (August–September)
Trinity Alps (August–September)

GENTIAN, HIKER'S or FRINGED GENTIAN   *Gentianopsis simplex*
Gentian family

DESCRIPTION: 4–12 inches. One tubular flower at tip of stem. Four deep-blue petal lobes, usually ragged at edges, flare out of flower tube windmill-like. Petal lobes often twisted.

NOTE: The ragged and often twisted petal lobes make it seem that maybe something is a bit askew.

HABITAT: Moist, grassy meadows (4,000–9,500 feet); found in northwest mountains, north coast ranges, Cascades, Sierra, northeast corner, Transverse Ranges.

WHERE AND WHEN:
Lakes Basin (August)
Trinity Alps (August)
Pohono Trail in Yosemite (August)
Desolation Wilderness in Tahoe (August–September)
Warner Mountains (August–September)
San Bernardino Mountains (August–September)

Hiker's gentian

Western
eupatorium

EUPATORIUM, WESTERN   *Ageratina occidentalis*
Aster family
DESCRIPTION: 0.5–2.5 inches. Soft-looking, roundish flower heads of long, slender, tubular, pink or lavender disk flowers. No rays. Broadly triangular, toothed leaves.
NOTE: When these lovely plants cascade in the hundreds down rock cliffs and talus slopes, the hard rock softens and brightens with cheer.
HABITAT: Rocky slopes, cliffs (6,500–11,500 feet); found in northwest mountains, north coast ranges, foothills, Cascades, Sierra, east of the Sierra, northeast corner, Transverse Ranges.
WHERE AND WHEN:
Lakes Basin (August)
Pole Creek in Tahoe (August–September)
Lassen National Park (August–September)
San Gabriel Mountains (August–October)
Tenaya Creek in Yosemite (August–September)
Warner Mountains (August–September)

FUCHSIA, CALIFORNIA   *Epilobium canum*
Evening primrose family
DESCRIPTION: 0.5–2 feet. Subshrub with many long-tubular, scarlet flowers from the leaf axils on the upper stems. Four notched petals. Long-protruding, scarlet pistil with four-lobed stigma.
NOTE: Although fuchsia begins blooming in July in some of the southern mountains, it is such a dominant and spectacular member of the northern fall flora beginning to bloom in August that I have included it here as well.
HABITAT: Cliffs, talus, rock crevices (to 10,000 feet); found in much of California (except northeast corner and eastern edge).

WHERE AND WHEN:
Santa Rosa Plateau (August–October)
Lakes Basin (August–September)
Pole Creek in Tahoe (August–September)
Mount Shasta (August–September)
Warner Mountains (August–September)
Santa Lucia Range (August–October)

California fuchsia

CORYDALIS, SIERRA
Corydalis caseana
Poppy family

DESCRIPTION: 2–3 feet. Long raceme of 50 or more white or pink, tubular, spurred, four-petaled flowers horizontal to stem in all directions (like a weathervane in a swirling wind). Deeply pinnately dissected leaves.

NOTE: These plants often form extensive jungles in shaded seep areas and along creeks, filling the air with their grape fragrance and filling your heart with their unusual beauty.

HABITAT: Shaded seeps, along creeks (6,000–10,000 feet); found in Cascades, Sierra, northeast corner.

WHERE AND WHEN:
Antoine Meadows in Tahoe (August)
Modoc Plateau (August)
Lassen National Park (August)
Butte Meadows (August)
Susanville area (August)
Clicks Creek (August)

Sierra corydalis

Alpine gentian

GENTIAN, ALPINE *Gentiana newberryi*

Gentian family

DESCRIPTION: 1–5 inches. Solitary tubular flower (to 1.5 inches) at tip of short stem. Tube and five flaring petal lobes white (sometimes blue) with green spots. Fringes between petal lobes. A few spoon-shaped leaves.

NOTE: Despite the large size of this beautiful flower, it is easy to overlook, for it sits practically on the ground and can be at least partly hidden by surrounding grass.

HABITAT: Wet meadows (4,000–13,100 feet); found in northwest mountains, Cascades, Sierra, east of the Sierra.

WHERE AND WHEN:

Mount Tallac in Tahoe (August)

Trinity Alps (August)

Tuolumne Meadows in Yosemite (August–September)

north of Mount Eddy (August–September)

Lassen National Park (August–September)

White Mountains (August–September)

LEWISIA, DWARF or ALPINE LEWISIA *Lewisia pygmaea*

Miner's lettuce family (previously included in Purslane family)

DESCRIPTION: 1–3 inches. Dwarfed plant with several small flowers on very short stems cradled by basal rosette of narrow, fleshy, almost wormlike leaves. Five to nine translucent white or pink petals with maroon sepals with jagged edges.

NOTE: The rosettes of fleshy leaves are like starfish clinging to the rocky ground.

HABITAT: Wet, rocky places (6,000–13,000 feet); found in northwest mountains, north coast ranges, Cascades, Sierra, east of the Sierra, northeast corner, Transverse Ranges.

Dwarf lewisia

WHERE AND WHEN:
Tioga Crest in Yosemite area (August)
San Bernardino Mountains (August)
Desolation Wilderness in Tahoe (August)
Mount Whitney (August)
Warner Mountains (August)
White Mountains (August)

TWAYBLADE, BROAD-LIPPED   *Listera convallarioides*
Orchid family

DESCRIPTION: 4–12 inches. A few small, greenish flowers along short stem. The five similar petals are narrow and swept back toward the pedicel; the one different petal is broader, heart-shaped, and projecting forward.

NOTE: The odd-shaped greenish flower resembles some kind of delicate insect trying to fly off the stem.

HABITAT: Moist openings in woods, stream banks (to 8,000 feet); found in northwest mountains, coast ranges, Cascades, Sierra, northeast corner, Transverse Ranges, Peninsular Ranges.

Broad-lipped
twayblade

WHERE AND WHEN:
Modoc Plateau (August)
San Jacinto Mountains (August)
San Bernardino Mountains (August)
Trinity Alps (August)
Santa Lucia Range (August)
Yolla Bolly-Middle Eel Wilderness (August–September)

SEPTEMBER

Rabbitbrush at Tahoe

THE COLORS ARE MUTED, browns and golds replacing the wider spectrum of summer. There is a crispness in the air even on the warmest days, and a tinge of moldering and passing. The spectacular golds and yellows and oranges of the turning trees (most notably the aspens) are still a few weeks away, but the flowering herbs and shrubs are already creating their own miniature version of the fall colors.

Especially in northern California, a few of the plants that started blooming in August may still be in their last phases of blooming, but most of the year's blossoms have gone. It is a wonderful time to explore the world of fruits and seeds—such a wide range of pods, siliques, burrs, berries, drupes, plumes, and parachutes, and other fascinating forms of fruit.

> There comes a time in every life to pass along the bloom,
> To cycle back, to simplify, to rest in nature's womb,
> To leave behind a part of you, a glimmer from your past,
> So the wisdom from your long, good life will have a chance to last.
> So with your love you form a seed and plant it in the earth,
> And settle back to enjoy the life that starts anew with birth.

There is, however, one last floral hurrah—a golden salute to the other golds of fall on the way. The golden "brushes" of **rabbitbrush** paint open hillsides and road edges with soft but bright autumnal hues. The insects are grateful, as are we, for one last morsel before the great sleep.

Flowers

RABBITBRUSH *Ericameria nauseosa* or *Chrysothamnus nauseosus*
Aster family

DESCRIPTION: 1–3 feet. Much-branched shrub covered with brushlike flower heads of yellow disk flowers. Narrow, unlobed leaves covered with gray, woolly hairs.

NOTE: These golden-flowered shrubs help us make the transition from flowers to winter, for they are late-fall bloomers that retain some of their (dried) color even into the winter months.

HABITAT: Dry flats and slopes, sagebrush scrub (3,300–9,500 feet); found in much of California (except Central Valley).

WHERE AND WHEN:
Carson Pass (September)
Trinity Alps (September)
San Jacinto Mountains (September)
Freel Peak (September–October)
San Gabriel Mountains (September–October)
King's Canyon/Sequoia (September–October)

Rabbitbrush

OCTOBER–EARLY JANUARY

Fall color in Yosemite

THE FLOWERS ARE GONE, but the brilliant golds, bronzes, yellows, and oranges, and occasional reds of the leaves of the mountain deciduous trees—aspen, willow, alder, cottonwood, maple—are a warm farewell to another colorful wildflower year. The glorious turning of the leaves eases us into winter and its joys before the flowers stir again in only a few months. With the endings always come beginnings and another turn of the great circle of life.

> Oh Earth, such a gift you bring to us all—
> The leaves are the wisdom of plants,
> So green in the spring and so gold in the fall,
> They tell of life's circular dance.
> With the warming of days and sweet spring in the air,
> The leaves are the flower's fresh start,
> But as you turn once again and for winter prepare,
> The leaves and the blossoms depart.
> Things come and things go all through our long years,
> So we can't demand that they stay,
> Instead, praise the joy and taste the sweet tears,
> And welcome all life on the way.

FEATURED FLOWERS AND THEIR LOCATIONS

Alpine gold White Mountains

Arnica, heart-leaf Warner Mountains

Baby blue eyes, white Bodega Head

Blazing star, Lindley's State Route 58

Bleeding hearts Drum Powerhouse Road

Blue curls, woolly Pinnacles National Monument

Blue flag, western Carson Pass

Buckwheat, coast Dunes of Arcata

Camas lily Sagehen Creek

Canterbury bells Joshua Tree National Park

Canterbury bells, wild San Gabriel Mountains

Chuparosa Anza-Borrego Desert State Park

Clarkia, bilobed Ponderosa Way

Clarkia, ruby chalice Edgewood Preserve

Clarkia, speckled Kern River Canyon

Clarkia, Williamson's Yankee Jim's Road

Columbine, alpine Mosquito Flat to Mono Pass Trail

Coreopsis, Bigelow's Gorman Hills

Coreopsis, giant Santa Monica Mountains

Corn lily Castle Peak

Dahlia, sea Torrey Pines

Daisy, hillside Wind Wolves Natural Preserve

Desert gold Death Valley National Monument

Downingia, toothed Jepson Prairie

Downingia, two-horned Boggs Lake

Dudleya, coast Salt Point

Evening primrose, beach Nipomo-Guadalupe Dunes

Gentian, explorer's Lake Tahoe Basin

Gilia, bird's eye Camp Nine Road

Globe lily, Mount Diablo Mount Diablo

Harebell, California Smith River

Heather, pink mountain Mount Shasta

Ithuriel's spear Phoenix Park

Lacepod Buttermilk Bend Trail

Larkspur, Parry's Carrizo Plain

Lily, adobe Bear Valley

Lily, chocolate Santa Rosa Plateau

Lily, leopard Lakes Basin

Lily, sand Modoc Plateau

Lily, Washington Lassen National Park

Lupine, grape soda California Desert Conservation Area

Lupine, spider Electra Road

Mallow, apricot Topaz Lake

Mariposa lily, Tiburon Ring Mountain

Monkeyflower, Bigelow's Benton Area

Monkeyflower, bush Feather River Canyon

Monkeyflower, Lewis Trinity Alps

Mule ears, El Dorado Pine Hill Ecological Preserve

Mustard Pleasants Valley Road

Nemophila, five-spot Red Hill Road

Onion, Lemmon's Monitor Pass

Phacelia, Scott Mountain Kangaroo Lake

Phlox, showy Independence Trail

Pitcher plant, California Butterfly Valley

Pond lily Grass Lake

Poppy, annual Hite's Cove Trail

Poppy, California Antelope Valley California Poppy Reserve

Rhododendron, Pacific Kruse Rhododendron State Reserve

Rock fringe Kearsarge Pass in King's Canyon National Park

Sandblossoms Alabama Hills

Saxifrage, Tolmie's Freel Peak

Sedum, dwarf cliff Table Mountain

Shooting star, foothill China Camp State Park

Sky pilot Yosemite National Park

Slink pod Muir Woods

Wallflower, Franciscan San Bruno Mountain

Windflower Redwood National and State Parks

PLANTS IN THIS BOOK THAT ARE ENDEMIC TO CALIFORNIA

(Endemic to California = occurs only in California.)

Aesculus californica
Allium cratericola
Allium crispum
Allium dichlamydeum
Allium hyalinum
Allium lacunosum
Allium obtusum
Aquilegia pubescens
Arabis blepharophylla
Arctostaphylos imbricata
Aristolochia californica
Armeria maritima
Calochortus albus
Calochortus amabilis
Calochortus luteus
Calochortus pulchellus
Calochortus tiburonensis
Calochortus umbellatus
Castilleja lemmonii
Castilleja mendocinensis
Castilleja nana
Chamaebatia foliolosa
Chorizanthe douglasii
Cirsium occidentale
Clarkia biloba
Clarkia breweri
Clarkia concinna
Clarkia cylindrica
Clarkia rubicunda
Clarkia unguiculata
Clarkia williamsonii

Clarkia xantiana
Delphinium purpusii
Delphinium variegatum
Dicentra formosa
Dicentra pauciflora
Dichelostemma volubile
Downingia bella
Downingia concolor
Downingia cuspidata
Downingia ornatissima
Draba lemmonii
Draperia systyla
Dudleya cymosa
Eriodictyon crassifolium
Erysimum franciscanum
Erysimum insulare
Erythronium purpurascens
Eschscholzia caespitosa
Fremontodendron californicum subsp. *decumbens*
Fritillaria liliacea
Fritillaria pluriflora
Gilia cana
Gilia millefoliata
Hackelia velutina
Iris hartwegii
Lathyrus littoralis
Layia fremontii
Lepechinia calycina
Leptosiphon montanus (Linanthus m.)
Leptosyne bigelovii (Coreopsis b.)
Lilium pardalinum
Lilium parvum
Linanthus dianthiflorus
Linanthus parryae
Lupinus benthamii
Lupinus chamissonis
Lupinus croceus
Lupinus densiflorus var. *densiflorus*
Lupinus grayi
Lupinus stiversii
Mentzelia lindleyi
Mimulus angustatus
Mimulus bicolor
Mimulus kelloggii
Mimulus torreyi

Monardella crispa
Monolopia lanceolata
Narthecium californicum
Nemophila maculata
Nolina parryi
Opuntia phaeacantha
Paeonia californica
Penstemon grinnellii
Perideridia parishii
Phacelia californica
Phacelia campanularia
Phacelia dalesiana
Phyllodoce breweri
Polemonium eximium
Primula suffrutescens
Ranunculus hystriculus (Kumlienia hystricula)
Ribes roezlii
Romneya coulteri
Salvia leucophylla
Salvia spathacea
Scoliopus bigelovii
Sidalcea calycosa
Spiraea splendens var. *splendens (S. densiflora)*
Stachys bullata
Triphysaria eriantha subsp. *rosea*
Triteleia peduncularis
Wyethia reticulata (Agnorhiza r.)
Zeltnera venusta (Centaurium venustum)

PLANTS IN THIS BOOK ON THE CALIFORNIA NATIVE PLANT SOCIETY INVENTORY OF RARE AND ENDANGERED PLANTS

This list includes rare, endangered, and threatened plants, and plants of limited distribution.

Abronia maritima
Arabis blepharophylla
Arctostaphylos imbricata
Calochortus pulchellus
Calochortus striatus
Calochortus tiburonensis
Calochortus umbellatus
Castilleja mendocinensis
Chorizanthe douglasii
Clarkia breweri
Coreopsis maritima
Darlingtonia californica
Delphinium purpusii
Enceliopsis covillei
Erysimum franciscanum
Fremontodendron californicum subsp. *decumbens*
Fritillaria liliacea
Fritillaria pluriflora
Gilia millefoliata
Monardella crispa
Monotropa uniflora
Pedicularis contorta
Phacelia dalesiana
Romneyi coulteri
Salvia funerea
Sidalcea malachroides
Thermopsis macrophylla
Veronica cusickii
Wyethia reticulata

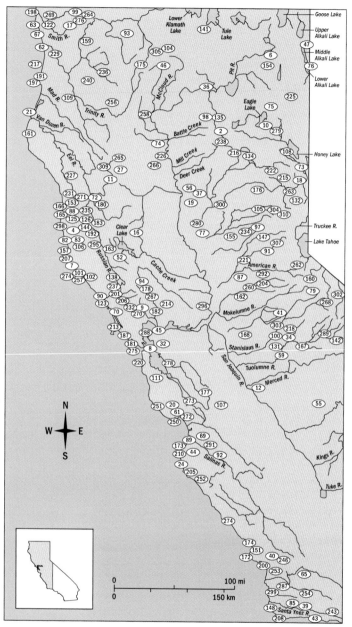

Map of other flower locations indicated in the text. For the names of the locations numbered in the map, see the pages that follow.

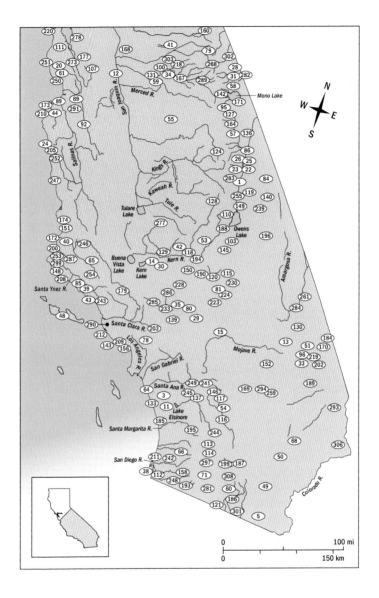

OTHER FLOWER LOCATIONS INDICATED IN THE TEXT

Italics = southern or central California. No italics = northern California. For the maps that pinpoint the locations numbered below, see the page spread previous to this one.

1. *Aberdeen—EAST OF THE SIERRA: U.S. 395 south of Big Pine*
2. Adobe Flat—CASCADES: east of Lassen National Park
3. *Agua Tibia Mts.—PENINSULAR RANGES: inland (east) from San Clemente*
4. Albion River—NORTH COAST RANGES: reaching the coast south of Mendocino
5. *Algodones Dunes—SONORAN DESERT: just north of border with Baja, California*
6. Alturas—NORTHEAST CORNER: U.S. 395 west of Warner Mountains
7. Anchor Bay—NORTH COAST: along SR-1 north of Gualala
8. *Angel Island—CENTRAL COAST: in San Francisco Bay south of Tiburon*
9. Annadel State Park—NORTH COAST RANGES: north of Petaluma
10. Antelope Mountain—NORTH COAST RANGES: north of Susanville
11. Anthony Peak—NORTH COAST RANGES: east of Covelo
12. *Arena Plains—SAN JOAQUIN VALLEY: SR-140 area south of Modesto*
13. *Baker—MOJAVE DESERT: western edge of Mojave National Preserve*
14. *Bakersfield—SAN JOAQUIN VALLEY: just north of Mojave Desert*
15. *Barstow—MOJAVE DESERT: I-15 west of Mojave National Preserve*
16. Bartlett Springs Road—NORTH COAST RANGES: extending west from Bear Valley
17. Bear Basin Butte Botanical Area—NORTHWEST MOUNTAINS: 30 miles east of Gasquet
18. Beckwourth Pass—EAST OF THE SIERRA: SR-70 east of Portola
19. Bidwell Park—SACRAMENTO VALLEY: in Chico
20. *Big Basin Redwoods State Park—CENTRAL COAST RANGES: north of Santa Cruz*
21. Big Lagoon County Park—NORTH COAST: north of Eureka
22. *Big Pine—EAST OF THE SIERRA: south of Bishop*

23. *Big Pine Creek—SOUTHERN SIERRA: running east to Big Pine*
24. *Big Sur—CENTRAL COAST RANGES: south of Monterey*
25. *Bishop—EAST OF THE SIERRA: U.S. 395 south of Mammoth*
26. *Bishop Creek—EASTERN SIERRA: running east to Bishop*
27. Black Rock Mountains—NORTHWEST MOUNTAINS: Yolla Bolly Wilderness
28. Bodie Hills—EAST OF THE SIERRA: east of Bridgeport
29. *Boron—MOJAVE DESERT: along north edge of Edwards Air Force Base*
30. *Breckenridge Mountain—SOUTHERN SIERRA: east of Bakersfield*
31. Bridgeport—EAST OF THE SIERRA: U.S. 395 north of Mono Basin
32. *Briones Regional Park—CENTRAL COAST RANGES: San Francisco east bay*
33. *Bristol Mountains—MOJAVE DESERT: in Mojave National Preserve*
34. *Buck Meadows—CENTRAL SIERRA FOOTHILLS: SR-120 west of Yosemite*
35. *Buckhorn Dry Lake—MOJAVE DESERT: on Edwards Air Force Base*
36. Burney—CASCADES: between Mount Shasta and Lassen National Park
37. Butte Meadows—NORTHERN SIERRA FOOTHILLS: SR-32 east of Chico
38. *Cabrillo National Monument—SOUTH COAST: in San Diego*
39. *Cachuma Lake Recreational Area—SOUTH COAST RANGES: north of Santa Barbara*
40. *California Polytechnic University Campus—CENTRAL COAST: in San Luis Obispo*
41. *Calaveras Big Trees State Park—CENTRAL SIERRA FOOTHILLS: southwest of Bear Valley*
42. *California Spring—SOUTHERN SIERRA FOOTHILLS: north of Kern River Canyon*
43. *Canada Honda Creek—SOUTH COAST: Santa Barbara area*
44. *Carmel—CENTRAL COAST: just south of Monterey*
45. *Carquinez Strait Regional Seashore—CENTRAL COAST RANGES: northeast of San Francisco*
46. Cedar Basin Research Natural Area—CASCADES: just southwest of Mount Shasta
47. Cedarville—NORTHEAST CORNER: U.S. 395 just east of the Warner Mountains
48. *Channel Islands—SOUTH COAST: off the coast in the Los Angeles area*
49. *Chocolate Mountains—SONORAN DESERT: between Salton Sea and Arizona border*
50. *Chuckwalla Mountains—SONORAN DESERT: just southeast of Joshua Tree*
51. *Clark Mountains—MOJAVE DESERT: in Mojave National Preserve*
52. Clear Lake—NORTH COAST RANGES: southeast of Ukiah
53. *Clicks Creek—SOUTHERN SIERRA: south of Sequoia National Park*
54. *Coachella Valley—SONORAN DESERT: just north of Salton Sea*
55. *Coarsegold—SOUTHERN SIERRA FOOTHILLS: SR-41 north of Fresno*

56. Cohasset Ridge—NORTHERN SIERRA FOOTHILLS: north of Chico
57. *Convict Lake—EASTERN SIERRA: just south of Mammoth*
58. *Conway Summit—EAST OF THE SIERRA: U.S. 395 just north of Mono Basin*
59. *Coulterville—SOUTHERN SIERRA FOOTHILLS: SR-49 east of Modesto*
60. *Coyote Mountain—SONORAN DESERT: just south of Anza-Borrego State Park*
61. *Coyote Ridge—CENTRAL COAST RANGES: in the Santa Cruz Mountains*
62. Cozy Dell Trail—NORTH COAST: in Requa north of Redwoods National Park
63. Crescent City—NORTH COAST: U.S. 101 near Oregon border
64. *Crystal Cove State Park—SOUTH COAST: in Newport Beach*
65. *Cuyama Valley—SOUTH COAST RANGES: east of San Rafael Mountains*
66. *Cuyamaca Mountains—PENINSULAR RANGES: east of San Diego*
67. Del Norte Redwoods—NORTH COAST RANGES: U.S. 101 just south of Crescent City
68. *Desert Lily Preserve—MOJAVE DESERT: SR-177 just east of Joshua Tree*
69. *Diablo Range—SOUTH COAST RANGES: inland from Monterey and Salinas*
70. Dillon Beach—NORTH COAST: north of Point Reyes
71. *Dos Cabezas—SONORAN DESERT: just southwest of Anza-Borrego State Park*
72. Dos Rios—NORTH COAST RANGES: northeast of Fort Bragg
73. Doyle—EAST OF THE SIERRA: U.S. 395 north of Reno
74. Dye Creek Preserve—SACRAMENTO VALLEY: south of Redding
75. Eagle Lake—NORTHEAST CORNER: just north of Susanville
76. Eagleville—NORTHEAST CORNER: just east of Warner Mountains
77. East Park Reservoir—SACRAMENTO VALLEY: west of Yuba City
78. *Eaton Canyon Nature Center—TRANSVERSE RANGES: San Gabriel Mountains*
79. *Ebbetts Pass—CENTRAL SIERRA: SR-4 southwest of Markleeville*
80. *Edwards Air Force Base—MOJAVE DESERT: south of Ridgecrest*
81. *El Paso Mountains—MOJAVE DESERT: just southwest of Ridgecrest*
82. Elk—NORTH COAST: south of Fort Bragg
83. Elk Creek—NORTH COAST: south of Fort Bragg
84. *Eureka Dunes—MOJAVE DESERT: just north of Death Valley*
85. *Figueroa Mountain—TRANSVERSE RANGES: north of Santa Barbara*
86. *Fish Slough—EAST OF THE SIERRA: just north of Bishop*
87. Folsom Lake—NORTHERN SIERRA FOOTHILLS: just north of Sacramento
88. Fort Bragg—NORTH COAST: north of Mendocino
89. *Fort Ord—CENTRAL COAST: on Monterey Bay*
90. Fort Ross—NORTH COAST: north of Point Reyes
91. French Meadows Reservoir—NORTHERN SIERRA: on American River east of Foresthill

92. *Gabilan Range—SOUTH COAST RANGES: just west of Pinnacles National Monument*
93. Gazelle Mountain—CASCADES: south of Yreka
94. Geyser Peak—NORTH COAST RANGES: northwest of Calistoga
95. Glass Mountain—EAST OF THE SIERRA: north of Mammoth
96. *Granite Mountains—MOJAVE DESERT: in Mojave National Preserve*
97. Grass Valley—NORTHERN SIERRA FOOTHILLS: SR-49 northeast of Sacramento
98. Gray's Valley—CASCADES: north of Lassen National Park
99. Green Pass—NORTHWEST MOUNTAINS: just south of Oregon border
100. *Groveland—CENTRAL SIERRA FOOTHILLS: SR-120 west of Yosemite*
101. Gualala—NORTH COAST: south of Manchester
102. Gualala River—NORTH COAST: south of Manchester
103. *Haiwee Reservoir—EAST OF THE SIERRA: south of Olancha on U.S. 395*
104. Heart Lake—CASCADES: in the Mount Shasta area
105. Hell's Half-Acre—NORTHERN SIERRA FOOTHILLS: just outside Grass Valley
106. Hendy Woods—NORTH COAST RANGES: between Ukiah and Manchester
107. *Henry Coe State Park—CENTRAL COAST RANGES: southeast of San Jose*
108. Honey Lake—NORTHEAST CORNER: dry lake southeast of Susanville
109. Horse Mountain—NORTHWEST MOUNTAINS: east of Arcata off SR-299
110. *Horseshoe Meadow Road—EASTERN SIERRA: southwest of Lone Pine*
111. *Huddard Park—CENTRAL COAST RANGES: in the Santa Cruz Mountains west of Woodside*
112. *Imperial Beach—SOUTH COAST: south of San Diego*
113. *Imperial Highway (S2)—SONORAN DESERT: runs along west edge of Anza-Borrego*
114. *Imperial Valley—SONORAN DESERT: near the Mexican border*
115. *Indian Wells Valley—MOJAVE DESERT: just northwest of Ridgecrest*
116. *Indio—SONORAN DESERT: just south of Joshua Tree National Park*
117. *Indio Hills—SONORAN DESERT: just east of Palm Springs*
118. *Inspiration Point Botanical Area—SOUTHERN SIERRA: in the Lake Isabella area*
119. *Inyo Mountains—EAST OF THE SIERRA: just west of Death Valley*
120. *Inyokern—MOJAVE DESERT: just west of Ridgecrest*
121. *Jacumba—SONORAN DESERT: just south of Anza-Borrego State Park*
122. Jedediah Smith Redwoods State Park—NORTHWEST MTS: SR-199 east of Crescent City
123. Jenner—NORTH COAST: north of Point Reyes
124. *John Muir Wilderness—CENTRAL SIERRA: just north of King's Canyon National Park*

125. Jughandle Creek—NORTH COAST: just south of Fort Bragg
126. Jughandle State Reserve—NORTH COAST: just south of Fort Bragg
127. *June Lake—EAST OF THE SIERRA: north of Mammoth Lakes*
128. *Kern Hot Spring—SOUTHERN SIERRA: in Sequoia National Park*
129. *Kern Plateau—SOUTHERN SIERRA: northeast of Bakersfield*
130. *Kingston Range—MOJAVE DESERT: northeast of Baker*
131. *Knight's Ferry—CENTRAL SIERRA FOOTHILLS: SR-120 east of Modesto*
132. Kyburz Flat—NORTHERN SIERRA: off SR-89 north of Truckee
133. *Laguna Coast Wilderness Park—SOUTHERN COAST: south of Los Angeles*
134. Lake Almanor—CASCADES: southeast of Lassen National Park
135. Lake Britton—CASCADES: north of Lassen National Park
136. *Lake Crowley—EAST OF THE SIERRA: just east of Mammoth*
137. *Lake Elsinore: SOUTH COAST RANGES: I-15 east of Los Angeles*
138. *Lake Sonoma—NORTH COAST RANGES: just southwest of Cloverdale*
139. *Lancaster—MOJAVE DESERT: just east of Antelope Valley California State Poppy Reserve*
140. *Last Chance Range—MOJAVE DESERT: northern Death Valley*
141. Lava Beds National Monument—NORTHEAST CORNER: Modoc Plateau along SR-139
142. *Lee Vining Canyon—CENTRAL SIERRA: SR-120 on eastern edge of Sierra*
143. *Leo Carillo Beach—SOUTH COAST: west of Santa Monica*
144. Leonard Lake—NORTH COAST RANGES: southeast of Mendocino
145. *Little Lake—MOJAVE DESERT; U.S. 395 north of Ridgecrest*
146. *Little San Bernardino Mts.—MOJAVE DESERT: southwest edge of Joshua Tree*
147. Loch Leven Lakes—NORTHERN SIERRA FOOTHILLS: I-80 at Big Bend exit
148. *Lompoc—CENTRAL COAST: northwest of Santa Barbara*
149. *Lone Pine—EAST OF THE SIERRA: south of Bishop*
150. *Long Canyon Research Natural Area--SOUTHERN SIERRA: Lake Isabella area*
151. *Los Osos—CENTRAL COAST: just south of Morro Bay*
152. *Ludlow—MOJAVE DESERT: SR-40 southwest of Mojave National Preserve*
153. MacKerricher State Park—NORTH COAST: just north of Fort Bragg
154. Madeline—NORTHEAST CORNER: SR-89 south of Alturas
155. Maidu Interpretative Center—NORTHERN SIERRA FOOTHILLS: in Marysville
156. *Malibu Lagoon/Creek State Parks—SOUTH COAST: northwest of Santa Monica*
157. Manchester Beach—NORTH COAST: south of Mendocino, just south of Manchester
158. *Manzanita Indian Reservation—SONORAN DESERT: I-8 east of San Diego*

159. Marble Mountains—NORTHWEST MOUNTAINS: west of Yreka
160. Markleeville—EAST OF THE SIERRA: SR-89 south of Lake Tahoe
161. Mattole Beach—NORTH COAST: south of Eureka
162. Mather Field—NORTHERN CENTRAL VALLEY: in the Sacramento area
163. Mayacmas Range—NORTH COAST RANGES: just west of Clear Lake
164. *McGee Creek—EASTERN SIERRA: running east into Lake Crowley*
165. Mendocino—NORTH COAST: SR-1 south of Fort Bragg
166. Mendocino Headlands State Park—NORTH COAST: at Mendocino
167. Merced River Canyon—NORTHERN SIERRA FOOTHILLS: SR-140 west of Yosemite
168. *Milton Road—CENTRAL SIERRA FOOTHILLS: crossing SR-4 east of Stockton*
169. *Mission Creek Preserve—MOJAVE DESERT: west of Twenty-Nine Palms*
170. *Mojave National Preserve—MOJAVE DESERT: south of Death Valley*
171. *Mono Lake Basin—EAST OF THE SIERRA: just east of Yosemite*
172. *Montana del Oro—CENTRAL COAST: just south of Morro Bay*
173. *Monterey Peninsula—CENTRAL COAST: south end of Monterey Bay*
174. *Morro Bay—CENTRAL COAST: just northwest of San Luis Obispo*
175. Mount Eddy—NORTHWEST MOUNTAINS: west of I-5 and south of Klamath River
176. Mount Fillmore—NORTHERN SIERRA: La Porte area
177. *Mount Hamilton Range—CENTRAL COAST RANGES: just east of San Jose*
178. Mount Hood—NORTH COAST RANGES: east of Santa Rosa
179. *Mount Pinos—SOUTH COAST RANGES: inland from Santa Barbara*
180. Mount Sanhedrin—NORTH COAST RANGES: south of Covelo
181. *Muir Beach—CENTRAL COAST: north of San Francisco Bay*
182. Napa—NORTH COAST RANGES: SR-128 north of San Francisco
183. Navarro River—NORTH COAST RANGES: running west to ocean south of Fort Bragg
184. *New York Mountains—MOJAVE DESERT: eastern Mojave National Preserve*
185. *Oceanside—SOUTH COAST: north of San Diego*
186. *Ocotillo—SONORAN DESERT: just south of Anza-Borrego State Park*
187. *Ocotillo Wells—SONORAN DESERT: west of Salton Sea*
188. *Olancha Peak—SOUTHERN SIERRA: west of U.S. 395 and Olancha*
189. *Old Woman Mountains—MOJAVE DESERT: south of Mojave National Preserve*
190. *Onyx—MOJAVE DESERT: SR-178 west of Ridgecrest*
191. Orick—NORTH COAST: in Redwood National Park
192. Orr Spring Road—NORTH COAST RANGES: from Mendocino to just north of Ukiah
193. *Otay Mountains—PENINSULAR RANGES: east of San Diego*
194. *Owens Peak—SOUTHERN SIERRA: just north of Walker Pass*

195. *Palomar Mountain/Palomar State Park—PENINSULAR RANGES: east of Oceanside*
196. *Panamint Range—MOJAVE DESERT: western edge of Death Valley*
197. Patrick Point State Park—NORTH COAST: north of Eureka
198. Pelican State Beach—NORTH COAST: just south of the Oregon border
199. *Pinyon Mountains—SONORAN DESERT: in Anza-Borrego State Park*
200. *Pismo Beach—CENTRAL COAST: just south of San Luis Obispo*
201. Pitkin Marsh—NORTH COAST RANGES: east of Jenner
202. *Piute Mountains—MOJAVE DESERT: south edge Mojave National Preserve*
203. *Placerita Canyon—SOUTH COAST RANGES: east of Santa Clarita*
204. *Placerville—CENTRAL SIERRA FOOTHILLS: SR-49 south of Auburn*
205. *Plaskett Meadow—CENTRAL COAST RANGE: south of Big Sur*
206. Pocket Canyon—NORTH COAST: along the Russian River
207. Point Arena—NORTH COAST: south of Manchester
208. *Point Arguello—CENTRAL COAST: just south of Lompoc*
209. *Point Dume State Beach—SOUTH COAST: in Malibu*
210. *Point Lobos—CENTRAL COAST: Carmel area*
211. *Point Loma—SOUTH COAST: on San Diego Bay*
212. *Point Magu State Park—SOUTH COAST: just south of Oxnard*
213. *Point Reyes National Seashore—CENTRAL COAST: just north of San Francisco*
214. Pope Valley—NORTH COAST RANGES: wine country north of San Francisco
215. Portola—EAST OF THE SIERRA: SR-70 southeast of Quincy
216. Potato Patch Campground—CASCADES: west of Lake Almanor
217. Prairie Creek Redwoods State Park—NORTH COAST: north of Eureka
218. *Preston Falls Trail—CENTRAL SIERRA FOOTHILLS: Groveland area*
219. *Providence Mountains—MOJAVE DESERT: southern part of Mojave National Preserve*
220. *Pulgas Ridge—CENTRAL COAST RANGES: just south of Edgewood Preserve*
221. Quarry Trail—NORTHERN SIERRA FOOTHILLS: off SR-49 just south of Auburn
222. Quincy—NORTHERN SIERRA: SR-89 south of Lake Almanor
223. *Rand Mountains—MOJAVE DESERT: southwest of Randsburg*
224. *Randsburg—MOJAVE DESERT: just south of Ridgecrest*
225. Ravendale—NORTHEAST CORNER: U.S. 395 north of Susanville
226. Red Bluff—SACRAMENTO VALLEY: on I-5 south of Redding
227. Red Mountain North—NORTH COAST RANGES: just northeast of Leggett
228. *Red Rock Canyon—MOJAVE DESERT: north of California City*
229. Requa—NORTH COAST: north of Redwood National Park
230. *Ridgecrest—MOJAVE DESERT: west of Death Valley National Park*
231. Rodeo Lagoon—NORTH COAST: SR-1 north of Fort Bragg

232. Rohnert Park—NORTH COAST RANGES: southwest of Santa Rosa
233. *Rosamund—MOJAVE DESERT: SR-14 northeast of Los Angeles*
234. Rough and Ready—NORTHERN SIERRA FOOTHILLS: west of Grass Valley
235. Russian Gulch State Park—NORTH COAST: just north of Mendocino
236. Russian Peak Wilderness—NORTHWEST MOUNTAINS: northeast of Eureka
237. Russian River—NORTH COAST RANGES: reaching the coast at Jenner
238. Said Valley Reservoir—NORTHEAST CORNER: east of Mount Lassen National Park
239. *Saline Valley—MOJAVE DESERT: northwest part of Death Valley*
240. Salmon Mountains—NORTHWEST MOUNTAINS: east of Arcata
241. *San Bernardino Valley—TRANSVERSE RANGES: south of San Bernardino Mts.*
242. *San Diego River—SOUTH COAST RANGES: flows southwest from Cuyama Mts*
243. *San Emigdio Range—SOUTH COAST RANGES: northeast of Santa Barbara*
244. *San Felipe Valley—PENINSULAR RANGES: just west of Anza-Borrego*
245. *San Jacinto River—SOUTH COAST RANGES: south of Los Angeles, flowing northeast then west*
246. *San Luis Obispo—CENTRAL COAST: southeast of Morro Bay*
247. *San Simeon—CENTRAL COAST: north of Morro Bay*
248. *San Ysidro Mountains—PENINSULAR RANGES: east of San Diego*
249. *Santa Ana Mountains—PENINSULAR RANGES: southwest of Riverside*
250. *Santa Cruz—CENTRAL COAST: north end of Monterey Bay*
251. *Santa Cruz Mountains—CENTRAL COAST RANGES: just inland from Santa Cruz*
252. *Santa Lucia Range—CENTRAL COAST RANGES: south of Monterey*
253. *Santa Maria River—CENTRAL COAST: drains the southern part of the Nipomo Dunes*
254. *Santa Ynez Mountains—SOUTH COAST: north and inland from Santa Barbara*
255. *Sawmill Pass Trail—EASTERN SIERRA: off U.S. 395 north of Independence*
256. Scott Mountain—NORTHWEST MOUNTAINS: north of Weaverville
257. Sea Ranch—NORTH COAST: south of Manchester
258. Shasta Lake—CASCADES: western foothills north of Redding
259. *Sheephole Mountains—MOJAVE DESERT: just north of Joshua Tree National Park*
260. *Shingle Springs—CENTRAL SIERRA FOOTHILLS: U.S. 50 west of Placerville*
261. *Shoshone—MOJAVE DESERT: just southeast of Death Valley*
262. Showers Lake—NORTHERN SIERRA: Carson Pass area
263. Sierra Valley—NORTHERN SIERRA: north of Sierraville

264. Siskiyou Mountains—NORTHWEST MOUNTAINS: near Oregon border

265. Snow Basin Ck—NORTHWEST MOUNTAINS: Yolla Bolly-Middle Eel Wilder.

266. Snow Mountain—NORTH COAST RANGES: southwest of Red Bluff

267. Sonoma Valley Regional Park—NORTH COAST RANGES: southeast of Santa Rosa

268. *Sonora Pass—CENTRAL SIERRA: SR-108 west of Sonora Junction*

269. South Kelsey Historical Trail—NORTHWEST MOUNTAINS: east of Crescent City

270. Spring Lake—NORTH COAST RANGES: Santa Rosa area

271. Standish-Hickey Redwood State Park—NORTH COAST RANGES: north of Fort Bragg

272. *Steven's Creek Canyon—CENTRAL COAST RANGES: Santa Cruz Mountains*

273. *Stevens Trail—CENTRAL COAST RANGES: in Cupertino*

274. Stewart's Point—NORTH COAST: south of Gualala

275. Stinson Beach—NORTH COAST: just west of Mount Tamalpais

276. Stony Creek Bog—NORTHWEST MOUNTAINS: east of Crescent City

277. *Success Lake—SOUTHERN SIERRA FOOTHILLS: Porterville area*

278. *Sunol Regional Park—CENTRAL COAST RANGE: east of Hayward*

279. Susanville—NORTHEAST CORNER: U.S. 395 east of Lassen National Park

280. Sutter Buttes—SACRAMENTO VALLEY: just west of Yuba City

281. *Sweeney Pass—SONORAN DESERT: east of San Diego*

282. Sweetwater Mountains—EAST OF THE SIERRA: east of U.S. 395 north of Bridgeport

283. *Taboose Pass—EASTERN SIERRA: west of Big Pine*

284. *Tecopa—MOJAVE DESERT: north of Baker*

285. *Tehachapi Mountains—MOJAVE DESERT: south of Bakersfield*

286. *Tejon Ranch—MOJAVE DESERT: in the Gorman area*

287. *Temblor Range—CENTRAL COAST RANGES: eastern edge of Carrizo Plain*

288. *Tiburon—CENTRAL COAST: north across Bay from San Francisco*

289. *Tioga Pass Road—CENTRAL SIERRA: just east of Yosemite*

290. *Topanga State Park—SOUTH COAST: in the Santa Monica Mountains*

291. *Toro Park—CENTRAL COAST: in Salinas*

292. *Traverse Creek Botanical Area—CENTRAL SIERRA FOOTHILLS: north of Placerville*

293. *Turtle Mountains—MOJAVE DESERT: south of Needles*

294. *Twenty-Nine Palms—MOJAVE DESERT: just north of Joshua Tree National Park*

295. Ukiah—SACRAMENTO VALLEY: U.S. 101 east of Mendocino

296. Vacaville—SACRAMENTO VALLEY: I-80 southwest of Sacramento

297. *Vallecito Stage Station—SONORAN DESERT: just west of Anza-Borrego*

298. Van Damme State Park—NORTH COAST: just south of Mendocino
299. *Vandenberg Air Force Base—CENTRAL COAST: in Santa Maria*
300. Vina Plains Preserve—SACRAMENTO VALLEY: south of Oroville
301. *Volcanic Hills—SONORAN DESERT: near Mexico border east of San Diego*
302. Walker—EAST OF THE SIERRA: U.S. 395 south of Topaz Lake
303. *Ward's Ferry Road—CENTRAL SIERRA FOOTHILLS: north of Groveland*
304. Washington—NORTHERN SIERRA FOOTHILLS: off SR-20 east of Nevada City
305. Weed—CASCADES: just west of Mount Shasta
306. *Whipple Mts.—SONORAN DESERT: southeast nose of California on Arizona border*
307. Wright's Lake—SIERRA: west of the Tahoe Basin
308. *Yaqui Well—SONORAN DESERT: bordering Anza-Borrego State Park*
309. Yolla Bolly-Middle Eel Wilderness—NORTHWEST MOUNTAINS:
310. Yuba River Canyon—NORTHERN SIERRA FOOTHILLS: North I-80 west of Truckee

REFERENCES

Baldwin, Bruce. *The Jepson Desert Manual*. Berkeley: University of California Press, 2002.

Beauchamp, R. Mitchel. *A Flora of San Diego County, California*. National City, Calif.: Sweetwater River Press, 1986.

Beidelman, Linda, and Eugene Kozloff. *Plants of the San Francisco Bay Region*. Berkeley: University of California Press, 2003.

Belzer, Thomas. *Roadside Plants of Southern California*. Missoula, Mont.: Mountain Press Publishing Co., 1984.

Best, C. *A Flora of Sonoma County*. Sacramento, Calif.: CNPS, 1996.

Blackwell, Laird. *Tahoe Wildflowers: A Month-by-Month Guide*. Guilford, Conn.: Globe Pequot Press, 2007.

Blackwell, Laird. *Wildflowers of the Eastern Sierra and Adjoining Mojave Desert and Great Basin*. Edmonton, Alberta, Canada: Lone Pine Press, 2002.

Blackwell, Laird. *Wildflowers of Kirkwood Mountain Resort*. Mountain View, Calif.: Mountain View Printing, 2007.

Blackwell, Laird. *Wildflowers of the Sierra Nevada and the Central Valley*. Edmonton, Alberta, Canada: Lone Pine Publishing, 1999.

Blackwell, Laird. *Wildflowers of the Tahoe Sierra*. Edmonton, Alberta, Canada: Lone Pine Publishing, 1997.

Bossard, Carla, John Randall, and Marc Hoshovsky. *Invasive Plants of California's Wetlands*. Berkeley: University of California Press, 2000.

Botti, Stephen. *An Illustrated Flora of Yosemite National Park*. El Portal, Calif.: Yosemite Association, 2001.

Botti, Stephen, and A. Mendershausen. *Wildflowers of the Hite's Cove Trail*. Fresno, Calif.: Pioneer Publishing, 1985.

Coffeen, Mary. *Central Coast Wildflowers*. San Luis Obispo, Calif.: EZ Nature Books, 1993.

Corelli, Tony. *Flowering Plants of Edgewood Natural Preserve*. Half Moon Bay, Calif.: Monocot Press, 2004.

Croissant, Ann, and Gerald Croissant. *Wildflowers of the San Gabriel Mountains*. Glendora, Calif.: San Gabriel Mountains Regional Conservancy and Stephens Press.

Dale, Nancy. *Flowering Plants of the Santa Monica Mountains*. Santa Barbara, Calif.: Capra Press, 1986.

Ertter, Barbara, and Mary Bowerman. *The Flowering Plants and Ferns of Mount Diablo, California*. Sacramento, Calif.: CNPS, 2002.

Faber, Phyllis, ed. *California's Wild Gardens*. Sacramento, Calif.: CNPS, 1997.

Fauver, Toni. *Wildflower Walking in Lakes Basin*. Orinda, Calif.: Faver and Steinbach, 1992.

Fauver, Toni. *Wildflower Walks and Roads of the Sierra Gold Country*. Grass Valley, Calif.: Comstock Bonanza Press, 1998.

Ferlatte, Wilma. *A Flora of the Trinity Alps of Northern California*. Berkeley: University of California Press, 1974.

Ferris, Roxana. *Death Valley Wildflowers*. Death Valley, Calif.: Death Valley Natural History Association, 1983.

Ferris, Roxana. *Flowers of Point Reyes National Seashore*. Berkeley: University of California Press, 1970.

Game, John, and Richards Lyon. *Fifty Wildflowers of Bear Valley*. Colusa County. San Francisco, Calif.: American Land Conservancy Publication, 1996.

Gillette, George, John Thomas Howell, and Hans Leschke. *A Flora of Lassen Volcanic National Park*, California. Sacramento, Calif.: CNPS, 1995.

Gubernick, D., and Vern Yadon. *Wildflowers of Monterey County*. Carmel, Calif.: Carmel Publishing Co., 2002.

Hickman, J., ed. *The Jepson Manual of Higher Plants in California*. Berkeley: University of California Press, 1993.

Horn, E. *Coastal Wildflowers of the Pacific Northwest*. Missoula, Mont.: Mountain Press Publishing Company, 1993.

Howell, J. *Marin Flora*. San Francisco: California Academy of Sciences, 2007.

Ingram, Stephen. *Cacti, Agaves, and Yuccas of California and Nevada*. Los Olivos, Calif.: Cachuma Press, 2008.

Jaeger, Edmund. *Desert Wildflowers*. Stanford, Calif.: Stanford University Press, 1969.

Jones, Alice. *Flowers and Trees of the Trinity Alps*. Weaverville, Calif.: Trinity County Historical Society, 1986.

Knute, Adrienne. *Plants of the East Mojave*. Barstow, Calif.: Mojave River Valley Museum Association, 2002.

Liskow, George. *Wildflowers of the Mount Wilson Trails and San Gabriel Mountains*. 1990. No publisher.

Llond, Robert, and Richard Mitchell. *A Flora of the White Mountains of California and Nevada*. Berkeley: University of California Press, 1973.

Lyons, Kathleen, and Mary Beth Cuneo-Lazaneo. *Plants of the Coast Redwood Region*. Boulder Creek, Calif.: Looking Press, 1988.

Mackay, Pam. *Mojave Desert Wildflowers*. Guilford, Conn.: The Globe Pequot Press, 2003.

Mackey, Samantha, and Albin Bills. *Wildflowers of Table Mountain, Butte County, California*. Chico, Calif.: Studies from the Herbarium of California State University–Chico, 2003.

Matthews, Mary Ann. *An Illustrated Field Key to the Flowering Plants of Monterey County*. Sacramento, Calif.: CNPS, 1997.

McClintock, Elizabeth, Paul Reeberg, and Walter Knight. *A Flora of the San Bruno Mountains*. Sacramento, Calif.: CNPS, 1990.

McLeod, Malcolm. *The Dune Mother's Wildflower Guide to the Dunes of Coastal San Luis Obispo and Santa Barbara Counties, California*. Sacramento, Calif.: CNPS, 2001.

Morgenson, Dana. *Yosemite Wildflower Trails*. Yosemite, Calif.: Yosemite Natural History Association, 1975.

Morhardt, Sia, and Emil Morhardt. *California Desert Flowers*. Berkeley: University of California Press, 2004.

Nakamura, Gary, and Julie Nelson. *Selected Rare Plants of Northern California*. Oakland: University of California Agriculture and Natural Resources, 2001.

Oswald, Vernon. *Vascular Plants of Upper Bidwell Park, Chico, California*. Chico, California: The Herbarium of California State University–Chico, 1986.

Oswald, Vernon. *Selected Plants of Northern California and Adjacent Nevada*. Chico, Calif.: Studies from the Herbarium of California State University–Chico, 2002.

Parker, Reny. *Wildflowers of Northern California's Wine Country and North Coast Ranges*. Cloverdale, Calif.: New Creek Ranch Press, 2007.

Redbud Chapter of California Native Plant Society. *Wildflowers of Nevada and Placer Counties, California*. Sacramento, Calif.: CNPS, 2007.

Ritter, Matt. *Plants of San Luis Obispo*. Dubuque, Iowa: Kendall/Hunt Publishing Co., 2006.

Roberts, Fred. *A Checklist of the Vascular Plants of Orange County, California*. Encinitas, Calif.: F.M. Roberts Publications, 1998.

Roberts, Fred. *The Vascular Plants of Western Riverside County, California*. San Luis Rey, Calif.: F.M. Roberts Publications, 2004.

Rundel, Philip, and Robert Gustafson. *Introduction to the Plant Life of Southern California*. Berkeley: University of California Press, 2005.

Sharsmith, Helen. *Flora of the Mount Hamilton Range of California*. Berkeley: CNPS, 1962.

Showers, Mary Ann, and David Showers. *A Field Guide to the Flowers of Lassen Volcanic National Park*. Mineral, Calif.: Lassen Loomis Museum Association, 1996.

Smith, Clifton. *A Flora of the Santa Barbara Region*. Santa Barbara, Calif.: Santa Barbara Botanic Garden and Capra Press, 1998.

Smith, Gladys. *A Flora of the Tahoe Basin and Neighboring Areas and Supplement*. San Francisco, Calif.: University of San Francisco, 1984.

Smith, Gladys, and Clare Wheeler. *A Flora of the Vascular Plants of Mendocino County, California*. San Francisco, Calif.: University of San Francisco, 1997.

Spellenberg, Richard. *Sonoran Desert Wildflowers*. Guilford, Conn.: Globe Pequot Press, 2003.

Stearns, P. *A Journey in Time*. Ukiah, Calif.: Peter Stearns Enterprises, 2007.

Stewart, Jon Mark. *Colorado Desert Wildflowers*. Palm Desert, Calif.: Jon Stewart Photography, 1993.

Stewart, Jon Mark. *Mojave Desert Wildflowers*. Palm Desert, Calif.: Jon Stewart Photography, 1998.

Thomas, John. *Flora of the Santa Cruz Mountains of California*. Stanford, Calif.: Stanford University Press, 1961.

Twisselmann, Ernest. *A Flora of Kern County, California*. Sacramento, Calif.: CNPS, 1995.

Ulrich, Larry, and Susan Lamb. *Wildflowers of California*. Santa Barbara, Calif.: Companion Press, 1994.

Weise, Karen. *Sierra Nevada Wildflowers*. Helena, Mont.: Falcon Publishing, Inc., 2000.

Witham, Carol. *Field Guide to the Vernal Pools of Mather Field, Sacramento County*. Sacramento, Calif.: CNPS, 2006.

ADDITIONAL CAPTIONS

PAGE I Coast dudleya at Salt Point.

PAGE III Sierra rein orchid and tiger lily in Tahoe Basin.

PAGE VI Globe gilia and California poppy at Gorman Hills.

PAGE 1 Baby blue eyes and phacelia.

PAGE 11 California poppies near Lancaster.

PAGE 79 Our Lord's candle and California prickly phlox in the Santa Monica Mountains in April.

INDEX OF COMMON NAMES

Torrey's, 437
wide-throated, 215
yellow-and-white, 315
monkshood, 425
monolopia, common. *See* daisy, hillside
monument plant. *See* deer's tongue
morning glory
beach, 94
purple, 136
western, 136
mosquito bills. *See* shooting star, foothill
mountain bells, spotted. *See* fritillary, purple
mountain misery, 327
mountain pride, 364
mouse ears, purple. *See* monkeyflower,
Douglas
mouse-on-a-stick. *See* pasqueflower
mule ears
El Dorado, 216
woolly, 385
mullein, moth, 258
mustang clover, 243
mustard, field, 153

nama, Rothrock's, 473
navarretia, needle, 328
nemophila
five-spot, 244
vari-leaf, 245
white, 245
nettle, stinging, 337
nightshade, Parish's purple, 86
nolina, Parry's, 328

ocotillo, 95
old man's whiskers, 438
old-man-in-the-ground. *See* cucumber, wild
onion
Cascade, 195
coast, 290
crater, 195
crinkled, 365
desert, 289
dwarf, 460
flat-stemmed, 366
fringed, 289
glassy, 246
Lemmon's, 366
pitted, 404
red Sierra, 460
rosy, 290
Sierra, 367
swamp, 439
volcanic, 195
onion weed. *See* garlic, wild

ookow. *See* hyacinth, wild
orchid
calypso, 290
phantom, 460
Sierra rein, 461
stream, 253
our Lord's candle, 246
owl's-clover, purple, 195

paintbush
alpine, 486
Applegate's, 439
coast, 96
desert, 291
fuzzy, 196
great red, 487
hairy, 487
Lemmon's, 488
Mendocino coast, 368
wavy-leaf, 439
wooly, 196
pancake, beach. *See* verbena, magenta
pansy, yellow. *See* violet, golden
paperbag bush. *See* bladder sage
parsley, desert, 334
parsnip, lace, 253
partridge foot, 509
pasqueflower, 462
pea
perennial sweet, 256
rock, desert, 116
silky beach, 292
peach, desert, 292
pennyroyal, 463
penstemon
alpine, 474
Bridge's, 440
climbing, 197
Davidson's, 474
desert, 345
Eaton, 197
Grinnell's, 293
heart-leaf, 197
hot-rock, 510
Palmer's, 294
rosy, 368
royal, 346
scarlet, 440
scented, 294
showy, 346
woodland, 426
peony
California, 146
western, 417
peppergrass, yellow, 216

thistle
  Anderson's, 493
  cobweb, 299
  Drummond's, 412
  dwarf, 412
  elk, 412
  Mojave, 374
  peregrine, 411
  stemless, 412
tickseed, Bigelow's. *See* coreopsis, Bigelow's
tidy tips, Fremont's, 223
tincture plant. *See* Chinese houses, white
tobacco brush, 465
tofieldia, 466
toothwort, California. *See* milk maids
trillium
  giant, 142
  western, 142
turtleback, 118
twayblade, broad-lipped, 524
twinberry, 224
twinevine, fringed. *See* milkweed,
    climbing
twinflower, 444

velvet, desert. *See* turtleback
verbena
  coastal sand, 320
  common sand, 204
  desert sand, 102
  magenta, 101
  purple sand, 204
  red sand, 101
  sticky sand, 102
  yellow sand, 320
veronica, Cusick's, 476
vetch
  spring, 256
  winter, 254
violet
  Beckwith, 271
  Douglas, 224
  early blue, 179
  fan, 321
  golden, 119
  Great Basin, 271
  Macloskey's, 412
  mountain, 388
  pinewoods, 388
  Shelton, 321

small white, 412
  western dog, 179
virgin bower, 143

wake-robin, western. *See* trillium, western
wallflower
  dune, 225
  Franciscan, 251
  sand dune, 120
  western, 120
wally basket. *See* Ithuriel's spear
whiskerbrush, 204
whispering bells, yellow, 226
whiteheads, swamp. *See* ranger's buttons
willow, desert, 375
willowherb, Watson's, 299
windflower, Columbia, 413
windmills, 102
wintergreen
  bog, 494
  one-sided, 517
  white-veined, 515
wishbone bush, 144
  California, 103
witches' teeth. *See* lotus, bicolored
woodbalm. *See* sage, pitcher
woodland star
  fringed, 145
  San Francisco, 145
woolly star, giant. *See* heavenly blue

yampah, Parish's, 515
yarrow, golden, 121
yellow carpet, 121
yellow cups, 226
yellow eyes, 271
yellow head, 122
yellow mats. *See* footsteps-of-spring
yellow throats, 179
yellowdome. *See* yellow head
yellow-eyed grass, California, 389
yerba mansa, 251
yerba santa
  California, 414
  thick-leaved, 180
youth-on-age, 418
yucca
  banana, 414
  chapparal. *See* our Lord's candle
  Mojave, 332

INDEX OF SCIENTIFIC NAMES

ABOUT THE AUTHOR

Author's front yard in winter

My wife, Melinda, and I now live in Washoe Valley, Nevada, bordering a wildlife area and looking out at the dramatic, precipitous eastern escarpment of the Carson Range. We share our one-and-a-half acres with horses, alpaca, chickens, dogs, cats, and a miniature donkey, not to mention gardens of flowers and vegetables. Now that's sharing!

After 30 years as a professor of psychology, literature, and wildflowers at Sierra Nevada College at Lake Tahoe, I continue to love teaching there, although I'm beginning to think about transitions.

This current wildflower book is the latest in a long series of such books for various parts of the American West, and in some ways is a culmination of many years of fascination with our floral companions. I hope that you will appreciate the flowers as I do—as gifts of beauty and as fellow journeyers and guides through life.

Composition:	Bytheway Publishing Services
Text:	9/11 Minion
Display:	ITC Franklin Gothic Book and Demi
Prepress:	Embassy Graphics